A METAHISTORY OF THE CLASH
OF CIVILISATIONS

ARSHIN ADIB-MOGHADDAM

A Metahistory of the Clash of Civilisations

Us and Them Beyond Orientalism

Columbia University Press
New York

Columbia University Press
Publishers Since 1893
New York   Chichester, West Sussex
Copyright © Arshin Adib-Moghaddam, 2011
All rights reserved

Library of Congress Cataloging-in-Publication Data

Adib-Moghaddam, Arshin.
  A metahistory of the clash of civilizations : us and them beyond
Orientalism / Arshin Adib-Moghaddam.
      p. cm.
  Includes bibliographical references and index.
  ISBN 978-0-231-70212-6 (alk. paper)
  ISBN 978-0-231-80048-8 (eBook)
  1. East and West. 2. Culture conflict—History. 3. Civilization, Western.
  4. Islamic civilization. 5. Western countries—Relations—Islamic countries.
  6. Islamic countries—Relations—Western countries. I. Title.

CB251.A24 2010
909'.09821—dc22

                                        2010036466

∞

Columbia University Press books are printed on permanent and durable acid-free paper. This book is printed on paper with recycled content.
Printed in India

c 10 9 8 7 6 5 4 3 2 1

References to Internet Web sites (URLs) were accurate at the time of writing. Neither the author nor Columbia University Press is responsible for URLs that may have expired or changed since the manuscript was prepared.

Of one Essence is the human race,
Thusly has Creation put the Base;
One Limb impacted is sufficient,
For all Others to feel the Mace.

Saadi Shirazi
Thirteenth-century poet

CONTENTS

ABOUT THE AUTHOR

Arshin Adib-Moghaddam is University Lecturer in Comparative- and International Politics at the School of Oriental and African Studies, University of London where he convenes postgraduate courses on the 'International Politics of the Middle East' and 'Islamic Political Thought'. He was born in the Taksim area of Istanbul to Iranian parents and was raised in Hamburg/Germany. In Hamburg he attended the Wichern School—a German-evangelical private institution and Persian and Arabic language courses at the Imam Ali mosque in the same city. His academic education began at the University of Hamburg where he read Political Science, Psychology and Economics culminating in a Masters Degree in Political Science in 2000. Between 1997 and 1998 he was a scholarship student at the American University in Washington DC. In the summer of 2000, a generous scholarship by the Cambridge European Trust Society, Trinity College under the auspices of HRH the Duke of Edinburgh and the Elizabeth Cherry Fellowship at Hughes Hall enabled him to pursue his academic studies at the University of Cambridge. Supervised by Charles Jones and mentored by Yezid Sayigh he was awarded an MPhil in late 2001 and a PhD in International Relations in early 2004 (accepted without corrections). His viva voce was examined by the late Peter Avery, OBE and Raymond Hinnebusch at the former's legendary fellows' suite at King's College, Cambridge. After his PhD, Adib-Moghaddam lived, researched and lectured extensively in Iran. In 2005, he was elected the first Jarvis Doctorow Junior Research Fellow in International Relations and Peace Studies at St. Edmund Hall and the Department of Politics and International Relations, University of Oxford. Two years later in 2007, he accepted his current tenured position at SOAS. Adib-Moghaddam is

ABOUT THE AUTHOR

the author of *The International Politics of the Persian Gulf: A cultural genealogy* (Routledge, 2006, 2009), *Iran in World Politics: The question of the Islamic Republic* (Hurst/Columbia University Press, 2008, 2010) and numerous research articles which have been published in leading peer-reviewed journals. Adib-Moghaddam's writings have been translated into many languages and he keeps a busy national and international lecture schedule. A member of several anti-war organisations, his commentary and opinion pieces appear regularly in the mainstream and alternative press in Europe, Asia, the United States and Latin America.

PREFACE

As I was finishing the final manuscript of this book, I received a curious leaflet through my letterbox at home in Cambridge. It was titled 'Urgent and Important: What will you leave behind for the children?' Upon closer inspection, it turned out to be a part of a 'marketing' initiative by the 'Creation Science Movement', which presents itself—further research reveals—as the oldest creationist movement in the United Kingdom. The leaflet was folded into a six–page article on Charles Darwin, which attempts to prove the compatibility of the theory of evolution with the creation of Adam and Eve. The authors of the leaflet emphasise that 'Britain is a country founded on the Christian faith' and alert us about the 'serious deterioration' of the 'general conduct of society' compared to 'forty years ago'. One of the main causes for this moral and social malaise, we are warned, 'is the worship of false gods and idols such as Allah, the Islamic god, or the Virgin Mary. Muhammad ... based the religion of Islam originally around the superstition of worship of the "moon god"'. This explains, according to the authors, the crescent moon on the flag of many Islamic nations. 'One only has to read the Qur'an (Koran) to see the aggressiveness of Muhammad'. Towards the end of the leaflet the authors anxiously add that '[f]uture generations of Britons are in danger of Islamic totalitarian intentions'. The only way to prevent this impending Islamic conquest is for parents to 'plead for recovery of Biblical truth in this nation for their children'.[1]

I am not quoting from this intense and angry leaflet because I deem it in any way representative of public opinion in Britain, of course. The

[1] 'Urgent and Important: What will you leave behind for the children?' Essex: Moral Recovery U.K., September 2008.

attitude displayed in it does not drive a political movement with mass appeal. It is as marginal to the consciousness of the rational majority in this country and beyond, as the message of Al Qaeda is in Muslim-majority societies. You will have surmised that the authors of the leaflet do not represent 'Christianity', not even 'Evangelicals', the German-protestant variant of which I learned to appreciate during my *Gymnasium* years in Germany. Nor can they be considered well versed in the symbolism of 'Islam'. But the message is a minor surface effect of a shifting, yet historically surprisingly stable setting that no amount of scholarly aloofness can ignore. For not only do leaflets like that arouse our revulsion over the arbitrary semantic ambiances that continue to be exercised over complex systems such as 'Islam' or 'Christianity' itself, but we are also immediately transposed into the real world, there to battle with, if not the whole politico-cultural apparatus behind it, then at least the most central institutions and norms in which those angry narratives are spun.

Any discussion of that battle beyond the micro-politics of my home cannot ignore a larger constellation encapsulated in the seemingly uncanny idea of a 'clash of civilisations'. When one mentions it, many self-respecting scholars have as dismissive and violent a reaction as the leaders of Al Qaeda have to women—to lash out, to call for disciplinary action, for confinement and enclosure. However, is it possible to think about contemporary (world) politics, the international media, and some proto-fascist discourse on the intransigent right-wing here and there without taking the clash idea into consideration analytically? It seems to me that if historians, in the near future, would come together in order to enquire into the development of world order in the twenty-first century, they would most certainly find it unavoidable to evaluate the interventions of some of the surprisingly contagious ideas suggesting that we are in the middle of some sort of 'clash of civilisations', especially, we are told, between Islam and the 'West'.

One would have thought that the clash idea is too atrocious and too unspecified to make rational sense. It is all the more surprising that it continues to have a presence in many political discourses. Consequently, this study focuses on the way a range of talented, occasionally callous, certainly influential orators, academics, journalists, polemicists, politicians, propagandists have habituated us to believe in the normality of conflict between 'us' and 'them'. By all the conventional wisdom available, the disciples of this pervasive idea should not be so successful. Surely, their prominence cannot be due to the ethical strength of their argument. Surely, trying to persuade us that the conflict between 'us' and 'them' is inscribed in human nature is not an alluring or convincing prospect. So why is it that we are continuously confronted with the idea that we are embroiled in some eternal clash, between civilisations or other imagined concepts? This question is central to this book and will be engaged from a theoretical, epistemological, ontological and empirical angle.

It is my proposition that the argument put forward by Huntington in his highly influential *Foreign Affairs* essay in 1993 and his subsequent book is the product and element of a 'regime of truth' that sustains the clash idea today.[2] I will explain the term 'regime of truth' which I have derived from Foucault more fully in the introduction. Suffice to say at this stage that the 'regime of truth' under focus here, refers to the apparatus of techniques, the strategies, policies, ideas and disciplinary constellations that compel 'us' into believing in some seemingly inevitable clash with 'them'. It is that 'clash regime' that suggests a 'clash of civilisations' and whose aim is nothing less than political quiescence into the importance of a permanent war against the 'other'. As we will see, the transmutation from myth to 'pseudo-reality' has been the task of the 'clash regime' and its disciples for a long time now. In order to investigate how we got to where we are, we have to write a metahistory of the 'objectification' of this 'clash regime' facing us at the very moment at which I ask these questions: In what ways has the 'clash regime' been engineered and reified throughout history? How does it appear, and in which disciplines and discourses does it anchor its structural force? How did formative events in history, for instance the Persian-Greek wars, the emergence of Islam in the seventh century AD, the Crusades, colonialism and imperialism, the 'War on Terror' contribute to the making of that clash regime? What is it that makes us believe in dichotomous constellations in the first place? To what extent have we overcome stringent notions of 'our' and 'their' 'identity'? What are some of the strategies to battle with the structural violence of the clash regime?

If there is a cultural pre-disposition within society that delivers the clash idea and its corresponding mindset, as I have suggested, then we

---

[2] See Samuel P. Huntington, 'The Clash of Civilisations?', *Foreign Affairs*, vol. 72, no. 3 (1993), pp. 22–49 and idem., *The Clash of Civilisations and the Remaking of World Order*, London: Simon & Schuster, 1997.

should be able to locate the institutions, norms and systems of thought, that perpetuate that idea. If the artificial engineering of the clash of civilisations from innumerable loci suggests its ontological force; if people from all walks of life—Silvio Berlusconi, Osama bin Laden, Martin Amis, Ayman al-Zawahiri, Christopher Hitchens, Geert Wilders, Glenn Beck to name a few—believe they can 'see' the clash between 'Islam' and the 'West', than there must be a cultural constellation out there that valorises an inevitable conflict between 'us' and 'them'. So in order to be able to analyse the giant historical field and institutional geography in which the idea of a clash is continuously cultivated, we have to step back and look at History from a fresh perspective. Such 'histories of History' (or metahistories) have only emerged very recently and this book intends to make a contribution to the many critical schools that have proliferated in opposition to mainstream writings of the past and present. Thus, the opportunity exists to resist and to emphasise that the making of our 'self' is entirely dependent on the 'other', and that our inevitable, quite biological and genetic interdependence—like any other sibling relationship—demands a politics of empathy. Killing the 'other', we have to protest, always also means killing a part of our 'self' much in the same way as killing a member of our family constitutes an act of genealogical self-mutilation. We should be aware that a world depleted of 'otherness' is the 'ideal' order that the racist imagines. In this order, which can only be delivered through a sustained, blood-trenched *Gleichschaltung* (synchronisation), the self would be entirely 'purified', depleted of any otherness. I for one would not want to live in such a sterilised world, would you?

So we stand in front of an awesome truth constellation, a system of control, constituted by many discourses, permeated by entrenched ideologies, and many disciplines including some of those that are being taught at this very moment, all of which ensure a permanent reactivation of the clash regime and its 'us' versus 'them' mentality. Today, we continue to be disciplined in valorising a continuous war against the 'other'. At this very moment, we can see that the geography of violence has been seriously expanded in the 'War on Terror' and bin-Laden's corresponding global terrorism campaign, from Kandahar, Kabul, Peshawar and Baghdad, to Tavistock Square, Fort Hood and Manhattan. But the regime of truth producing and sustaining the idea that we are embroiled in an all-encompassing, zero-sum clash is less visible. And yet it is 'everywhere' inducing, on a continuous basis, factual validity to some clash of civilisations. To that end, a technique of enmeshment is employed. Disparate conflicts, all with their own very specific historical and political dynamics, are artificially aggregated in order to legitimate and prescribe violence. The bombing of the World Trade Centre in 1993, the bomb attack on the Paris Metro (St. Michel Station) in 1995, the attacks on American military personnel in Riyadh in November 1995, and Dharan in June 1996, the US embassy bombings in Nairobi and Dar es Salaam in 1998, the suicide attack on the USS *Cole* in the Port of Aden in December 2000, 11 September 2001, the bombing of the US Consulate and Marriott Hotel in Karachi in 2002, the Bali bombings in the same year, the war in Afghanistan, the invasion of Iraq in March 2003, the three bombings of railroads in Madrid in November 2004, the attacks on London in July 2005, the bloody siege of the Taj Mahal hotel in Mumbai in December 2008, Abu Ghraib and Guantanamo are not at all indicative of some clash of civilisations. Rather, the fact that some of us think they are, is indicative of the persistence of a clash regime that *suggests* a clash of civilisation, nothing more and nothing less. Hence, for my generation, it must be a priority to investigate how the clash regime has been constituted and perpetuated and to debunk its violent logic at the same time.

What many of the proponents of the 'clash regime', in East and West, North and South, have done is by far more decisive to world politics and global history more generally than one would think. Those who enlist an individual's mind to the cause of conflict against another group command awesome powers. That is not necessarily because they swing the sword or wield the sceptre, but because of the devastating influence of their ideas; the disciples of the 'clash regime' are primarily interested in coding the way we think about difference. The wars of ideas thus engendered have devastated empires, enslaved whole continents and colonised cultures. So it must be an ambition of this book to identify these men and women and to delve into their discourses and theories in order to fight them from within.

What is strange is that in a world shaken by recurrent conflicts in the name of group affiliations—the 'West', 'Islam', the 'nation', 'the free world'—we do not know enough about the way these conflicts are produced in the first place. One would have thought that in a world that continuously worries about war and terror and talks of the tensions between 'Islam' and the 'West' in particular, the individuals who have lured us into this treacherous territory and their way of thinking would be constantly challenged by the rational majority. Instead, they are offered columns in daily newspapers, magazines and enough airtime on TV to preach their angry message and to fog the brains of their consumers. The omnipresence of the clash regime is not at least a product of today's global media culture that has catapulted the Osama bin Ladens of this world to unenviable stardom. But it is also an indication of the retreat and disempowerment of the University and critical discourse more generally.

It is the creation and legitimation of war and conflict that is the ultimate goal of the engineers of the clash regime. In order to combat this vast constellation at its contemporary sites—academia, the international media, History, Hollywood, discursive formations (or systems) such as Islamism or the 'West'—this book presents a journey through the ideas, norms, institutions and myths that have habituated us to accept the current status quo as normality. It is a book that pays particular attention to the complex interaction between representations of 'self' and 'other', 'us' and 'them' during formative periods of world history. It practises comparative politics in a metahistorical mode. To that end, we will encounter not only scholars on our way, but many revolutionaries, warriors, philosophers, orators, many propagandists both megalomaniac and brilliant, and even here and there the self-conscious terrorist. At the same time, I am aware that our subject matter is spread out on a vast canvas, and that the sketches holding the pages of this book together need to be redrawn in future studies.

No discourse is innocent, every idea has a political connotation, and any system of thought affects us all the way down to our very consciousness and preferences. This text battles with these rapturous powers unleashed primarily by the identity inducing cultures surrounding us. Ultimately, it is a book written in the middle of—yet in opposition to a period of major trepidation and rage; both here and over there.

The 'rump' of the argument of this book was first contemplated rather sketchily in two articles: 'A (short) history of the clash of civilisations', *Cambridge Review of International Affairs*, vol. 21, no. 2 (June 2008), pp. 217–234 and 'Islamutopia (Post)Modernity and the Multitude', in Patrick Hayden and Chamsy El-Ojeili (eds), *Globalisation and Utopia: Critical Essays*, London: Palgrave, 2009, pp. 137–155. I would like to thank Gilbert Achcar for his ideas on the plight of the *Muselmann*. Gilbert has been a reliable companion and brilliant interlocutor since his arrival at SOAS, and he reserved much time to comment on the whole manuscript. I am grateful to Fatemeh Kesha-varz for her verification of some of the quotes on Rumi (Mowlana). I am also grateful to Michael Dwyer, Richard Jackson, Corinna Mullin-Lery and Morten Valbjørn for their critical comments and advice, and the team at Hurst and Columbia University Press who facilitated the production of this book with patience and professionalism. The Department of Politics and International Studies at SOAS, with the 'Middle East' section staffed with Salwa Ismail, Laleh Khalili and Charles Tripp and the armada of critical students from all over the world that roam our corridors and enrich our seminars, has been the perfect place to reflect on an interdisciplinary study like the present one. I am grateful for being a part of this academic culture. I owe a special thank you to the librarians of the SOAS library, the Bodleian at Oxford University, and the staff at the University Library at Cambridge University who have been very patient with my requests and my chal-lenges to the opening hours. For the past five years, this project has taken a huge chunk out of my life. Without the love, intelligence and artistic mind of my wife Elham, I couldn't have made it.

There is no uniform way of transliterating Persian and Arabic terms. For the sake of consistency and clarity I have used the most prevalent spelling and kept it throughout the study. All translations are mine unless indicated otherwise in the references.

Arshin Adib-Moghaddam   Cambridge/London
                                                         January 2010

INTRODUCTION

THE CLASH REGIME AND ITS PATHOLOGIES

1. *On the 2nd December, 1947, the Council of al-Azhar University proclaimed a world-wide holy war in defence of Arab Palestine, and it is perhaps worth noting that the appeal was to 'Arabs and Muslims'.*

2. *The origin of the institution of Jihad, or holy war, is to be found in several of the suras of the Quran revealed to the Prophet Muhammad... Out of these ordinances and 'traditions' associated with the Prophet and the early Muslim period, there gradually evolved a general religious duty of performing the jihad incumbent on all free adult Muslims who had means of reaching the army. This duty had two aspects: the advancement of Islam by arms and the repelling of evil from the Muslims. Thus, if a Muslim country is invaded by unbelievers a general summons may be issued calling all Muslims to arms. And as the danger grows, so may the width of the summons grow until the whole Muslim world is involved. However, it must be remembered that the Islamic world, except in the first stages of its history, has never responded in its entirety to such a summons.*

From Volume 7, Air Commodore K. Buss, *Foreign Office Research Centre*,
12 December 1947, 'Partition in Palestine and the Declaration of a Jihad'

The first thing one notices apropos of the idea of the clash of civilisations is its contagious nature: the way many tend to engage with its premises, sometimes mockingly, sometimes in compliance, but always with an understanding that such phenomena are contemplated. 'There is a partial truth to the notion of a "clash of civilisations" attested here', writes even as self-consciously a 'leftist' writer as Slavoj Žižek. 'Two philosophical references immediately impose themselves apropos of this ideological antagonism between Western consumerism and

1

Muslim radicalism: Hegel and Nietzsche'. According to Žižek, 'we in the West are the Nietzschean Last Men, immersed in stupid daily pleasures, while the Muslim radicals are ready to risk everything, engaged in the struggle up to the point of their own self-destruction'.[1] There is no suggestion here that Žižek wholeheartedly believes in, or promotes the idea of an inevitable clash between 'Islam' and the 'West' of course. But even when he says that 'this notion of the "clash of civilisations" must be thoroughly rejected: what we are witnessing today is rather clashes within each civilisation'; the way he uses the term 'each' is deceptive. It seems that he accepts the idea that 'Islam' and the 'West' are essentially and evidently conflicting 'civilisations'; that there exists some kind of innate epistemological difference between 'us' and 'them' that corroborates the clash idea.[2] Žižek does not tell us how such antagonism is facilitated or how we can mitigate it intellectually. That would imply some engagement with discourses of Islam and an understanding of the ways they represent self and other, a path that Žižek is not prepared to take. In his emphasis on a Judeo-Christian discourse in near total detachment of its Islamic sibling,[3] in his 'leftist plea for Eurocentrism',[4] in his Hegelian methodology, Islam appears only as a footnote or subject of world history that remains centred around Europe. 'The political sympathy Žižek shows towards Islam—its faith, followers and cultures', one tends to agree with one of his critics, 'constantly carries concealed within itself this risk, the Hegelian inheritance of a 200–year-old "Mohammedanism", dynamic and unreflective, fanatical and sublime'.[5] When Muslims do appear in

---

[1] Slavoj Žižek, *The Universal Exception: Selected Writings*, London: Continuum, 2006, p. 277.

[2] Ibid., p. 278, emphasis in original.

[3] See especially, idem., 'Neighbors and Other Monsters: A Plea for Ethical Violence', in Slavoj Žižek, Eric L. Santner and Kenneth Reinhard, *The Neighbor: Three Inquiries in Political Theology*, Chicago: The University of Chicago Press, 2005, pp. 134–190; and *The Fragile Absolute or Why is the Christian legacy worth fighting for?*, London: Verso, 2000, especially p. 2 where Žižek states that 'there *is* a direct lineage from Christianity to Marxism' (emphasis in original) and pp. 107 ff. where he makes the case for a 'Judeo-Christian logic'.

[4] See Žižek, *The Universal Exception*, pp. 183 ff.

[5] Ian Almond, *The New Orientalists: Postmodern Representations of Islam from Foucault to Baudrillard*, London: I.B. Tauris, 2007, pp. 192–193.

INTRODUCTION

his writings, they are typically treated in a blissfully reductionist manner, for instance when Žižek argues that underlying the protests against a cartoon series of the Prophet Mohammed, which were published by the Danish newspaper *Jyllands-Posten* in 2005 and which many Muslims deemed derogatory, is the 'Muslim belief in the sacred status of writing (which is why, traditionally, Muslims don't use paper in their toilets)'. The next step in the argumentation of Žižek is typical: 'A mocking of divinity', he states with the establishment of boundaries in mind, 'is part of European religious tradition itself, starting with the ancient Greek ritualistic ridiculing of the gods of Olympus'.[6]

As we will see in the following chapters, such artificial establishment of gated epistemological territories, which always also engender a euphoric, if claustrophobic sense of superiority, is characteristic of the processes of 'othering' at stake in this study. If vocal proponents of the (new) 'left' such as Žižek do not move beyond what Homi Bhaba aptly terms 'binary oppositions or polarities through which we think cultural difference'.[7] If a philosopher who was raised in a country that brought together different communities, including a sizeable Bosnian-Muslim population, does not mitigate otherness, what can we expect from the 'bin-Ladenesque fundamentalist' or the 'neoconservative crusader' whose understanding of the 'other' is engineered in—and articulated by a perversely violent and oppressively one-dimensional mindset that is entirely devoid of dialectical empathy?

I have chosen to start with a sketch of some of the ideas of one of the most frequently cited public intellectuals in the contemporary social sciences in order to indicate that the issues at stake here are largely divisive and why it is, to the surprise of many of us who live and think on the porous borders of East and West, North and South, that the idea that we are in the middle of some epic struggle between 'Islam' and the 'West' continues to be so fervently discussed and reproduced. Undoubtedly, the terrorist attacks on the United States in September 2001 and the 'neo-imperial' rhetoric surrounding the invasions of Afghanistan in 2001 and Iraq in 2003 have played their part in this unwelcome come-back. But as I will argue in this book, the marking of

6 Slavoj Žižek, *Violence: Six Sideways Reflections*, London: Profile Books, 2009, p. 90.
7 See further Homi K. Bhaba, *The Location of Culture*, London: Routledge, 1994, p. 182.

'self' and 'other' feeding into the 'clash regime' today and its corresponding us-versus-them logic has a diverse archive. We have not only failed to escape that logic. Our academic disciplines, movies, journalists, institutions, our whole cultural constellation is susceptible to accentuating the inevitability of conflict between supposedly homogenous constructs, especially between 'Islam' and the 'West', but also between other imagined collectivisations.[8] Expressed by elites and disseminated through powerful institutions, it is this regime of truth that is implicated in the ubiquitous, if artificial claim that some 'clash of civilisations' is inevitable, that violence between 'us' and 'them' is a 'natural' fact of history, or that our differences demand subjugating the 'other'. The aim of this book is to offer some suggestions for a more comprehensive critique of this 'clash regime'. This can only be done through an interrogation of History, for it is in the past that this system of thought anchors its institutionalised power to produce images of 'us' and 'them' that legitimate war and destruction. As such, the argument being presented here is a part of a growing literature in the social sciences in general, and in 'critical international relations' in particular which draw inspiration from a series of studies which have focused on the inter-relationship between discourse, power and knowledge.[9] It is not concerned with a chronology of Muslim-Western atrocities against each other or a straightforward history of the 'clash of civilisations' idea, from its supposed beginnings to its end. Rather, it presents an inquiry into the ways the revival of that idea became possible in our age; within what material and ideational constellations it has been produced; on the basis of which ideas it could appear, travel,

---

[8] I think Anderson's by now classic definition still holds. These collectives or communities are imagined 'because the members of even the smallest nation will never know most of their fellow-members, meet them, or even hear of them, yet in the minds of each lives the image of their communion'. See Benedict Anderson, *Imagined Communities: Reflections on the Origin and Spread of Nationalism*, revised edition, London: Verso, 1983, p. 6.

[9] Some of the recent studies include: David Campbell, *Writing Security: United States foreign policy and the politics of identity*, Manchester: Manchester University Press, 1992; and idem. *Politics Without Principle: Sovereignty, Ethics, and the Narratives of the Gulf War*, London: Lynne Rienner, 1993; Richard Jackson, *Writing the War on Terrorism: Language, Politics and Counterterrorism*, Manchester: Manchester University Press, 2005; and Corinna Mullin, *Constructing Political Islam as the New Other: America and its Post-War on Terror Politics*, (London: I.B. Tauris, forthcoming 2010).

INTRODUCTION

metamorphose and objectify itself. Ultimately, I am writing a metahistory of the making of the clash regime. The clash of civilisations thesis as it appears to us today is only a factor of this grander betrayal committed by those, who have written our history in such a violently divisive manner.

My point of departure is that the 'clash regime' is a cultural artefact of a very special and pervasive kind. I deem it 'cultural' because it is posited in different strata of society and institutions, because it claims historical depth and normative salience, because it is constituted by a range of interdependent discourses that disperse into society, at this very moment, an overwhelmingly powerful 'clash mentality'. To understand and battle with this structural power we are compelled to find out where the clash regime has been located, in what ways it has established its archives, and why today, it commands such immense ideological authority. At the same time, I am not claiming to capture the comprehensive history of the clash regime in the past or to construct a teleological stepping ladder to the present. Instead, I will attempt to explain why and how it could become a major part of today's national and international political culture. To that end, I will examine constructions of self and other in 'western' and 'Islamic' historiography, in Greek and Persian mythology, in Enlightenment discourse, in disciplines such as International Relations (IR) and Anthropology, in Islamist narratives, in the idea of the nation-state and in US foreign policies. In addition to issues of theory, epistemology and methodology, I consider discourse-power-knowledge relations that have an impact on political practice and on our very thinking about the 'other'.

Cultural artefacts such as the clash regime are comparable to nationalisms, imperialisms, or religious fundamentalisms. They are systemic. They articulate and produce, they animate and make things happen. They command a truly productive force. They make us believe in things, in justice, the nation, war. As such, the clash regime refers to more than a metanarrative. It is more powerful than organising principles which promise to give comprehensive meaning to aspects of our surrounding social world. It is even more powerful than discursive formations, more consequential than systematic patterns of narratives and statements which are bound up with each other. We are not dealing with something trivial here. We are faced by a structural giant. As such the clash regime is closer to what Michel Foucault calls a 'regime of truth':

Each society has its regime of truth, its 'general politics' of truth—that is, the types of discourse it accepts and makes function as true; the mechanisms and instances that enable one to distinguish true and false statements; the means by which each is sanctioned; the techniques and procedures accorded value in the acquisition of truth; the status of those who are charged with saying what counts as true.[10]

Foucault understands 'truth' to be a 'system of ordered procedures for the production, regulation, distribution, circulation, and operation of statements'.[11] Such truth is bound up 'in a circular relation', that is not strictly ordered, 'with systems of power that produce and sustain it, and to effects of power which it induces and which extend it'.[12] In other words, discourses not only represent a particular issue, nor do they only produce meaningful knowledge about it, which in turn affects social and political practices; they are a part of the way power operates, reveals itself and is contested. Once a particular discourse sustains its effectiveness via disciplinary constellations and in practice, it can be conceptualised as a regime of truth. It is through this under-standing of discourse, power and knowledge and their amalgamative interaction, that I have derived the concept of the clash regime, which is a major building block of the argument of this book.

Moreover, my analysis is informed by Foucault's claims inasmuch as I will discuss different exclusionary discourses inspired by 'Islamism', the 'West' and to a lesser extent other binary constellations such as Orient vs. Occident, East vs. West, civilisation vs. barbarism that sometimes operate alongside one another, sometimes in opposition, and sometimes in detachment. In the process of threading through the archives, I found that it is the clash regime itself that produces the object about which it deliberates. It is that regime of truth, that gives credence to the idea that we have always been in the middle of some clash between 'us' and 'them', Orient and Occident, Islam and the West, civilisation and barbarism. The clash is exactly non-existent out-side of such discourses suggesting it. The clash is exactly non-existent without the terroristic narratives spun by Al Qaeda; it does not exist without the hate-manuals of the resurgent right-wing parties in Europe;

---

[10] Michel Foucault, 'Truth and Power', in idem., *Power: Essential Works of Foucault, vol.* 3, James D. Faubion (ed.), Rober Hurley et. al. (trans.), London: Penguin, 2002, p. 131.

[11] Ibid., p. 132.

[12] Ibid., p. 132.

it is not existent without the violence of (neo)colonialism, (neo)imperialism and other forms of systematic oppression. The clash of civilisations as it appears to us today is a surface effect of all that has been invented about 'us' and 'them' in all the histories, statements, books, pamphlets, dialogues that have ruminated about the inevitability of inter-group conflicts. As such, the clash regime has become one of the most perennial and pernicious cultural artefacts of human history.

A history of the objectification, of the making into a 'reality' of the clash regime, I believe, must avoid reifying the prejudiced cultural context from which it draws sustenance. I am not identifying the clash regime so that at the end of this study its structural salience remains as it is. In order to avoid such a tautological own-goal, this study has to be positioned, from the outset, in that entirely hybrid and polluted area, in which the 'self' and the 'other' submerge. So even when I focus on very real clash situations—between warring states, between nations, between empires—I am aware that I am right in the middle of a social arena, that is to say that a) the opposing collectives take each other into account when they contemplate their actions and their very imagination as a group and b) they operate on the basis of a stock of shared knowledge acquired through direct or indirect interaction with the other side. When Walter Benjamin famously commented that there is 'no document of civilisation that is not at the same time a document of barbarism',[13] he was not only referring 'to the barbaric acts of history done in the name of civilisation, but also to the necessary interdependence and entanglement between civilisation and barbarism in the mutually defining opposition that is supposed to set them apart'.[14] This 'mutually defining opposition' is exactly the place where 'us' and 'them' emerge as entirely interdependent, where our sibling relationship is genealogically conjoined.

The letter written by sixty prominent US intellectuals, including Samuel Huntington, in reaction to the terrorist attacks of September 2001 and the responses it provoked in the Islamic worlds may serve as an example here. In the letter, the authors link the 'War on Terror' to

[13] Walter Benjamin, 'Theses on the Philosophy of History', in *Illuminations*, Hannah Arendt (ed.) and Harry Zohn (trans.), New York: Schocken Books, 1968, p. 256.

[14] Robert J.C. Young, *Colonial Desire: Hybridity in Theory, Culture and Race*, London: Routledge, 1995, p. 32.

the just war principles of Augustinian Christian philosophy stating that a 'just war can only be fought by a legitimate authority with responsibility for public order',[15] an implicit reference to the United States' role as the global 'policeman'. I will delay the discussion of the politico-ideological effects of such self-designations until Chapter 3, where I will focus on the relationship between discourse, power and violence in the context of US foreign policies. What concerns me at this stage is that the letter elicited immediate reactions in the Islamic worlds, in Saudi Arabia, Turkey, Indonesia, Algeria, Morocco, Egypt, Pakistan, Iran, Malaysia and beyond and that the responses by some of these self-proclaimed authorities operated along a similar structure, creating yet another instance for the conflict between 'us' and 'them' constitutive of the clash regime. Yet it is central to note here that even an angry response, such as the following by Abul Bara, opens up an interdependent field in which the Muslim self and the 'infidel' other are entirely co-constitutive:

It is not astonishing that crusaders have the impudence to attack Islam, a religion that deserves to be followed and to be spread as a priority for the world. What is shocking is that people who follow Islam have told the infidels that they want to coexist. It is shocking particularly because it comes at a moment in which the infidels are attacking and scorning Islam and launching a crusader war against Islam. It is shocking when we know that the answer of our intellectuals is a call for coexistence, and a comprehensive and just peace.[16]

Delineating the infidel from the pious, civilisation from barbarism, juxtaposing a 'free world' to an 'evil empire', presenting an Islam in opposition to a West, differentiating the in-group from the out-group, does not refer to or cause detachment. Such processes of 'othering' do not result in autonomy; 'we' and 'they' continue to inhabit a social field, our 'self' continues to be entirely interdependent with the 'other'. One cannot be the 'leader of the free world' without some understanding about the realm beyond this zone. One cannot be 'civilised' without inventing the attributes of the 'barbarian' other. One cannot

---

[15] 'What we're fighting for: A letter from America, 60 intellectuals', in David Blankenhorn, Abdou Filali-Ansary, Hassan I. Mneimneh, and Alex Roberts (eds.), *The Islam/West Debate: Documents from a global debate on terrorism, U.S. Ppolicy, and the Middle East*, Oxford: Rowman & Littlefield, 2005, p. 27.

[16] Abul Bara, 'Please Prostrate Yourselves Privately', in Blankenhorn et. al. (eds.), *The Islam/West Debate*, p. 82.

INTRODUCTION

meaningfully clash with someone else without presuming some understanding of who he/she is and what he/she stands for in the first place.
The history of the clash regime is not a history that has created detachment. Rather the contrary. We will find that it is a history that has
created a common genetic code in which we are entirely dependent on
each other. Today, who can think about Islam without the West? Who
can think about the West without Islam? Certainly, the proponents of
the clash regime cannot.

Yet at the same time, in any regime of truth, including the clash
regime at stake here, historically engineered collective representations
of the self and the other acquire a life of their own. They represent and
disseminate into society collective beliefs and anticipations that are
stable even as their properties are contested. It is in terms of this us-
versus-them logic constituted by the clash regime that individuals and
societies define their selves and others, rather than within a situation
that is neutral. The result is a logic of interaction between 'us' and
'them' that is based on inventions, rather than 'our' and 'their' 'actual'
qualities. Here, it should become immediately clear that I go beyond a
'fatalistically' deconstructive analysis that would disregard the 'quasi-
objective' status the clash regime has carved out for itself within society and the constitutive effects it has on our thinking about the other.
A metahistory of the objectification of a particular regime of truth cannot end before the object appears as autonomous, before the clash
regime escapes its engineers, before the clash of civilisation is accepted
as a 'fact'. To explain this paradox further we have to delve into the
realms of theory where deceptive realities are made, where everything
in our surrounding world has been concocted.

How do we think of the clash of civilisations as being real? Objectification implies that the invented clash regime appears external to its
makers. Reified as something distinctive, it becomes entirely capable of
sustaining a presence of its own that cannot simply be wished away.
And since structure and agency (or subjectivity) are always weaved
together; the clash regime also commands a clash mentality . Its sociological vigour cannot be detached from its psychological pathologies.
Its structural salience is meant to have a disciplining effect on the way
we think about the other. Its density turns us from culture maker to
culture taker. 'There exists a correspondence between social structures
and mental structures', writes Pierre Bourdieu, 'between the objective
divisions of the social world—particularly into dominant and dominated in the various fields—and the principles of vision and division

that agents apply to it'.[17] Bourdieu refers here to the mutual co-constitution of societal norms and individual cognitions with particular reference to the stratification of society into dominant and dominated. The other would always be pushed into the latter position and the idea that we are in conflict with them is very functional to that end. A fundamental psychological process ensues: the exponential historical exposure to the clash regime facilitated by elites engrains in society a set of salient and virulent dispositions that internalise the exclusionary precepts of that extant cultural artefact engraving in the very cognition of the individual agent its exclusionary logic. In turn, this guided reflexive interpenetration of social structures and mental cognitions, this pathological dialectic in which the clash regime sustains its parasitical existence, implies a moment of 'self-mutilation': the makers and takers of the clash regime are also its victims. The processes of externalisation, objectification, internalisation always also imply and engender a moment of 'introjection', exactly because culture and cognition are linked. Introjection implies that the socially engineered clash regime that classes, Muslims, Europeans and other self-conscious collectives sustain, are believed to be 'really' inevitable and necessary, rather than the outcome of particular historical circumstances, outright lies, racism, imperial competitions or a strategy of governments to sustain societal order or ideological cohesion within the 'nation'. In a Marcuseian sense the clash regime is thus a particularly violent, highly functional element of the reification of forms of discipline and dominance, which help to constitute today's proto-typical 'one-dimensional' individual who reveals himself as a disciple of war whenever the politics of the day demands it:

One-dimensional thought and behaviour are systematically promoted by the makers of politics and their purveyors of information: their universe of discourse is populated by self-validating hypotheses, which, incessantly and monopolistically repeated, become hypnotic definitions or dictations. ... Reason is turned into submission to the facts of life and to the dynamic capability of producing more and bigger facts of the same sort of life. The politico-technical apparatus and its totalitarian rationality and productivity militate against change, they blunt the recognition that facts are made, mediated by Subjectivity (a recognition long since incorporated into scientific method).[18]

[17] Pierre Bourdieu, *The State Nobility: Elite Schools in the field of power*, Lauretta C. Clough (trans.), Cambridge: Polity Press, 1996, p. 1.
[18] Herbert Marcuse, *Towards a Critical Theory of Society*, Douglas Kellner (ed.), London: Routledge, 2001, p. 55, emphasis in original.

INTRODUCTION

The political economy marking Marcuse's one-dimensional universe is comparable to the societal constellations producing 'truths' that Foucault relentlessly criticises (or the inter-relationship between 'field' and *habitus* in Bourdieu's 'reflexive sociology'). 'There is a battle "for truth" or at least "around truth"' which is understood as 'the ensemble of rules according to which the true and the false are separated and specific effects of power attached to the true'. According to Foucault, 'it's not a matter of a battle "on behalf" of truth but of a battle about the status of truth and the economic and political role it plays'.[19] Marcuse emphasises more explicitly the materialist aspects of power than Foucault, its introjective force, its power to subsume, to dominate, to enslave. Understood in this sense, the clash regime is 'deposited' within society as yet another form of authority over truth and suppression of counter-truths. Methodologically, it waxes and wanes within a circular universe composed of ongoing dialectical 'moments': externalisation (the incitement/production of a particular exclusionary discourse), objectification (the reification of that discourse), internalisation (the absorption of that discourse by agents and society), and introjection (the indoctrination of those agents and society by that discourse).[20] In this way, the clash regime occupies and holds on to an overbearing one-dimensional habitat from which the critical difference (the counter-regime), the power of negation is excluded.

One has to be very careful not to force or imply a direct, causal link between the clash regime and its corresponding clash mentality. There is no suggestion here that the agents of the clash are inevitably coded to think in dichotomous terms. At any point of time society creates counter-discourses which challenge and modify the exclusionary logic underlying the clash regime. Society can never be subsumed under one all encompassing logic, be it that of the clash regime, Islamism, fundamentalism, modernity or other. The structural composure within the clash regime does not refer to an arbitrary aggregation of conflicts between 'us' and 'them' that are 'natural' and inevitable. Nor does it relate to a historical conspiracy to that end that we cannot escape. The clash regime presents itself within society as a source of probable conflict which always implies a measure of indeterminacy. At the same

[19] Foucault, *Power*, p. 132.
[20] See also further my *Iran in World Politics: The Question of the Islamic Republic*, New York: Columbia University Press, 2008.

time, the clash regime has exhibited a rather strong gravity which it forces upon society and individuals who enter in it. The last part of the previous sentence ('who enter it') is crucial. Despite the pressures of the clash regime on society and individual cognitions about the other, thinking in dichotomous terms, believing in some clash of civilisations continues to be a choice. We all may carry the seeds of the clash regime within us, we all may be predisposed to ostracise the other, to positively distinguish ourselves from him/her as cognitive psychologists and neurophysiologists argue. But there is no automatism that triggers these attitudes and turns them into hatred and fear of the other. We will find out that historically, the triggering devices are composed of powerful inventions that accentuate conflict in the name of national, civilisational or religious group affiliations.

The structural quality of the clash regime and its systematic marketing today requires a cultural genealogy to survey where its exclusionary tenets have been located. As we will see, history is but one of the sites where the violent logic of the clash regime is reproduced. The international media and our educational institutions are others. I am aware that my focus on the structural depth of the clash regime and its corresponding psychological efficacy is open to the criticism that I am vastly exaggerating the pervasive power of this cultural artefact. But I think it is a qualified emphasis. As I hope to demonstrate in the following chapters: contemporary society is exposed to the clash regime as preconditioned by its exclusionary premises which have been sustained and enriched from innumerable loci throughout human history. Some of us think of the clash of civilisations today, in short, because we are coded to do so.

The implication of treating the clash as a 'regime' is not that it is a part of the natural order of things, that it has any 'real' and inevitable truth content beyond its production, but rather that it derives its socially constructed status from particularly privileged human beings (in East and West or North and South) who have objectified and disseminated it to enforce their political, economic, cultural and social agendas. The clash regime functions for a tiny strata of society that benefits from conflict and war, for instance politically (i.e. parties fanning xenophobia against immigrants in order to gain votes), ideologically (i.e. states and networks benefitting from group constellations that enhance their claim to lead the 'in-group' such as the free world, or the 'Muslim nation'), and/or materially (i.e. the military-industrial complex). The individuals, the 'clash agents' embedded within these strata of society, function as incubators of cognitive integration. They mould and remould the violent logic of the clash on a continuous basis. In this way, they manage to promote the political and social homogenisation of an oppressive system: the injustice of contemporary society—domestic and international—is decisively reproduced by the reification of binary categories which, being conducive to sustain the divisions of the prevalent order (e.g. class divisions) and therefore amenable to the interests of the ruling elites, are made readily available to all of us. In short, the clash regime can hover above and exist within society because many individuals, and the institutional sites that formalise their power, want it to.

It was Edward Said, of course, who referred to the ideas of Foucault in *Orientalism*, in order to represent that discipline as a discourse rather than a 'natural' reality. According to Said, 'without examining Orientalism as a discourse one cannot possibly understand the enormously systematic discipline by which European culture was able to manage—and even produce—the Orient'.[21]Although Orientalism asserts factual validity, even a scientific status, Said points out that it is the product of ideological fiction with no real linkage to the cultures and peoples it claims to explain. Beyond this, Said took seriously Foucault's idea that power and knowledge are joined together: Orientalism does not only constitute a particular discourse, it produces the Orient 'politically, sociologically, militarily, ideologically, scientifically, and imaginatively during the post-Enlightenment period'.[22]

Furthermore, it follows for Said that Orientalism has muted the Orient intellectually and discursively. The object (the Orient) is ostracised from the discourse of Orientalism; it does not speak, it is not present within its articulation. 'If we use the Napoleonic expedition (1798–1801) as a sort of first enabling experience for modern Orientalism', Said writes, 'we can consider its inaugural heroes—in Islamic studies, Sacy and Renan and Lane—to be builders of the field, creators of a tradition, progenitors, of the Orientalist brotherhood'. Said attributes maximum structural salience to this discursive formation:

What Sacy, Renan, and Lane did was to place Orientalism on a scientific and rational basis. This entailed not only their own exemplary work but also the

[21] Edward Said, *Orientalism: Western Conceptions of the Orient*, London: Penguin, 1995, p. 3.
[22] Ibid., p. 3.

creation of a vocabulary and ideas that could be used impersonally by anyone who wished to become an Orientalist. Their inauguration of Orientalism was a considerable feat. It made possible a scientific terminology; it banished obscurity and instated a special form of illumination for the Orient; it established the figure of the Orientalist as central authority for the Orient; it legitimised a special kind of specifically coherent Orientalist work; it put into cultural circulation a form of discursive currency by whose presence the Orient henceforth would be *spoken* for; above all, the work of the inaugurators carved out a field of study and a family of ideas which in turn could form a community of scholars whose lineage, traditions, and ambitions were at once internal to the field and external enough for general prestige.[23]

It is this thesis, itself inspired by Foucault's own effort to show how civilisation has banished the other, in his case the mad and insane, that provoked the wrath of the 'Orientalist' establishment on the one side, whilst inspiring a corpus of 'subaltern' studies which represent the voice of the 'oppressed' on the other.[24] In the main, it will become apparent that my own thinking has been seriously affected by Said's scholarly corpus. Yet in what follows in this book, I go beyond the idea that the other was muted, that discourse functions according to a strict inclusion-exclusion logic. Discourses and their corresponding knowledge-power dynamics cannot be possessed, organised or shut down by one social agent (e.g. individuals, institutions, disciplines) or the other. They are, in this sense, gliding phenomena; heterogeneous, rather than homogeneous, capillary rather than hierarchical, progressive rather than conservative. In the orthodox view, power emerges from the state (or a discursive constellation such as Orientalism in Said's case) and exercises its fulminate force onto society (or the colonised); it operates in a top-down fashion. But Foucault draws our attention to the diffusion of power, its 'relayed' locality within society, the individual and our psychological and physical existence:

Do not regard power as a phenomenon of mass and homogenous domination—the domination of one individual over others, of one group over others, or of one class over others; keep it clearly in mind that unless we are looking at it from a great height and from a very great distance, power is not something that is divided between those who have it and hold it exclusively, and

---

[23] Ibid., p. 122, emphasis in original.
[24] See further on this issue Robert J.C. Young, *White Mythologies: Writing, History and the West*, London: Routledge, 1991; or Zachary Lockman, *Contending Visions of the Middle East: The History and Politics of Orientalism*, Cambridge: Cambridge University Press, 2004.

those who do not have it and are subject to it. Power must, I think, be analysed as something that circulates, or rather as something that functions only
when it is part of a chain. It is never localised here or there, it is never in the
hands of some, and it is never appropriated in the way that wealth or a commodity can be appropriated. Power functions. Power is exercised through
networks, and individuals do not simply circulate in those networks; they are
in a position to both submit to and exercise this power.[25]

In their collaborative study of the entanglement between power,
resistance and space, Ronan Paddison, Chris Philo, Paul Routledge and
Joanne Sharp, mention the prison of Long Kesh (also H-Blocks and
The Maze), as a site where power—in this case the power of the state
exercised through incarceration/confinement—intersected with the
power of resistance. The length of the hunger strike of the ten Republican prisoners led by Bobby Sands, who eventually passed away from
the effects, did not only contribute to the restructuring of the political
strategy of the Irish Republican Army (IRA) by a younger generation
of leaders, including Gerry Adams; the very spatiality of the prison, the
caging together of hundreds of prisoners for surveillance and discipline, created new spaces for resistance and communication. 'The
particular spatiality of domination within Long Kesh', the authors
point out, 'enabled an articulatory and strategic space of Republican
resistance to be created'.[26]

The point of that short foray into the proliferating field of 'critical
geography' is to indicate that the power to resist, or indeed to narrate,
is possessed by everyone: prisoner, colonised, subject, Oriental, Occidental, Muslim, European, North American. 'Power is everywhere; not
because it embraces everything, but because it comes from everywhere'.[27] This does not mean that there are no power discrepancies of

[25] Michel Foucault, *Society Must be Defended: Lectures at the Collège de
France*, Mauro Bertani and Alessandro Fontana (eds), David Macey (trans.),
London: Penguin, 2004, p. 29.
[26] Ronan Paddison, Chris Philo, Paul Routledge and Joanne Sharp, *Entangle-
ments of Power: Geographies of Domination/Resistance*, London: Routledge,
1999, p. 28. On critical approaches to geography and space see also Jeremy
W. Crampton and Stuart Elden (eds.), *Space, Knowledge and Power:
Foucault and Geography*, London: Ashgate, 2007; and Edward W. Soya,
*Postmodern Geographies: The Reassertion of Space in Critical Social
Theory*, London: Verso, 1989.
[27] Michel Foucault, *The Will to Kowledge: The History of Sexuality*, vol. 1,
Robert Hurley (trans.), London: Penguin, 1998, p. 93.

course, that men are not suppressing women in patriarchal societies, that imperial force does not devastate whole continents, that discrimination and racism are not very real obstacles holding minorities back. What it means is that power and resistance are intermingled, that the site of power cannot be detached from its source, that master and slave, subject and object, us and them are equally entangled with the forces of power. We are alerted that 'power is not an institution, and not a structure; neither is it a certain strength we are endowed with; it is the name that one attributes to a complex strategical situation in a particular society'.[28] In short, power is promiscuous; we are all entirely interdependent subjects of particular power constellations. In order to explain how power functions and is exercised, we need to identify the particular points and agents through which it passes, for instance, governments, Mullahs, journalists, scholars, academic disciplines, political and socio-economic institutions, political parties, preachers, marketing managers, etc. At the same time, it is necessary to look at the entanglements of power and resistance, and to try to detect the 'power of the powerless', their latent ability to subvert and dislocate their position within the dialectics of master and slave, husband and wife, core and periphery, state and society, system and individual, subject and object.

The effect of such understanding of the inter-relationships between discourse, power and knowledge is to question the validity of the natural truthfulness of 'facts' and focus attention instead on the mechanism of persuasion, which reveals the 'hidden agenda' of a particular writer or political movement. So instead of the clash regime being considered a fact of nature, deriving, for example, from a 'real' clash between 'Islam' and the 'West', we would be able to conceive it as the product of innumerable narratives suggesting that such a clash exists. Consequently, questions such as: what were the main battles between the West and Islam, what is the history of conflict between these civilisations, why does Islam clash with the West and vice versa, must be substituted by questions of a different kind; in a specific cultural, socioeconomic, political and historical context, how do Islamic/western narratives extract themselves? How do different societal settings make possible the discourses about Islam/the West, how do they inhibit their powers? How is an Islam and a West positioned as a binary formation? What are the logocentricisms/methodologies/epistemologies that simu-

---

[28] Ibid., p. 93.

16

late internal, civilisational coherence and difference to the other? In short, rather than attempting to excavate the true, eternal essence of ideas, such as the clash of civilisations and their composite binaries, we are compelled to comprehend the composition of expanding narratives about them within specific contexts.

The clash of civilisations has been alternatively termed 'the clash of barbarisms' by Gilbert Achcar, 'the clash of fundamentalisms' by Tariq Ali and the 'clash of definitions' by Edward Said.[29] Indeed, international literature on 'Islam' and the 'West' has multiplied in the past few years, which by itself indicates the importance attached to the subject. In the German academic context, the clash of civilisations thesis is criticised by Kai Hafiz, Andreas Meier, Udo Steinbach and in a rather more reluctant way by Bassam Tibi.[30] In France, both Gilles Kepel and Olivier Roy have written extensive tracts about the dangers and failures of some politico-Islamic discourses, some would say in a rather sweeping manner.[31] In Britain, where there is substantive breeding ground for rather nefarious polemics on the 'Islamic menace' in influential and widely read newspapers (particularly in the 'tabloid press'),

[29] Gilbert Achcar, *The Clash of Barbarisms: The Making of the New World Disorder*, London: Paradigm, 2006; Tariq Ali, *The Clash of Fundamentalisms: Crusades, Jihads and Modernity*, London: Verso, 2003; Edward Said, 'The Clash of Definitions', in idem, *Reflections on Exile and other Essays*, Cambridge, MA: Harvard University Press, 2000. Others have used comparable concepts. See, for instance, Ken Booth and Tim Dunne (eds.), *Worlds in Collision: Terror and the Future of Global Order*, London: Palgrave, 2002.

[30] See amongst others Kai Hafez (ed.), *The Islamic World and the West: An Introduction to Political Cultures and International Relations*, Leiden: Brill, 2000; Andreas Meier (ed.), *Der politische Auftrag des Islam: Programme und Kritik zwischen Fundamentalismus und Reformen—Originalstimmen aus der islamischen Welt*, Wuppertal: Peter Hammer Verlag, 1995; Bassam Tibi, *The Challenge of Fundamentalism: Political Islam and the New World Disorder*, Berkeley: University of California Press, 1998.

[31] See Gilles Kepel, *Allah in the West: Islamic Movements in America and Europe*, Cambridge: Polity, 1997; idem. *Jihad: The trail of political Islam*, London: I.B. Tauris, 2002; and idem. *The Roots of Radical Islam*, London: Saqi, 2005; Olivier Roy, *The Failure of Political Islam*, Carol Volk (trans.), London: I.B. Tauris, 1999; idem., *Globalised Islam: The Search for a New Ummah*, London: Hurst, 2002; and idem. *The Politics of Chaos in the Middle East*, Ros Schwartz (trans.), London: Hurst, 2007.

Fred Halliday is amongst the most strident academic critics of the myth of an Islamic threat.[32] In the United States, the high tide of anti-Islamic sentiments after 9/11 is contained by the sober and balanced writings of John Esposito amongst others.[33] In policy terms, the clash of civilisations thesis even provoked a symbolic counter-approach in the form of the 'Dialogue among Civilisations' initiative, suggested by the former Iranian President Mohammad Khatami and adopted by the United Nations as the political motto in 2001.[34] Since then it has metamorphosed into the 'Alliance of Civilisations' sponsored, amongst others, by the Turkish Prime Minister Recep Tayyip Erdogan. Likewise, US President Barack Obama felt compelled to point out on a trip to Turkey in April 2009 that the 'United States is not at war with Islam'.[35] In a similar spirit, Alastair Crooke who was an adviser to EU High Representative Javier Solana and who was involved in negotiations with Islamist movements in Palestine, has recently finished a perceptive book on Islamic views of the 'West'.[36] The Archbishop of Canterbury, Rowan Williams, has also been concerned with the idea of a clash between Islamic and western values.[37] His comments that the British state should consider incorporating elements of sharia law sparked angry rebuttals by many British commentators with right-wing leniencies. Leaders of other denominations are equally unsettled by the status quo. Indeed, so topical is the idea of an ongoing clash of civilisations that the chief rabbi of the United Hebrew Congregations of the

---

[32] See Fred Halliday, *Islam and the Myth of Confrontation*, London: I.B. Tauris, 1995.

[33] See John L. Esposito, *The Islamic Threat: Myth or Reality*, Oxford: Oxford University Press, 1999.

[34] See further Mohammad Khatami, *Islam, Dialogue and Civil Society*, Canberra: Centre for Arab and Islamic Studies, The Australian National University, 2000; and beyond within the Iranian context, see, Mojtaba Amiri (ed.), *Theory of Clash of Civilisations: Huntington and his critics*, Tehran: Foreign Ministry Publishing House, 1995.

[35] The speech is available at <http://news.bbc.co.uk/1/shared/bsp/hi/pdfs/06_04_09_obamaspeech.pdf> [Last accessed 19 April 2009].

[36] Alastair Crooke, *Resistance: The essence of the Islamist revolution*, London: Pluto, 2009.

[37] 'Sharia law in UK is "unavoidable"', BBC News, 7 February 2008, Available at <http://news.bbc.co.uk/1/hi/uk/7232661.stm> [Last accessed 22 February 2009]. See also <http://www.archbishopofcanterbury.org/1581> [Last accessed 22 February 2009] for a full exposé on the subject.

Commonwealth, Jonathan Sacks, felt compelled to dedicate a whole book to measures on how to avoid it.[38]

Huntington's methodological omissions and empirical flaws have been convincingly revealed especially in the studies of Esposito and Mottahedeh.[39] Consequently, I believe I can set aside the civilisational component. There is no such thing as a coherent western or Islamic civilisation that could/would clash. Civilisations are not tectonic plates that move against each other. Having said that, those authors mentioned above, who have rephrased the clash of civilisations, appear to acknowledge that there are some factors at conflict here. Undoubtedly, there exist powerful discursive constructions that signify Islam and the West as such, and which have penetrated our cultural systems, and our understanding of selfhood and the other. Indeed, this study intends to show how a Manichean world-view has been promoted by 'power brokers' throughout history in both the western and the eastern worlds.

We cannot simply wish away the clash regime. It is too convenient to ignore that there are influential clash disciples out there. Why is it that the idea continues to be weaved into a range of discourses and disciplinary apparatuses, if it is a myth, if it is irrational, if it is illogical? In order to address this question the epistemological context in which the clash regime grounds its fulminate force and thereby manifests itself as a pervasive attitude permeating the mindsets of influential decision and opinion makers, needs to be brought into focus. In this analysis, what should crystallise are those structural signposts which

---

[38] Jonathan Sacks, *Dignity of Difference: How to Avoid the Clash of Civilisations*, London: Continuum, 2003.

[39] See Esposito, *The Islamic Threat*, 1999; Roy P. Mottahedeh, 'The Clash of Civilisations: An Islamicist's critique', *Harvard Middle Eastern and Islamic Review*, Vol. 2, No. 1 (1995), pp. 1–26;. Other recent studies dealing with the clash thesis include: Fawaz Gerges, *America and Political Islam: Clash of Cultures or Clash of Interests?* Cambridge: Cambridge University Press, 1999; Graham E. Fuller and Ian O. Lesser, *A Sense of Siege: The geopolitics of Islam and the West*, Boulder, CO: Westview 1995; Amin Saikal, *Islam and the West: Conflict or Cooperation*, London: Palgrave, 2003; Mark B. Salter, *Barbarians and Civilization in International Relations*, London: Pluto, 2002; and S. Sayyid, *A Fundamental Fear: Eurocentrism and the emergence of Islamism*, London: Zed, 1997. For a critique of Sayyid from the 'Left' see Susan Buck-Morss, *Thinking Past Terror: Islamism and critical theory on the Left*, London: Verso, 2003, pp. 44 ff. and 105 ff.

have given rise to the clash regime, that is the transnational ideas, institutions, norms and ideological constellations that have reified the self-fulfilling message of an inevitable crisis between 'us' and 'them'. At the end of this journey we should arrive at a tentative anatomy of the clash regime that goes beyond existent concepts. And since it is parts of 'Islam' and the 'West' that we put on the operating table, their body of thought will be dissected so that we can better identify their constituent parts and the way they have been assembled. This may be a first, very small step towards cutting out some of the mutations affecting them along the way.

In this sense, the contemporary presence of the clash regime is due to its historically engineering in the name of the 'West' and 'Islam' and other imagined collectivisations. As a cultural artefact, the clash regime is the outcome of an apparently immutable, incestuous consensus amongst influential strata of European, North American and Muslim majority societies: they are all in agreement that there is a perennial and inevitable conflict between the secular Occident and the Muslim Orient, between *dar al-Islam* and *dar al-harb* between the West and the rest—you are either with us, both sides proclaim, or against us. The present study will show that ultimately there is no epistemological, methodological or psychological antagonism here. Rather, what we have is a particular form of mimesis, an immediate identification of the clash disciples with the normality and necessity of some 'clash' between collectives or, if necessary in order to 'purify' the in-group, within them. Thus, the transnational clash regime is constituted dialectically. It is homologous because the clash disciples here and there depart from the same cognitive disposition: the warring factions are genetically and genealogically linked to the same regime. They are certainly not detachable in a psychological sense because both need each other to exist. Their 'I am' is entirely intertwined with the other, with the 'He/She is'. The ideal-types, East and West, Occident and Orient are co-constitutive. The clash disciples are not only entirely dependent on each other because the other has become the referent for determining the self—the other inhabits the self.

So imagined collectivisations such as 'Islam' and the 'West', Orient and Occident, are asymmetrical formations that are not at all reducible to a single, autonomous logic or a coherent political, cultural or socio-economic regime. Several studies, authored by scholars from different disciplinary backgrounds, have corroborated this inevitable interdependence: to the social anthropologist Jack Goody, Islam is an integral part of Europe;[40] the political scientist John M. Hobson declares that 'the deceptively Eurocentric view is false for various reasons, not the least of which is that the West and East have been fundamentally and consistently interlinked through globalisation ever since 500 CE'.[42] Similar scepticism towards the linear development of civilisations and their seemingly coherent histories has been expressed by Martin Bernal, Jerry Brotton, Peter Burke, Andre Gunter Frank and others.[42] These critical approaches point to the interconnections between East and West, North and South thus debunking the familiar symmetries on which overbearing regimes of truth, such as the one under scrutiny here, depend.

But it is not only that Orient and Occident have been co-constitutive on cultural, ideational, historical, economic or ethical grounds. There has also been cross-fertilisation of the discourse of 'othering' which has been strengthened in this process of interaction. It is true that '[n] either the West nor Islam can be understood without reference to the other'.[43] But this does not mean that as discursive formations, Islam and the West have lost their signifying vigour; that they have ceased to claim plausibility. The fact that Islam has been in the West and that the West has been in the Islamic worlds does not mean that Islam and the West are the same. Globalisation has not advanced to the degree that it has created universal sameness. The fact that there are approximately 20 million Muslims living in the European Union and that the 'Middle East' cannot be conceived of without the 'West' has not created a common ideational field in which the categories 'West' and 'Islam' have ceased to exist. Islam and the West retain their gravitating

[40] See Jack Goody, *Islam in Europe*, Cambridge: Polity, 2004.

[41] John M. Hobson, *The Eastern Origins of Western Civilisation*, Cambridge: Cambridge University Press, 2004, p. 2.

[42] See Martin Bernal, *Black Athena: Tthe Afroasiatic Roots of Classical Civilizations,*. Vol. 1: *The Fabrication of Ancient Greece 1785–1985*, London: Free Association Books, 1987; Jerry Brotton, *The Renaissance Bazaar: From the Silk Road to Michelangelo*, Oxford: Oxford University Press, 2002; Peter Burke, *The European Renaissance: Centres and Peripheries*, Oxford: Blackwell, 1998; Andre Gunter Frank, *ReOrient: Global Economy in the Asian Age*, Berkeley: University of California Press, 1998.

[43] Tarak Barkawi, *Globalisation and War*, Lanham, MD: Rowman & Littlefield, 2005, p. 140.

powers which they impose on objects and agents which enter into their realms. This does not mean that accentuating difference is the same as calling for a clash. Difference can be celebrated, negotiated, mitigated and tolerated. Not all the personalities and constellations that I will examine are supportive of a clash only because they accentuate difference or because they play the game of identity politics. What I accept is that for a great many people categories such as Islam or the West, continue to be accepted as Lacanian *points de capiton* or nodal points; master signifiers with immense identity inducing properties.[44] For a great many less, whose destructive powers are nonetheless exponentially higher, they continue to be worth dying and killing for. And for yet others they, or related sub-concepts such as 'humanitarian intervention', the 'caliphate' or the 'free world', function as ready-made formulas to legitimate aggression and murder. The latter two groups 'inhabit' the clash regime and have immediate analytical value for this study. In one way or another they are busy remoulding disparate issues, for instance the Rushdie affair, the cartoon controversy in Denmark, 9/11 and the current wars in Iraq and Afghanistan, into the quasi-reality that the clash between Islam and the West is inevitable.

Hence it must be captured analytically that both the political economy sustaining the clash regime (and its historical 'underbelly') and tendencies towards radical transformations persist and that radical political change may eventually be possible. Consequently, this study will vacillate throughout between two contradictory realities. On the one side, it will show that there have existed throughout history alternative forms of experience and ideas which have stressed inclusiveness, and which have divorced themselves from Manichean categories such as East versus West, Occident versus Orient or Islam versus Christianity. So I am aware that next to the reoccurring episteme of civilisational superiority and distinctiveness there were counter-discourses of an inclusive kind which accentuated integration and the oneness of the human species. No hegemony of thought is all encompassing; everything surrounding us is constantly challenged; nothing worldly remains eternally dominant.[45] One only needs to consider Goethe's East-Western

---

[44] See Sayyid, *Eurocentrism*, pp. 45 ff.

[45] With regard to this oppositional conception of the possibility of—and necessity for social change I am borrowing from Raymond Williams, especially his *Marxism and Literature*, Oxford: Oxford University Press, 1977, pp. 113. ff.

Divan, Jalal ad-Din Rumi's poetic musings about the enveloping powers of love or Aldous Huxley's beautifully metaphysical style in *The Perennial Philosophy* to appreciate that there have been constant and quite successful efforts to transcend dichotomous reasoning, to move beyond the limitations of Manichean categories. All the more surprising that the clash regime continues to be so vividly contemporaneous; that we have not managed to find a consensus that could signify a common fate for humanity.

On the other side, there will be an intense focus on the 'clash disciples', who generally found themselves in a hegemonic position, in charge of immense ideational and material power resources, and who were thus capable to contain the counter-regime and its nascent power of negation. Although the primary focus of the analysis is on the clash regime, on the personalities, narratives, ideologies, norms, social institutions, disciplines that have operated on and perpetuated its one-dimensional premises, I will also attempt to sketch the discursive nuances within and interconnections between formations such as 'civilisation' and barbarity, Islam and Christianity and Islam and the West. The fact that there will be more material on the clash side of things, especially in discourses signifying the 'West', is not a matter of choice or due to convenient cherry picking. Rather it is an empirical indicator of the hegemony of such discourse in the different epochs covered. The 'counter-regime' to the clash mentality has been weak and, alas, has not been dominant. Having said that, it is precisely the vision of 'what could be' which is discussed more extensively in the last chapter that dramatises the gloomy reality of 'what is'; the two concepts are juxtaposed in the same chapter and throughout the book.

From that juxtaposition between reality and 'utopia', a critical position is extracted. One-dimensional thought derives its norms, narratives, and ideology from the regime of truth constituted by the vast corpus of 'clash-conducive' productions. The critique of it resists the status-quo thus sustained and reproduced. At the same time, a critical alternative cannot profess 'concepts which could bridge the gap between the present and its future; holding no promise and showing no success, it remains negative'.[46] It is this negativity that turns criticism into an endemic practice. Very much inspired by that productive

---

[46] Herbert Marcuse, *One-Dimensional Man: Studies in the Ideology of Advanced Industrial Society*, London: Routledge, 1991, p. 257.

pessimism, the present book should thus be conceived of as a metahistorical critique of the clash regime, an exercise in theory and political philosophy rather than descriptive history. I am convinced with Said and Foucault that history comes after discourse, that theory precedes reality. Hence, you will find that my historical examples follow particular, thematically structured discourses about the meaning of the 'West', Islams, Orients and Occidents. This study is not chronologically ordered in strict terms because of that suspicion towards the tales and imagined historical 'realities' it faces.

Let me quickly summarise the composition of what follows. In the next chapters, I will attempt to bring into focus some of the issues that have habituated us to think in a particularly divisive mode. I will start with a discussion about the way 'self' and 'other' were signified in the discourses of Antiquity, before moving on to a perusal of Christian and Islamic inventions (Chapter 1). Chapter 2 delves into the depth of the grammatical structure of the clash regime. In its wealth of exclusionary dictums the clash regime circulates around a set of syntactical, epistemological and methodological devices. These can be discerned from the writings of 'guild' historians, as well as from the books and pamphlets of colonial functionaries, and in response to them, in the tracts of Islamists. The nuances, tensions, differences and commonalities between those attitudes cannot be satisfactorily deciphered, it is argued in this chapter, without going through the pains of identifying their 'syntactical' structure. At the end of this process, we may be better positioned to place ourselves beyond the grammar of the clash regime and change our language in relation to the other. Chapter 3 locates the clash regime in the contemporary international system with a particular emphasis on US foreign policies, the backlash in the Muslim worlds and its impact on world order. Finally, in the last chapter, I will peruse instances of the clash regime today and engage with 'contrapuntal' signposts of a counter-regime: 'negative dialectics' that suggest alternative ways of thinking about the other.

In all of this the present study attempts to reflect on, and at times challenge ideas such as Islamism, the West, Orientalism, Occidentalism, without claiming to discover some kind of 'grand paradigm' that we can all agree upon. Only because I am interested in shacking the discursive and ideological scaffolding of the clash regime, it does not mean that I am willing to, or indeed capable of, erecting something equally structural in its place. Of course, I am aware that dispelling the myth of the clash of civilisations cannot be attempted without a certain intransigent fanaticism about revealing what is merely engineered, criticising what is taken as a given, and 'exploding' what is monolithically crafted. One ends up 'terrorising' teleological theory, planting 'bombs' wherever one encounters rigid building blocks of thought that threaten to compound existing hierarchies, asymmetries and relations of domination. And yet, the purpose of juxtaposing the ideological functions of the clash idea here and there in one analysis is not to invent a homogenous counter model; it is not in my interest to create a clash versus dialogue binary. The idea of a 'dialogue of civilisations' is as dependent on the myth of undisturbed civilisational entities as the 'clash of civilisations'. To think in stark dichotomies is both utterly irrational and devastatingly provincial. This book seeks to engage with a set of questions that are pertinent to contemporary (world) politics to that end: Why do so many people in the twenty-first century continue to believe, with so much devastating passion and destructive anger, that conflict between imagined collectivisations is inevitable? What is it in these ideas that perpetuate the clash regime? Why hasn't western modernity (or Islam for that matter) created 'coherence' between us and them?[47] Isn't that universal brotherhood part of what they promised us, at times with the authority of God behind them?

Of course, there is a normative ambition behind all this, naturally I am interested in attacking the clash regime, and believe that intellectuals have a particular duty in this regard. We can afford the luxury to rebel, at a time when many people surrounding us have been de-politicised to the degree that they get more excited by the Paris Hiltons of this world than the politics of their own country; the very politics that determines their place in society and the future of their children. Many quarters of (international) society have been politically marginalised in this way and rebellion seems to me to be the only way to make our voices heard.

To that end, allow me to speak.

---

[47] On the congruence of the 'socialist' and 'capitalist' utopia and its common roots in modernity see Susan Buck-Morss, *Dreamworld and Catastrophe: The Passing of Mass Utopia in East and West*, Cambridge, MA: MIT, 2000.

1

THE PASSIONS OF HISTORY

We grasp the significance of a moment in the past. It is meaningful insofar as in it a connection with the future was made, through an act or an actual event (Erlebnis).

Wilhelm Dilthey

Self and Other, Us and Them

I have started to argue that the clash regime refers to a vast system; that its exclusionary logic is re-inscribed into society and that its structural tenets have not emerged recently.[1] The issue to be noticed about the logic of this regime, which continuously accentuates and legitimates the necessity of conflict, is how strategically important it has been, how often its exclusionary violence has been invoked in order to legitimate domestic and international aggression, how successful it has been in reifying memories of war and oppression. History is central here. By continuously attempting to persuade us that the supposed conflict between, 'us' and 'them', especially between 'Islam' and the 'West', has always existed, the disciples of the regime concoct a historical field in which the exclusionary logic of the clash can reveal itself as such. Deliberately placed within it, we are continuously alerted to the undue presence of the 'other'. If the clash regime successfully sustains

---

[1] Parts of this section have appeared in 'A (short) History of the Clash of Civilisations', *Cambridge Review of International Affairs*, vol. 21, no. 2, Summer 2008, pp. 217–234.

its structural power and psychological efficacy today, it is because it is repeatedly positioned within an ideational tradition rooted in the past. 'Inventing traditions', write Eric Hobsbawm and Terence Ranger, 'is essentially a process of formalisation and ritualisation, characterised by reference to the past, if only by imposing repetition'.[2] Michel Foucault agrees that tradition gives a 'special temporal status to a group of phenomena that are both successive and identical ...' enabling us 'to isolate the new against a background of permanence'.[3] This idea of 'permanence' in turn is very close to what Paul Ricoeur means when he argues that 'to live in human time is to live between the private time of our mortality and the public time of language'.[4] These authors alert us to the effects that appeals to the past are designed to have: they are meant to create artificial territories populated with seemingly contingent truth conditions that permanently reify the logic of a particular idea. They are meant to create 'pseudo-realities'. Hence we are told that the clash between 'Islam' and the 'West' has always been there, that it is inevitable, that there is normality to the confrontation; that we are merely born into it and so on. The truth regime thus created invents a grammar and syntax that translates the statement of a clash of civilisation into a seemingly highly realistic fact.

In a particularly striking section in *Writing and Difference*, Derrida 'wonders whether history itself does not begin with [some] relationship with the other'.[5] Derrida seeks to emphasise here the interdependent dynamics of history. He attempts to set himself apart from Levinas' emphasis on the absolute alterity of the other which would place the self-other delineation thus totalised beyond philosophical and historical mitigation. Derrida argues that rather than the otherness of the other being absolute and infinite, the other always also inhabits the self: *J'est un autre*—I is an other. Without this interdependency, alterity could not be established in the first place. 'Just as ... simple internal consciousness could not provide itself with time and with the absolute

---

[2] Eric Hobsbawm and Terence Ranger (eds), *The Invention of Tradition*, Cambridge: Cambridge University Press, 1983, p. 4.

[3] Michel Foucault, *The Archaeology of Knowledge*, London: Routledge, 1989, p. 23.

[4] Paul Ricoeur in R. Kearney, *Dialogues with Contemporary Continental Thinkers*, Manchester: Manchester University Press, 1984, p. 20.

[5] Jacques Derrida, *Writing and Difference*, new edition, London: Routledge, 1990, p. 94.

alterity of every instant without the irruption of the totally-other, so the ego cannot engender alterity within itself without encountering the other'.[6]

Such notions of otherness as expressions of mutually interdependent differences have only been theorised very recently. With Derrida (and Deleuze), the other becomes an opportunity that we can appreciatively embrace and that we have to acknowledge in order to make our 'self' visible in the first place. This discourse is a particularly valuable one, but it only emerged with the 'post-modern' *zeitgeist* enveloping some creative minds, primarily in continental Europe. The narratives accentuating conflict between self and other that we will peruse in the following paragraphs are different; not only in terms of their political message, but also in the way they are assembled. Some of them think difference absolute and immitigable, some of them necessary and expedient. All of them implode within the hyphen between the self-other dialectic thus provoked. Hence they open up a vast space that we think unbridgeable. We will find that to that end, particular methodical and grammatical 'devices' are used. The force of those disjunctive attitudes suggests to some of us today that the natural order of things is Manichean, that everything beyond the confines of what we have been habituated to claim as 'our' realm, must be other to us. But on closer inspection we find that this is rather more reminiscent of a fictitious order as the etymology of the term Manichean itself implies. Surely we don't live in the mythical world of the ancient Persians who divided the universe between realms of goodness and light (governed by Ahura Mazda) and of darkness and evil (governed by Ahriman).

Why is such Manichaeism fictitious? Why is any clash of civilisations imagined? What constitutes the 'false consciousness' that animates the clash disciples today? As I have argued in the introduction: any interaction between self and other, even in the most violently divisive mode, can only function in a social arena where we can constitute the otherness of the other on the basis of a stock of shared knowledge about him in the first place. Viewed from the outside, the clash regime is a social system, even if it is not recognised as such by its 'inhabitants'. From this outside perspective, it becomes apparent that it is the other that presides over the spatial organisation of the clash regime into subject and object, barbarian and civilised, us-and-them and over

[6] Ibid., p. 94.

the transitive interactions between them. The binaries only exist through the possibility with which the presence of the other fills them. Even when violence towards the other is presented as necessary, that is to say as a pre-emption against his lingering threat, this *violence of the Other* is not an objective reality except in the sense that it exists in all men as the universal motivation of counter-violence; it is nothing but the unbearable fact of broken reciprocity and of the systematic exploitation of man's humanity for the destruction of the human'.[7] Understood in this Sartrean sense, their violence against the other is merely a symptom of their perverted and dysfunctional relationship to their self.

So if we are all genetically linked, the purpose of this chapter must be to dissect some of the narratives informing and sustaining the idea that the clash between 'us' and 'them' has an ancient presence, that it was there before Adam and Eve, before Mani, before Babel, before Chinese cosmology established the polarised forces of Yang (positive action) and Yin (negative passivity), that it has been with us since the first self-consciously social group defined another group as its referential object. To that end, I start by explaining notions of exclusion and commonality in the ancient world and throughout the following centuries. What I try to establish are the nuances within and between the constructs we have called 'civilisation', 'barbarism', 'Islam', the 'West', 'Christianity' and other in order to show how the clash regime is based on a questionable epistemology that has served particular political interests—that it is not simply inevitable. Understanding where notions of the inevitability of inter-group conflict come from is the first step towards chasing the clash regime down to its tribal 'epicentre'. Once we have reached that plateau, we may be better positioned to comprehend its seismic force and build viable constructs to contain its awesome power.

It is within that framework that I will start to sketch and challenge three artificial binaries that have been used in order to sustain the clash regime today: barbarian versus civilised that has been distilled out of the interaction between Greeks and Persians in antiquity; Islam versus Christianity that was signified during successive periods of imperial

---

[7] Jean-Paul Sartre, *Critique of Dialectical Reason, Volume 1: Theory of Practical Ensembles*, Alan Sheridan-Smith (trans.), Jonathan Rée (ed.), foreword by Frederic Jameson, London: Verso, 2004, p. 133, emphasis in original.

rivalry between Muslim and Christian rulers especially during the medieval period; and finally West versus Islam that emerged more forcefully in the eighteenth and nineteenth century.

Thermopylae versus Persepolis, barbarian versus anarya

The emergence of ideas, norms, and other cultural artefacts constituting a regime of truth is always dependent upon the presence of authorities, 'guild' historians who are qualified and sufficiently legitimated via institutions to write the history of the self and the other, to maximise difference and to legitimate violence. The historian acts here as a narrator who redefines a particular period of time or event in relation to a fictive present. He inscribes a timeless element into his narration, as if what happened were both inevitable and of endemic endurance. Herodotus of Halicarnassus' (Bodrum, modern day Turkey) differentiation of world affairs into the Greek speaking world and the 'barbarians' beyond these confines has been regarded as the first prominent employment of a 'tribal' method at the service of a particular political interest, i.e. in this case the pan-Hellenic unification of the warring Greek city-states against the Persian empire. Herodotus was not interested in signifying some grand clash of civilisation and barbarism, but without his systematic inquiries the figure of the 'barbarian' would not have gained such prominence at quite an early stage of human history. And as we will see, the barbarian continues to figure prominently in successive clash scenarios until today.

Cicero called Herodotus the father of history in the first century BC. Certainly, he assumed this title when History was institutionalised as a discipline in the modern University. Yet Herodotus' historical tracts were not only systematic in analytical terms, they were also systematically mythical. He did not manage to free himself entirely from the traditions surrounding him, from the Greek Gods and their tantalising myths. It was Thucydides who perfected the art of writing 'objectivised' history at a later stage. Thucydides managed to record the Peloponnesian War without adopting Herodotus' uncritical narrative style that mixed quasi-factual tale telling with fantasy and entertainment. It is not only that Herodotus writes in chapter 186 of the *Histories* that the Persian king Xerxes, the son of Darius, brought 5,283,220 men to the battles at Sepias and Thermopylae, who then fought 300 Spartans in a heroic battle in which the Spartan leader Leonidas distinguished himself as one of the most brave and brilliant military leaders in human history. The whole book is permeated by Greek mythology. Indeed, the battle at Thermopylae itself is presaged by the oracle of the Pythoness:

For when the Spartans, at the very beginning of the war, sent to consult the oracle concerning it, the answer which they received from the Pythoness was, 'that either Sparta must be overthrown by the barbarians, or one of her kings must perish'. The prophecy was delivered in hexameter verse, and ran thus:

'O ye men who dwell in the streets of broad Lacedaemon!
Either your glorious town shall be sacked by the children of Perseus,
Or, in exchange, must all through the whole Laconian country
Mourn for the loss of a king, descendant of great Heracles.
He cannot be withstood by the courage of bulls nor of lions
Strive as they may; he is mighty as Zeus; there is nought that shall stay him,
Till he have got for his prey your king, or your glorious city'.

The historical account of the events during the battle at Thermopylae follows the 'prophecy' of the oracle:

So the barbarians under Xerxes began to draw nigh; and the Greeks under Leonidas, as they now went forth determined to die, advanced much further than on previous days, until they reached the more open portion of the pass. ... Now they joined battle beyond the defile, and carried slaughter among the barbarians, who fell in heaps. Behind them the captains of the squadrons, armed with whips, urged their men forward with continual blows. Many were trampled to death by their own soldiers; no one heeded the dying. For the Greeks, reckless of their own safety and desperate, since they knew that, as the mountain had been crossed, their destruction was nigh at hand, exerted themselves with the most furious valour against the barbarians.

By this time the spears of the greater number were all shivered, and with their swords they hewed down the ranks of the Persians; and here, as they strove, Leonidas fell fighting bravely, together with many other famous Spartans whose names I have taken care to learn on account of their great worthiness, as indeed I have those of all the three hundred. There fell too at the same time very many famous Persians: among them, two sons of Darius, Abrocomes and Hyperanthes, his children by Phratagune, the daughter of Artanes.[8]

'Greek' heroism and steadfastness is juxtaposed here to Persian cruelty and disorganisation. Herodotus writes history from an obviously biased disposition, one that is constituted and necessitated by the

---

[8] Herodotus, *Histories*, George Rawlinson (trans. with notes), Ware: Wordsworth, 1996, p. 595.

politico-cultural *zeitgeist* enveloping him. So if Herodotus can be considered the father of history, it must follow quite logically that history was born in myth and out of political considerations. The oracle, the idea of the 300 Spartans fighting a heroic battle against over 5 million Persians, all of this appears unacceptable to the critical mind. Herodotus' *Histories* served the important purpose to narrate the imperial rivalry between Greece and Persia, in favour of the former. From our contemporary perspective, we would consider Herodotus one of the first 'organic' intellectuals who wrote in the service of a newly devised, confessional ideology.

The pan-Hellenist agenda thus signified—an early form of 'identity politics'—was already introduced in 472 BC with the staging in Athens of Aeschylus's play *The Persians*. The theme of the play focused on the effect on the Persian royal family of the news of the defeat of their armies in the battle of Salamis. Aeschylus was a veteran of the battle against the Persians at Marathon, so his representation of the Greeks as free, emancipated and chivalrous in contrast to the Persian king who is shown to be hubristic, decadent, a totalitarian master of slaves, had a very particular political function. Ultimately, the historicised narration of this period, facilitated by Herodotus and later on by Xenophon (ca. 430–354 BC) in his accounts of the 'Ten Thousand', was meant to solidify the boundaries between the newly established Greek 'entity' and its equally imagined 'Persian' competitor and to imprint this binary into the 'public' consciousness. The theatrical performances had a similar purpose. Thus, the category 'barbarian' became a marker of a fictitious identity, an ideological device to delineate the Greek-speaking world from the rest—not only from Persians but also from Lydians, Phrygians, Egyptians and others who were now disqualified by the emergent Hellenocentric discourse. The us-versus-them binary thus dispersed into the field of politics and society was also expressed through sexual allegories. A famous vase depicting the battle on the Eurymedian River in the early 460s BC, for instance, shows a Greek warrior advancing with an erect penis in hand towards a Persian who is bending over (looking rather helpless). An inscription on the vase identifies the Persian as 'Eurymedon', after the name of the river where Cimon won a battle against the Persians. Given that homosexuality was a socially accepted practice in the Greek speaking worlds (and in parts of Persia, contemporary Iran/Iraq), he may be considered one of the first 'pin-ups' exemplifying the sexually charged representation of the other: 'Eurymedon' may be the first prominent victim of the licentious passions of history.[9]

Some of these early reactions towards the other have been touched upon by Edward Said of course. As early as in Aeschylus's *The Persians* and in *The Bacchae* of Euripides, he writes:

a line is drawn between two continents. Europe is powerful and articulate; Asia is defeated and distant. Aeschylus *represents* Asia, makes her speak in the person of the aged Persian queen, Xerxes' mother. It is Europe that articulates the Orient; this articulation is the prerogative, not of a puppet master, but of a genuine creator, whose life-giving power represents, animates, constitutes the otherwise silent and dangerous space beyond familiar boundaries.[10]

Said investigates how this 'Orientalist vision, a vision by no means confined to the professional scholar, but rather the common possession of all who have thought about the Orient in the West', has constituted the discursive formation termed 'Orientalism'.[11] From the depictions of Xerxes as the leader of the 'barbarians' in Aeschylus's *The Persians* to Mohammed's location in the 'eighth of the nine circles of Hell, in the ninth of the ten Bolgias of Malebolge, a circle of gloomy ditches surrounding Satan's stronghold in Hell',[12] what Dante called the *seminator di scandalo e di scisma* in *Inferno*, to modern, 'social-scientific' inquiries into the 'Muslim mindset', Said threads through the maze of often denigrating representations of the other 'Oriental' by European and (at a later stage) American scholars.

At least since antiquity, the self-other delineation that Said emphasises has been strengthened from innumerable loci. It was not only the Greeks who started to rewrite their history, to concoct seemingly well

---

[9] For the self-other delineation in antiquity and its consequences for Western historiography see Paul Cartledge, *The Greeks: A Portrait of Self and Others*, Oxford: Oxford University Press, 2002; John Coleman and Clark Walz (eds), *Greeks and Barbarians: Essays on the Interactions between Greeks and Non-Greeks in Antiquity and the Consequences for Eurocentrism*, Bethesda: CDL Press, 1997; Edith Hall, *Inventing the Barbarian: Greek Self-definition Through Tragedy*, Oxford: Oxford University Press, 1989; Thomas Harrison (ed.), *Greeks and Barbarians*, Edinburgh: Edinburgh University Press, 2002; Benjamin Isaac, *The Invention of Racism in Classical Antiquity*, Princeton: Princeton University Press, 2004.

[10] Edward W. Said, *Orientalism: Western Conceptions of the Orient*, London: Penguin, 1995, p. 57, emphasis in original.

[11] Ibid., p. 69.

[12] Ibid., p. 68.

cloistered 'genealogical' territories, to invent their self in accordance with a set of myths. The Persians were equally adamant about their 'special' status. For them anyone who did not believe in the fusion of cosmic, moral and political order, the precepts of Ahura Mazda (the Zoroastrian God) manifested in the Persian king of kings (*shahanshah*) was deemed 'barbarous' and wicked; *anarya* or 'other' as opposed to *arya* or 'pertaining to ourselves'.[13] This attitude, expressing as it does an undoubted sense of religiously endowed superiority, can be discerned from the cuneiform writings inscribed in the rock of a massive mountain 66 metres above ground level, the Bisitun or 'place of gods' in old Persian which is situated in the Kermanshah area of today's Iran. It exhibits a relief depicting Darius' ascension to the throne of Persia, his triumph over his enemies, and his endorsement by Ahura Mazda and is supplemented by a large amount of accompanying text in the three main languages of the Persian empire: Babylonian, Old Persian, and Elamite:

I am Darius the Great King, King of Kings, King in Persia, King of countries, son of Hystaspes, grandson of Arsames, an Achaemenian.

Darius the King says: My father was Hystaspes; Hystaspes' father was Arsames; Arsames' father was Ariaramnes; Ariaramnes' father was Teispes; Teispes' father was Achaemenes. ... For this reason we are called Achaemenians. From long ago we have been noble. From long ago our family had been kings. ... By the favour of Ahuramazda I am King; Ahuramazda bestowed the kingdom upon me. ... These are the countries which came to me; by the favor of Ahuramazda I was king of them: Persia, Elam, Babylonia, Assyria, Arabia, Egypt, (those) who are beside the sea, Sardis, Ionia, Media, Armenia, Cappadocia, Parthia, Drangiana, Aria, Chorasmia, Bactria, Sogdiana, Gandara, Scythia, Sattagydia, Arachosia, Maka: in all, 23 provinces. ... These are the countries which came to me; by the favor of Ahuramazda they were my subjects; they bore tribute to me; what was said to them by me either by night or by day, that was done. ... This is what I did in both the second and the third year after I became king. A province named Elam became rebellious. One man named Atamaita, an Elamite—they made him chief. Thereupon I sent forth an army. One man named Gobryas, a Persian, my subject—I made him chief of them. After that, Gobryas with the army marched off to Elam; he joined battle with the Elamites. Thereupon Gobryas smote and crushed the Elamites, and

---

[13] See further Mary Boyce, *A History of Zoroastrianism, Vol. 1: The Early Period*, Leiden: Brill, 1975; François Hartog, *The Mirror of Herodotus: The Representation of the Other in the Writing of History*, Janet Lloyd (trans.), Berkeley: University of California Press, 1988.

captured the chief of them; he led him to me, and I killed him. After that the province became mine. ... Those Elamites were faithless and by them Ahuramazda was not worshipped. I worshipped Ahuramazda; by the favor of Ahuramazda, as was my desire, thus I did to them.

Superiority is claimed here both religiously, through the viceregency of the Zoroastrian god Ahura Mazda that Darius assumes as a source of legitimacy, and ethnically, based on Darius' obvious bias in favour of his 'Persian' subjects. Those rebellious Elamites, whose chief Darius is said to have killed, were reproached primarily because they were amongst the few non-Iranian people during that period who did not accept Ahura Mazda as their God and who rejected, by implication, the sovereignty of Darius. In turn, those Elamites who yielded to Persian suzerainty were rewarded. Cuneiform tablets from Persepolis, the ancient capital of the Achaemenid kings, suggest how these 'good' Elamites received wine and food and how they offered them to the Iranian divinities. In short: the *anarya* were incorporated into the 'Persian' narrative as long as they accepted the Irano-centric sovereignty expressed therein.

Myth making, hierarchies, the privileging of the in-group (in this case 'Persians) against the out-group (non-Persians) in order to express an imperial claim is not a prerogative of a particular culture. The modalities of oppression, the idea of superiority, the power of subjugation all of which have been inscribed in the archives of the clash regime, go very deep and are much more indiscriminate than it seems. If one fails to account for the circularity of them, one risks overemphasising one form of hegemony over the other. In this case it has to be acknowledged, and captured analytically, that the other existed for the Persians, or so it appeared to the imagination of the Persian kings and notables, whose relationship to their subjects was either hierarchical or immediately hegemonic.

It is out of this period that a particular idea of Iran emerges. Especially during times of imperial competition, this idea tended to license a discourse that was formulated from within its confines, the ideational contours of which were rendered pseudo-authentic either through religious designations (e.g. Zoroastrianism), racial factors (e.g. Iran, land of the Aryans) or linguistic delineation (e.g., the 'Pahlavi' script). Some of these sentiments are fused rather brilliantly in the *shahnameh* (Book of Kings) or *namey-e bastan* (the ancient epistle) written by Ferdowsi in the eleventh century. Alexander of Macedonia is presented here as the legitimate and eldest son of the Persian emperor Darab (Darius). In other words, he is turned from conqueror to lost heir, from Macedonian invader, to Persian prince in a display of phantasmal 'historical' re-engineering. Ferdowsi, an ardent romantic and outstanding narrator, implies that a heroic figure like Alexander must have been Iranian, that this would explain his great success as a conqueror. So suggestive were Ferdowsi's tales that they continue to function as a point of reference for many contemporary Iranian nationalists, who would emphasise that the *shahnameh* is almost entirely depleted of Arabic terms and that pre-Islamic Persia is truly representative of the 'Iranian-Aryan' spirit. Simply because Ferdowsi heralded Iran's pre-Islamic kings (*shahs*) does not mean that he was racially biased towards Iranians of course or even inherently anti-Arab, despite his rather negative depiction of the Muslim invasion of Sassanid Iran. But he does reserve, with immense mythical and poetical vigour, a privileged position for the Iranian/Persian self that has been strong enough to function as an ingredient in the construction of Iranian identity until today. To link this paragraph to our previous argument: distinguishing the self from the other via historical concoctions was not the prerogative of Herodotus or Aeschylus. Such pronounced articulations of identity can also be discerned from narratives signifying the meaning of Persia or Iran, in many ways until today. None of this has turned the human condition into a perpetual clash of civilisations of course, but repeatedly into a war between brothers and sisters: it has created a bond of fraternity between 'us' and 'them' which is violently interdependent.

The reification of the other from all sides indicates why contemporary adherents to the clash have recourse to an ideationally diverse and historically deep regime of truth. Their aim is to continuously reinvigorate the early antecedents of the clash regime, to persistently organize an archive in which what matters is primarily identities, tribes and permanent cultures, with all their claims to causality and 'objective' validity. From this perspective, at least since the Persian-Greek wars at Marathon, Salamis and above all Thermopylae, history is the field of identity production and myth-making. That there is enough material to choose from only accentuates the salience of the regime of truth, thus constituted.

No regime of truth could function without the empirical inference of an archive. The power of the clash regime emanates from the salience of its constitutive discourses which are 'thickened' via innumerable narratives situated within that socially engineered constellation. The particular talent of the clash disciples today is to mould these discourses together into a historical teleology. They are aided by the way history has been written in this regard. In other words, the regime of truth sustaining the clash regime today seems to emerge from 'everywhere', out of the innumerable narratives accentuating exclusion which are scattered around the archives of human thought and practice, because a whole range of prominent poets, writers, academics and other elite groups have not suggested otherwise. The fact that Herodotus' assertion that at Thermopylae, a tiny Greek holding force fought a heroic battle against over five million Persians could be picked up by Lord Byron (1788–1824) in a poem written in protest of Turkish occupation of Greece in the nineteenth century is yet another indicator for the structural continuities I am alluding to:

> The mountains look on Marathon—
> And Marathon looks on the sea;
> And musing there an hour alone,
> I dreamed that Greece might still be free;
> For standing on the Persians' grave,
> I could not deem myself a slave.
> A King sate on the rocky brow
> Which looks o'er sea-born Salamis;
> And ships, by thousands, lay below,
> And men in nations;—all were his!
> He counted them at break of day—
> And, when the Sun set, where were they?
> And where are they? and where art thou,
> My Country? On thy voiceless shore
> The heroic lay is tuneless now—
> The heroic bosom beats no more!
> And must thy Lyre, so long divine,
> Degenerate into hands like mine?
> 'T is something, in the dearth of Fame,
> Though linked among a fettered race,
> To feel at least a patriot's shame,
> Even as I sing, suffuse my face;
> For what is left the poet here?
> For Greeks a blush—for Greece a tear.

> Must *we* but weep o'er days more blest?
> Must *we* but blush?—Our fathers bled.

Earth! render back from out thy breast
A remnant of our Spartan dead!
Of the three hundred grant but three,
To make a new Thermopylæ![14]

That the myth-making apparatus in antiquity (e.g. Herodotus), could be carried over throughout the centuries (e.g. by Lord Byron), and continues to make inroads into contemporary culture through Hollywood blockbusters like *300* is yet another indicator for the structural linkages at stake here.[15] The myth of Thermopylae, or what Edgar Allan Poe called 'the Glory that was Greece', has travelled a long way: It can be found in a famous 'rebel' poem entitled 'A Nation Once Again' written by the Irish nationalist Thomas Osborne Davis (1814–1845); it was taught in the British public school system since Victorian times and well into the twentieth century; it appears in the novels of Charles Dickens (*The Mystery of Edwin Drood*, 1870), Edward Bulwer Lytton (*Pausanias, the Spartan*, 1873) and Steven Pressfield (*Gates of Fire*, 1998); it fed into Nazi race theories on the one side and Greek resistance to Mussolini's attempt to occupy Greece in 1940–1941 on the other; and it inspired anti-Soviet propaganda movies produced by Hollywood most vividly exemplified by the Cinemascope film *The 300 Spartans* (1962) which depicted, rather typically for this particular genre, the independent Greek city-states as 'the only stronghold of freedom remaining in the then known world' (*viz.* the United States), holding out against the 'slave empire' of the Persians (*viz.* the Soviet Union).

---

[14] Ernest Hartley Coleridge (ed.), *The Works of Lord Byron, volume 6*, Ebook, The Project Gutenberg. Available at http://www.gutenberg.org/files/18762/18762–h/18762–h.htm [Last accessed 21 January 2008]. On Lord Byron and Islam see also Seyed Mohammad Marandi, 'The Oriental World of Lord Byron and the Orientalism of Literary Scholars', *Critique: Critical Middle Eastern Studies*, vol. 15, no. 3, Fall 2006, pp. 317–337.

[15] The movie *300* (2006), directed by Zack Snyder and based on the graphic novel of Frank Miller, provoked protests from many quarters in Iran and beyond. The movie was criticized for depicting Persians as 'bloodthirsty, underdeveloped zombies' feeding into 'racist instincts in Europe and America'. Other film critics described it as 'a textbook example of how race-baiting fantasy and nationalist myth can serve as an incitement to total war'. See further Gary Leupp, 'A Racist and Insulting film: 300 vs. Iran and Herodutus', *Counterpunch*, Weekend Edition, 31 Mar./1 Apr. 2007.

But we have to intervene in our argument here. The myth of Thermopylae has had a rather more central function for the discourse of the 'West' and the pronounced will to signify hegemony contained therein, than the 'glory of Persepolis' has had for the discourse of Iran or some Orient. Indeed, this nationalist narrative of Iran that is premised on the mythification of the Achaemenid kings, their Aryan ideal-type, the narrative style of the *shahnameh* etc. never really developed a systematic 'anti-western' connotation, or any ideological vigour that would signify the 'East' in its entirety. Rather, during the rule of the Pahlavi dynasty (1925–1979) in the twentieth century and in many ways before, it served to delineate the 'Persian self' from the 'Arab-Muslim other' and to signify Iran's supposed natural affinity with Europe and its 'Indo-European' syntax. There was immense 'Occidentalist' breeding ground for such narratives to gain currency amongst the elites of the country, a whole range of nationalist myths which have survived throughout the centuries and which have been repeatedly tapped into in order to define, somewhat metaphysically, the national narrative in Iran. The Pahlavi monarchs were fascinated by the imperial history of pre-Islamic Persia, and found its historical vigour conducive to legitimate their rule. To that end, they invoked the myth that their dynasty was somehow related to Xerxes, Cyrus and Darius, the legendary Kings of the Achaemenid Empire. Thus, Mohammed Reza Shah adopted the official title *aryamehr* or light of the Aryans, celebrated 2,500 years of Iranian monarchy in a lavish festival in Persepolis in 1971 and subsequently abandoned the Islamic solar *hegra* calendar in favour of an imperial one, suddenly catapulting Iran into the year 2535 (based on the presumed date of the foundation of the Achaemenid dynasty). In the imagination of the shah, this was the beginning of a new era for Iran, an era that was meant to set the country apart from its Islamic heritage, fast-forwarding it to the gates of a 'great civilisation' (*tamadon-e bozorg*).[16]

So it was primarily in the western discourse that the imperial competition between Persia and the Greek city-states has been turned into an artificial cultural and civilisational marker between East and West.

---

[16] I have elaborated on the functions of the identity politics of the Pahlavi state recently. See 'Discourse and violence: The friend-enemy conjunction in contemporary Iranian-American Relations', *Critical Studies on Terrorism*, vol. 2, no. 3, Dec. 2009, pp. 512–526.

THE PASSIONS OF HISTORY

It was this imperial rivalry, in other words, that created the historical archives of the clash regime in the West, its conceptual framework around notions of us-versus-them, its paradoxical emphasis on total difference, its imagination of fixed identities, its objectifying ideology and deceptive cultural coherence. The reason why it was possible for Huntington and others to replant this idea in the twentieth century and for their argument to gain such prominence is exactly because it was nurtured within this regime of truth that has been located in those real and imagined early encounters. The clash regime is nourished and sustained by this circulation of myths and their institutionalisation. This regime—de-centralised, heterogeneous, and yet structurally salient— has accustomed us to accept demarcations between us and them as a way of introducing order especially during periods of crisis and upheaval. By far more divisive than the polemicists of the ancient and medieval period, contemporary proponents of the clash regime avoid drawing things together by circumventing possibilities of kinship, attraction and affinity. Their argument is rather dependent on discrimination; that is, on an epistemology that accentuates conflict with the other, who is thought to be absolutely detached from the self. By necessity of its exclusionary nature, this type of discourse simulates boundaries, contracts the various forms of the other, erects total systems instead of hybrid structures, and produces deceptive binaries: Orient versus Occident, barbarian versus civilised, West versus Islam. This type of discourse is retroactive, not only because of its ideological content; it is in fact directly retroactive.

The Muslim presence within Christianity

An alternative history of the classical world could have engendered a counter-hegemonic model. But only recently have historians embarked on the project to emphasise more fully the interconnections between different civilisations and to debunk the spatial compartmentalisation of Europe, Africa and Asia. One of the most prominent efforts in that direction has been made by Martin Bernal in *Black Athena*.[17] Bernal challenges the idea that Greek civilisation was founded by Aryan set-

---

[17] Martin Bernal, *Black Athena: The Afroasiatic Roots of Classical Civilisation, Vol. 1: The Fabrication of Ancient Greece 1785–1985*, London: Free Association Books, 1987.

41

tlers from the North emphasising instead the interpenetration of Greek culture by Phoenicia and Egypt (hence the suggestive subtitle of the book *The Afroasiatic Roots of Classical Civilisation*). According to Bernal, these inter-civilisational linkages were suppressed by the emergence of the 'Aryan model' in the eighteenth/nineteenth century which popularised the misguided belief in the Indo-European/Aryan nucleus of Greek civilisation from which the idea of Europe and the 'West' more generally would derive.[18] From this perspective, the 'Aryan model' is based on a racist stratification of history that has detached the idea of Greece (and by extension the West) from Egypt and Levantine influences. In a wide-ranging comparison of the philological linkages between the different languages of antiquity, Bernal goes as far as to say that Greek religion is essentially Egyptian.

Jack Goody expresses similar doubts about the Hellenocentric viewpoint and its racial precepts.[19] According to him, the marginalisation of Phoenician and Carthaginian influences on ancient Greece are obvious examples of that bias. He emphasises the communication and trade links during the classical period, the fact that Phoenician traders travelled throughout the Mediterranean, and that the cedars of Lebanon voyaged as far as to Cornwall. Goody agrees with Bernal that 'racial factors' have played a significant part in the Hellenocentric writing of history in the eighteenth/nineteenth century. But he also cautions that these factors have a 'much more long-standing origin than he suggests' and that they are 'linked to notions of cultural as well as racial superiority'.[20]

Goody is right to point out that the us-versus-them stratification of world history precedes the eighteenth/nineteenth century. As we have seen, the barbarian is presumed to threaten the confines of our polis at least since antiquity. What happened in the following centuries? What was the impact of the emergence of Islam on the stratification of history?

In *Islam and the West: The Making of an Image*, Norman Daniel aptly demonstrates how the emergence of Islam in the seventh century was greeted with both ignorance and fear by Latin Christians. In sub-

[18] Ibid., p. 442.
[19] Jack Goody, *The Theft of History*, Cambridge: Cambridge University Press, 2006, p. 63.
[20] Ibid.

sequent centuries, Muhammad was seen as the 'great blasphemer' and the 'Qur'an became the object of their ridicule because it was unfamiliar'.[21] As a consequence, 'Islam took its place rather dramatically, but inevitably, in the historical sequence as a prefiguration of Antichrist, for as long as political, economic and military requirements dominated European thought upon the subject'.[22] Islam became an image against which Christendom, and at later stage 'Europe', organised itself in terms of military development, cultural preferences and ideational constitution. Within the emergent discourse thus created, the Muslims were accused of turning the Orient from light to darkness, from good to evil, from civilisation to barbarity. Such views are encapsulated very forcefully in the songs and poems compiled in *The Song of Roland*, from the period of the first crusades in the twelfth century:

> the ruler of that land
> men call the Hills of Darkness ...
> In that land, they say,
> the sun shines not, nor rain nor gentle dew
> fall from the heavens, and not a grain of corn
> may ripen. No rock is there that isn't solid black;
> some say it is the devil's habitation.[23]

The Song of Roland is one of the many signposts that show the centrality of some Islam in the making of western Christendom and Europe. This is the topic of a new study by David Levering Lewis.[24] Lewis chronicles the meteoric rise of Islam in the seventh century and identifies the defeat of the Muslim armies at Poitiers (present day France), as a turning point in the Christian-Islamic rivalry. From then on, Lewis argues, Europe started to define itself in opposition to Islam. The emerging discourse of a holy war against the barbarian infidels emerges more forcefully when Charlemagne (742–814) ascends the throne of the Franks in 768. The myth of Roland, the idea that he was

---

[21] Norman Daniel, *Islam and the West: The Making of an Image*, Edinburgh: Edinburgh University Press, 1960, pp. 77; 107.

[22] Ibid., p. 193.

[23] Quoted in Angeliki Laiou, 'The Just War of Eastern Christians and the Holy War of the Crusaders', in Richard Sorabji and David Rodin, *The Ethics of War: Shared Problems in Different Traditions*, London: Ashgate, 2006, pp. 36–37.

[24] David Levering Lewis, *God's Crucible: Islam and the Making of Europe 570–1215*, London: W.W. Norton and Co., 2009.

the ultimate 'noble' Christian, emerged out of this historical context. Through the creation of such folkloric heroes, history was increasingly framed in terms of an inevitable and continuous struggle between Christianity and Islam, good versus evil. Islam was conceived of as the ultimate other to be combated, not only by religious and political leaders in Europe, but also by the cultural elite. Ultimately, the elite consensus thus created explains the power of such normatively and emotionally charged notions like 'veneration', 'chivalry', 'piety' and 'duty of the West' in the discourse of the Crusades, the uniting force of which motivated Shakespeare (1564–1616) in the beginning of Henry IV, Part I, as a symbol of the 'sanctified' resolution of English civil strife:

> Therefore friends
> As far as to the sepulchre of Christ,-
> Whose soldier now, under whose blessed cross
> We are impressed and engaged to fight,-
> Forthwith a power of English shall we levy,
> Whose arms were moulded in their mother's womb
> To chase these pagans in those holy fields
> Over whose acres walk'd those blessed feet
> Which fourteen hundred years ago were nailed
> For our advantage on the bitter cross.[25]

This passage is a particularly striking example of the way the Crusades were romanticised from a distant perspective in order to serve particular political agendas, in this case to contribute to an ending of the civil war that was ravaging England. Shakespeare did not have an immediate conception of Islam; he did not encounter cultures under Muslim suzerainty. This sets him apart from his contemporary Cervantes (1547–1616) and explains the superficial and harmlessly biased way the 'moors' are treated in his plays. Cervantes thought he could afford the luxury of a rather more pronounced representation of the Muslim other whom he encountered as a soldier in his battles with the Ottoman naval fleet in the Gulf of Lepanto and during his captivity in Algeria. These experiences fed into his novels, certainly into *Don Quixote*, but perhaps more forcefully into plays such as *Los Banos de Argel* and *El Trato de Argel*. Conversely, Shakespeare's disgust at the insatiable 'lust of the Turks' and the enmity that they displayed against

---

[25] William Shakespeare, *The Works of Shakespeare*, vol. 1, Howard Staunton (ed.), London: Routledge, Warne & Routledge, 1862, p. 510.

Christianity, was driven by ignorance, fear and out of political considerations. True, from our contemporary perspective, the physically distinctive depiction of the typical *moro molto valoroso* (the moor, a very valiant man), the blackening of the moor, for instance in *Othello*, provoke charges of a racialised representation of the other. But such representations were not driven by racism per se, not at least because systematic, scientific theories of race only emerged at the beginning of the eighteenth century.

According to Daniel, the otherness ascribed to Islam in medieval Europe also created a 'western' approach to Islam over the field of morality. He pays particular attention to this development, especially to the 'theoretical, and almost legalistic, character that it assumes'.[26] A fundamental fear was artificially inscribed into this discourse: as a result of the emergence of Islam, the whole moral episteme of Christianity could find its foundational place in history modified. In particular, the epistemology of Christ as the ultimate sign of God, which early Christians saw as absolute and eternal. This whole idea of the infinitude of the biblical revelations threatened to take on a dramatic new configuration. This Christian-Islamic rivalry that feeds into the clash regime today is, in short, a competition over history and temporal sequences of humanity. It is our time that Islam and Christianity have been competing for, both in the present and in the hereafter.

The Christian sense of time and history is perhaps encapsulated in Genesis 9:1, where God tells Noah and his sons to start the collective, 'to be fruitful and multiply and replenish the earth'—to form the ingroup. It is surely central to the following chapters 'where the job of populating is done, and the peoples, lineages, and cities of the world are created, already too ambitious, and consequently scattered by God into a great linguistic diversity, the nations'.[27] This early emphasis on a distinctive community is re-accentuated in the parables of Jesus which, according to the evangelist Mark, were told with an understanding that they may not be understood by those outside the trusted circle. The followers of Jesus must have been convinced that with them a particular sequence of human existence and human history was coming to an end, and that from the depths of the transcendental revelation of Jesus another epoch was approaching. This new era was

---

[26] Daniel, *Islam and the West*, p. 160.
[27] David Gary Shaw, 'Modernity Between Us and Them: The Place of Religion Within History', *History and Theory*, Theme Issue 45, Dec. 2006, p. 1.

considered to be contingent in terms of both its transcendental *and* historical claim. It did not allow for the possibility of an alternative temporality such as the one presented by Islam. It allowed only one Logos who 'passes out of eternity into time for no other purpose than to assist the beings, whose bodily form he takes, to pass out of time into eternity'.[28] In this specific sense Christianity was exclusive, both in terms of its belief in the one, eternally valid revelation and its emphasis on an exclusive temporality:

If the Avatar's appearance upon the stage of history is enormously important, this is due to the fact that by his teaching he points out, and by his being a channel of grace and divine power he actually is, the means by which human beings may transcend the limitations of history.[29]

In this way, the Christian revelation introduced what Ricoeur calls 'the upper limit to the process of the hierarchisation of temporality'.[30] 'For Augustine and the whole Christian tradition', he explains, 'the internalising of the purely extensive relations of time refers to an eternity where everything is present at the same time'.[31] In order to decrease the distance between the individual and that divine eternity, the good Christian was obliged to hold firm, to 'smooth out', the vicissitudes of history: 'Then I shall be cast and set firm in the mould of your truth' said Augustine.[32] Indeed, if we follow the main themes of Augustine's *Confessions*, we find that the temporal sequence of the world was central to the self-understanding of early and medieval Christianity. It constituted Christian cosmology and its doctrinal legitimations all the way down to the individual's communication with God:

Suppose that I am going to recite a psalm that I know. Before I begin my faculty of expectation is engaged by the whole of it. But once I have begun, as much of the psalm as I have removed from the province of expectation and relegated to the past now engages my memory, and the scope of the action which I am performing is divided between the two faculties of memory and expectation, the one looking back to the part which I have already recited, the

---

[28] Aldous Huxley, *The Perennial Philosophy*, London: Chatto & Windus, 1950, p. 62.

[29] Ibid.

[30] Paul Ricoeur, *Time and Narrative*, vol. 1, London: The University of Chicago Press, 1984, p. 86.

[31] Ibid.

[32] Saint Augustine, *The Confessions*, R.S. Pine-Coffin (trans.), London: Penguin Books, 1961, Book 11, 30: 40.

other looking forward to the part which I have still to recite. But my faculty of attention is present all the while, and through it passes what was the future in the process of becoming the past. As the process continues, the province of memory is extended in proportion as that of expectation is reduced, until the whole of my expectation is absorbed. This happens when I have finished my recitation and it has all passed into the province of memory.[33]

The central terms in this paragraph are action (*actionis*), engaged (*tenditur*), divided (*distenditur*), attention (*attentio*), passes (*traicitur*) and continues (*agitur et agitur*). They all refer to the central issue, *viz.* time. They also constitute Christians as subjects of history, by placing them onto a temporal sequence starting from the birth of Jesus and ending on Judgment Day. 'The Christian apprehends the world as one term of a Metaphor', elaborates Hayden White, 'the other and dominant term of which, that by which the world is given its meaning and identity, is conceived to exist in another world'.[34] Within this temporal sequence there was no place for competing faiths which made it impossible for early Christian thinkers to regard Muhammad as an authentic prophet. For them, an authentic universal prophet 'had his place in the evangelical preparation for the coming of Christ ... But Muhammad came after the event to which the line of universal prophets pointed, and he foretold no events in the future'.[35] If many Christian priests and monks were hostile to the emergence of Islam, it was not because they were hostile to Islam and Muhammad per se then, but because Islam threatened to disperse the units and time sequences claimed by Christianity. If Muhammad could not be positioned within the Christian universe and its sense of history and time, then he could only be considered the 'Antichrist' who heralds the end of the world. Thus, Muhammad's claim that Islam introduced the last stage of the human experience of God was taken to threaten the very *raison d'être* of Christianity because Islam claimed to engender a new temporal sequence in God's revelation to humankind. Islam threatened to make it apparent that the dialectic between man and God had more than one or two rounds, much in the same way that Christianity

[33] Ibid., 28; 38.
[34] Hayden White, *Metahistory: The Historical Imagination in Nineteenth Century Europe*, Baltimore: Johns Hopkins Press, 1973, p. 125.
[35] Albert Hourani, *Europe and the Middle East*, London: Macmillan, 1980, p. 8.

confronted Judaism with a new transcendental sequence in human history.[36]

Such theological factors were important, but they became sources of conflict primarily due to political considerations. Within two years of Muhammad's death in 632, Islam fought with the Byzantine Empire at the battle of Ajnadayn and moved on to establish the foundations of the first Islamic empire from its new base in Damascus. During the rule of the second caliph Omar, the Islamic domain spread further into Egypt and Persia. By the end of the tenth century Muslim rulers had established a firm foothold in Southern and Eastern Europe. Before these immediate imperial confrontations, there was confined interest in Muhammad in Europe. But by the end of the eleventh century, the *reconquista* of the lost territories in al-Andalus, and the offensive of the Normans in Southern Italy and Sicily, turned him into an object of immense agitation. The Normans, the Christians of Northern Spain and the knights of Europe who carried the first crusade into the Muslim heartland in western Asia, were enveloped with a theo-politico-cultural ideology that would successfully demonise not only the persona of Muhammad, an early instance of character assassination, but also that new religion called Islam. The narrative of 'Mahound', that wicked imposter, charlatan and pervert emerges out of this historical constellation. The wild fervour of the papal crusades could only be delivered in an ideological universe that was rendered radically dichotomous.

So in the battle over territory and imperial supremacy, Christian elites resorted both to military force and to a whole set of polemics, theories and rhetoric in order to legitimate their cause. The oft-cited tale of the Christian monk 'Perfectus' and the 'martyr movement' that he is said to have inspired in Cordoba serves as an entry into this topic. The tale goes like this: in 850, walking through the streets of Cordoba, the capital of Umayyad al-Andalus, 'Perfectus' was asked by a group of Muslims whether he deemed Jesus or Mohammed to be the greater prophet. We are told that Perfectus was aware about the capital punishment that any insult to Mohammed would have wrought upon him, so he initially responded cautiously. But further down the conversation Perfectus started to hurl abuse at Mohammed calling his lifestyle las-

[36] See further, Raymond Schwab, *La Renaissance orientale*, Paris: Payot, 1950; Kurt Goldhammer, *Der Mythus von Ost und West: Eine Kultur-und religionsgeschichtliche Betrachtung*, München: Ernst Reinhardt, 1962.

THE PASSIONS OF HISTORY

civious and his religious claim bogus. Brought in front of the judge (*qadi*) he was asked to retract his blasphemy and accept the prophetic status of Muhammad or to face the death penalty. Perfectus replied with an attack on Muhammad that was even more vociferous than before. Subsequently, he was executed.

What makes Perfectus so special? Why did this individual reserve a particular place in histories about Christian 'clashes' with Islam until today? Who told us about him in the first place? His fame cannot be due to the fact that he was killed because of his beliefs of course. Throughout history millions of individuals have been executed because of their dissent, not only since the emergence of Islam, but before during and after that period. What has inscribed Perfectus' name into the annals of history is the political function that he served for another monk, Eulogius, who was, by all secular standards available, presenting Perfectus and the other martyrs as the inspiration for a new movement against Muslim suzerainty in Cordoba. It was him who chronicled the so called 'Cordoban Martyrs Movement' in his *Memoriale Sanctorum* and who pointed to the 'sexual degeneracy' and 'madness' of Muhammad. On the former issue he writes:

In what manner can he be considered one of the prophets, how can he avoid being punished by a curse from heaven, who, blinded by the beauty of Zainab, the wife of Zaid, one of his countrymen, and taking her on the basis of some barbaric law, as if an irrational horse or mule, joined himself to her in adultery, and claimed to have done it at the command of an angel?[37]

And on Islam and those who considered it a true religion he had the following to say:

O head empty of brains and heart occupied with the privilege of Satan! O corrupt vessel and abode of unclean spirits! O tongue worthy of being cut in two by a sword! O instrument of the demons and symphony of the devil! What madness and insanity compel you to be polluted with such blasphemies? What, O sewer of filth, snare of perdition, abyss of iniquity and cesspool of all vice, has deprived you of your human senses?[38]

Eulogius narrative is replete with terms such as *praecursor antichristi* and *pseudopropheta* which are readily employed in order to question

---

[37] Kenneth Baxter Wolf, *Christian Martyr's in Muslim Spain*, The Library of Iberian Resources Online, p. 59. Available at http://www.documentacatholicaomnia.eu/03d/sine-data, Wolf._Kenneth,_Christian_Martyrs_in_Muslim_Spain,_EN.pdf [Last accessed Jan. 2009].

[38] Ibid.

Muhammad's prophetic claim. At the same time he hails the glorious bravery of the martyr's movement in the face of this obvious evil. In order to dramatise and legitimate the strategy espoused, Eulogius had to emphasise the cruelty of the Muslim rulers in southern Spain and the false prophetic claim of Muhammad. From our contemporary perspective, the method followed by those monks resembles what we would call 'propaganda by deed', a political strategy to radicalise the Christian community living in Cordoba, and here especially those Christian authorities who argued that since the Christian community was not systematically persecuted, there was no need to disturb the relative peace.[39] The strategy was cunning: Christian monks would openly denounce and denigrate Muhammad and Islam knowing very well that the law prescribed execution for such blasphemy. Thus, they would display their willingness to die for their cause and provoke the violence of the state at the same time.

Eulogius' *Memoriale Sanctorum* had the ideological function to unify the Christian community in southern Spain against their Muslim rulers much in the same way that Herodotus' *Histories* was instrumental in forging a Hellenocentric identity suitable to ward off intrusions by the Persian Empire. The dichotomous narrative in Cordoba thus inflamed had also cultural connotations which are discernable from Paul Alvarus' (d. 859) writings. Alvarus was an ardent defender of the martyrdom movement, a friend of Eulogius and his biographer, and a passionate admirer of Perfectus. So he had a particular political stake in criticising the growing exchange of ideas and the build up of libraries with books in Arabic. '[H]ardly one can write a passable Latin letter to a friend', he lamented, 'but innumerable are those who can express themselves in Arabic and can compose poetry in that language with greater ease than the Arabs themselves'.[40] Apart from his cultural consternation, Alvarus also turned out to be a particularly divisive 'historian':

At the time when the savage rule of the Arabs miserably laid waste all the land of Spain with deceit and imposture, when King Mohammad with unbelievable rage and unbridled fury determined to root out the race of Christians, many terrified by fear of the cruel king and hoping to allay his madness, by a cruel

---

[39] See further Daniel Baraz, *Changing Perceptions: Late Antiquity to the Early Modern Period*, New York: Cornell University Press, 2003, pp. 53 ff.
[40] Ibid., p. 93

use of evil will endeavoured to assail Christ's flock with various and ingenious temptations. Many by denying Christ threw themselves into the abyss; others were shaken by severe trials. But others were established and confirmed in flourishing virtue. ... For some who were holding the Christian faith only in secret by God's grace brought out into the open what they had concealed, and without being searched out they sprang forward to martyrdom and snatched their own crown from the executioners. Among these was blessed Christopher, of an Arab family, the story of whose passion we plan to write in another place. Among them also were blessed Aurelius and holy Felix, who having practised Christianity in secret, came forward with their wives to the glory of martyrdom. Another of them was the blessed virgin Flora, who indeed flowered with virtues, and despising the transitory pomp of the world won an eternal crown. Our holy director Eulogius described the combat of each of these and wrote their lives and acts in a brilliant style.[41]

Gender conscious readers will note the way the image of 'the virgin' is abused here as a means to underline the religious purity and glory of the movement. Of course, such imagery has been repeatedly used throughout history in order to inflame the ideological fervour of the nation or, in this case, the 'Christian race'. Alvarus intends such sentiments not only as an immediate political mobilisation of the Christian community, but as a moral marker that would position the martyr's movement in the larger scheme of an enduring confrontation between Christianity and the forces of evil represented by Islam. Moreover, Alvarus' emphasis on the cruelty of the Muslim rulers, that is Abdalrahman II and Muhammad I respectively, was not only meant to organise the Christian community in Cordoba. It was also a very conscious effort to legitimate their martyrdom strategy in theological terms. Both Eulogius and Alvarus were adamant to suggest that the Muslim rulers were cruel persecutors of the ancient Roman type in order to defend their suicide tactics against the accusations of other Christian authorities who deemed them illegitimate.[42]

It does not come as a surprise that the hegemonic discourse sponsored by the Muslim rulers of al-Andalus—hegemonic because it benefitted from the full administrative power of the state—displayed comparable discursive biases in favour of the 'in-group'. The effort to

---

[41] Paul Alvarus, 'Eulogius and the Martyr's of Cordoba' in Olivia Remie Constable (ed.), *Medieval Iberia: Readings from Christian, Muslim, and Jewish Sources*, Philadelphia: University of Pennsylvania Press, 1997, p. 51.

[42] Michael Gerli, *Medieval Iberia: An Encyclopaedia*, London: Routledge, 2002, p. 312

legitimate the suzerainty of successive Muslim dynasties in Cordoba and beyond was based on a distinction between Muslim and Christian that was less pronounced than in the discourse of the martyr's movement, but that was nonetheless filled with enough attitude and vigour to signify Muslim superiority. At least three recurrent themes can be distilled from the historical documents available: the authenticity of the prophetic status of Muhammad, the central role of the Caliphs as his legitimate successors and defenders of his *sunna* (in opposition to the Shia); and the sovereignty of Islam over other religions. The ever more complete narration of the meaning of Islam and Christianity, the establishment of archives, the reorganisation of world politics from the emergence of Islam in the seventh century onwards, all these developments represent not so much the inevitability of the clash regime, as a way of its political utility for those strata of society whose primary aim has been to legitimate their hegemony.

I would like to interrogate the argument of the preceding paragraphs with a question now: what is the difference between the identity politics underlying the Christian-Islamic rivalry and those underpinning the nineteenth century French notion of *la mission civilisatrice*, based on a belief in the inherent superiority of some cultures and their 'natural' entitlement to dominate others? Could one compare Christian-Islamic efforts to express their superiority and colonise the 'other' to this colonial concept? Is it possible to link the emphasis on the prominence of one's own civilisation to the writings of St. John of Damascus who considered Islam to be a forerunner of the Antichrist: *Prodromos tou Antichristou* in the seventh century? Aren't there parallels to be drawn between this mindset and Ibn Hazm's (994–1064) criticism of the Christian (and Jewish) scriptures in his *al-fasl fi-l-milal wa-l-ahwa wa-l-nihal* (Discerning between religions, ideologies and sects),[43] or Ibn Taymiya's (1263–1328) critique in *al-jawab as-sahih li-man baddaka din al-masih* (The true answer to those who falsified the religion of Jesus) in which he argues that the historical parts of the Bible are forged and that Christian exegesis has misinterpreted the legislative parts?[44] We have to ask these questions in order to be better positioned

---

[43] On Ibm Hazim's writings, see Anwar G. Chejne, *Ibn Hazm*, Chicago: Hazi, 1982; J. Windrow Sweetman, *Islam and Christian Theology*, part one, vol. 2, London: Lutterworth Press, 1955, pp. 178–262.

[44] See further, Thomas F. Michel (ed.), *A Muslim Theologian's Response to Christianity: Ibn Taymiyya's al-Jawab al-Sahih*, Delmar, NY: Caravan Books,

to identify both the continuities and ruptures in 'Oriental' and 'Occidental' representations of the other.

True, a broader perspective from which one can view the making of the Christian-Islamic binary and from which the intimate dialectic between one and the other may be observed, reveals an immensely rich archive accentuating the superiority of one group over the other. The signposts of this Christian-Islamic dialogue can be traced through the centuries. They were especially pronounced during the period beginning with the first crusades shortly before 1100, which engendered a surprisingly adaptable field, suggesting some irrefutable clash between Islam and Christianity. So Nestorians such as Elias of Nisibis (975–1046) or the philosopher and physician Abdallah bin al-Tayyib, Christian Arabs such as Bartholomew of Edessa, start to write long treatise refuting the theological tenets of Islam. On the other side of the cognitive divide Muslim philosophers like al-Ghazzali (1058–1111), al-Qarafi (d. 1285), al-Iskandarani (d. 1320), Ibn Taymiya and Ibn Qayyim al-Djawziyya (1292–1350) refute Christian ordinances, and here especially the emphasis on the holy trinity and the divinity of Jesus. Examples of the 'micro-politics' of this Christian-Islamic dialectic reveal comparably antagonistic attitudes. Consider how Usamah Ibn Munqidh (1059–1188) refers to the 'kind of jurisprudence and legal decisions the Franks have' in his memoirs in the twelfth century, by describing a duel between a blacksmith and an old man, which ends with the smith knelling down over the old man trying to 'stick his fingers into the eyes of his adversary' which he failed to do 'because of the great quantity of blood flowing out'.[45] Or his disgust with the execution of a young, blind Muslim whose eyeballs were pierced 'with red-hot awls'—to him a typical example for the 'Frankish way of procedure'.[46] From Ibn Munqidh's perspective, the sudden appearance of the *militia Christi* in his Syrian homeland during the first Crusades in the eleventh century had a comparably shocking and disruptive

---

1985; M. Perlman, 'Notes on anti-Christian Propaganda in the Mamluk Empire', *Bulletin of the School of Oriental and African Studies*, University of London, vol. 10, no. 4, 1942, pp. 843–861; Jaques Waardenburg, *Muslims and Others: Relations in Context*, Berlin: Walter de Gruyter, 2003, especially chapter 5.

[45] Quoted in Philip K. Hitti, *Islam and the West: A Historical Cultural Survey*, Princeton: D. Van Nostrand Company Inc., 1962, p. 186.

[46] Quoted in ibid., p. 187.

effect as the appearance of Islam in Europe for the Latin Christians must have had. Ultimately, it was in reaction to this period of the Crusades that such antithetical Quranic terms and phrases such as *mushrikun* (polytheists) and *kuffar* (infidels) or *ahl al-shirk* and *ahzab al-kufr* (parties of unbelief) gained prominence. It was the imperial rivalry between Muslim and Christian empires, in other words, that signified the seemingly disparate epistemological fields in which notions of Islam and Christianity were placed and in which they are imagined to confront each other inevitably. In this emphasis on a duality and the claim to dominate and educate in the name of an ideal-type (Islam, Christianity) there seems to be some resemblance to the perspective of *la mission civilisatrice*.

Indeed, Nabil Matar has recently paid particular attention to the way that discourse developed in the period between 1578 and 1727. Matar shows that beginning in 1578 with a major Moroccan-Muslim victory over a invading army from Portugal, there was considerable engagement between various Muslim and Christian rulers and that some of their political, commercial and military goals were shared. According to Matar, this period reveals 'Arabic historiography that was both complex and not—not yet, at least—essentialised, a historiography that had been epistemologically moulded by the ongoing engagements and encounters with the European *nasra*'.[47] His study also indicates that North-African Muslims established their own field in which to enclose the 'infidel other', primarily out of political expediency and in reaction to the ongoing wars in the Mediterranean area. The following passage taken from a letter written in 1578 by the reformist Genoan convert to Islam, Radnan al-Janawy al-Fasi, addressed to the victorious Moroccan ruler Ahmad al-Mansur who had just repelled the Portuguese from the territory he claimed, serves as an example:

In the name of God the Merciful, the Compassionate. The prayer of God on our lord Muhammad and his family and companions: may they be safeguarded. ... May God help you and us to protect His charge, uphold what he has entrusted us of His laws, and assist us in fulfilling our trust as He has decreed. Amen. Thanks be to God and thanks again for His manifold blessings: for giving victory to Islam and its people, for defeating infidelity and its people, and for destroying the infidels and breaking their necks. There is no

[47] Nabil Matar, *Europe Through Arab Eyes 1578–1727*, New York: Columbia University Press, 2009.

blessing greater than the glory of religion [Islam] and the humiliation of its faithless adversaries. May God increase your endeavour and joy, so you continue in your endeavour until it becomes your mission and vocation. It was the vocation of your grandfather, peace and prayer of God upon him and his honourable companions, who spent their lives in fighting the infidels, and dispensed their wealth and gave up their lives for their beloved Prophet. They persevered until they rectified religion—following the path of the Lord of Messengers, may God be pleased with them all.[48]

It is not some coherent Islam that has inevitably clashed with Christianity that explains the Muslim versus infidel binary in al-Fasi's letter. It was the political competition between the Morroccan-Muslim ruler Ahmad al-Mansur and the Portuguese crusaders, i.e. a very particular competition over power between two dynasties, which suggests that binary. Once we look below it more closely, we find that during that same period goods and peoples circulated throughout the Mediterranean, that individuals intermingled within the domains claimed by their rulers as exclusively 'Muslim' or 'Christian'. It is risky, I am aware, to abstract from a set of examples from different historical epochs, but it seems to me that ultimately, in all the above cases, expressing the superiority of one's own civilisation was a reactive gesture vis-à-vis the assertive other which opened up a central ideological opportunity: to organise collective passions for religious war against the barbarian infidel. Here as well the discourse equips itself with sexual connotations, emphases on the 'immorality' of the other. Typically, these are linked to indictments of sexual licentiousness and libidinous lasciviousness. Thus, in early writings about Islam, it is asserted that in the 'Muslim sect any sexual act at all is not only not forbidden, but allowed and praised',[49] whilst the Muslim historian Asnawi (writing in the fourteenth century) held 'the Christians responsible for the spread of moral laxity, for wine drinking, seduction of Muslim women, etc'.[50] Such designations show the imposition of sexuality on the legitimacy of violence. The important issue with regard to this gendered layer of the clash regime is that in passing from political competition to a conflict over *sharaf* (honour) and *namus* (virtue), the very biologi-

[48] 'Letters of Radwan al-Janawy on Muslim Captives', in *Tuhfat al-Ikhwan*, Rabat National Library: 1578, MS Kaf 154, fols. 423–424; 427–428. Translated in Matar, *Europe Through Arab Eyes 1578–1727*, pp. 141–142.
[49] Quoted in Hitti, *Islam and the West*, p. 146.
[50] Perlman, 'Notes on anti-Christian Propaganda', p. 851.

cally coded reciprocity between us and them is subdued. Instead, we are tempted by a distinction presumably so fundamental and primordial as to make mitigation seemingly impossible.

And yet, it would be wrong to assume that the rivalry between Christianities and Islams in Europe, North Africa and Western Asia in the medieval period is synonymous to the ruptures engendered by the European colonialists, which are encapsulated in the perspective of *la mission civilisatrice*. As we will see in the following sequences of this book, colonialism was premised on a racially charged discourse that was filled with immense causal violence, a discourse that rendered differences essentially immitigable. The Christian-Islamic rivalry of the medieval period was by far less sophisticated. We see here a binary system which functions primarily in a politico-theological mode, both as an ideological instigator and as a religious marker of difference. A schematic binary differentiating the polis and the barbarian (or the Aryan and the inferior non-Aryan) already existed during antiquity. This was the first time in that area that the world was cut in two and that binaries were mixed with ideational reference points such as language and race. The Christian-Islamic dialectic adds a new dimension. It made it possible to write history in terms of a confrontation between institutions, administered armies, and formalised religious world-views and their interpretation by theo-political authorities. This is a binary that emerged out of the political and military reaction to the emergence of Islam, not out of some primordial hatred towards the Oriental other. With the colonial period the us-versus-them logic is not only legitimated on the grounds that the non-Islamic world has to ward off intrusions from the 'outside'. European colonialists call for subjugation as an absolute necessity. They think it their duty to spread civilisation, *la mission civilisatrice, missão civilizadora*, the white man's burden in Kipling's words. The justification for violence is not signified by some romantic martyr's movement in Cordoba, it does not call for action in the name of justice, piety or an inclusive order for humanity. It becomes a vital strategy to rescue the white man from the vicissitudes of history, to detach him from the other once and for all. *La mission civilisatrice*: a particularly violent manifestation of a historical period endorsing a permanent war against the other until her ultimate annihilation from the self.

Inventions of and by the 'West'

I have argued earlier in this chapter that there emerged a hegemonic discourse that represented Muslims as the 'other' *par excellence*, because Islam injected a new sense of time into the cosmology of humankind. For many writers who identified themselves as Christians, the new revelation seemed to shatter the articulated unity of the three ecstasies of time proposed by Ricoeur—the having-been, the making-present and the coming towards.[51] Because this dialectic was played out in a temporal sequence where Muhammad came after Abraham, Moses and Jesus, the discourse thus created, purported that mainstream Christianity (and Judaism) did not acknowledge the prophetic claim of Muhammad, in the same way the Jews did not accept the prophetic sovereignty of Jesus.

A second dynamic can now be added to this process: what became known as the 'West' was also pushed away historically, with immense force at least since the eighteenth century. There emerged a salient discourse constituted by interdependent narratives and methodologies suggesting that civilisation as such only matured in the 'Occident'. Modernity afforded the 'West' with the mandate to complete the history of humanity initiated in the 'East'. This newly infused temporal succession was central to the methodology of Hegel, Marx, Weber and other canonical figures of western modernity. The 'West', in other words, was perceived to be at the receiving end of history. It was imagined that its historical consciousness superseded that of the East. This means that in terms of revelation and history, the latter was thought to be forever beyond the former; that Occidentals and Orientals were irreducible to the synchrony of temporal sameness. 'Time is not the accomplishment of an isolated and lone subject', writes Levinas, 'but it is the subject's very relation with the Other ...'[52] There have been systematic efforts to suspend this relational function of time in order to ostracize the Orient in general and Muslims in particular from 'western' cosmology. No wonder then that anti-Islamic polemics, and at later stages 'Orientalist' writings, emphasise the backwardness of the Muslim Orient, its retroactive superstitions, archaic cultures and outdated fundamentalisms. Christianity was exclusive. With the advent

---

[51] Ricoeur, *Time and Narrative*, vol. 1.

[52] Emmanuel Levinas, *Time and the Other, and Additional Essays*, R. A. Cohen (trans.), Pittsburgh: Duquesne University Press, 1987, p. 17.

of modernity, the 'West' as well was turned into a distinct ideational marker. Inevitably, the temporal superiority thus afforded pushed the 'other' back in time rewinding the clock of history in favour of Europe.[53] This negation of the other is one of the most fundamental legacies of western modernity.

And so European history oscillated between Christian exclusivity and western distinctiveness. To make matters even more acute, the emerging Islamic empires co-opted geographically the very habitat and birthplace of Christian culture—they shook the orientation of the Christian discourse to its spatial core. Indeed, from the period of the second century, it was customary both in the eastern and western church to pray facing towards the east. Augustine traced this practice, which appeared early in the Christian church, to the custom observed by the 'heathens'. The altars of the Christian churches were situated in the same manner, and the dead were buried so that the eyes might be turned in the same direction. In the baptismal ceremony it was customary to turn first towards the west as the region of darkness, where the prince of darkness was supposed to dwell, to renounce with solemnity the devil, and then to turn east and to covenant with Christ.

But with Muhammad, the east was not exclusive to Jesus anymore. What came with his emergence was the idea that Islam had dismantled the great unity of Christianity, that Islam was responsible for the spatial and political dispersal of the Christian community. 'Re-territorialising' Christianity away from the East, which after Muhammad and the Muslim conquests fell from grace, became a theo-political necessity. From now on, Christianity had to be re-territorialised away from its Oriental birthplace, where the Antichrist was thought to have established his satanic rule. From now on the fact that Jesus as well as Moses and Abraham, were 'Orientals' and that their presence in Islam is central, had to be glossed over. Protap Chandra Mazumdar, one of the co-organisers of the first World Parliament of Religions (1893), demonstrated as early as in 1883 how the 'Oriental Christ' was artificially detached from its original habitat in order to function as an ideological source of inspiration for European-ness.[54] The effort to invent a 'white Jesus' is not only reflected in depictions of him as blue-

---

[53] See further, Johannes Fabian, *Time and the Other: How Anthropology Makes its Object*, New York: Columbia University Press, 1983.

[54] P.D. Mazumdar, *The Oriental Christ*, Boston: George H. Ellis, 1883.

eyed and fair-skinned which was central to the romantic musings of the artists of the Renaissance. It is also exemplified by contemporary efforts of the Catholic Church to emphasise the 'Hellenistic', 'European' and 'western' character of Christianity. According to Pope Benedict XVI:

The inner rapprochement between Biblical faith and Greek philosophical inquiry was an event of decisive importance ... Given this convergence, it is not surprising that Christianity, despite its origins and some significant developments in the East, finally took on its historically decisive character only in Europe. We can also express this the other way around: this convergence, with the subsequent addition of the Roman heritage, created Europe and remains the foundation of what can rightly be called Europe.[55]

There is no suggestion here that the artificial fortification of Europe can be directly linked to an inevitable clash between 'East' and 'West' or 'Christianity' and 'Islam'. What is rather more important for my line of argument is that institutionalised religion has always politicised identity in order to fulfil a particular agenda, in this case the invention of Europe. The Pope and a whole range of Islamic clerics today benefit from creating artificial boundaries between 'us' and 'them'. Such delineation re-inscribes their sovereignty over their flock, which is the 'sanctified' in-group. In the case of Christianity the making of such 'deified sovereignty' was pursued at least since Roman Emperor Constantine, who was only just baptized on his deathbed, issued the Edict of Milan in 313 proclaiming religious tolerance in the Empire. From now on 'European Christianity became less a grassroots movement and more an imperial system'.[56] In subsequent centuries, 'Islam' became very functional to the political advancement of that imperial system. The Muslim other became the irresistible reference point for the Christian self, creating a dense Muslim-Christian field that is entirely conjoined historically. Hence during times of crisis, such as the sixteenth century when Catholic princes were forced into negotiations and alliances with the Ottoman Empire, whose armies were at the gates of Vienna in 1529; the battle against the 'Turkish' Antichrist became the rallying call for both Protestants and Catholics. Martin Luther's cam-

[55] Pope Benedict XVI, 'Three Stages in the Program of De-Hellenization', 12 Sept. 2006. Available at www.zenit.org [Last accessed 17 Jan. 2008].
[56] Ali Mazrui, *Cultural Forces in World Politics*, Oxford: James Currey, 1990, p. 33

paign against the papacy and his aversion to the sanctification of violence did not prevent him from depicting war against the Ottoman forces as *gotselig* ('godly spirited'). Neither did he refrain from attacking '*Mahmet*', that is Muhammad himself, as the apostle of the devil, as the *grobe Teufel* (rude devil) whose followers, the '*Mahmetisten*', did not deserve to be called human. Other central figures such as Erasmus of Rotterdam (1466–1536) and Thomas More (1478–1535) were equally unequivocal in their denigration of the Turks and their 'abominable sect'.[57]

I should immediately reemphasise that I am not implying that these attitudes were all-encompassing. They couldn't be, because as I have suggested in the introduction, any hegemonic discourse provokes and implies a dialectic relationship with opposing discourses. So we 'must make allowance for the complex and unstable processes whereby discourse can be both an instrument and an effect of power, but also ... a point of resistance and a starting point of an opposing strategy'.[58] Foucault implies here that at any given moment counter-discourses exist. Discourse power, and resistance are circular, decentralised:

Discourse transmits and produces power; it reinforces it, but also undermines and exposes it, renders it fragile and makes it possible to thwart it. In like manner, silence and secrecy are a shelter for power, anchoring its prohibitions, but they also loosen its holds and provide for relatively obscure areas of tolerance.[59]

Indeed, standing aback with awe at the conquests of the Ottoman Muslims, the Islamic presence in Europe also engendered self-reflection. Many perceptive clergymen and/or theologians in the colleges of Oxford (and Cambridge of course!) such as William Laud, Archbishop of Canterbury (1573–1645, Archbishop 1633–1645), or Matthias Pasor (1599–1658) asked themselves what it was that made this 'Muslims sect' so successful. English Unitarians, such as Stephen Nye, ostracised from mainstream Christianity because of their rejection of the

---

[57] See further Tomaž Mastnak, 'Europe and the Muslims: The Permanent Crusade', in Emran Qureshi and Michael A. Sells (eds), *The New Crusades: Constructing the Muslim Enemy*, New York: Columbia University Press, 2003, pp. 205–248.

[58] Michel Foucault, *The Will to Knowledge: The history of sexuality*, vol. 1, Robert Hurley (trans.), London: Penguin, 1998, p. 101

[59] Ibid., p. 101.

Holy Trinity, even looked at Islam's principle of *tawhid*, or the oneness of God, as a source of inspiration:

They will have it that Mahomet [Muhammad] meant not his religion should be esteemed a new religion, but only the restitution of the true intent of Christian religion. They affirm moreover that the Mahometan [Muslim] learned men call themselves the true disciples of the Messias or Christ: intimated thereby that Christians are apostates from the most essential parts of the doctrine of the Messias; such as the unity of God; and that he is to be worshipp'd without images or pictures, in spirit and in truth. But whatsoever the design of Mahomet [Muhammad] was 'tis certain Mahometism [Islam] has prevailed over greater numbers and more nations than at the day profess Christianity: nay, it has worn Christianity out of great part of Europe, most of Asia, and all of Roman Africa; not by force and the sword, for the Mahometans [Muslims] grant liberty of religion to the conquered provinces of Christians, but by that one truth in the Alchoran [Qur'an], the unity of God.[60]

So there has been considerable movement in the representations of Islam from the seventh century onwards, some of it driven by ignorance, some of it by fear, some of it by religious fanaticism and some of it by recognition of the achievements of Islamicate civilisation. Ultimately, however, there did not emerge a discourse that would be powerful enough to accentuate affinity and empathy. Rather the contrary. The otherness of Islam was artificially inflated. By implication, narrating what Islam 'was' became very functional to delineating what Europe was not. It is out of this process of re-invention that the idea of the 'West' emerged. In other words, the implication of the preceding analysis is that the 'western' historical consciousness has been achieved via a discursive process of re-engineering. Islam assumed a prominent role within this process, not only because of its imperial expansion into Europe until the eighteenth century, but because its appearance in Western Asia in the seventh century necessitated the creation of a new discourse that would re-locate Christianity away from its eastern origin: It was the Muslim other, in short, who ordered the syntax of Europe and its western derivative. It was some imagined Islam that made the making of 'the West' possible.

Whether or not the 'West' as an imaginary construct assumed a new status in the Christian world-view because of the institutionalisation of the church in Rome and the development of the Catholic papacy needs

[60] Stephen Nye, *Letter of Resolution Concerning the Doctrine of the Trinity and the Incarnation*, London, 1690, p. 4.

to be further investigated by scholars better qualified to do so than I am. Beyond the discussion offered above, I am rather more confident to link the imagination of a 'West' in its modern sense to the events after 1492, that is to the period after the 'discovery' of the 'new world'. According to Couze Venn:

The year 1492 is the date when the Moors are finally expelled from Spain, as Columbus himself notes in the first paragraph of his log book, it is also the year in which the Jews are brutally deported to North Africa. 'Ethnic cleansing', and, with Columbus and his backers, the fantasy of Christianising the world whilst amassing untold riches—an irresistible combination—forms the backdrop to New World colonialism and the othering of the other. This splitting of the people is repeated in the history of the becoming of the West; its iteration can be detected in the tropes of East and West, civilised and (new) barbarians, humans and non-or sub-humans, them and us, subjects and non-subjects.[61]

Robert Young goes one step further:

It was after the fall of Granada in 1492 that Ferdinand and Isabella were attracted by the prospect of an anti-Islamic crusade that would make contact with the fabled Christian kingdom of Prester John in the east and deal a decisive blow to the Muslim enemy whose colonisation of Spain they had just ended with the *Reconquista*. ... [T]he discovery of America was the result of what was intended to be the last crusade against Islam. It was funded by the wealth acquired from the expulsion of the Jews and Moors from Granada two months after Ferdinand and Isabella had secured the city. European colonial expansion began simultaneously with the institution of the Catholic Inquisition that replaced centuries of Islamic multiculturalism. It was a symptomatic beginning.[62]

Venn and Young pay particular attention to the ruptures that 1492 engendered. Especially Venn seems to imply that the making of the 'West' was only possible by relocating the temporal basis of it away from the 'lost' Orient. In other words, he suggests that the struggle to invent a 'West' has been a struggle to reorganise its temporal and territorial locus. It is in this light that we can better comprehend why the 'West' has been consciously 'retemporalising/re-territorialising' with one hand what it was 'detemporalising/de-territorialising' with the

---

[61] Couze Venn, *Occidentalism: Modernity and Subjectivity*, London: Sage, 2000, p. 113
[62] Robert J. C. Young, *Postcolonialism: An Historical Introduction*, Oxford: Blackwell, 2001, p. 21.

other. The idea of a 'West' could only function because the 'new world' gave it a life line, a new space away from the Orient where it could invent itself without being challenged by Buddha, Muhammad, Master K'ung (Confucius), or the spirit of Brahman. For this, the system of reference of the native population had to be broken, a process referred to as 'the enterprise of deculturation' by Frantz Fanon: 'Expropriation, spoliation, raids, objective murder', he famously noted, 'are matched by the sacking of cultural patterns, or at least condition such sacking'. It is through this process that the native's 'social panorama is destructured; [that] values are flaunted, crushed, emptied'.[63]

Divested of their independent history, i.e. independence from the 'West', the subjugated Aztecs, Mayas and other natives were either wiped out altogether or co-opted into the epistemological order of Europe. The colonial process functioned as a temporal re-sequencing machine, which attempted to transplant what came to be known as 'Latin' America into the western/Christian spatiality. The 'modern' discursive territory thus engendered accentuated sameness along the western continuum thus established. From now on, the western discourse invented a temporality for itself and for America that made it both younger and yet older than the rest of the world: since it was the 'West' that established the new order it had extended the upper limit of its own finitude. But since it was in the murder of other peoples that the 'West' was constituted, reified, narrated, the idea of a 'West' itself was condemned to be affected by the reincarnation of the native consciousness. If the newly signified, western discourse from then on battled with itself, it was because after dispersing with the 'other' through colonialism and the ensuing imperial world order, it had reduced its syntactical structure to similitude and sameness. The discourse thus created condemned it to a destiny of endless wandering within its own *episteme* until the end of history would rescue it from this fate.[64]

---

[63] Frantz Fanon, *Toward the African Revolution: Political Essays*, Haakon Chevalier (trans.), Harmondsworth: Penguin, 1970, p. 43.

[64] On the specific issue of Islam and modernity, see also Mahmut Mutman, 'Under the Sign of Orientalism: The West vs. Islam', *Cultural Critique*, no. 23, Winter 1992–1993, pp. 165–197; Elizabeth Shakman Hurd, 'Appropriating Islam: The Islamic Other in the Consolidation of Western Modernity', *Critique: Critical Middle Eastern Studies*, vol. 12, no. 1, Spring 2003, pp. 25–41.

1492: the emergence of western modernity, the expunction of the other and the violent signification of the 'West'.

What are the methodological and epistemological tenets of that novel discourse? What is their implication for the clash regime? I would like to engage with these questions by turning to some of the canonical authorities of western modernity: Hegel, Marx and Weber. This digression is necessary in order to show how the idea of the West was epistemologically solidified, how it was theorised, how it was professionally imagined.

In *The Phenomenology of Spirit* (1807), Hegel puts forward a concept of historical development that was particularly dependent on temporal sequences. He differentiates between four phases in the birth and demise of civilisations: the period of birth and original growth, that of maturity, that of 'old age', and that of dissolution and death. Thus, for instance, the history of Rome is conceived of as passing through the phase from its foundation down to the Second Punic War in the first phase; from the second Punic War to the consolidation of the Principate by Caesar in the second phase; from this consolidation to the triumph of Christianity in the third phase; and from the third century to the fall of Byzantium in the last phase. Similarly, he argues that ancient Oriental history can be differentiated according to four 'sub-phases', manifesting themselves in four political orders: the 'theocratic-despotism' of China, the 'theocratic-aristocracy' of India, the 'theocratic-monarchic' culture of Persia, and finally the dichotomization of spirit and matter attributed to the civilization of ancient Egypt. He concludes that Egyptian culture, and by implication the Orient, failed in its mission to solve the 'riddle of man' for humankind. The solution to it, and to history as a whole, is found in the West. That is why according to the Oedipus myth, the Sphinx travelled to Greece and why the Owl of Minerva spread its wings in the Orient only to settle finally in the Occident. According to these metaphors and Hegel's methodology:

The History of the World travels from East to West, for Europe is absolutely the end of history, Asia the beginning. The History of the World has an East … (the term East in itself is entirely relative); for although the Earth forms a sphere, History performs no circle around it, but has on the contrary a determinate East, viz. Asia. Here rises the outward physical Sun, and in the West it sinks down: here consentaneously rises the Sun of self-consciousness, which diffuses a nobler brilliance. The History of the World is the discipline of the uncontrolled natural will, bringing it into obedience to a Universal principle and conferring subjective freedom. The East knew and to the present day knows only that *One* is free; the Greek and Roman world, that *some* are free; the German World knows that *All* are free.[65]

To Hegel, the East is in a state of 'unreflected consciousness—substantial, objective, spiritual existence ... to which the subject will sustain a relation in the form of faith, confidence, obedience'.[66] Thus when Hegel likens the Orient in general to a childhood in history, when he argues that the 'religion of Islam ... hates and proscribes everything concrete' and that 'its God is the absolute One, in relation to whom human beings retain for themselves no purpose, no private domain, nothing peculiar to themselves',[67] he assumes that the West has transcended the Orient, that humanity has overcome its original predicament, that the cycle of history from childhood to adolescence has left the Orient at some infantile stage. By contrast, Europe has freed itself from the determinations of that temporality. Now that it has entered the new age, its civilization is timeless and universal. There is a very pronounced mathematical calculus behind Hegel's conceptualisation of Europe's newly acquired temporal infinity. This is particularly apparent in the Platonic theme permeating *The Science of Logic*:

[T]he mathematical infinite is important because underlying it, in fact, is the notion of the genuine infinite and it is far superior to the ordinary so-called metaphysical infinite on which are based the objections to the mathematical infinite ... The consideration of these justifications and characteristics of the mathematical infinite ... will at the same time throw the best light on the nature of the true Notion itself and show how this latter was vaguely present as a basis for those procedures.[68]

As the contemporary French philosopher Alain Badiou points out: Hegel's 'mathematical concept of the infinite was historically decisive in the break with the ordinary metaphysical concept of the infinite'.[69] But not only that: Hegel's invention of a mathematical infinite was also

---

[65] Georg Wilhelm Friedrich Hegel, *The Philosophy of History*, New York: P.F. Collier & Son, 1902, p. 164

[66] Ibid., p. 105.

[67] Georg Wilhelm Friedrich Hegel, *Lectures on the Philosophy of Religion*, Peter C. Hodgson, J. Michael Stewart and HS Harris (eds), Berkeley: University of California Press, 1985, p. 243.

[68] Georg Wilhelm Friedrich Hegel, *Hegel's Science of Logic* Vol. I, Book I, Section 2, Chapter 2, (c), A.V. Miller (trans), Atlantic Highlands, NJ: Humanities Press, 1989, pp. 241–243.

[69] Alain Badiou, *Theoretical Writings*, London: Continuum, 2006, p. 35.

central to transcending the limitations of time and history, to artificially divorce the new dawn from everything that preceded it, including the Orient and its metaphysical 'superstitions'. Ultimately, the mathematical infinite complements methodologically the proclaimed, historical superiority of the West: the Orient is turned into a dependent, intervening variable that is entirely relative to the Occident. In this way Hegel's mathematical infinite is nothing but the false promise that the end of history had dawned and that is can be deciphered by a mnemonic calculus.

A similar logic can be discerned from the writings of Karl Marx. Marx was a keen student of the Hegelian methodology in firmly believing in the newly acquired superiority of western civilisation. Whereas Hegel likened this superiority to the constitution of 'historical consciousness' in Europe, Marx explained it in terms of Europe's superior means of production. In *The Communist Manifesto*, history itself is reduced to a 'history of class struggles' in which the various classes of all previous societies 'stood in constant opposition to one another' and 'carried on an uninterrupted, now hidden, now open fight'.[70] It must follow quite causally that the industrially underdeveloped 'East' is at the receiving end of this process. If you get into the habit of thinking that western men (nineteenth century thinkers are quite literally gender specific) will bring about a worldwide socioeconomic revolution, the cooption of Oriental men and women (no gender discrimination here) is then made acceptable as a means of rescuing the natives from their self-inflicted backwardness. This view is especially pronounced in Marx's article 'The British Rule in India', published in the *New York Daily Tribune* on 25 June 1853. Here, Marx adheres to Hegel's view that India had lost its 'claim' to history. Hindu society as a whole is characterized as 'undignified, stagnatory and vegetative'.[71] Because the West was in the process of perfecting the modes of production, 'English steam and English free trade' would eventually undermine the material base of Hindu society: Inevitably, this process would lead to 'the greatest, and to speak the truth, the *only* social revolution *ever*

[70] Karl Marx and Friedrich Engels, *The Communist Manifesto*, London: Penguin, 2002, p. 219.

[71] Karl Marx, 'The British Rule in India', *New York Daily Tribune*, 25 June 1853, reprinted in A. L. Macfie (ed.), *Orientalism: A Reader*, Edinburgh: Edinburgh University Press, 2000, p. 16.

heard in India'.[72] The pains and sufferings of the natives had to be accepted in order to hasten that grand project:

Now, sickening as it must be to human feeling to witness those myriads of industrious patriarchal and inoffensive social organisations disorganised and dissolved into their units, thrown into a sea of woes, and their individual members losing at the same time their ancient form of civilisation and their hereditary means of subsistence, we must not forget that these idyllic village communities, inoffensive though they may appear, had always been the solid foundation of Oriental despotism, that they restrained the human mind, within the smallest possible compass, making it the unresisting tool of superstition, enslaving it beneath traditional rules, depriving it of all grandeur and historical energies. We must not forget the barbarian egotism which, concentrating on some miserable patch of land, had quietly witnessed the ruin of empires, the perpetration of unspeakable cruelties, the massacre of the population of large towns, with no other consideration bestowed upon them than on natural events, itself the helpless prey of any aggressor who deigned to notice it at all. We must not forget that this undignified, stagnatory, and vegetative life, that this passive sort of existence evoked on the other part, in contradistinction, wild, aimless, unbounded forces of destruction, and rendered murder itself a religious rite in Hindustan. We must not forget that these little communities were contaminated by distinctions of caste and by slavery, that they subjugated man to external circumstances instead of elevating man to be the sovereign of circumstances, that they transformed a self-developing social state into never changing natural destiny, and thus brought about a brutalising worship of nature, exhibiting its degradation in the fact that man, the sovereign of nature, fell down on his knees in adoration of Hanuman, the monkey, and Sabbala, the cow.

England, it is true, in causing a social revolution in Hindustan, was actuated only by the vilest interests, and was stupid in her manner of enforcing them. But that is not the question. The question is, can mankind fulfil its destiny without a fundamental revolution in the social state of Asia? If not, whatever may have been the crimes of England she was the unconscious tool of history in bringing about that revolution.[73]

In analysing this passage we must not overemphasise, as Said did, that this type of discourse expresses a particular bias against the Orient.[74] India was pasted onto a larger paradigm that accentuated the integrative force of the social revolution of the proletariat. Marx thought that English imperialism unconsciously gave impetus to this

[72] Ibid., p. 16 emphasis added.
[73] Ibid., pp. 16–17.
[74] Said, *Orientalism*, pp. 153–157.

process. So when he accentuated that England had to 'fulfil a double mission in India: one destructive, the other regenerating—the annihilation of the Asiatic society, and the laying of the material foundations of Western society in Asia',[75] Marx was expressing, above all else, his belief in the transformative powers of the industrial revolution. Moreover, for Marx, significant causal efficacy follows from this industrial revolution in the West to the underdeveloped East, by a direct, not a dialectical path. 'Thus, for Marx, the emergence of the industrial proletariat is taken as the principal cause, because it is also what bears the "cause" to be defended'.[76] Within that historical configuration, the West was obliged to reintegrate Asia into the new age. There may occur a lag between the causal forces that promote the social and economic transformations and cultural changes, but this lag will finally be overcome. Now that the communist revolution was about to happen, the religiously sanctioned forms of both Oriental consciousness and praxis could be re-established according to the determinations of the new reality in new laws, a new government, a new religion, a radical art, a new culture and so on. Whilst in theory, for both Marx and Hegel, 'men can contribute through their failures and defeats to the human knowledge of the laws that govern both nature and history',[77] their methodologies are clearly biased in favour of the 'Occident'. For both thinkers the essential historical dynamics emerged from the West. For both, the Orient was yesterday, the West today and tomorrow.

Such temporal discrimination can also be discerned from an extended footnote that Engels added to an article on the history of early Christianity which he published in 1894 in Karl Kautsky's *Die Neue Zeit*. 'Islam is a religion adapted to Orientals, especially Arabs, i.e. on the one hand to townsmen engaged in trade and industry, on the other to nomadic Bedouins', Engels writes. 'Therein lies, however, the embryo of a periodically recurring collision' he adds. 'The townspeople grow rich, luxurious and lax in the observation of the "law". The Bedouins, poor and hence of strict morals, contemplate with envy and covetousness these riches and pleasures'. Forthwith thirteen decades of supposedly coherent 'Islamic history' are reduced to one material dynamic: The economically disadvantaged Bedouins 'unite under

---

[75] Karl Marx, *Surveys from Exile*, David Fernbach (ed.), London: Pelican, 1973, p. 320.
[76] Ricoeur, *Time and Narrative*, vol. 1, p. 119.
[77] White, *Metahistory*, p. 329.

a prophet, a Mahdi, to chastise the apostates and restore the observation of the ritual and the true faith and to appropriate in recompense the treasures of the renegades'. Yet those Khaldunian cyclical struggles do not bring about progress, they do not yield anything new. Rather, in 'a hundred years', the Bedouins 'are naturally in the same position as the renegades were: a new purge of the faith is required, a new Mahdi arises and the game starts again from the beginning. ... All these movements are clothed in religion but they have their source in economic causes'. But we are reminded that in Muslim societies these economic causes and the ensuing historical dynamics they provoke have not brought about any lasting changes in the political or socio-economic order. Rather, 'the old situation remains unchanged and the collision recurs periodically'. In this, we are told, Islam is fundamentally different from the 'Christian West' where 'the religious disguise is only a flag and a mask for attacks on an economic order which is becoming antiquated'. So quite contrary to the Islamic world, which remains trapped in that retroactive circuit, in the Christian West the economic order 'is finally overthrown, a new one arises *and the world progresses*'.[78] In this final act, Engels establishes the historical superiority of the Christian West. This historical superiority emerges quite directly from his materialist understanding of what progress is and what it should be in the first place.

In the writings of Max Weber, we find mediation between the materialist emphasis of Marx and Engels and the focus on 'historical consciousness' intrinsic to the methodology of Hegel. The reasoning employed in *The Protestant Ethic and the Spirit of Capitalism* satisfies the quest for historical distinctiveness exactly, with one very important difference: Weber's emphasis on the irreconcilability of Oriental beliefs with western rationality. In other words, whereas the theories of Marx and Hegel were essentially inclusive—that is they both believed that human action everywhere could provide the basis for the transcendence of the status quo—Weber's understanding of civilisational development and rationality was rather more exclusive to the Occident:

Only the Occident knows the state in the modern sense, with a constitution, specialised officialdom, and the concept of citizenship. Beginnings of this

---

[78] Frederick Engels, 'On the History of Early Christianity', in Karl Marx and Frederick Engels, *On Religion*, Moscow: Progress Publishers, 1975, p. 275, emphasis added.

institution in antiquity and in the Orient were never able to develop fully. Only the Occident knows rational law, made by jurists and rationally interpreted and applied, and in the Occident is found the concept of citizen (civis Romanus, citoyen, bourgeois) because only in the Occident does the city exist in the specific sense of the word. Furthermore, only the Occident possesses science in the present-day sense of the word. Theology, philosophy and reflection on the ultimate problems of life were known to the Chinese and the Hindu, perhaps even of a depth unmatched by the European; but a rational science and in connection with it a rational technology remained unknown to those civilisations.[79]

Marx and Hegel do not express a conscious Orientalist bias towards their East. Their historical verdict in favour of Europe emerges from their methodology which is *a priori* to their appropriation of the Orient in general and Islam in particular. It follows from this, that history is projected from the East to the West, where the final destiny of mankind would be realized. This was temporality worked out through the introjection of the other into western time. The other is necessarily seen as 'left behind' only to be reanimated within the new age. In this context, the other becomes the site of western temporality: the retroactive East is finally turned into the recipient of the civilising mission of the West. A comparable methodological emphasis is found in Weber, with the difference that the achievements of the Occident—the protestant ethic and capitalism—are deemed to be exclusive to western civilization. No dialectical historical consciousness or revolutionary cell could transfer it to the Orient. Faithful to the causal merits of abstraction, Weber not only leaves the Orient behind; he renders it non-existent—an artefact of history that is forever trapped in its 'Oriental despotism'. The causal connection between the protestant ethic and the spirit of capitalism is central to this verdict, because it provides the structure for an historical consciousness that imagines itself to be thoroughly independent of both the ancient civilisations of China, India, Persia, Egypt and the Islamic worlds. Both capitalism and Protestantism were considered distinctively western inventions. Hence, Weber does not only separate 'the specific component of the work ethic on the one side of the religious phenomenon and, on the side of the economic phenomenon, the spirit of acquisition characterised by rational calculation',[80] he positions both on a causal chain in a distinct juxta-

---

[79] Max Weber, *General Economic History*, New York: Collier Books, 1961, pp. 232–233.
[80] Ricoeur, *Time and Narrative*, vol. 1, p. 191.

position to the Orient in general and Islam in particular. Within such a constellation, tracing the development of history from East to West, central to the methodology of Marx and Hegel, is irrelevant. The West is yesterday, today and tomorrow all in one; it has established its own distinctive temporality.[81]

Affinities with contemporary theories such as Arnold Toynbee's *Civilisation on trial* (1948) and especially Francis Fukuyama's *The End of History* (1992) are not coincidental, of course.[82] Whilst Toynbee makes a general argument that the culminating impact of western culture points to the eventual evolution of a universal civilisation, Fukuyama is self-consciously Hegelian, re-enacting the end of history thesis in our contemporary epoch by locating it within the historical context after the demise of the Soviet Union and the apparent assimilation of the core values of western civilisation—capitalism and liberalism—on a global scale. At last it appears, according to Fukuyama, that the West has managed to rewind the clock of history rendering alternative politico-economic models useless. After several millennia, after superimposing itself on the rest of the world, the West has positioned itself beyond the ancient empires of the East, even beyond history. Via colonialism and the capitalist world order, the Orient has been either coerced or habituated into accepting the new temporality, which may explain why in many countries in the East, from Turkey to China, we are officially in the year 2010.

It should be pointed out that I don't think that Marx, Hegel, Weber, Fukayama or Toynbee were/are somehow intentionally prejudiced towards Asia or Islam. Their abstractions emerge out of their methodological propensities, not from the archives of Orientalism. Granting the other a historical space and time normatively en par with the West, would have seriously undermined the all-encompassing claim intrinsic to their sense of history, for it would pluralise and relativise it. In

---

[81] On Weber and Islam see also Afshin Matin-Asgari, 'Islamic Studies and the Spirit of Max Weber: A Critique of Cultural Essentialism', *Critique: Critical Middle Eastern Studies*, vol. 13, no. 3, Fall 2004, pp. 293–312; Toby E. Huff and Wolfgang Schluchter (eds), *Max Weber and Islam*, New Brunswick: Transactions, 1999; Bryan S. Turner, *Weber and Islam*, London: Routledge, 1974.

[82] See Francis Fukuyama, *The End of History and the Last Man*, New York: Free Press, 1992; Arnold J. Toynbee, *Civilisation on Trial*, Oxford: Oxford University Press, 1948.

methodologies like these, the othering of the 'East' is a central function of theorisation, not an instance of a coherent 'Orientalist vision' as Said seems to suggest in *Orientalism*.[83] I will return to the relationship between epistemology, methodology and argument in Chapter two. Suffice it to add to our understanding of the clash regime at this stage, that the making of the 'West' seriously deteriorated the distance between 'us' and 'them' and that it filled our relationship with the 'other' with immense violence.

Discourses of Islam

The imagination of the writers in antiquity, the medieval period and modernity did not produce a counter-hegemonic discourse that could have revealed the mythical and fictitious structure of some of the narratives that have signified convenient totalisations such as Christianity, the 'West' or 'Islam'. There would have been enough material to fight for such a discourse which could have created its own martyr movement, its own momentum towards the radical procurement of critical knowledge. Marx tried, but he did not provide for any space where Islamic (or eastern) notions of capital and communitarianism could have revealed themselves and enriched his analysis. Hegel was very thorough in forging his historical teleology and he was certainly not ignorant of the 'Oriental' contribution to civilisation, but he simply did not believe that the East had anything to offer to history anymore. Equally, for Weber, Islam and the Orient in general were utilised as methodological reference points suitable to buttress his argument. All three authors were imbued with the *zeitgeist* of the Enlightenment: their methodologies were compromised by the pronounced arrogance towards the other that their period suggested.

Weber's idea that Islam does not purport a concept of the individual as a rational agent is particularly false. Of course, rationality was central to the philosophy of Ibn Sina (980–1037), Ibn Rushd (1126–1198) Abu Nasr Farabi (d. 950) and fed into the sociology and historiography of Ibn Rushd (1332–1406) as well. The classical philosophers of Islam, the former two of whom escaped Dante's eight circle of hell in which Muhammad was placed, distilled particularly critical notions of rationality out of the Aristotelian corpus. John Hobson has recently

[83] Said, *Orientalism*, p. 154.

remarked that '[i]t was the Muslims (especially the Mutazilites) who propagated the idea that man was a free and rational agent—supposedly one of the *leitmotifs* of modern European thinking'.[84] This is true. Indeed, the discourse of the classical philosophers of Islam would have been a good place to debunk the idea that Islam is ultimately different and to point out, on the contrary, that it developed epistemologically adjacent, and frequently intrinsic to the West. It is not only that the philosophy of Plato and Aristotle, supposedly distinctly European, would have been lost in Europe's 'dark ages' if their ideas would not have been reinterpreted and seriously advanced especially by Farabi and Ibn Sina and subsequently translated, preserved and archived in the libraries of Cordoba, Toledo and Palermo. It is not only that the Perso-Iraqi-muslim scientist Ibn al-Haytham (965–1039) published the *kitab al-manazir* (Book of Optics) which revolutionised the fields of optics and visual perception and which laid the groundwork for modern physics. It is not only that Razi's groundbreaking publications on medicine were translated and reprinted in Europe about forty times in the period of 1498–1866. It is not only the very immediate impact that Ibn Sina's *Canon of Medicine* and *The Book of Healing* had on the emergence of medicine as a modern discipline at least since the eighteenth century onwards.[85] It is not only that in the writing of orthodox history these linkages are subdued or rejected. Consideration of the abstract treatise of the classical philosophers of Islam would have revealed fertile ground for a truly comparative theorisation of the political, social, intellectual and scientific developments in 'Eurasia'. This has not happened until today, certainly not in any systematic and comprehensive manner in the field of comparative politics or international studies. Instead, the hand that Muslim philosophers had in the invention of modernity has been largely chopped off in the 'West' due to the widespread prejudice—expressed as early as in Moses Maimonides' (1135–1204) *Guide of the Perplexed*—that they merely copied ideas developed by the ancient 'Greek' philosophers, and, in the Islamic worlds, because of the subversive substance of their critical ideas and the emergence of a literalist discourse of Islam that was depleted of intellectualism, especially after the successful Mongol invasions in

---

[84] John M. Hobson, *The Eastern Origins of Western Civilisation*, Cambridge: Cambridge University Press, 2004, p. 177.
[85] Ibid., p. 179.

1258. Yet the presence of Ibn Arabi, al-Kindi, Razi, Zahrawi, Farabi, Ibn Sina, Ibn Rushd within the vast discursive fields claimed by Islam, illuminates a very important epistemological factor with as yet untapped pedagogical value: that there is a wide range of theories and ideas which have been absorbed by and emerged from the Islamic field; that Islam, the *sunna* or the Quran have not always functioned as a starting or end-point for theorisation; that the Mullah, *mujtahid*, *qadi* or the Imam was not the only authority signifying the meaning of Islam.

In the writings of the classical philosophers, a concrete notion of Islam is almost entirely absent. Islam emerges as an *a priori*, an entirely abstract nodal point that was yet to be conquered intellectually. We must therefore distinguish between this '*a priori* Islam' of the classical philosophers and the 'concrete Islam' of the so called 'Islamic revivalists' from the nineteenth century onwards. *A priori* Islam disperses with political utilitarianism and the politics of identity, it cannot afford a fundamentalist or literalist reading of the Quran, it is not ideological. It does not refer to a multiplicity of syntheses, every one of which constitutes an individual discourse articulated towards some concrete notion of the meaning of Islam. Islam is there, a desired object, yet it is *a priori* to our existence, it is not a concrete definition of a place we can easily venture to. Islamic ontology, the Islam we think we can see, is not that of a totality, but rather that of an engineered totalisation which changes in accordance with the determinations of history and time. Thus, the ontology of any Islamic field must be entirely dependent on the process of human construction. The classical philosophers were central to illuminating this *a priori* existence of Islam that does not yield a significant boundary between self and other. In their writings the ontology of Islam is stretched so thin, resembling an infinite horizontal line, that the points of contact with adjacent discursivities are exponentially multiplied.

The immediate expansion of the Islamic empire and its corresponding success as a religion was an important factor for the absence of an urgency to define Islam as a source of unambiguous identity in the writings of the classical philosophers of Islam. The Abbasids, especially since the reign of Harun al-Rashid (786–809), administered a growing empire and nurtured the sciences with intense vigour, not at least in order to set themselves apart from the narrow ethno-centric ideology of the Umayyad caliphate. Undoubtedly, it was this inclusive historical context that allowed some of the classical Muslim philosophers to move beyond the tedious world of empirical reality and enter the fantastic realm of spiritual exigency. The politics of the day signalled to them that the former was conquered with immense authority. Conversely, the realm of spirituality, the desire that was created by a conceptualisation of God and his/her Islamic conduit as *a priori*, posited an unending field of intellectual possibilities. So Muslim philosophers, as early as adherents to the Peripatetic or *mashshai* school that developed out of the writings of al-Kindi in the ninth century, developed a particular propensity for 'transcendental' or 'prophetic' philosophy, 'a philosophy that recognizes beyond reason and the senses, the channel of revelation ... as means of gaining access to knowledge of the most elevated level'.[86]

In the philosophy of Farabi and especially in Ibn Sina's seminal *danish-namaha-ye alai* (Treatise on Knowledge) philosophy takes on a forward-looking modality adequate to this idea of the capacity for change towards the transcendental object. In his *uyun al-hikmah* Ibn Sina writes that '*al-hikmah*, (which he uses as being the same as philosophy) is the perfection of the human soul through conceptualisation (*tasawwur*) of things and judgment (*tasdiq*) of theoretical and practical realities to the measure of human ability'.[87] He went on in his later writings to distinguish between Peripatetic philosophy and what he called 'Oriental philosophy' (*al-hikmat al-mashriqi'yah*) which was not based on ratiocination alone, but included revealed knowledge (it also set the stage for the influential treatises of Sohravardi, and here especially his *kitab hikmat al-ishraq*). There is a particularly striking poem by Ibn Sina about the fate of the human soul, which exemplifies this emphasis on congruence between rational analysis and spiritual opportunity which was central to the canons of the classical philosophers of Islam:

> Until when the hour of its homeward flight draws near,
> And 'tis time for it to return to its ampler sphere,
> It carols with joy, for the veil is raised, and it spies
> Such things as cannot be witnessed by waking eyes.

[86] Seyyed Hossein Nasr and Mehdi Aminrazavi (eds), *An Anthology of Philosophy in Persia*, vol. 1, Oxford: Oxford University Press, 1999, p. 85.
[87] Ibn Sina, *Fontes sapientiae (uyun al-hikmah)*, Abdurrahman Badawied (ed.), Cairo, 1954, p. 16.

On a lofty height doth it warble its songs of praise
(for even the lowliest being doth knowledge raise).
And so it returneth, aware of all hidden things
In the universe, while no stain to its garment clings.[88]

The ultimate object here is the perfection of the intellectual faculties of the individual, who does not carry an exclusive identity, who is only presumed in his or her physical constitution. There is no realm of knowledge that is exclusive to Muslims in the writings of Ibn Sina, no discernible schematic dichotomy that permeates his narratives. Ibn Sina searches for a supreme truth, not a supreme civilisation or race. He and many of his contemporaries managed to write the intellectual archives of the *umma* without the emergence of a discourse that would legitimate subjugation of the other, without a hysterical call for arms.

The reason I have dealt with some ideas of the classical philosophers of Islam in such a sketchy manner, is that I wanted to show the absence of a 'clash mentality' in their tracts and to indicate what a systematically comparative engagement with their philosophy, the theoretical opportunities of which I will explore more fully throughout this study, would entail. The syntax of Islamic philosophy in the Farabian/Avicennian tradition has not lent itself to the making of a coherent 'Islam' and an equally coherent evil 'other', even during the period when Islam expanded into a world empire. Whereas in the 'West', especially from the eighteenth century onwards, there developed a close relationship between the production of knowledge and the exercise of power, between the archive and the state, in the Islamic worlds such intimate integration has not happened, in many ways until today. But what is it then that inflated the 'Islamicity' within the discourse of Islam? Where did the signification of the field that came to be known as Islamic come from, if not out of the writings of the classical philosophers of Islam who were not really interested in accentuating their identity as I have claimed?

Some of the experiences of time and history and their effects on the clash regime today that I would like to set out in the following paragraphs are rather comparable to what I discussed in the previous section. Whereas many philosophers and historians in Europe restructured the temporal sequence of history in favour of their 'Occident', Islam

---

[88] Quoted in Richard Walzer, *Greek into Arabic: Essays on Islamic Philosophy*, Cambridge, MA: Harvard University Press, 1962, p. 26.

developed its own 'temporal distinctiveness', its own 'mandate of history'. The logos of this historical mandate lie in the Quran where it is expressed that this new religion 'seeks to abrogate the excrescences that came to disfigure truth in the course of time, because the generations that had gone before had failed to preserve the earlier revelations'. With the emergence of the discourse of Islam, Muslims are placed within the continuum of a new temporality which would supersede that of their Abrahamic precursors. 'Prophets had come in various societies at different times and had preached the same essential truth, but there had grown errors and misunderstandings … and divine revelation had become clouded. … If the past has an impact on the present the message of Muhammad has to be made functional throughout the future'.[89] Several *ayats* refer to this historical process privileging Islam: 'Do they not travel through the earth to see what was the end of those nations before them' it is written in Surah 30: 9.

They were more distinctive in strength and they cultivated more lands and built more buildings more than what this people have made; their Messengers came to them with evident Signs and Miracles but they denied them and caused their own perdition; Allah did not wrong them, but they wronged themselves. (Surah 30: 9)

Surah 5 (al-Maidah), verses 68 to 70 are equally specific in their emphasis on Islam's place within the prophetic revelations and genealogy of mankind:[90]

Say [O, Messenger]: "O, people of the book! You do not stand on anything until you stand fast by the Taurat [Torah] and the Injil [Bible] and what has been sent down to you from your creator. …" (68)

Surely, those who believe [in Islam] and those who are the Jews and the Sabians and the Christians and whoever believes in Allah and the Last Day and do good, no fear shall be upon them and nor shall they grieve. (69)

Verily, We took a covenant from the Children of Israil and We sent to them Messengers with that [of Decrees] which they did not like, they called some of them liars and some others, they killed. (70).

A rash interpretation of these verses would highlight their ideological vigour in conjunction with other *ayats* where 'violence' against

[89] M. M. Sharif (ed.), *A History of Muslim Philosophy: With Short Accounts of Other Disciplines and The Modern Renaissance in Muslim Lands*, vol. 2, Wiesbaden, Germany: Otto Harassowitz, 1966, p. 1198.

[90] Quotations from the Qur'an are based on *The Holy Qur'an*, 4th edition, Tahereh Saffarzadeh (trans.), Tehran: Sooreh Mehr, 2002.

Jews and Christians is legitimated. This is not a luxury that we can afford here. True, there is an attitude of 'temporal superiority' vis-à-vis others inscribed in these passages. Moreover, from the perspective of the early Muslims, their imperial success must have been taken as evidence that the new continuum created by Islam would subsume the whole world. If Islam could have transmuted from those events in Arabia into a global movement, Muslims must have been granted the torch of history. If Islam was revealed in order to usurp Christianity's supersessionist claims over Judaism, Muslims were obliged to carry their divinely mandated universal mission to all corners of the world. Until the devastating Mongol invasion in the thirteenth century, Islam occupied an area that was heir to the ancient civilizations of Egypt, Mesopotamia and Persia. Muslim armies had pushed into Africa and Europe. Islamicate civilisation was endowed with a prophetic religion with universal claim on top of the pre-existing heritage of the ancient civilisations it conquered.[91] Surely, this *zeitgeist* must have imbued Muslims with the attitude that they were granted the torch of human history much in the same way that Enlightenment thinkers were animated by the exuberance of their period.

Yet there is an obvious difference between the othering of Christianity within the discourse of Islam and the othering of Islam within the discourse of Christianity. The discourse distilled out of the Quran, and here especially out of those *ayats* quoted above, establishes the difference of Islam as an interdependent, not autonomous, not detached community. To be more precise, Islam is consciously placed within the genealogy of Judaism and Christianity. Muhammad was presented as a part of the same prophetic revelation that was handed over to the Jewish prophets. Difference is expressed here as an opportunity to embrace the other, whose otherness is within the Muslim self. It is initially in Abraham and Jesus and through them that the difference of Islam is created. For Islam the Jewish prophets merge into those others that Deleuze invokes; the others that preside 'over the organisation of the world into objects and over the transitive relations of these objects. These objects exist only through the possibilities with which Others filled up the world'.[92] In short: the Muslim universe could never exist

[91] See further, Marshal G. S. Hodgson, 'The Role of Islam in World History', *International Journal of Middle East Studies*, vol. 1, no. 2 (1970), pp. 105 ff.
[92] Gilles Deleuze, *The Logic of Sense*, London: Continuum, 2004, p. 351.

without the presence of the other; the Christian and Jewish siblings could never be entirely cleansed from the discourse of Islam.

So we have to establish a fundamental difference to the views of history which emerged amongst those canonical writers in eighteenth/nineteenth/twentieth century Europe which I have sketched above. From their perspective it was easier to ignore Islam as a continuous historical force, even to negate it as Weber suggests, because from the outset, Islam was not considered part of the 'western' cosmos. Muslims did not populate Augustine's *City of God*; neither did they appear in the three ages of history described in the *Everlasting Gospel* of Joachim of Fiore (1132–1202). By virtue of its ordinances, Christian dogma did not accommodate Islam theologically, which made it that much easier to ignore it historically in the making of the 'West'. Conversely, the discourse of Islam, could not afford total isolation; it could never really refute Jesus, Moses and Abraham *tout court*. Islam's othering of Christianity has always been relative to the presence of Jesus in the Islamic syntax. Thus, during the Umayyad period of the Islamicate caliphate (661–750), Umayyad writers attacked particular ordinances of Christianity, namely the Holy Trinity, the crucifixion of Jesus and the doctrine that he was the son of God, but they did not challenge his prophetic status. True, during the Abbasid dynasty (750–1258), the period when Islam was institutionalised and relations with others were formalized, Christians, Jews (and Zoroastrians) were designated as *dhimmis*, the ones who would only enjoy the protection of the Islamic state in return for their allegiance to it and payment of a special 'poll' tax (*jizya*). Moreover, although they were regarded as 'People of the Book' (*ahl-al kitab*), their evidence was not accepted against that of Muslims in the burgeoning *sharia* courts, their accession to political power was limited and they could not marry Muslim women. It is also true that polemics by Muslims writers such as the Afro-Arab scholar al-Jahiz (ca. 776–868), Ali al-Tabari (ca. 838–870) or Ibn Sayyar al-Warraq (ca. ninth century) and refutations of Christian dogmas by the Zaydi Shia al-Qasim ibn Ibrahim (785–860), the Asharite theologian Abu Bakr al-Baqillani (ca. 950–1013) and the Mutazilite theologian Abd' al-Jabbar (ca. 935–1024) engendered a dense group of arguments against Christianity that were soon to be archived, indexed and researched in the *madrasas* of Baghdad, Isfahan, Cairo and Damascus. Yet even in the most polemical treatise written about Christianity, Jesus himself is referred to respectfully as the messiah (al-masih). Consider the aforementioned Ibn Qayyim al-Djawziyya (1292–1350), one of the most devoted disciples of Ibn Taymiya in this regard:

And they [the Christians] saw that the Jews believed Jesus was a mad magician [sahir, majnun] and a bastard, so they said: "He is God perfect and the son of God"; and they saw that all the Jews were being circumcised so they dropped circumcision completely; and they noted that the Jews exaggerated the laws of purification, so they abandoned them altogether ... and they took notice of their prohibition [of the meat] of swine, so they made it lawful food and even started to regard it as the symbol [shi'ar] of their religion; and they saw them refraining from much of slaughtered meat and [many] animals, so they made it lawful [to eat] everything that is smaller than an elephant even unto a mosquito [Ma duna-l-fil ila-l-ba'uda] and said: "just eat what you wish and leave what you wish—no objection"; and they saw the Jews facing Jerusalem in their prayer, so they started facing the east ... and they saw them keep the Sabbath, so they choose Sunday, and desecrated the Sabbath, although they admitted that the Messiah [al-masih] glorified the Sabbath and kept [its laws].[93]

The allegation of tahrif, the falsification of the holy scriptures, i.e. the Torah and the Bible, by the Jews and the Christians, and in this case the misconceptions of the culinary preferences of the latter, did not entail a personal attack on Jesus. If there is a common thread permeating the tahrif discourse, it is Islam's refutation of the Holy Trinity, the crucifixion of Jesus and the doctrine that he was the son of God, rather than the total rejection of the Christians as a religious community or the negation of Jesus' status as a prophet. Hence, the discourse distilled out of the Quran has never really been functional to signify a 'Muslim race' or systematic efforts to ethnically cleanse the other. A minority of contemporary historians have touched upon this issue:

The Muslims tolerated Christianity but they disestablished it; henceforth Christian life and liturgy, its endowments, politics, and theology, would be a private not a public affair. By an exquisite irony, Islam reduced the status of Christians to that which the Christians had earlier thrust upon the Jews, with one difference. The reduction in Christian status was merely judicial; it was unaccompanied by either systematic persecution or blood lust, and generally, though not everywhere and at all times, unmarred by vexatious behaviour.[94]

---

[93] Ibn Qayyim al-Djawziyya, Hidayat al-Hayara fi-l Radd ala-l-Yahud wa-l-Nasara (The Guidance of the Perplexed in Answering the Jews and the Christians), Sayf al-Din al-Katib (ed.), Beirut: Manshurat Dar Maktabat al-Hayat, p. 196.

[94] Francis E. Peters, 'The Early Muslim Empires: Umayyads, Abbasids, Fatim-

Consider also the views of Marshall G.S. Hodgson on this matter:

Many of the religious disputes that were agitated among Christians and Jews in the region at large found an echo at Mecca and Medina. It is possible to interpret much of the Qur'an as an attempt to get behind those disputes to common basic essentials, to the faith of Abraham who was before Jews and Christians. Almost immediately after Muhammad's death in 632, his community made itself master of the whole region from Nile to Oxus. In doing so, it did not enter essentially alien territory. When Islam was announced there, the new doctrine did not seem strange, and indeed increasing numbers found it a quite logical further step in their own religious development.[95]

A digression seems to be necessary now: the reader should be aware that I have not deduced a 'western, European or Christian perception of history' from the samples sketched above and juxtaposed it with an 'Islamic' one. I would like to emphasise that I am not indulging in a total comparison here. What I have tried to establish are the nuances which are conducive to inform and challenge the clash regime within and between the constructs we have come to call 'Islam' and the 'West'. Thus far I have argued that there is an obvious difference between a discourse, whose theological tenets constantly alert it that it has been born within a pre-existent genealogy of prophetic revelations (Islam), and one that refutes any prophet coming after it (Christianity). I could not find a systematic philosophical school in Islam or even a coherent narrative of Islam that negates Jesus, in spite of refutations of Christianity as an incomplete religion. Certainly not in the early writings, but neither in the political manifestos of the 'Islamic revivalists' such as al-Afghani, Mawdudi, Iqbal, Qutb, al-Banna, or Khomeini with whom we will engage more fully in the following chapter. Rather the contrary, Jesus, as well as Abraham and Moses, have been of constitutive importance to the master-discourse of Islam, both to the religious self-understanding of the *umma* and to its imagination as a historical force. Without the Jewish prophets, Muhammad could not have claimed the seal of prophecy and his supersessionist claim in the first place.

The displacement of Christianity and Judaism into Islam was not merely deductive; it was not merely passively copied from the verses of

---

ids', in Marjorie Kelly (ed.), *Islam: The Religious and Political Life of a World Community*, London: Praeger, 1984, p. 79.

[95] Hodgson, 'The Role of Islam in World History', pp. 105–106.

the Quran. Abraham et al. have been continuously conceptualised as vital ingredients of many discourses that were deemed Islamic. This explains why they could have a presence in the philosophy of Abu Yaqub Ishaq ibn Ahmad Sijistani (d. ca. 971), the pioneer of Ismaili thought in the fourth Islamic century who placed Abraham, Moses and Jesus, together with Adam, Noah, Muhammad and the *qa'im* or Messiah, within the sacred history of religion which, according to him, is divided into seven cycles, each founded by a speaker prophet or *natiq*.[96] It also explains why Ayatollah Khomeini could emphasise the 'revolutionary character' of Jesus and Abraham during the Iranian Revolution in 1978–1979, why both were central to the writings of Ali Shariati and why even the ideologues of Al Qaeda do not attack him personally. Likewise, as Matar argues:

Magharibi jurists and Sufis appropriated Mary and Christ into their religious culture, invoking the hadith of the Prophet Muhammad that told about "*sayyidna 'Isa, 'alayhi al-salam*"/our Lord Jesus, peace be upon him. Jesus served as an inspiration to Muslims so much so that mosques in North Africa were named after al-Masih/Christ, showing how much the Islamic discourse redefined and co-opted the central figure in the Christian revelation. Many Muslims read Christian books which they then employed in their theological reformulations. ... Some Moriscos [Muslims of al-Andalus] integrated Christian material in their worship, including invocations to Jesus and Mary, while others wrote anti-Catholic polemics in Spanish for their exiled coreligionists in North Africa—polemics that were not too different in argument and theological content from contemporary Protestant (and later Unitarian) polemics.[97]

Ultimately, the central presence of Jesus, Mary, Abraham etc. within the discourse of Islam even explains why until the present day many Muslims have supposedly 'Christian' or 'Jewish' names such as Maryam (Maria), Yussef (Joseph), Ibrahim (Abraham) or Mussa (Moses). So the effort to place Islam outside of the Judeo-Christian universe and by extension outside of the 'West' is entirely artificial and contrary to their shared Abrahamic and historical roots. And yet despite the available sources for a potent counter-regime, the detachment of the discourse of Islam from the West has been rather successful. This is not only exemplified by the fact that today there are not many Christians named Ali, Muhammad, Omar or Hussein, of course. On the particu-

---

[96] See Abu Yaqub Sijistani, *Kashf al-mahjub*, H. Corbin (ed.), Paris-Tehran: Institut Francais de Recherche en Iran, 1949, pp. 2–96.

[97] Matar, *Europe through Arab Eyes*, p. 32.

lar issue of the prophetic claim of Muhammad and the religious merits of Islam there exists, a systematic regime accentuating exclusion. One can easily deduce that total refutation from the writings of Theodore Abu Qurra (c. 740–c.826) who used Greek philosophy, and in particular Aristotelian logic to negate both Islam and Judaism; the writings of St. John of Damascus (also Yuhanna Ibn Mansur d. c.749), who treated Islam in chapter 101 of his book on heresies which is part of his influential treatise *Pege tes gnoseos*; from Thomas Aquinas's accusation that Muhammad delivered his message first to 'men not learned in divine method ... but bestial people living in deserts';[98] from the characterisation of Muhammad by Constantine Porphyrogenitus (905–959) who described him as a 'wicked imposture' who was quite obviously 'crazy' and 'deluded';[99] from the observation of Guibert of Nogent in his early twelfth century chronicle of the First Crusade, *Gesta Dei per Francos*, that 'it is safe to speak evil of one whose malignity exceeds whatever ill can be spoken;'[100] from Voltaire's designation of him as a 'sublime et hardi charlatan';[101] from comments made by contemporary leaders of Christian denominations such as the prominent Baptist preacher Jerry Falwell who asserted on the popular CBS news show '60 minutes' that the Prophet 'Muhammad was a terrorist' and that he was 'a violent man, a man of war',[102] or the remarks of Pope Benedict XVI at the University of Regensburg in September 2006 in which he quoted the fifteenth century Byzantine Emperor Manuel II Palaeologus: 'Show me just what the Muhammad brought that was new', Palaelogus said in a passage quoted by Benedict, 'and there you will find things only evil and inhuman'.[103]

Obviously, Christianity could not afford accepting Muhammad's prophetic claim without questioning or even threatening its own legiti-

---

[98] Gordon Leff, *Medieval Thought: St. Augustine to Ockham*, Harmondsworth: Penguin, 1958, p. 218.

[99] Quoted in Chris Brown, Terry Nardin, N.J. Rengger, *International Relations in Political Thought*, Cambridge: Cambridge University Press, 2002, p. 146.

[100] R.W. Southern, *Western Views of Islam in the Middle Ages*, Cambridge: Harvard University Press, 1962, pp. 30–31.

[101] Quoted in Hourani, *Europe and the Middle East*, p. 28.

[102] See 'Jerry Falwell Apologises for Mohammad Criticism', *Reuters*, 12 October 2002.

[103] Pope Benedict XVI, 'Three Stages in the Program of De-Hellenization', op cit.

macy. Much of the personal attacks on Muhammad are explained by that competition for transcendental supremacy. But what I found surprising, nonetheless, is that there did not develop a potent counter-discourse that would engage with the transcendental claim of Islam and that would establish a similarly qualitative exchange between Christianity and Islam, that the Judeo-Christian dialectic afforded. Why is it, to put it bluntly, that we are not talking about a Judeo-Christian-Islamic field today? Of course, exactly because such a field has not been signified intellectually and theologically yet. Rather the contrary, despite the advances in the human sciences, the very necessary theo-philosophical inclusion of Islam into the Judeo-Christian monopoly over Abraham's legacy has not been achieved.

Even in the most sophisticated, contemporary treatments of Muhammad's life methodically problematic efforts are employed to place him outside the transcendental realm that he and his followers have claimed. Such an effort is most eloquently and perceptively pursued in Maxime Rodinson's influential biography of him. In a particularly revealing section, Rodinson considers the theme that Muhammad was epileptic:

> It may be ... that as a child Muhammad had some mental experience of the kind known to many shamans of north and central Asia, and also to Australian magicians: at the moment of their initiation they feel that a spirit has taken away their internal organs and replaced them with fresh ones. However that may be, the Prophet certainly suffered from attacks of some kind in adult life. Hostile Christians put it down to epilepsy. If this were so, it was a benign form. What is much more probable is that Muhammad's psycho-physiological constitution was basically of the kind found in many mystics.[104]

The methodology espoused by Rodinson, at times Marxist, at times Freudian, exhibits a form of argumentation that allows him to speak with a rather more pronounced authority than the one expressed by the Christian polemicists perused above, one that is intrinsic to the confident language of western modernity. Equipped with the privilege—inherited from Marx via Hegel—that we can construe a causal version of history that would be impervious to disappointment, Rodinson empowers himself to suggest a psychological diagnosis of his object who lived fourteen centuries before him in a place and culture

---

[104] Maxime Rodinson, *Muhammad: Prophet of Islam*, London: I.B. Tauris, 2002, p. 56.

that was rather different from the one enveloping the author in the Paris of the 1950s:

One has only to dip into psychology text-books to find a hundred perfectly bona fide cases of people in a state of hallucination hearing things and seeing visions which they claim quite genuinely never to have seen or heard before. And yet an objective study of their cases shows that these are simply fresh associations produced by the unconscious working on things which have been seen and heard but forgotten. Facts of this kind we now take for granted. It is therefore conceivable that what Muhammad saw and heard may have been the supernatural beings described to him by the Jews and Christians with whom he talked. It is understandable that, in the words that came to him, elements of his actual experience, the stuff of his thoughts, dreams and meditations, and memories of discussions that he had heard should have re-emerged, chopped, changed and transposed, with an appearance of immediate reality that seemed to him proof of some external activity which, although inaccessible to other men's minds, was yet wholly objective in its nature.[105]

It is clear what Rodinson attempts here. He is trying to present a 'scientific' analysis of the reasons why Muhammad may have thought that he had contact with some transcendental deity called Allah via the Archangel Gabriel. Once we begin to focus on the way Rodinson constructs his argument, we find that the reader is disqualified from engaging with the prophetic claim of Muhammad, not only because it is suggested that it may be superstitious to do so, but because Rodinson's methodology does not allow for a discussion of that prophecy as a social factor or a philosophical system rather than as a claim that could be measured in the laboratory. In Rodinson's *Muhammad* there is no escaping this dominating narrative and since it is Islam's prophet that is subsumed in it, he emerges out of the book without any powers left to speak for himself. The methodology of Rodinson disqualifies him and any theo-philosophical conceptualisation of his transcendental claim. Rodinson's objectivised discourse is not conducive to a serious engagement with Islam, especially with those notions of Islam that are actually active in the political and socio-economic struggles engulfing Muslim societies until today.

There rages at the time of writing an illuminating controversy about the merits of such methodologies as the one espoused by Rodinson. On the one side of the debate we find adherents to the panaceas of causal positivism such as Richard Dawkins, Christopher Hitchens and

[105] Ibid., p. 77.

Daniel Dennett, who would link Rodinson's attitude to the power of scientific enquiry. Conversely, critics such as Terry Eagleton would counter that the evidence on which such arguments are based is compromised, that it is necessary to rediscover the transcendental realm as an object of rational enquiry. I would like to place the following sentences somewhere between the two ends of this spectrum of opinions, not as a conjunction but as a discontinuity. What is important for my line of argument, to be more precise, is that after the 'Enlightenment' there emerged a strong tendency in the 'West' to transfer Muhammad, Jesus, Moses and everybody else with a transcendental mandate to the laboratory. In this process, Nietzsche famously proclaimed, God died in the Occident; the dialectics between man, God and being were transformed into a dialectic between individual, society and history. The discourse that retained some notion of Islam as a nodal point metamorphosed into a different direction. The discourse of Islam, in its many manifestations, retained God as an object, not only as an object of primary theological enquiry, but also as a source of ideological vigour. Let me start with a passage taken from Khaled Abou El Fadl's inquiries into forms of authority in Islam, which serves as an entry into my argument in the following paragraphs:

The issue is not simply the authenticity of any particular tradition. It is possible to come to the conviction that the Prophet had no role whatsoever in the production of a particular tradition and, therefore, we might determine that this tradition is inauthentic. But this determination is of limited utility. The much more pertinent issue is to evaluate the historical context that generated the authorial enterprise and to analyse the cumulative and evolving process that led to the development of communities of interpretation around that enterprise. In terms of analysing the work product of communities of interpretation, we must inquire into the extent to which such communities constructed or were constructed by their respective historical contexts, and we must inquire into the nature of a community's understanding of the authorial enterprise and its historical context. In addition, we must analyse the interpretive community's understanding of the role of the Prophet in that enterprise.[106]

El Fadl focuses here on the evolution of Islamic jurisprudence (*fiqh*) and the interpretation of *sharia* law by epistemic, interpretive communities during different historical periods. He implies that it is the historical context and its signification by elites, primarily those with

---

[106] Khaled Abou El Fadl, *Speaking in God's Name: Islamic Law, Authority and Women*, London: One World Publications, 2003, p. 110.

institutionalised legal authority, that signals whether a particular law is *sahih* (authentic) or *mawdu* (fabricated). El Fadl is right to point out that the components of Islamic law and jurisprudence are not static, uni-linear or monopolised in accordance with a set of easily identifiable rules that have remained unchanged throughout history, and in his study he provides a range of empirical material to substantiate his case. But what has to be emphasised more fully is what makes this field and its constituting discourse 'Islamic' in the first place. Is this not the historical axis established by Muhammad? It seems to me that no Islamic law, however abstractly and secularly formulated, could afford to lose this reference point without losing its 'Islamicity'. What I am saying is that any discourse of Islam could not discard Muhammad and the Quran without losing its 'Islamic' object. Hence it makes sense to speak of a particular discourse of Islam rather than of an Islam that would exist in and of itself. This does not mean that the discourse thus Islamicised is by necessity religious or theocratic, but that it would retain Muhammad and the Quran, however conceptualised, as some abstract reference point that signifies the Islamic order as such. The genealogical point I am making is not that notions of Islam offer one comprehensive, religious or theocratic attitude towards history, but that they entail terms and concepts with which some Islam could be signified either as a seemingly concrete and coherent discourse or one that is entirely diffuse and abstract. At the extreme end of the latter possibility, that is opened up occasionally in the philosophy of Farabi and Ibn Sina, and the poetry of Rabia Balkhi, Khayyam, Hafiz and Rumi, the seeming paradox of an Islamic order that is entirely 'secular' diffuses itself in a process of grand metaphysical syntheses.

Self and other beyond Orientalism

The Muslim subject: she moves beyond the *ahl al-kitab* (people of the book) taking with her a part of their identity. She causes a rift in the universe and the order of the world. A whole spectrum of objects constitutes her substance, each object transferring its quality to the newly constituted Muslim subject. Abraham and Jesus merge in Muhammad and as such no longer exist autonomously. Hinduism, Buddhism, western modernity submerged in Islamicate civilisation and seized to function independently. The Muslim subject is the effect of its disqualified objects; the disqualified objects are affected by the Muslim subject.

That Muslim subject that we think other to our self, is in actual fact within our self, she is a sibling not a double. So engaging with her constitution becomes an act of anthropological necessity; it is literally essential in order to comprehend the constitution of our own self in the first place. That alerts us against a 'fundamentalist' reading of Said's *Orientalism*. If we read Orientalism as a discursive formation that was objectified as true and internalised as real in a linear process. If we assume that this discourse has created an inevitable and all-encompassing reality called the 'Orient'. If we think that there is no way to go beyond that discourse, we will become paralysed by it. Consequently, we would refrain from looking at the field the Oriental subject has tried to carve out for herself. This is where the voice talking to us is articulated and which places the other within *our* self. Said acknowledges in his later writings, that in 'the Islamic world there has been a resurgence of rhetorics and movements stressing the inimicability of Islam with the West, just as in Africa, Europe, Asia, and elsewhere, movements have appeared that stress the need for excluding designated others as undesirable'.[107] He seems to acknowledge that the otherness of the Orient as represented by the 'West' threatens to undervalue the interventions in this process by the Orient itself.

But this is not all that is happening here. In his writings Said is primarily concerned with the way the 'West' represents the Orient in general and Arabs and Muslims in particular and not with the manner the Orient narrated itself. In his oeuvre the philosophy of Ibn Sina, the *shahnameh* of Ferdowsi or the *Muqqadimah* (or Prolegomena in Greek) of Ibn Khaldun is marginal; it is not what the argument of Orientalism encompasses. But it seems to me that the strident methodology employed in *Orientalism* suggests not only the primacy of the colonial period in the constitution of the Orient and its Arab-Muslim sub-stratum, but also the complete centrality of the West as a *ghul*, a giant with all-enveloping powers. The danger is that as a result of a hegemony thus rearticulated, the 'subaltern' may stop speaking to us as an agent (maker and taker) of history. She threatens to be silenced by the authoritarian voice of the West propounded through a discourse called Orientalism. A self-fulfilling prophecy may thus ensue.

---

[107] Edward W. Said, 'The Clash of Definitions: On Samuel Huntington', in idem. *Reflections on Exile and Other Essays*, Cambridge, MA: Harvard University Press, 2000, p. 576.

But I think if we listen carefully, beyond the cacophony expounded by the makers of the 'West', the 'altern' speaks to us with an enticing and charming accent. We find ourselves transposed back into history to the seventeenth century and into the culture of Ottoman Istanbul that delivered the multicultural language of Katib Çelebi (1609–1657). I have chosen Çelebi because I believe that it is with him that the other is systematically discovered both within Islamic theory and in practice in many ways for the first time in such a methodical manner. Çelebi was a keen follower of the polymath Ibn Khaldun, who was born and raised in Tunis during a period of intense engagement and rivalry between dynasties that ruled in the name of Christianity and Islam. Ibn Khaldun's *Muqqadimah* masterfully captures these vicissitudes in a dialectic that suggests the cyclical rise and fall of civilisations in accordance with the degree of strength of their *asabiya*, the internal cohesion of their community. Çelebi adopted and reinterpreted Ibn Khaldun's theory in order to explain why it was that the Ottoman Empire retained its power for so many centuries, and why Ottoman expansion into Europe had now been halted.

Çelebi systematically followed his credo 'to acquire knowledge and become acquainted with the division of mankind into various sorts, and with the state and condition of every part'.[108] He sponsored the translation of Latin and Arabic chronicles, produced a 'Guide for the Perplexed on the History of the Greeks, Byzantines, and Christians', authored cartographic works such as the *Cihannüma* and the *Tarh-i Hindi garbi*, treatise on tobacco and coffee, Ottoman naval matters, encyclopaedias, world histories and so on.[109] What strikes me as different to the writings of the classical philosophers of Islam and the polemicist who wrote against Christianity, is that Çelebi is self-conscious about his exploration of the other. Çelebi is so adamant to catch up on knowing the other, something that he felt Ottoman historians had failed to do, that he allows us to see his footprint in history not as a muted Oriental, but as an erudite Ottoman-Muslim who was entirely capable of expressing himself in the language of his day and age. The other appears in Farabi, Ibn Hazm and Ibn Taymiya. But with Çelebi

---

[108] Katib Chelebi, *The Balance of Truth*, Geoffrey L. Lewis (trans.), London: George Allen and Unwin Ltd., 1957, pp. 29–30.

[109] See further, Suraiya Faroqhi, *The Ottoman Empire and the World Around it*, London: I.B. Tauris, 2005, pp. 199 ff.

the other is explored systematically. Ultimately, what emerges through his discoveries is a frightening possible world that is already in the irresistibly modern mode. For Çelebi and the adherent of his school of thought, the other must have appeared as a reality that was presumed to be possible before its knowledge, but which was now revealing itself to be possibly outrageous. For them Europe emerged as the horizon of a frightening reality which could not be known without the annihilation of the one preceding it. To put it bluntly: the resistance to the emerging hegemony of the West begins with the discomforting discovery of it by Çelebi and his followers. It is with them that *dar al-harb* (the abode of war) and *dar al-Islam* (the abode of Islam/peace) begin to merge more forcefully.

An unproblematic ascription of causality to the discourse of Orientalism, threatens to undervalue the ability of the 'Oriental' to revert to her own epistemological devices in order to write her history. I don't think that this has been merely in reaction to the 'imperial gaze' of the nineteenth century as Said suggests in his later writings, but a parallel process with comparatively ancient manifestations as its Occidental pendant.[110]

Allow me to zigzag, these are molar, segmented lines, through the centuries in order to demonstrate the point I am making more fully. It is true as Said argues that in the nineteenth century, the East in general and Islam in particular were densely narrated. The Orient had a prominent place in the imagination of Schlegel, Humboldt, Goethe in the German context, Chateaubriand, Lamartine, Nerval, Flaubert, Renan in France and the Victorian travellers in the English speaking worlds, especially in Sir Richard Burton's *Personal Narrative of a Pilgrimage to al-Madinah and Meccah*, Austen Layard's *Discoveries in the Ruins of Nineveh and Babylon* (1851), Eliot Warburton's *The Crescent and the Cross* (1844), Robert Curzon's *Visit to the Monasteries of the Levant*, Thackeray's *Notes of a Journey from Cornhill to Grand Cairo* (1845) and the writings of Blunt, Doughty and T.E. Lawrence.[111] Moreover, Albert Hourani has rightly pointed out that scholars such as I.

---

[110] See his 'The Clash of Definitions: On Samuel Huntington', in Said, *Reflections on Exile and Other Essays*, p. 575.

[111] See Said, *Orientalism*, pp. 193 ff.; Thomas J. Assad, *Three Victorian Travellers: Burton Blunt and Doughty*, London: Routledge & Kegan Paul, 1964, p. 5.

Goldziher (1850–1921) and Snouck Hurgronje (1857–1936) first established 'Islam' as a field of enquiry in Europe and North America, that the study of Islam was departmentalised a generation later with C.H. Becker (1876–1933) and W. Barthold (1869–1930)[112] and that it was institutionalised in England beyond Cambridge and Oxford with the establishment of the School of Oriental and African Studies (SOAS) in London in 1916.[113]

The merit of Said's analysis lies in the way he brings out the dense structural vigour of this period that lent legitimacy to the dispersal and subjugation of millions of people. But the disparity of power does not imply that the East was silent, intellectually muted before, during and after the institutionalisation of Orientalism. The other side made the 'Occident, Europe, the West, Christianity' available as well. Such designations of the other were interpreted, abstracted and contracted by 'Orientals' before, during and after colonialism. Consider the Persian travel narrative of *safarnameh*, which grew in Iran during the rule of Fath Ali Shah (1797–1834) and here especially during the period of the *nezam-e jadid* (or 'new system') introduced by Crown Prince Abbas Mirza in the early-nineteenth century.[114] In Mirza Saleh Shirazi's travelogues of Europe, for instance, he commends the magnificence of the Bodleian Library at Oxford and acknowledges the shared drive for learning in Iran and England, which he had the luxury of comparing as a part of an official delegation sent by Abbas Mirza, the Iranian Crown Prince.[115] At the same time, he points to the arrogance of the Vice Principal (Reverend Frodsham Hodson, 1770–1822) and the 'extreme pomp' of an Oxford degree ceremony, which appeared to him as 'nothing but

---

[112] See Hourani, *Europe and the Middle East*, p. 162.

[113] See Albert Hourani, *Islam in European Thought*, Cambridge: Cambridge University Press, 1991, pp. 65 ff.

[114] See further Monica M. Ringer, 'The Quest for the Secret of Strength in Iranian Nineteenth-Century Travel Literature: Rethinking Tradition in the *Safarnameh*', in Nikki R. Keddie and Rudi Matthee (eds), *Iran and the Surrounding World*, London: University of Washington Press, 2002, pp. 146–161; Juan R. I. Cole, 'Invisible Occidentalism: eighteenth-century Indo-Persian constructions of the West', *Iranian Studies*, vol. 25, issue 3 and 4, 1992, pp. 3–16.

[115] See further, Mohammad R. Ghanoonparvar, *In a Persian Mirror: Images of the West and Westerners in Iranian Fiction*, Austin: University of Texas Press, 1993, p. 18.

tomfoolery and excess'.[116] Nineteenth century chroniclers such as 'Abd al-Rahman al-Jabarti (1825), Niqula al-Turk (1828) and Haydar al-Shihabi (1835) developed a comparable ambiance vis-à-vis Europe in general and the French in particular, expressing their admiration for the personality of Napoleon whilst deprecating the violence and antireligious tone of the French revolutionaries.[117] Further back in history, Ibn Batoutah's writings in the fourteenth century emphasises the superiority of Islamic civilisation, which, according to him, transformed Gibraltar into a 'supreme' city,[118] whilst the chronicles of Ahmed Sinan Celebi in the fifteenth century accentuate the immorality of the Christian monarchs.[119] We may even discern an eastern penchant for Orientalist views on the 'tedious' sameness of 'Muslim cities'[120] translated into 'Occidentalist' terms in the writings of the Qajar monarch Nasir ed-Din Shah (1831–1896), for whom 'the cities of Firangistan (Europe in general) all resemble one another. When one has been seen', the Shah emphasised with immense 'Occidentalist' authority, 'the arrangement, condition, and scale of the others is in one's possession'.[121]

Let us also consider the writings of Seyyed Fakhrodin Shadman, and here especially his most important work entitled *taskhir-e tamaddon-e farangi* (*The conquest of western civilisation*), published in Tehran in 1948. Shadman makes the case for *farangshenasi*, or 'Occidentalism'

[116] Mirza Saleh Shirazi, *majmu'ah-e safarnamahha-ye Mirza Saleh Shirazi*, Gholam Hussein Mirza Saleh (ed.), Tehran: Nashr-e Tarikh-e Iran, 1364/1985, pp. 321–324.

[117] See Ibrahim Abu-Lughod, *Arab Rediscovery of Europe: A Study in Cultural Encounters*, Princeton: Princeton University Press, 1963, pp. 26 ff.

[118] See C. Defrémery and B.R. Sanguinetti, *Voyages d'Ibn Batoutah, texte arabe accompagné d'une traduction*, vol. 4, Paris: Imprimerie Nationale, 1879.

[119] See Brigitte Moser (trans. and ed.), *Die Chronik des Ahmed Sinan Celebi genannt Bihisti: Eine Quelle zur Geschichte des Osmanischen Reiches unter Sultan Bayezid II*, Beiträge zur Kenntnis Südeuropas und des Nahen Orients, München: Dr. Dr. Rudolf Trofenik, 1980.

[120] 'Nothing is more foreign to a Muslim town in the Maghreb', writes Roger Le Tourneau, 'than the rectilinear avenues of a Roman or a modern city: an aerial photograph of any Muslim city makes us think of a maze, or a labyrinth'. See his *Cités musulmanes d'Afrique du Nord*, Alger: La Maison de livre, 1957, p. 20. See also on this subject, Albert Hourani and S. M. Stern (eds), *The Islamic City*, Oxford: Oxford University Press, 1970.

[121] J.W. Redhouse (trans.), *The Diary of H.M. The Shah of Persia*, London: John Murray, 1874, p. 105.

in Iran, much the same way Lord Curzon and others stated the case for Oriental Studies as a means to fill the gap in the 'national equipment' of England 'which ought emphatically to be filled'.[122] Indeed, Shadman himself makes the analogy between Occidentalism and Orientalism rather explicit:

The vastness of the precise science of farangshenasi was revealed to me in England when I first realised how difficult a task it was. But inquiry into the conditions of other nations, particularly farangi ones, is so beneficial that it is worth the trouble. I believe this subject is so important that it must be taught in all Iranian schools. ... The task of a *farangshenas* has at least ten times more importance, variety, and hardship than that of an Orientalist. It is a pity that in all of Iran there are not even ten farangshenas [while] for us to get acquainted with farangi civilisation, we need thousands of enlightened, Persian speaking Iranians who are [both] *Iranshenas* and farangshenas.[123]

Scholars of contemporary Iranian history have studied how that systematic critique of the 'West' was integral to the process of identity formation amongst revolutionary Iranian intellectuals in the twentieth century.[124] Especially, the pro-western policy and Aryan-centric identity discourse of the Pahlavis (1925–1979) that I mentioned at the beginning of this chapter was counter-acted with a mixture of leftists, Islamic and Iranian-Shia symbols and imagery which were strong

---

[122] George Nathaniel Curzon, *Subjects of the Day: Being a Selection of Speeches and Writings*, London: George Allen & Unwin, 1915, pp. 191–192.

[123] Quoted in Mehrzad Boroujerdi, *Iranian Intellectuals and the West: The Tormented Triumph of Nativism*, Syracuse: Syracuse University Press, 1996, p. 58.

[124] See further Boroujerdi, *Iranian Intellectuals*; Hamid Dabashi, *Theology of Discontent: The Ideological Foundation of the Islamic Revolution in Iran*, New York: New York University Press, 1993; Behrooz Ghamari-Tabrizi, *Abdolkarim Soroush, Religious Politics and Democratic Reform*, London: I.B. Tauris, 2008; Ali Gheissari, *Iranian Intellectuals in the 20th Century*, Austin: University of Texas Press, 1998; Mehran Kamrava, *Iran's Intellectual Revolution*, Cambridge: Cambridge University Press, 2008; Ali Mirsepassi, *Intellectual Discourse and the Politics of Modernization: Negotiating Modernity in Iran*, Cambridge, MA: Harvard University Press, 2000; Negin Nabavi, *Intellectuals and the State in Iran: Politics, Discourse and the Dilemma of Authenticity*, Gainesville: University of Florida Press, 2003; Mohammad Tavakoli-Targhi, *Refashioning Iran: Orientalism, Occidentalism and Historiography*, New York: Palgrave, 2001; Farzin Vahdat, *God and Juggernaut: Iran's Intellectual Encounter with Modernity*, Syracuse: Syracuse University Press, 2002.

enough to merge on a pivotal revolutionary goal: the downfall of the Shah and the end of Iranian dependence on the 'West' in general and the United States in particular. A quick perusal of this literature reveals that this rigorous picture of the 'West' has been intensified in innumerable ways: in Ali Shariati's emphasis on the archetypical difference between the spiritual orientation of the Orient and the empirical quest of the Occident;[125] in Jalal-al e Ahmad's deprecation of the state of *gharbzadegi*, the 'westtoxification' of Pahlavi Iran in the 1960s which he likened to a cultural disease;[126] in the economic theories of Ayatollah Taleghani which contrast the 'morality' intrinsic to 'Islamic economics' to the injustices caused by western capitalism;[127] in the influential writings of Abolhasan Jalili, Ehsan Naraghi, Seyyed Hossein Nasr and Dariush Shayegan; and in contemporary philosophical controversies in post-revolutionary Iran between Reza Davari-Ardakani (pen name Davari)—who argues that the 'West' must be seen as the ultimate other against which an Islamic identity must be construed—and Hosssein Faraj-Dabagh (pen name Abdolkarim Soroush)—who argues that the 'West' is integral to the 'East', that it is epistemologically flawed to invent the 'West' in isolation of the Islamic worlds in general and Iran in particular.[128] Moreover, this intellectual representation of the Occident has been re-enacted in the cultural sphere. The English, especially, have had a particular place in the cultural imagination of Iranians. Their presence amongst Persians in the different epochs of mutual relations is typically reduced to acts of plethoric materialism, imperial conspiracy, elitist arrogance, political amorality or ethical inferiority: 'The English are always the enemy of those, who

---

[125] For his writings in English see Ali Shariati, *Man and Islam: Lectures by Ali Shariati*, Ghulam M. Fayez (trans.), Mashhad: University of Mashhad Press, 1982; Ali Shari'ati, *On the Sociology of Islam: Lectures by Ali Shari'ati*, trans. Hamid Algar, Berkeley: Mizan Press, 1979; Ali Rahnema, *An Islamic Utopian: A Political Biography of Ali Shariati*, London: I.B. Tauris, 2000; Lloyd Ridgeon (ed.), *Religion and Politics in Modern Iran: A Reader*, London: I.B. Tauris, 2005 and writings published at http://www.shariati.com.

[126] See Jalal Al-e Ahmad, *Plagued by the West (Gharbzadegi)*, Paul Sprachman (trans.), New York: Caravan, 1982.

[127] For a comprehensive analysis of economic discourses of Islam see Charles Tripp, *Islam and the Moral Economy: The Challenge of Capitalism*, Cambridge: Cambridge University Press, 2006.

[128] See further Kamrava, *Iran's Intellectual Revolution*.

love their homeland'.[129] This is a famous quote taken from the 1970s television series based on Iraj Pezeshkzad's best-selling novel *Dai jan Napoleon* ('My dear uncle Napoleon'). It has been vividly reproduced in Iranian culture until today.

And now I feel that I have to stop and assess my interpretation of the historical and empirical material marshalled. Have I not obscured the differences between Orientalism, an institutionalised academic field, and Occidentalism, an aggregation of statements culminating in narrative, cultural and ideological representations of the 'Occident'? Have I not overstated the parallels between the 'Occidentalisation' of the West by Orientals and the 'Orientalisation' of the East by Occidentals? Is it not true that Orientalism is 'thicker' than its Occidental pendant, that 'the very presence of a "field" such as Orientalism, with no corresponding equivalent in the Orient itself, suggests the relative strength of Orient and Occident', that the 'crucial index of Western strength is that there is no possibility of comparing the movement of Westerners (since the end of the eighteenth century) with the movement of Easterners westwards'?[130]

One must agree with Said in quantitative terms: Orientalism has a rather more pronounced presence due to the sheer volume of representations produced about the East in general and Islam in particular which is a strong indicator for the discrepancy of power between the European empires and their colonial subjects during that period. But the relatively low number of travellers to Europe in the nineteenth century does not divorce Orientals from the epistemological pressures of their own narratives.[131] There continuously existed ideas which created their own field in which to enclose the 'Westerner', their own caricatures of the self; their own stage in which to enact their parodies of the other. There were representations of the Macedonians as 'wicked' and 'wild' which Persians found confirmed in of the most recited tragedy of ancient Iranian history: the burning of the grand Archimedean capital Persepolis in fourth century BC on the orders of Alexander; there was the Muslim denial of the Christian Holy Trinity

---

[129] See further Ahmad Ashraf, 'The Appeal of Conspiracy Theories to Persians', *Interdisciplinary Journal of Middle Eastern Studies*, vol. 5, Fall 1996, pp. 57–88.

[130] Said, *Orientalism*, p. 204.

[131] Those travels have been considered in Abu-Lughod, *Arab Rediscovery of Europe*, especially pp. 76–77, 84–86, and 96 ff.

and the emphasis on *tawhid*, the oneness of God instead; there was the representation of Islam and the Prophet Muhammad as the seal of humanity and the *Endziel* of History in Ibn Khaldun's historical treatise five centuries before Hegel's Owl of Minerva spread its wings, and six centuries before Francis Fukuyama attempted to re-enact the Hegelian motif in our era; there was the refutation of the Greek Peripatetics in Ibn Sina's *mantiq al-mashraqiyyin* ('The Logic of the Orientals') in the eleventh century; there was the Islamic call for a world *umma*; there was Saladin's criticism of 'Christian' military strategy; there was Butrus al-Bustani's protestation of 'western' culture and its corrupting influence on Syrian/Lebanese society in the nineteenth century; and there is a self-conscious emphasis on the spirituality of the 'East' and the materialism of the 'West' in Tawfiq al-Hakim's famous Arabic novels *The Return of the Spirit* (1933) and the *Bird of the East* (1938).

What we may establish then is a pattern of representations of the other that is structural: a diffuse 'Occidentalist' archive that is informed, even constituted, from the narratives that belong to those experiences: *these are some of the lenses through which the Occident is experienced, and they have repeatedly shaped the language, perception, and form of the encounter between East and West.*[132] And as we have seen and will continue to investigate, some sections of this archive have also signified instances of conflict between the fictitious Islamic in-group and the imagined western out-group .

So a nuanced approach to the argument in *Orientalism* is warranted. Only if we believe in a totalitarian historicism that deletes historical memory from consciousness and subliminal awareness, only if we believe that nineteenth century 'Orientals' were somehow detached from the ideas of their ancestors, only if we believe in the thorough, unthreaded distinctiveness of historical epochs, can we sustain the notion that there exists no comparably powerful 'pendant' to Orientalism in non-western discourses. Did not the Muslim scholar writing in the nineteenth century have recourse to the encyclopaedic treatises of Muslim historiographers of previous centuries? Do not Islamic institutions like the al-Azhar in Egypt, or the seminaries in Isfahan, Qom, Najaf, Samarkand and Mashhad claim historical continuity? Do not

---

[132] This is a quotation from Said's, *Orientalism*, p. 58. All I have done is substituting Orient with Occident in order to accentuate the relative interchangeability of the discourse of Orientalism.

their libraries and archives hold books, articles, declarations and so on that go farther back than the nineteenth century? It appears to me that for the 'Oriental' the nineteenth century did not occur in an entranced suspension of history; that the singularity of the discourse of Orientalism threatens to obscure the 'Oriental' presence in history during, before and after that period. The Islamic worlds continued to both socially engineer their own image of the other and to endeavour an ontological presence apart from his imagination. Such an understanding of our interdependencies is not only central to qualify what I have termed the co-constitution of the clash regime, but also for the plotting of strategies suitable enough to heave us out of our self-inflicted mess.

At the same time, as a means of summary, we have to establish a very important difference to the discourses that have signified the imperialisms that emerged in Europe, Orientalism included. Until the nineteenth century, the discourse of Islam did not develop an all-encompassing ideology as devastating as the one signifying European imperialisms/colonialisms. The syntax of Islam did sanction military expansion, hegemonic dominance of Jews, Christians, Hindus and other minorities. It did also legitimate occasional outbursts of concerted violence, but not an attempt to racially dissect the Muslim self from its significant others. The Islamic archive did not serve the same function as Orientalism did for western imperialisms. The discourses of Islam, in their many variations, did not deliver an ideology that would sanction the mass killing of individuals because of their race. In none of the narratives perused in this chapter can we discern an absolute detachment that would have been effected and institutionalised as an overarching ideology suitable to legitimate mass murder. We will see in the following chapters that mass killings in the name of some Islam is a particularly modern phenomenon.

If I have started this chapter with a paragraph on the functions of history, if I have stressed connections between past and present, if I have sketched the strategies of exclusion employed by Muslims and Christians, Persians and Greeks, I have done so not to reify seemingly insurmountable differences that would corroborate some eternal clash of civilisation, but rather to point out interdependencies; to stress that the clash regime, even when it accentuates insurmountable differences, remains a social system, even if its proponents do not recognise it as such. To the rational majority, it should be clear that the clash regime 'creolizes', that it is hybrid, that it refers to overlapping identities and intertwined memories, not the fond memories that are subdued because of their immediately ameliorating force, but those memories of death and violence that bind us together as well. Even the particularly strident trend to divorce Islam from the 'West' and vice versa that was dramatised by the discourse of western modernity and that I will explore more fully in the next chapter has not erased this inevitable bond. Our irreducible interdependence remains inherent even to the angriest notions of friend and enemy, master and slave, us and them. And yet, so strong is the clash regime today, that even talking about organising joint memorial ceremonies that would commemorate the Muslims, Christians and others who died during the Crusades or the conquests of Muslim rulers in Europe, would provoke—most probably—ridicule or a massively violent reaction from many sides.

2

THE TEMPTATIONS OF GRAMMAR

The attributes of things are of two kinds—the essential and the accidental. The former is an attribute which is essential for a conception of that object, so much so that we cannot conceive that object without first conceiving that attribute.

Omar Khayyam

To be or not to be?

The preceding chapter presented a 'tabula rasa argument'. It discussed some of the ideas that have been used to give meaning to the clash regime facing us today. It also introduced some of those rare narratives that would/could challenge its structural salience. To that end, I focused on the constructed nature of some of the principal binaries holding the clash regime together. Metahistories of regimes of truths are adequately explained not according to measures of 'factuality', but rather to how their deep ideological structure operates—what effects they have on our understanding of selfhood and otherness. So I have tried to draw attention away from the idea that the clash regime has an existence in and of itself, that it is inevitable, or immutable. At the same time I did not suggest that no alternative discourses existed. Neither did I sketch a discourse/counter-discourse symmetry. I believe I took seriously Foucault's premise that within a particular discourse, or a larger constellation such as a regime of truth, power and knowledge are linked together and that power entails resistance.[1]

The wide movement through time and space that I thought that I could afford in the last chapter has to be cut down now. It is not enough to question the writing of history; we have to screen the syntax underlying the clash regime as well. In their wealth of signification, words ascribe reality to objects that are otherwise 'lifeless'. At least since Bakhtin but certainly with Saussure and Derrida, the directedness of the sign, and language more generally, their ideological content and violent potentialities have been established.[2] It is one of the dilemmas of narration that we constantly have to re-invent the words we are using in order to make them relevant to the subject matter. It is the grammarian and writer in us, in other words, who weaves a particular argument out of the threads of language. It is she who has the powers to write the fairytales of history:

Language plays the dominant role in all the myths under discussion. It brings opposites together as 'natural'; it presents human types in scholarly idioms and methodologies; it ascribes reality and reference to objects (other words) of its own making.[3]

I am convinced with Said that words and their ascribed realities are deceptive, that the language that we use confers significance on otherwise meaningless phenomena. We know from Marx and Farabi, Ibn Sina and Hegel, that externalising ideas through language is an act of anthropological necessity. We speak to give meaning to our surrounding world and our very existence in it. But isn't discourse by definition also a dialogue between subject and object, self and other, the Orientalist and the Arab world that can never be entirely enveloped by Orientalism? That which has been sanctioned by a discourse, even a larger constellation such as a regime of truth, has an authority over us, over our attitudes and behaviour. But when a particular discourse such as Orientalism is produced, it does not disperse truth conditions—effects of its syntactical power—from which counter-hegemonic models can

---

[1] Michel Foucault, *The Will to Knowledge: The History of Sexuality*, vol. 1, Robert Hurley (trans.), London: Penguin, 1998, pp. 96 ff.

[2] See further Robert J. C. Young, *Torn Halves: Political Conflict in Literary and Cultural Theory*, Manchester: Manchester University Press, 1996, especially pp. 33–82.

[3] Edward Said, 'Shattered Myths' in A. L. Macfie (ed.), *Orientalism: A Reader*, Edinburgh: Edinburgh University Press, 2000, p. 100.

be excluded in their entirety. Neither is the language of such counter-hegemonies entirely coded by the authority of the dominant model they resist: Orientalism is resisted, the resistance is confronted by Orientalism; this is the dialectical struggle under focus here. This is why I found the argument of Said expressed in the latter sentences of the second part of the quoted paragraph less convincing:

> Mythic language is discourse, that is, it cannot be anything but systematic; one does not really make discourse at will, nor statements in it, without first belonging—in some cases unconsciously, but at any rate involuntarily—to the ideology and the institutions that guarantee its existence. *These latter are always the institutions of an advanced society dealing with a less-advanced society*. The principal feature of mythical discourse is that it conceals its own origins as well as those of what it describes. Arabs are presented in the imagery of static, almost ideal types, neither as creatures with a potential in the process of being realised nor as a history being made. The exaggerated value heaped upon Arabic as a language permits the Orientalist to make the language equal to mind, society, history, and nature. Undoubtedly the absence in Arabic of a full-fledged tradition of reported informal personal experience (autobiography, novel, etc.) makes it easier for the Orientalist to let the language as a whole have such uncontrolled significance; thus for the Orientalist the language speaks the Arab, not vice versa. There are historical and cultural reasons for this distortion.[4]

The critical argument expressed by Said is too focused on the impact of language on only one side of the discursive field, in particular its impact on representations of 'Arabs'. Such an emphasis works for Said, because it helps him to delineate Orientalism as an autonomous entity. But not only does he undervalue the resistance that the Orientalist discourse provokes, that very dialectic that Said himself pushed upon Orientalism with irresistible force and which has changed the Orientalist corpus ever since. He also neglects too readily that this resistance has access to a fertile 'Occidentalist' field, an interdependent epistemological area that Sadiq al-Azm and Aijaz Ahmad ponder. It seems to me that the latter is right when he observes that Said's 'ideal reader is the Western reader ... The non-Western reader is simply not addressed because that would bring up the question of what the structure of the histories of Asian and African countries have been'.[5] This is one of the reasons why notions of Islam are marginal to Said's writings, apart from their representations by 'Orientalists'. When you continuously

---

[4] Ibid., emphasis added.
[5] Aijaz Ahmad, 'Between Orientalism and Historicism', in Macfie (ed.), *Orien-*

emphasise the determining impact of the Orientalist discourse and the corresponding cultural prowess of the 'West', you reduce the agency of the other, her ability to speak beyond her representation in western scholarship. Pointing to the interdependencies between 'us' and 'them' that history has inevitably created is one thing. Assuming that the other is the only ideal-type that carries a hybrid identity is another.

In *Orientalism*, Said does not do justice to Foucault's dialectical notion of power and resistance and implies that language and the representation of the other tends to be agonistic and not dialectical, symmetrical and not cyclical. So when he quotes from Lord Cromer's two-volume work *Modern Egypt*, citing his emphasis on the inability of Egyptians to think logically, their propensity for contradictory explanations and their general tendency to 'break down under the mildest process of cross-examination',[6] in order to show that the Oriental is '*contained* and *represented* by dominating frameworks',[7] he underestimates the ability of Egyptians to express themselves, to write their own history, to narrate their sense of selfhood against the colonial odds. 'Power comes from below', writes Foucault, 'there is no binary and all-encompassing opposition between rulers and ruled at the root of power relations'.[8] Elsewhere Foucault is more explicit: '[w]e can never be ensnared by power: we can always modify its grip in determinate conditions and according to a precise strategy. ... The struggle is everywhere. ... [A]t every moment, we move from rebellion to domination, from domination to rebellion'.[9] This suggests that a powerful structural constellation such as Orientalism does not code the 'Oriental' all the way down to his cognitive constituency by necessity. The points of resistance that counteract such discursive formations are not only 'a reaction or rebound, forming with respect to the basic domination an underside that is in the end always passive, doomed to perpetual defeat. ... [N]either are they a lure or a promise that is of

---

talism, p. 293. Ahmad's criticism of Said, occasionally polemical, is contained within *In Theory: Classes, Nations, Literatures*, London: Verso, 1992.

[6] Edward W. Said, *Orientalism: Western Conceptions of the Orient*, London: Penguin, 1995, p. 38.

[7] Ibid., p. 40, emphasis in original.

[8] Michel Foucault, *The Will to Knowledge*, p. 94.

[9] Michel Foucault, *Society Must Be Defended: Lectures at the Collège de France*, London: Penguin, 2004, p. 280.

necessity betrayed'. Rather most of the time 'one is dealing with mobile and transitory points of resistance'.[10] Said's Orientalism implies a language of symmetry and of action/reaction, which helps to deny the subjectivity of the non-Western 'object'. Ultimately, Orientalism could *only* exist within a subject-object relationship that is deemed to be linear and one-directional. But overemphasising the subjective side (i.e. Lord Cromer, the West) of this relationship is dangerous, because it threatens to render analysis of the agency of the presumed object (i.e., Egyptians, Orientals) obsolete.

A history of Orientalism must always be accompanied by an account of the history of resistance to it, not least in order to show that the East (or the global 'South' for that matter) has continuously escaped attempts to freeze it as an unchanging totality, that even within a situation characterised by maximal power discrepancies, there remains the opportunity to resist. It is also necessary in order to emphasise that the 'West' and western modernity itself is a dialectical constellation constructed through the intimate interaction between Europe and its significant others, especially Islam which has a central position within its epistemological field, even though the colonial (false) consciousness did not recognise this reality as such.

Consider this exchange between the British Minister of War Lord Hartington and the Egyptian-Muslim reformer Mohammed Abduh (1849–1905) in that regard. 'Are the Egyptians not content that they are living in security and peace under the power of the English government', asked Hartington in typical colonial parlance. 'Are you not of the opinion, that our government is better for them than the government of the Turks and their Pashas?[11] Certainly not!' replied Abduh. 'The Egyptians are Arabs, and apart from a minority they are all Muslims. Amongst them there is no less love for the fatherland than amongst the English. None of them would contemplate subjugating themselves to the violence of those who have a different religion and race. What you have indicated about the distaste of foreign supremacy', Lord Hartington countered, 'is only related to the educated nations. Firstly', Abduh replied, 'the distaste for foreign rule, the diso-

---

[10] Foucault, *The Will to Knowledge*, p. 96.

[11] Lord Hartington refers to the dynasty of the Khedives in Egypt which was established by Mohammad Ali (1805–1848) after the Napoleonic invasion and which was operating within the Ottoman system.

bedience to be subjugated by its power is intrinsic to human nature and does not require further investigation. It is a human emotion, whose power manifests itself even amongst the most uncivilised peoples such as the tribes of the Zulus who have not forgotten how hard they were subjugated by you in their defence of their homeland.[12] Secondly', Abduh elaborated '[t]he Muslims whoever they may be and on whichever level of development they may be, never denigrate to such an inferior, uneducated status as in the imagination of your lordship. Because even the illiterate', Abduh maintained, 'are not alienated from knowledge due to the requirements of the [Muslim] religion'. Revealingly, Abduh than moved on to describe the independence and relevance of the sciences of Islam, the knowledge disseminated during Friday prayers and the lectures of preachers in the mosques which cater for the basic knowledge and education of society. 'In every little [Egyptian] village', Abduh elaborated, 'there is somebody who can read and write. The public news reaches them via Arabic newspapers. I don't think', he concluded, 'that in this they are different from other nations'.[13]

This conversation between Abduh and Hartington occurred in 1884, i.e. two years after the Orabi rebellion after which the British occupied Egypt militarily. Abduh's interpretation of Islam was influenced by his friend and mentor, Sayyid Jamal ad-Din al-Afghani (also Asadabadi, 1838–1897) with whom he founded the journal *al-urwa al-wuthqa* (The indissoluble Link) in Paris in 1884. Afghani himself had an oft-cited exchange with Ernest Renan in the *Journal Des Débats* in 1883 in which he refutes the argument of the former that Muslims in general and Arabs in particular were always opposed to science and philosophy and that their seemingly obvious subservience to Europe was due to their racial inferiority. Said interprets this exchange between Renan and Afghani within the context of the particular 'dynamic of dependency' characteristic of the colonial period.[14] Afghani's tone strikes Said as 'amiable'. 'In contrast to later resisters of imperialism' he points out,

[12] Abduh refers to the resistance of the Bantu nation to the Burs and English which was brutally crushed in the wars between 1878/79.
[13] Andreas Meier, *Politische Strömungen im Modernen Islam: Quellen und Kommentare* [Political Currents in Modern Islam: Sources and Commentaries], Bonn: Bundeszentrale für politische Bildung, 1995, pp. 46–48.
[14] Edward Said, *Culture and Imperialism*, London: Vintage, 1993, p. 317.

THE TEMPTATIONS OF GRAMMAR

'Afghani, like Indian lawyers in the 1880s, belongs to a stratum of people who, while fighting for their communities, try to find a place for themselves within the cultural framework they share with the West'.[15]

A deeper analysis of the anti-imperial activism of Afghani and Abduh and the epistemological field in which they placed themselves is sacrificed here for an explicit emphasis on the introjective powers of the colonial system and its Orientalist conduit. But do not the dialogues between Abduh and Hartington, Renan and Afghani also indicate that for every colonial thesis, there was a counter-thesis by the colonised that was not only rooted in the idioms of the discursive formation or even the historical period, but also in an epistemology that was older than the determinations of the colonial age? In the previous dialogue, Abduh resisted Lord Hartington's argument, in the Orabi revolt he fought against the British armies, in *al-urwa al-wuthqa* he forged a pan-Islamic, anti-imperial narrative provocative enough to lead to the ban of the journal a couple of months after its first publication; in a response to the accusation that he advocates a 'clash between Islam and the West' made by the French Minister of Foreign Affairs, Gabriel Hanoteaux, he refuted the idea that there is a link between the progress of Europe and the supposed Aryan origins of Europeans.[16] Abduh resisted in practice and in theory. His emphasis on the 'human emotion whose power manifests itself in the defence of the homeland' reveals itself as a strategy to turn the hypocrisy of his counterpart against himself. Do not think that we resist merely in the name of Islam, the Arab nation or Egypt, he implies. Our resistance is steeped in the same universalist premise through which you want to rule us. Thus, resistance is rendered teleological, natural, unending. It would continue even if you manage to nullify our Egyptian/Muslim/Arab identity. Abduh was sending a strong signal to Lord Hartington indeed.

Abduh did not fight as a unit determined by the colonial age, but a hybrid. His voice was expressed with a dialect. The colonial age imprinted its hybridity upon him. His day and age made it impossible to believe in the myth that he was coherent, racially distinct. He could

---

[15] Ibid. See also more recently Joseph A. Massad, *Desiring Arabs*, London: The University of Chicago Press, 2007, pp. 12 ff.
[16] See further Yvonne Haddad, 'Muhammad Abduh: Pioneer of Islamic Reform', in Ali Rahnema (ed.), *Pioneers of Islamic Revival*, London: Zed, 2005, pp. 37 ff.

not inhabit Lord Hartington's mythical world in which identities were presumed to be neatly delineated, in which the inevitable dialectics of history that delivered the hybridity of 'western man' in the first place was artificially subdued, even if he wanted to. European colonialism, in other words, did not constitute the other all the way down to the core of his (imagined) ideational existence. Reciprocity between subject and object, and the other way around, was not impossible. In actual fact the object-subject categorisation is entirely reversible: *Sie konnten sich vertreten und sie mussten nicht vertreten werden*, they could represent themselves and they needn't be represented! This is a reversal of the famous postulate expressed by Marx proclaiming that 'they can not represent themselves, so they must be represented', which was used by Said to emphasise the determining imprint of the Orientalist discourse. The relationship between coloniser and colonised, like Hegel's juxtaposition of the master and slave, was always dialectical: the master is constituted by the slave and vice versa. In this respect, the critique of Orientalism focusing solely on the way the 'slave identity' is objectified as real, can explain only one side of this dialectic.

A critique of the term 'post-colonial' is implicit in what I have claimed in the previous paragraphs. To be more precise, I tend to agree with those scholars who point out that employing the term 'post-colonialism' to structure the politico-cultural realities in Asia, Africa and Latin America is problematic because 'it is haunted by the very figure of linear development that it sets out to dismantle'. Metaphorically, the term post-colonialism marks history as a series of stages along an epochal road from 'the precolonial', to 'the colonial', to 'the post-colonial'. 'If post-colonial *theory* has sought to challenge the grand march of Western historicism', it is rightly observed, 'the *term* post-colonialism nonetheless reorients the globe once more around a single binary opposition: colonial-post-colonial. ... [T]he singularity of the term effects a recentring of global history around the single rubric of European time. Colonialism returns at the moment of its disappearance'.[17] Similar reservations have been expressed against the term 'post-modernity' which also implies a temporal lineage from the pre-modern, to the modern and finally to the post-modern condition. Postmodernism

---

[17] Anne McClintock, *Imperial Leather: Race, Gender and Sexuality in the Colonial Contest*, London: Routledge, 1995, pp. 10–11, emphases in original.

is indicted as a 'Euro-American western hegemony, whose global appropriation of time-and-place inevitably proscribes certain cultures as "backward" and marginal while co-opting to itself certain of their cultural "raw" materials'.[18] From such perspectives, concepts such as post-colonialism and post-modernism re-inscribe the authority of Euro-America into academic discourse: they establish yet another temporality that signifies western hegemony over the rest of the world.

A critical disposition can never afford the luxury of a unitary gaze. It alerts us to the fact that all of us, Muslim, Christian, white, black, American, British, Arab, are a fiction of language, grammar or a particular syntax that is interpenetrated. So when Seyyed Badiuz Zaman writes in 1956 that 'Islamic ideology is definite, concrete and clear-cut, whereas the ideology of the West is indefinite',[19] he is luring us into the same cloistered territory as the Orientalist H.A.R. Gibb, who accentuates the 'universal trait to divide mankind into the "we group" and the "they group"' which is especially pronounced within Muslim societies, 'because Islam has from the beginning ... institutionalised its sense of difference and of superiority' which according to Gibb 'may be related to its original Arab environment and Arab tribal attitudes to outsiders'.[20] The 'we group' that both authors indulge in is non-existent. It is not 'us' who are thinking and expressing ourselves here. Rather, Zaman and Gibb are trying to put words in our mouth, moulding our individual aspirations into a non-existent entity captured in the highly discriminatory term 'we'. Likewise, in the statement 'I think the clash of civilisations is true', the predicate 'think' requires a subject, as does every predicate. Proponents of the clash regime attempt to mislead us by declaring the 'I' to be the subject thus immediately rendering it the agent. Of course, it is the act of thinking that precedes the awareness of an 'I'. As Kant noted, in the Cartesian premise, *cogito ergo sum* (I think, therefore I am), the act of thought constitutes the actor. It is not the 'I' that is thinking, but rather the thinking that invents the 'I'.

Today many adherents to the clash regime have been so thoroughly duped by grammar and history, that they take myths such as the clash

---

[18] Stephen Slemon, 'Introduction', in Ian Adam and Helen Tiffin (eds): *Past the Last Post*, Hemel Hempstead: Harvester Wheatsheaf, 1991, p. viii.

[19] Syed Badiuz Zaman, *Islamic Literature*, Lahore, 1956, p. 32.

[20] Hamilton A. R. Gibb, 'The Heritage of Islam in the Modern World', *International Journal of Middle East Studies*, vol. 1, no. 1, Jan. 1970, p. 4.

of civilisations to be a 'fact of nature'. There is a very simple reason why the disciples of the clash regime continue to be so successful. Only a minority have dared to look more closely at the formation of a particular historical *Geist* or consciousness. We have been afraid of obliterating our sense of belonging, our self, our loyalty to the 'in-group', the invented histories that give us solace during periods of crisis. Once we dare to look more closely at the discourse that translates the clash idea into a seemingly highly realistic 'fact', we see that it is interwoven by facile unifying structures situated around the constitutive verb *to be*. The entire essence of the clash regime is concentrated in that singular term. Without it, the West, Christians, Hindus, Muslims, and Jews could not exist because they would not have been able to signify their difference. Without it, in short, the false idea of a dichotomy between us and them could not have been established in the first place.

Via grammar, history thus came out squarely in favour of the first part of the Shakespearian question, to be or not to be. Within each imagined camp, there emerged official representatives of that collective; talented tale tellers, who turned themselves into its historical animator. Their 'I', acting as the original point of agency, was more and more enmeshed into the 'we', acting as the extended version of the self. Understanding language is central to explaining this process because it invents supposedly well-defined cultural territories, or whole civilisations, because it ascribes life and content to dead and hollow word formations, because it invents reality and arouses destructive passions, nationalistic, religious or other. Let us delve deeper into the syntax of this tempting language now. What we will be trying to do, as far as possible, is to position ourselves between its conjunctions. These are the false harmonies that link us together into a totality, a wholeness that constantly threatens to rob us of our independent willpower.

Totalitarian methodologies and causal fallacies

The structural signposts of the clash regime that I have pondered thus far have been sustained by an epistemological emphasis on difference. We can consolidate that argument now by hinting towards a few common functions: the emphasis on difference is meant to make it possible to mould together—in an artificial unity—history, self-perception and group affiliation. This invented unity enables the respective author to use the newly invented 'we' in a causal relationship. This 'we' develops a seemingly autonomous identity which is thought to be strong enough to travel unchallenged through space and time. As such, an efficiently articulated epistemology of difference functions as a central signifier: it is essential to 'the Islam is …', 'the West is …' binary. By revealing itself in that fashion, accentuating difference is meant to mark the borderline between the self and the other and to contain the lines of contact between these imagined entities.

But the discourse thus created is not 'ego-logical'. It fails in its task to create a self-centred narration; it does not achieve total autonomy. Distance to the object whose 'otherness' it attempts to permanently produce with a set of exclusionary syntactic devices is a figment of the imagination of the author. Derrida is right when he says that difference forebodes a 'movement according to which language, or any code, any system of referral in general, is constituted historically as a weave of differences'.[21] A grammatology of language shows that *différance* folds into both sides of any binary, even the fundamental human/non-human divide. As such an epistemology of difference may create the illusion of a neatly delineated border between self and other. But in actual fact that border refers to an immense borderless grey area where divisions between self and other submerge in a great ocean of ideational hybridity.

Différance denotes an interdependent condition. There is no clear distinction between self and other. Hence difference becomes litigable. It is the myth, induced by epistemologies of difference, that otherness cannot be mitigated that turns our dialectic with the 'other' from a *natural contest* into a *violent rivalry*. In a natural contest, self and other remain consciously interdependent. In a violent rivalry, an artificial duality is implied. The other is not only pushed away from the self, she is (quasi)objectified as different. At the same time that the distance to the object is simulated, differences within the 'in-group' are minimised, one-dimensionality is promoted. This is the function of 'totalitarian methodologies'. They have to be distinguished from critical methodologies which pluralise and spread out the subject matter, which differentiate and relocate its 'nodal point' that animates the narratives surrounding it in the first place. Conversely, totalitarian methodologies are reductionist. They unite a set of statements at a given

---

[21] Jacques Derrida, *Margins of Philosophy*, Alan Bass (trans.), Brighton: Harvester Press, 1982, p. 12.

period of time, relate them in a causal fashion to the argument, formalise disparate objects into one iron-clad narrative and essentialise positions in a highly contingent, simplistic and positivistic manner. The object of a totalitarian methodology, in short, is a decrease in complexity. It is a retractile device suggesting hermetic consolidation through reduction: the shrinkage of the self and the other into neatly defined epistemological territories. This is the ultimate mode of persuasion underlying the us-versus-them logic and it is essential to understanding the spatial compartmentalisation of the clash regime.

With a totalitarian methodology, the optimism of knowledge assents complete fruition. The diversity of a particular issue is typically reduced to a single causality made possible by the conjunction 'because'. The discourse thus produced is mono-causal: why are we at war with them? Because they are different. Why is there a clash of civilisation? Because they are threatening us. 'One of the functions of the connective "because"', Ricoeur elaborates, 'is to set an agent's action within the framework of his "habitual" behaviour'.[22] Linking disparate issues together in such a way smoothes over dissonance and disregards heterogeneity; it presents complexity as analytically surmountable. This is why all prominent theorists of civilisations, from Fernand Braudel to Samuel Huntington, had to emphasise the longevity of civilisations, and why they used a static approach to culture in order to do so. For the former, civilisations claim 'a space, a cultural area', which explains their long time-span (*longue durée*), their capacity to endlessly re-adapt themselves, and to 'exceed in longevity any other collective reality; they outlive them all'.[23] Comparably, for Huntington, the 'differences among civilisations are not only real; they are basic',[24] which explains to him why the 'great divisions among humankind and the dominating source of conflict will be cultural'.[25]

In his emphasis on civilisational coherence, Braudel is not as deterministic as Huntington. Yet in both authors we find a deceptively ordered world in which civilisations retain their seemingly unspoiled identity.

---

[22] Paul Ricoeur, *Time and Narrative*, vol. 1, London: The University of Chicago Press, 1984, pp. 115–116

[23] Fernand Braudel, *On History*, Sarah Matthews (trans.), Chicago: Chicago University Press, 1980, p. 104.

[24] Samuel P. Huntington, 'The Clash of Civilisations?', *Foreign Affairs*, vol. 72, no. 3 (1993), p. 25.

[25] Ibid., p. 22.

If their conceptualisation of 'civilisation' is simplistic, then it should not come as a surprise that the great myth of uninhibited cultural continuities was also central to the methodology of post-Second World War Orientalism enveloping the writings of the most canonical figures in the discipline. Static notions of civilisations are one of the lamentable legacies of the modern human sciences, including their 'Orientalist' derivative. Neither Braudel and Huntington, nor Orientalists such as von Grunebaum were willing to break with scholarly tradition and to question the very concepts of 'civilisation' and 'cultural longevity'. The latter argues in a typically reductionist manner that it is:

essential to realise that Muslim civilisation is a cultural entity that does not share our primary aspirations. It is not vitally interested in analytical self-understanding, and it is even less interested in the structural study of other cultures, either as an end in itself or as a means toward clearer understanding of its own character and history. If this observation were to be valid merely for contemporary Islam, one might be inclined to connect it with the profoundly disturbed state of Islam, which does not permit it to look beyond itself unless forced to do so. But as it is valid for the past as well, one may perhaps seek to connect it with the basic antihumanism of this civilisation, that is, the determined refusal to accept man to any extent whatever as the arbiter or the measure of things, and the tendency to be satisfied with truth as the description of mental structures, or, in other words, with psychological truth.[26]

Von Grunebaum disperses his argument with immense syntactical authority. The paragraph starts with the phrase 'it is essential to realise' and 'is' appears four times in the first two sentences, pushing the paragraph into a rigorous grammatical structure. This mode of arguing helps von Grunebaum to emphasise the 'disturbed state of Islam' and the 'basic antihumanism of this civilisation' which 'does not share our primary aspirations'. In this way, he creates a contingent periodisation of the civilisational difference between his supposedly 'Western' thinking which *is* scientific, critical, rational, discursive and 'Muslim thinking' which *is* anachronistic, egocentric and obsolescent. Via this arbitrary inference, he empowers himself to capture the nature of that alien other through 'scientific' reasoning. Ironically, von Grunebaum quotes Anwar Sadat as an example of Oriental 'political aspiration' which, according to him, postulates the 'bankruptcy of the West' during a period 'when [its] technical as well as scientific-analytic supe-

---

[26] G.E. von Grunebaum, *Modern Islam: The Search for Cultural Identity*, Berkeley: University of California Press, 1962, p. 40.

riority ... though veiled by political concessions, has become more overwhelming than ever before'.[27] Intoxicated by his sense of analytical superiority, he fails to see how similar to his own mode of persuasion—in grammar and syntax—Sadat's argument really is:

The civilisation of the West and its heritage, for which both Europe and America fear, lives only on the debris of the East and would not be flourishing had they not sucked its blood. ... The East interprets civilisation as based primarily on values rather than on matter. We affirm that the Chinese, Egyptian, and Indian civilisations have created morality and literature, sanctified the family, organised the relations among individuals and of individuals with society and the government ... But these civilisations have not had as their sole product the establishment of human values; they have also produced the awakening of the sciences and the arts, of geometry and architecture, which have endured for thousands of years as so many witnesses of the permanence and superiority of these civilisations.[28]

Both von Grunebaum and Sadat base their argument on non-existent civilisational entities. Both refer to a highly contingent self. Both write in terms of unities. Both claim to know. Both attempt to hermetically shut down complex, mutually constituted cultural systems. Both attempt to produce a kind of grand discourse that one can travel over in any direction. For the sake of convenience and perhaps ideological conviction, variable issues are rendered independent and unchanging. Consequently, the whole structure of the argument is reduced to a set of mono-causalities: Why is the 'Muslim civilisation a cultural entity that does not share our primary aspirations'? Because 'it is not vitally interested in analytical self-understanding'. Why is the 'eastern civilisation' superior'? Because 'the Chinese, Egyptian, and Indian civilisations have created morality and literature'. Why are we exclusive? Because of these set of historical reasons.

The mono-causal inference that is at the heart of totalitarian methodologies creates urgency; it radically minimises time sequences. Reducing discourse to a set of discrete 'factors' is always the sign of a shortened and abbreviated explanation. 'Study books' in colleges and universities all over the world are full of definitions, summaries and tables not only because of very valid analytical reasons, but also because they represent the best way to condense knowledge and to present it in a way that is more digestible for the time-starved student

---

[27] Ibid., p. 140.
[28] Ibid.

juggling job, university and private life. It also helps to meet the demands of the modern mass University and its condensed curricula industrialising its relationship to its consumers in an efficient and highly capital effective way. This is not necessarily conducive to producing critical citizens, but it helps to speed up the educational process.

It should not come as a surprise then that minimising the logical gap between cause and effect is also very functional during conflict situations when the defence or extension of the 'homeland', religion or in-group is represented as particularly urgent. This is why in the build-up to war we will always be confronted by ideologues that narrow down complex constellations, such as world politics, to a pragmatic, easily-digestible us-versus-them dichotomy. The colonisation of Central/Southern America, Africa and Asia was one such period, the Cold War and the aftermath of the terrorist attacks on the United States in September 2001 were others.

So totalitarian methodologies are rather 'modern' phenomena. Their theoretical components—positivism, parsimony, realism—have become a cornerstone of the mainstream social sciences in many ways until today. There is a predominant belief that 'social science can establish universal laws of human behaviour, and thereby forecast the future development of mankind. ... For the Positivists, the advance of science is a sign of the progress of the human mind'.[29] In this sense, the paradigm of the clash of civilisation as well, displays typically modern features. It is highly positivistic for it is built on a rigid causal structure, dualities that are deemed insurmountable and civilisational traits that are rendered unchanging. The paradigm purports to explain a supreme truth, that is the clash of civilisations. It is highly parsimonious, elegant and slick. On this issue Huntington is rather nonchalant: 'a paradigm is disproved only by the creation of an alternative paradigm that accounts for more crucial facts in equally simple or simpler terms'.[30] Theoretical reductionism is presented here as a virtue. From this perspective, it is worthwhile to sacrifice critical integrity for accessible scholarship tailored to the 'skim reader', or in the case of Huntington, Fukuyama and others, to the policy world. But is this perception

[29] John Gray, *Al Qaeda and what it mean to be modern*, London: Faber and Faber, 2003 pp. 106–107.
[30] Samuel P. Huntington, 'If Not Civilisations, What? Samuel Huntington Responds to his Critics', *Foreign Affairs*, vol. 72, no 5 (1993), pp. 186–194.

not anti-democratic in the sense that it shuts down the subject matter? Does it not confine it to neat pigeon-holes? Is the idea that we can define our complex social worlds in terms of law-like causalities not utterly deceptive?

It was not scholarly arrogance that made Ibn Sina expound in his seminal *Mantiq al-mashraqiyyin* (the Logic of the Orientals) that '[o] nly the person who has thought much, has mediated deeply, and is not devoid of the excellence of intellectual intuition can make deductions from [this book]'.[31] It was his growing awareness that a simple reading of the reality surrounding him was no longer sufficient. From now on Ibn Sina liberated himself from external dictates. With *Mantiq al-mashraqiyyin*, he forcefully enters into the realm of radical dialectics that lead him (and others after him) to the negation of the status quo. Unwilling to narrow down his representations of 'reality' to easily digestible formulas, he urged the 'common crowd' to meet the philosopher 'half-way' in order to be able to digest the new terms and ideas he proposes. Ibn Sina would vent scorn on some of the 'pop-studies' in today's social sciences, which narrow down complex subjects to a few mnemonics in a blissfully anti-pluralistic way, rather than empowering the reader to appreciate the complexity of our surrounding habitat. Such 'pop studies' do not merely simplify, they stupefy society into submission. An uncultured society tolerates oppression because 'truths' are not sufficiently interrogated, but taken for granted. In Nietzsche, Ibn Sina's early laughter at the temptation to submit to the authority of such deceptive 'truths' resonates with equally irresistible, critical prowess:

What, then is truth? A mobile army of metaphors, metonyms, and anthropor-phisms—in short, a sum of human relations, which have been enhanced, seem firm, canonical, and obligatory to a people: truths are illusions about which one has forgotten that this is what they are; metaphors which are worn out and without sensuous power; coins which have lost their pictures and now matter only as metal, no longer as coins.[32]

---

[31] Ibn Sina, 'The Logic of the Orientals (Mantiq al-mashraqiyyin)', in Seyyed Hossein Nasr with Mehdi Aminrazavi (eds), *An Anthology of Philosophy in Persia*, vol. 1, Oxford: Oxford University Press, 1999, pp. 269–270.

[32] Friedrich Nietzsche, *Das Philosophenbuch: Theoretische Studien*, Paris: Aubier-Flammarion, 1969, pp. 180–182. I have used the translation contained in *The Portable Nietzsche*, Walter Kaufmann (ed. and trans.), New York: Viking, 1954, pp. 46–47.

We have seen that the 'truth' about an ongoing clash of civilisations that continues to have a presence in the subliminal consciousness of society is one of the biggest delusions of them all. Let us continue to cast it out of our minds by equipping ourselves with the tools to understand the way 'truths' are constructed and presented to us as historically inevitable and epistemologically contingent.

The syntax of the Enlightenment and the plight of the Muselmann

There is a more comprehensive case to be made that the very fact that the Christians and early Muslims were so intermingled, that because Christianity had a prominent presence within the Islamic body, stable and well-confined genealogies had to be invented in order to keep the siblings of the Abrahamic prophecy apart. A comparable 'politico-biological' strategy, a genetic manipulation of some sorts, enabled the elites in antiquity to establish boundaries between 'Persia' and 'Greece', despite the rather intimate dialectic that the Greco-Persian peoples were caught up in for many centuries. Of course, there is no suggestion here that these representations were thoroughly antagonistic. Was it not Xenophon, despite his political allegiance to the idea of 'Greece', who admired 'Cyrus the Great', who of all Persians who lived after him 'was the most like a king and the most deserving of an empire, as is admitted by everyone who is known to have been personally acquainted with him'?[33] Was not the same Cyrus charged with the enormous task of erecting the house of the Lord God of Israel and to protect the Jews from persecution in the Old Testament (Ezra 1:1–4, Ezra 6: 3–5, Isaiah 45:1–4)? Was he not the only 'Gentile' to be considered a messiah, a divinely anointed king in the Tanakh (Isaiah 45:1–6) because he succeeded in that task?[34] Was it not Alexander who 'married' a Persian princess and who actively encouraged cross-cultural 'marriages' between the Greeks and Persians? Did not the seventh Abbasid caliph, al-Ma'mun (813–833), found the *bayt al-hikmah* or

---

[33] Xenophon, *The Persian Expedition*, Rex Warner (trans.), London: Penguin 1949, p. 91.

[34] For a recent examination of the historical background of Cyrus's 'Davidic' mandate see Lisbeth S. Fried, 'Cyrus, the Messiah? The historical background to Isaiah 45:1', *The Harvard Theological Review*, vol. 95, no. 4, 2002, pp. 373–393.

'House of Wisdom' in Baghdad where among other things the works of Ptolemy, Archimedes and Euclid were taught? Did not the most formidable philosophers of Islam, Farabi, Ibn Sina, Razi, Ibn Rushd, enter into a fruitful dialogue with the philosophy of Plato and Aristotle, supposedly archetypal 'European' thinkers? The interdependent field with regard to the Persian-Greek interaction—a fertile field that could have engendered many histories accentuating mutuality—comes out hesitantly, but with sublime poetic vigour in the following verses composed by Byron:

> The antique Persians taught three useful things,
> To draw the bow, to ride, and speak the truth
> This was the mode of Cyrus, best of kings—
> A mode adopted since by modern youth.
> Bows have they, generally with two strings;
> Horses they ride without remorse or ruth;
> At speaking truth perhaps they are less clever,
> But draw the long bow better now than ever.
>
> The cause of this effect, or this defect,—
> 'For this effect defective comes by cause',—
> Is what I have not leisure to inspect;
> But this I must say in my own applause,
> Of all the Muses that I recollect,
> Whate'er may be her follies or her flaws
> In some things, mine's beyond all contradiction
> The most sincere that ever dealt in fiction.[35]

We cannot indulge in Byron's leisure not to 'inspect' the cause that leads to the effect, because we have seen how language, grammar and causal presumptions have been central to the process of othering. We know now that a causal argument always reduces the distance between cause and effect, that it speeds up explanations of complex systems duping us into believing in a single, independent and ongoing historical process. Only an argument encircled with causal myths can mark off a regime of truth suggesting some clash of civilisations as a discrete entity. In that way history threatens to become a self-fulfilling prophecy sustained and carried into society by self-perpetuating totalitarian methodologies.

[35] Ernest Hartley Coleridge (ed.), *The Works of Lord Byron, volume 6*, Ebook, Project Gutenberg. Available at http://www.gutenberg.org/files/18762/18762–h/18762–h.htm [Last accessed 21 January 2008].

We have to be careful not to enmesh distinct historical periods and personalities into our argument here. For all the talents of the Greek tragedians, historians and poets they did not have the semantic and scientific devices at hand to detach themselves completely from the rest of the world. For all the rhetorical sophistication of Gorgias of Leontini and Isocrates, their oratory skills did not create autonomous causal unities. They did not claim a space in total detachment from the realities surrounding them. In short, the ancient Greeks were conscious about the interdependence intrinsic to history, even if Herodotus deemed it necessary to suggest otherwise in order to unite the Greek city states against the assertive empire of the Achaemenid kings.

Yet on the threshold of the 'Renaissance', the 'West' is imagined as a separable formation filled with immense causal efficacy. According to Samir Amin, this period marks a break in the history of humanity because from that time on, 'Europeans become conscious of the idea that the conquest of the world by their civilisation is henceforth a possible objective'. According to him, this marks the birth of 'Eurocentrism'.[36] In other words, the emergence of an imperial mindset which enveloped the period of the Renaissance and western modernity was preceded by a 'positivistic' attitude that imbued Europe with a *zeitgeist* that was impervious to disappointment.

The politico-philosophical writings of Machiavelli (1469–1527) serve as one of the most prominent examples for this emergent attitude suggesting that everything was possible. In *The Prince*, he draws on the conquest of the 'kingdom of Darius' by Alexander, who could 'take his country for him' because the Persians did not revolt against his rule, in order to emphasise the possibility of conquering the 'government of the Turk'. '[O]nce the Turk has been conquered, and routed in the field in such a way that he cannot replace his armies', Machiavelli argues, 'there is nothing to fear but the family of the prince, and, this being exterminated, there remains no one to fear, the others having no credit with the people; and as the conqueror did not rely on them before his victory', he concludes, 'so he ought not to fear them after it'.[37]

---

[36] Samir Amin, *Eurocentrism*, Russell Moore (trans.), New York: Monthly Review Press, 1989, pp. 72–73.

[37] Nicolò Machiavelli, *The Prince*, W.K. Marriott (trans.), London: Encyclopaedia Britannica, 1952, p. 7.

Machiavelli's distinctive trust in the possibility of this mission could not be expressed without faith in causality, in the possibility to cause as difficult an effect as the conquest of the Ottoman Empire. According to Machiavelli, this effect (i.e. the conquest) could be realised without major repercussions for the conqueror. Machiavelli was writing during a period of intense organised violence in his native Florence and as a civil servant of the Florentine Republic, he had a particular interest in uniting the warring factions against the 'government of the Turk'. But the reason why he could express this strategic goal in the first place can be found in the way he objectifies the other without considering his reciprocity. Machiavelli may be considered the first prominent writer who freezes the other into oblivion. In his discourse, the sovereignty of the Prince is maximised because the power of retaliation of the other is minimised. In this way he got around the vicissitudes of his period via an articulation of an irresistible possibility: the conquest of the Ottoman Empire. This technique is typically modern. Machiavelli typifies a period in which the 'West' was artificially detached from the rest of the world. Interdependence was slowly turned into independence, into the 'liberal' ideal to create thoroughly autonomous territories. This rupture in human history, the detour from mutuality, the detachment from nature, the death of God and the birth of the ultra-rational scientist, all of these changes in the western discourse are innovatively chartered in Foucault's *The Order of Things*. The following, particularly pertinent passage deserves to be quoted in full:

It is true that History existed long before the constitution of the human sciences [in the nineteenth century]; from the beginnings of the Ancient Greek civilisation, it has performed a certain number of major functions in Western culture: memory, myth, transmission of the Word and of Example, vehicle of tradition, critical awareness of the present, decipherment of humanity's destiny, anticipation of the future, or promise of a return. What characterised this history—or at least what may be used to define it in its general features, as opposed to our own—was that by ordering the time of human beings upon the world's development (in a sort of great cosmic chronology such as we find in the works of the Stoics), or inversely by extending the principle and movement of a human destiny to even the smallest particles of nature (rather in the same way as Christian Providence), it was conceived of as a vast historical stream, uniform in each of its points, drawing with it in one and the same current, in one and the same fall or ascension, or cycle, all men, and with them things and animals, every living or inert being, even the most unmoved aspects of earth. And it was this unity that was shattered at the beginning of the nineteenth century, in the great upheaval that occurred in the Western *episteme* ... [From now on] [t]he human being no longer has any history: or rather, since he speaks, works, and lives, he finds himself interwoven in his own being with histories that are neither subordinate to him nor homogenous with him. By the fragmentation of the space over which Classical knowledge extended in its continuity, by the folding over of each separated domain upon its own development, the man who appears at the beginning of the nineteenth century is 'dehistoricised'.[38]

The ordering of the western *episteme* that Foucault highlights is heavily dependent, if not entirely constituted, by the premise of uninhibited causality. The possibility to establish 'an ordered succession between things, even non-measurable ones'[39] such as history, the humanities or the social sciences, could not be delivered without causal inference which always lets something else to follow on, thus simulating temporal succession. Indeed, every sentence that is linked up with the term 'because' creates such succession. It must follow that 'the order of things' that Foucault ponders is an effect of the sequential occurrence of events which could only be signified via causal conjunctions. The difference in the nineteenth century, according to Foucault, is that this period negates interaction between self and other. Western man seeks to detach himself from the interdependence forced upon him by history and attempts to establish himself without the other, as a 'dehistoricised', that is an autonomous entity, that is a causality that is cleansed from any impingement from the 'outside'.

Hayden White has a similar view on the changes in the western discourse. According to him, such methodological belief in 'cleansed' causal totalities is particularly strong in the late-eighteenth and nineteenth century galvanised by the emergence of 'realist' and 'positivist' approaches to history and the social and natural world more generally.[40] Starting with Count Henri de Saint-Simon (1760–1825) and carried over even more fervently by Auguste Comte (1798–1857), the vast majority of writers in this period had an almost fanatic trust in the merits of 'realist' and 'positivist' theories. It was this moment of intense controversy about the legitimate methods to explain human existence, White argues, which produced a conception of

[38] Michel Foucault, *The Order of Things: An Archaeology of the Human Sciences*, London: Routledge, 2002, pp. 401–402.

[39] Ibid., p. 63.

[40] Hayden White, *Metahistory: The Historical Imagination in Nineteenth Century Europe*, Baltimore: Johns Hopkins Press, 1973, p. 45.

rationalism derived from the (Newtonian) physical sciences. Enlightenment philosophers:

> approached the historical field as a ground of cause-effect relationships, the causes in question being generally conceived to be the forces of reason and unreason, the effects of which were generally conceived to be enlightened men on the one hand and superstitious or ignorant men on the other.

> The 'lexical' elements of this system were men, acting as individuals and as groups, who were 'grammatically' classifiable into the major categories of carriers of superstitious or irrational values and carriers of enlightened or rational ones. The 'syntax' of relationships by which these two classes of historical phenomena were bound together was that of the unremitting conflict of opposites.[41]

It should not come as a surprise then that the methodologically rigorous *zeitgeist* of the European Enlightenment affected the way Orientalism evolved as a guild faculty and ultimately as a disciplinary system. The treatment of the other as an object was fundamentally in accord with the extreme arrogance of the causal imperative that is at the heart of the positivist promise. Taken to its logical end, it disseminated into the discourse of the Enlightenment the idea that everything was possible and, by implication, that the 'West' had been granted the historical mandate to make it possible. Inevitably, to explain the Orient in general and Islam in particular became a strategy of showing that their essence can be deduced and hence predicted from observable and approachable natural laws. The thrust of these analyses not only served to widen the cognitive framework for the Manichean allegories of previous centuries (Christianity vs. Islam, barbarism vs. the Greek polis etc.), they claimed to objectify them as 'quasi-natural' verities, as real and inevitable. John Hobson elaborates:

> The major intellectual acrobatic here involved the reimagining of Greece. In a comparatively short space of time (from the late eighteenth to early nineteenth century) European thinkers suddenly elevated Ancient Greece to the birthplace of European civilisation, given its alleged democratic institutions and scientific rationality. Locating Greece within Europe was also crucial because of its alleged role within the all-important Renaissance (which supposedly created the 'European dynamic'). But this view of a pure European Greece was decidedly not how the Greeks saw themselves. They viewed Greece as fixed firmly within what was known as the 'Hellenic Occident'. That Europe has always been an idea as opposed to a geographical 'reality' is reflected in the fact that

[41] Ibid., p. 65.

'Europa' herself was in Greek mythology the daughter of Agenor, King of Tyre, situated on the coast of Lebanon. Note too that Troy was in fact east of the Dardanelles. ... But to admit either that Ancient Greece was in part oriental, or that the Renaissance was shaped or informed by Eastern (mainly Islamic) ideas, or that Greece was not especially democratic, would have been extremely confronting. For it would have undermined the emergent claim that Europe has always been uniquely progressive and ingenious—it would have interrupted the linear line of European progress that Eurocentric scholars had now invented or imputed.[42]

As a result, 'Oriental man' was invented as a subject for science. Studying him came to seem not only possible, but a primary goal of a range of academic disciplines. With regard to the clash regime, this emphasis on 'objective' history, theoretical self-consciousness and a thoroughly 'realistic' approach to science, by necessity of the positivistic premises thus created, reified a central dynamic: it artificially increased the distance of enlightened Europe from the rest of humanity and by implication from the Muslim worlds moulding Europe into a coherent entity that was perceived to be superior. At the centre of this process emerged a Eurocentric *Weltanschauung*. It was from this period onwards, in other words, that the idea of 'western man' was solidified, when he self-consciously carried the torch of humanity, when his very essence was genealogically cleansed from the undue impact of world history. That self-image that 'defines and constitutes him', argued the phenomenologist Edmund Husserl (1859–1938), was thought to be intrinsic to:

the idea of philosophy itself; the idea of a universal knowledge concerning the totality of being, a knowledge which contains within itself whatever special sciences may grow out of it as its ramifications, which rests upon ultimate foundations and proceeds throughout in a completely evident and self-justifying fashion and in full awareness of itself. Closely connected with this idea, whose first inception in Ancient Greece in the VIIth and VIth centuries B.C. marks the historical beginning of Western man, is the idea of a truly human, i.e., philosophical existence, an existence oriented towards the ideas, ideals and norms of autonomous reason, which alone permits Western man to live in conformity and at peace with himself.[43]

[42] John M. Hobson, *The Eastern Origins of Western Civilisation*, Cambridge: Cambridge University Press, 2004, pp. 227–228.
[43] Quoted in Aron Gurwitsch, 'The Last Work of Edmund Husserl', *Philosophy and Phenomenological Research*, vol. 16, no. 3, March 1956, pp. 381–382.

Husserl refers here to a 'phenomenology' of the idea of the West that he traces back to Ancient Greece. This period gave birth to philosophy and the historical beginning of the existence of 'western man' whose particular constitution thus effected allows him, and only him, 'to live in conformity and at peace with himself'. Along with this attitude comes a sense of entitlement, a sovereignty that is deemed to be exclusive to western civilisation. Husserl is confronting a *zeitgeist* that stood accused of anti-philosophical reasoning that alienated western man from himself. His phenomenological philosophy was meant to rectify this trend, and to re-establish philosophy as the master science of 'consciousness', a *Geisteswissenschaft*, suitable to explain the constitution of the 'West' in past and present. By inferring an unequivocal origin to the making of the West and by drawing on an epistemology divested of interdependencies with others, Husserl re-confirmed a central consensus of his period: the belief in the essential separateness of western man and his seemingly undisturbed genealogy. Husserl reserves for the 'West'—largely unconsciously—a privileged position of singularity with an immediate access to a superior truth. Again, this is a type of thinking that is typically modern.

In Husserl, the duality between the West and the rest is implicit, tampered by his discipline—philosophy—that retained its ingrained subtlety even during the exuberant period of the Enlightenment. Yet the idea of the 'West' was inflated more rigorously in other emerging fields, for instance in geography. Hobson has demonstrated how an attitude of 'spatial superiority' of the 'West' can be discerned from the Mercator world map which can be found in world atlases, school maps, airline catalogues, tourist guides etc. While the actual landmass of the southern hemisphere is twice that of the northern hemisphere, on the Mercator, the landmass of the North covers two-thirds of the map while the landmass of the South is limited to only a third. Hence Scandinavia, in actual fact about a third the size of India, is allocated the same amount of space on the map as the latter. The size of Greenland is inflated as well. Although the country is about one-fourth the size of China, it appears twice as big on the map.[44] Nowhere is this sense of spatial superiority better exemplified than in the naming of the Himalayan peak after Sir George Everest who directed the Trigonometrical Survey of India between 1818

[44] See Hobson, *The Eastern Origins*, pp. 5–6.

and 1840.[45] Everest himself expressed his opposition to naming the Himalayan peak after him to the Royal Geographical society in 1857 on the grounds that his name could not be written in Hindi, nor pronounced by the native Indian population. Nonetheless, Andrew Waugh, the British Surveyor General of India, made a successful case for it and in typical colonial parlance:

I was taught by my respected chief and predecessor, Colonel Sir George Everest to assign to every geographical object its true local or native appellation. But here is a mountain, most probably the highest in the world, without any local name that we can discover, whose native appellation, if it has any, will not very likely be ascertained before we are allowed to penetrate into Nepal. In the meantime the privilege as well as the duty devolves on me to assign ... a name whereby it may be known among citizens and geographers and become a household word among civilized nations.[46]

Such a notion of spatial superiority was not only expressed in maps and geographic designations. At least from the eighteenth century onwards, and more exponentially in the nineteenth century, there also emerged in Europe the spectacle of 'ethnographic shows'; world fairs and international expositions that were meant to objectify the racial superiority of the white man and to provide an 'anthropological' research agenda in which it could be measured scientifically. The 'savage' steps into history and into the clash regime out of this constellation. He becomes the natural man that makes civilised society possible. 'The savage—noble or otherwise', is not only the 'natural man whom the jurists or theorists of right dreamed up, the natural man who existed before society existed, who existed in order to constitute society'.[47] Foucault undervalues the degree of otherness ascribed to the savage here. The savage is not only exhibited as that obvious other that was left behind by history. He is conceptualised as that very missing link between the racially developed white man and the wild beast. The otherness of the savage is principally immanent to his being. Ultimately, he may turn out to be irreconcilable with the standards of the civilised world represented by Europe.

[45] See further C.A. Bayly, *The Birth of the Modern World 1780–1914: Global Connections and Comparisons*, Oxford: Blackwell, 2004, pp. 274–275.

[46] 'Papers relating to the Himalaya and Mount Everest', *Proceedings of the Royal Geographical Society of London*, no. 9, pp. 345–351, Apr.-May 1857.

[47] Foucault, *Society must be Defended*, p. 194.

Only recently have anthropologists established that the exhibition of native populations has a long history in the making of a Eurocentric consciousness. So we find that in his enquiries into the birth of the Zoo, Nigel Rothfels shows how Christopher Columbus 'returned to Spain in 1493 with seven Arawak Indians and reported that the masses of onlookers who came out to see his procession from Seville to Barcelona appeared to believe that he had returned with the inhabitants of another star'.[48] Let me link up with this proliferating literature with an eye on the 'bio-politics' of the clash regime. In the nineteenth century, the savage is not only a public spectacle; he becomes the site of intense excitement, an object of science and a source of income. As Carl Hagenbeck (1844–1913) states in 1876 after contracting out one of his animal catchers in Sudan to catch 'a number of really interesting natives':[49]

[I]n its totality the presentation of the caravan amounted to a sensation of the first order. Decorated only in their wild personalities, with their animals, tents, and household and hunting equipment, the guests offered a highly interesting, anthropological-zoological picture from the Sudan.[50]

Hagenbeck was a true 'celebrity' in the late nineteenth century and up until his death in 1913. Today, one of the main zoos in Germany, the 'Tierpark Hagenbeck' in Hamburg is named after him. *The New York Times* dedicated a major report to him after he passed away describing Hagenbeck as the 'wild animal king' lauding his extraordinary career from a 'humble fishmonger's boy' to the main 'source of supply for zoos, menageries, and circuses'.[51] But the report fails to mention that Hagenbeck did not only make his fame and fortune out of trading animals. He also professionalised 'human zoos', exhibitions of 'native savages' termed *Völkerschau* in German.[52] 'In 1874', writes Hagenbeck in his autobiographic *Beast and Men*:

---

[48] Nigel Rothfels, *Savages and Beasts: The Birth of the Modern Zoo*, Baltimore: The Johns Hopkins University Press, 2002, pp. 86–87.

[49] Quoted in ibid., p. 83.

[50] Quoted in ibid., p. 84.

[51] *The New York Times*, 20 Apr. 1913. Available at http://query.nytimes.com/mem/archive-free/pdf?res=9901EFD81139E633A25753C2A9629C946296 D6CF [Last accessed 12 May 2009].

[52] See further Raymond Corbey, 'Ethnographic Showcases, 1870–1930', *Cultural Anthropology*, vol. 8, no. 3, Aug. 1993, p. 345.

I happened to be importing some reindeer, and my friend, Heinrich Leute-mann, the animal painter, remarked that it would be most picturesque if I could import a family of Lapps along with them. This seemed to me a brilliant idea, and I therefore at once gave orders that my reindeer were to be accompanied by their native masters. The Lapps, conducted by a Norwegian, arrived at Hamburg in the middle of September, and Leutemann and myself went on board to welcome the little expedition. The first glance sufficed to convince me that the experiment would prove a success. Here was a truly interesting sight. On deck, three little men dressed in skins were walking about among the deer, and down below we found to our great delight a mother with a tiny infant in her arms and a dainty little maiden about four years old, standing shyly by her side. Our guests, it is true, would not have shone in a beauty show, but they were so wholly unsophisticated and so totally unspoiled by civilisation that they seemed like beings from another world. I felt sure that the little strangers would arouse great interest in Germany. The reindeer and the Lapps were safely disembarked, but on the way up to Neuer Pferdemarkt a rather fortu-nate accident occurred. The deer were, of course, unaccustomed to crowds, and two of them took fright and galloped away through the town, finally tak-ing refuge—not inappropriately—in the Zoological Gardens. My Lappic exhi-bition could scarcely have had a better advertisement than was afforded by this escapade. My optimistic expectations were fully realised, this first of my ethnographic exhibitions was from every point of view a huge success. I attribute this mainly to the simplicity with which the whole thing was organ-ised and to the complete absence of all vulgar accessories. There was nothing in the way of performance. The Laplanders themselves had no conception of the commercial side of the venture, and knew nothing of exhibitions. They were merely paying a short visit to the hustling-civilisation which they saw around them, and it never occurred to them to alter their own primitive habits of life. The result was that they behaved just as though they were in their native land, and the interest and value of the exhibition were therefore greatly enhanced. They took up their abode in the grounds behind my house at Neuer Pferdemarkt, and lived entirely out of doors. All Hamburg came to see this genuine 'Lapland in miniature'.[53]

Such ethnological exhibitions, which Hagenbeck organised in Europe and in the United States with immense success, do not only exemplify the way the 'altern' becomes the sight of attraction, amusement, sexual fascination and disgust, but they provide an insight into the spatial ghettoisation of the 'savage other', away from civilisation even within civilisation, in this case 'out of doors' behind Hagenbeck's house. A

---

[53] Carl Hagenbeck, *Beasts and Men: Being Carl Hagenbeck's Experiences for Half a Century Among Wild Animals*, Hugh S. R. Elliot and A. G. Thacker (abridged trans.), London: Longmans Green, and Co., 1912, pp. 18–19

second issue strikes out: the 'Lapps' are referred to as 'guests'. In this sense, they are an early manifestation of the *Gastarbeiter* in Germany; that foreign labourer who is invited to the country in order to contribute to the wealth of the nation, but who is not really considered a part of it. The savage as *Gastarbeiter* as spectacle has a practical, economic utility and a psychological, cognitive effect. He simulates a very particular deception. He causes the consciousness of the spectators to fold into an 'I am' (civilised, racially superior etc.), into a present that does not coincide with the object (the savage). Before I gazed at the savage there existed the theory of evolution that set me apart from him. Now I am provided with the 'empirical' evidence that he exists in an inferior mode. But I am immediately confronted with a paradox. If the savage exemplifies the ever present threat of a world that I thought I had left behind forever, how can he reciprocate my gaze? If I am at the pinnacle of the natural evolution, how much of that savage is still in me? How can I destroy his residues that I am carrying inside me? Even if the savage other is what makes civilisation possible, which renders my superiority scientific, can I ever entirely dispose of him?

Questions like these were forced upon the zoological-anthropological field, not only because European anthropologists began to challenge the merits of evolutionist theories or due to increased criticism of 'imperialism and racism'.[54] The idea that Europe has a history in and of itself is as mythical as the idea that it could rescue itself from that history without the 'other'. Rather, the anthropological-zoological field dreamed up by Hagenbeck and his contemporaries had to be re-imagined because it became a site of resistance. Revealingly, in *Beasts and Men*, Hagenbeck vents his scorn at 'Abdullahi Kalifat el-Mahdi, the false follower of a false prophet' who closed the 'animal paradise' in Egyptian-Sudan. Under his rule, Hagenbeck laments, '[n]one of the animals inhabiting the country could be brought to Europe … Nevertheless it would be a mistake', he adds, 'to suppose that these regions are inhabited by a fanatical, bloodthirsty population; for the savage barbarity which prevailed was entirely confined to the rulers'.[55] Hagenbeck refers here to Abdullah Ibn Muhammad (1846–1899), a devout follower of the 'Mahdi' movement in Sudan, who successfully and repeatedly repelled Anglo-Egyptian intrusions into his country until he was killed in

[54] Corbey, 'Ethnographic showcases', p. 358.
[55] Hagenbeck, *Beasts and Men*, p. 48.

November 1899. In short, Hagenbeck is lamenting the reciprocity of the other. Why is the savage capable of resistance? Does he not see that what we are doing is for the common good? He did not and he revolted. Consequently, what emerged during this period, scattered but ever more frequently, was the disturbing awareness that in the thick of the structures of imperial conquest, the savage would continue to claim disruptive articulation. He attained his counter-hegemonic force once he re-conquered the vast material and discursive spaces that were taken away from him with a mixture of violence and cunning trickery. He resisted not only in the formerly colonialised world, but also in the 'motherland' itself. It is out of this dialectic between power and resistance that there emerged civil rights movements and other effective forms of sustained revolt against the residues of the racist stratification of the societies that finally adopted the savage, transforming him into a citizen, albeit rather hesitantly. It is this dialectic, finally, that delivered the Mandelas, Kings, and Gandhis of this world.

That short foray into the identity politics underlying the discipline of Anthropology can now be related closer to the issues I have been discussing so far. The pronounced belief in the civilisational 'greatness' of the West, expressed in the spatial hegemonies touched upon above, by necessity of this inflated sense of being, confined the other to a limited, uncharted place thought to be entirely detached from civilisation; an ambiguous space that was open for colonial re-animation, the civilisational merits of which were considered to render the whole project entirely legitimate. The other was delimitated to an enigmatic, archaic, enchanting, callous, yet always indelible and germane, place, an object of scientific desire. A central feature of this type of discourse was the invention and military enforcement of a system of domination founded on the myth of naturally coded superiority of western civilisation. '[N]ineteenth century Orientalism', Said explains:

> was the distillation of essential ideas about the Orient—its sensuality, its tendency to despotism, its aberrant mentality, its habits of inaccuracy, its backwardness—into a separate and unchallenged coherence; thus for a writer to use the word *Oriental* was a reference for the reader sufficient to identify a specific body of information about the Orient. This information seemed to be morally neutral and objectively valid; it seemed to have an epistemological status equal to that of historical chronology or geographical location.[56]

---

[56] Said, *Orientalism*, p. 205, emphasis in original.

The latter sentence is crucial. Said argues that nineteenth century European narrations of the 'East' actively performed the essential turn toward a mode of thinking that created a self-fulfilling prophecy with regard to everything Oriental. The Orient was deemed to be genuinely objectified, it was there in the European mind external to its 'real' being, invented by history, but nonetheless claiming 'objective' validity. Thus, the Enlightenment made possible a very particular epistemological privilege: it arrogated to Europeans the luxury of interpreting, judging, evaluating and categorising the Orient from without, from the solace of an increasingly unified 'western' world-view. Even the most prominent and canonical thinkers, such as James Mill, indulged in this quintessentially modern attitude. Certainly, it made it easier for him to write what Peter van der Veer termed 'a frontal attack on both Indian traditional institutions and the British Orientalists whom he accused of defending a degraded and degrading society' in his three volume *History of British India* (1817), without having ever visited the country.[57] In his wide-ranging study, van der Veer identifies Mill as 'the first major thinker who identifies the need to push India into modernity as one of the main objectives of the East India Company'. The second was Marx of course, who concurred that it was necessary, even inevitable to subsume the East under the industrial force of western modernity despite the different historical and cultural context that he was immersed in.[58] That Mill's misrepresentation of India did not stem from prejudice—how could it be, he hadn't even visited the country— but from his blind faith in causal historical explanations can be discerned from Wilhelm Dilthey's note in his copy of Mill's *Logic*, where he laments that 'Mill is dogmatic because he lacks historical training'.[59] In other words, Dilthey, not a stranger to empiricist explanations himself, pays particular attention to Mill's positivistic attitude, the blind faith in causality. I think we can safely add to the existing literature on this issue that is this arrogant claim to know that turned Mill into one of the first prominent 'Orientalists'. This is the causal premise that

[57] Peter van der Veer, *Imperial Encounters: Religion and Modernity in India and Britain*, Princeton: Princeton University Press, 2001, p. 5. After publication of the book, Mill was employed by the East India Company as an 'expert' on Indian affairs.

[58] Ibid., p. 6.

[59] Quoted in Hans-Georg Gadamer, *Truth and Method*, 2nd edition, London: Continuum, 2004, p. 6.

made modernity happen, and by implication the unfinished project of the Enlightenment that Jürgen Harbermas ponders until today.

It has been argued that positivist methodologies empowered nineteenth centuries thinkers to negate the interdependencies of human history, to try to artificially detach themselves from the rest of humanity. No wonder then that imperial fantasies were turned into 'reality' without remorse. The colonial world became a 'world cut in two' in Frantz Fanon's words,[60] because blind faith in teleological reasoning and causal methodologies turned the Manichean world view into a 'quasi-reality'. This emergent epoch, Gadamer observes, was perceived to be the last 'step to objective knowledge of the historical world, which stands on a par with the knowledge of nature achieved by modern science'.[61] Adorno and Horkheimer are even more forthcoming than Gadamer in their radical critique of the hubristic attitudes engendered by the Enlightenment. According to them, 'calculating, instrumental, formal rationality led to the horrors of twentieth-century barbarism' including the horrors of the holocaust:[62]

Man's likeness to God consists in sovereignty over existence, in the countenance of the lord and master, and in command.

Myth turns into enlightenment, and nature into mere objectivity. Men pay for the increase of their power with alienation from that over which they exercise their power. Enlightenment behaves toward things as a dictator toward men. He knows them in so far as he can manipulate them. The man of science knows things in so far as he can make them. In this way their potentiality is turned to his own ends. In the metamorphosis the nature of things, as a substratum of domination, is revealed as always the same. This identity constitutes the unity of nature.[63]

Adorno and Horkheimer, followed by Giorgio Agamben today, argue that it was in the death of God that the Enlightenment was born. Inevitably thus, this period had to entail an element of arrogance and hubris, certainly towards the other. Hence, from now on producing

---

[60] Franz Fanon, *The Wretched of the Earth*, Constance Farrington (trans.), New York: Grove Press, 1963, p. 38.

[61] Gadamer, *Truth and Method*, p. 277.

[62] Martin Jay, *The Dialectical Imagination: A History of the Frankfurt School and the Institute of Social Research 1923–1950*, London: Heinemann, 1973, p. 265.

[63] Theodor W. Adorno and Max Horkheimer, *Dialectic of Enlightenment*, John Cumming (trans.), London: Verso, 1997, p. 9.

'alterity' was professionalised. A whole array of disciplines, chief amongst them anthropology, biology and later on the social sciences, were busy turning the 'otherness' of the non-European people into an 'objective reality' that could be scientifically measured. Books such as Robert Brown's *The Races of Mankind* (1873), Comte de Gobineau's voluminous *An Essay* on *the Inequality of Races* (1853–1855), Robert Knox's *The Races of Man* (1850), Carl Linnaeus's *Systema Naturae* (1735), Frederic Maryat's *Peter Simple* (1834), Josiah Nott and George Gliddon's *Types of Mankind* (1854), Edward B. Taylor's, *Anthropology: An Introduction to the Study of Man and Civilisation* (1881) or Johann von Tschudi's *Travels in Peru* (1847), created the archives of racial politics out of which modern political systems such as Apartheid in South Africa and Zionism in Israel emerged.[64] If the optimism of this age propelled the 'West' to solve the riddle of mankind, why should it not be possible to create a better world for everybody? If evolution delivered *homo sapiens* in Europe, why should natural perfection stop here and now? If England's historical progress could be linked to the 'Saxon race', as Benjamin Disraeli wrote in his novel *Tancred* (1847), it had to be imperative, for the sake of natural progress, to subjugate the lesser peoples of the world. Indeed, why might there not be a transcendental *homo sapiens*, an *Übermensch* representing the perfect biological type who would rescue mankind from his ignorance?

It would be too simplistic to link the triumph of Darwinism to Nietzsche's idea of the *Übermensch*, which was subsequently perverted by the Nazis and turned into the theory of the Aryan *Herrenrasse* or master race destined to rule over humankind. In *Ecce Homo* and *On the Genealogy of Morals*, the latter written one and a half years before his breakdown, Nietzsche himself qualified his concept of the *Übermensch* detaching it from Darwinism and locating the 'noble race' in the Italian Renaissance.[65] Darwin, on the other side, did locate man on the pinnacle of the organic scale pondering natural selection which 'acts solely by the preservation of profitable modifications' which is why 'extinction and natural selection' will always 'go hand in hand'.[66] But he also emphasised that he uses the term, 'Struggle for Existence',

---

[64] On the racist attributes of Zionist policies, see most recently Ilan Pappe, *The Ethnic Cleansing of Palestine*, Oxford: One World, 2006.

[65] See further Rüdiger Safranski, *Nietzsche: A Philosophical Biography*, London: Granta, 2003.

[66] Charles Darwin, *The Origin of Species*, Ware: Wordsworth, 1998, p. 133.

'in a large and metaphorical sense, including dependence of one being on another'.[67] So his brilliance and unwavering trust in theoretical constructions did not tempt him to overlook the inherent interdependency of the natural world and man's inevitable position within it. In fact, in his autobiography he turns his own theory into a critique of arrogance in the pursuit of scientific knowledge: 'Can the mind of man, which has, as I fully believe, been developed from a mind as low as that possessed by the lowest animal, be trusted when it draws such grand conclusions?'[68]

Despite Darwin's apparent scepticism, the idea that nature continuously progresses into something better, lends itself to the type of racial theorising that was characteristic for the colonial 'desiring machine' that Robert Young interrogates. According to him, it is sexual desire, 'constituted by a dialectic of attraction and repulsion' that carries along 'the threat of the fecund fertility of the colonial desiring machine, whereby a culture in its colonial operation becomes hybridised, alienated and potentially threatening to its European original through the production of polymorphously perverse people'.[69] From this proposition, Young moves on to charter the many racial typologies of the colonised peoples that were produced in the latter part of the nineteenth century, especially with regard to the inhabitants of South America. He shows how children with white fathers and negro mothers are classified as 'mulattos', a white father and an Indian mother produces 'mestizas' and a white father and mestiza mother, a 'creole' who could be identified by her pale-brownish complexion. Unsurprisingly, the list ends with the 'zambo-negro', the 'perfectly black' child of a black father and zamba mother.[70]

Such 'scientific' classification was not confined to the Americas, of course. Racism was a central legacy of colonialism/imperialism and continues to be a major component in the rationalisation of any clash with the 'other' in many ways until today, as we will establish later.

---

[67] Ibid., p. 50.
[68] Charles Darwin, 'The Descent of Man, and Selection in Relation to Sex', part 2, Paul H. Barrett and R. B. Freeman (eds), *The Works of Charles Darwin*, vol. 22, New York: New York University Press, 1989, p. 644.
[69] Robert J.C. Young, 'Colonialism and the Desiring Machine', in Gregory Castle (ed.), *Postcolonial Discourses: An Anthology*, Oxford: Blackwell, 2001, p. 87.
[70] Ibid., pp. 88 ff.

The literature produced during the nineteenth century and early-twentieth century is full of the lore of racial superiority despite the resistance of the natives. It is no accident then, that in his bestselling book about his travels through western Asia, the Tory Aristocrat, Mark Sykes presents a kind of comparative 'raciology' of the peoples he encountered, their 'puzzling faces', and their indistinguishable physiognomy. Although a 'Hill Kurd can be as easily distinguished from a Bedawi as a negro from an Englishmen', Sykes observes during his travels in and around Mosul (today's Iraq), 'the intermediate races present every combination of the two types. I have seen men known as Kurds', he elaborates, 'exhibiting every Arab characteristic, and Egal-wearing village Arabs so coarse-featured as to make one doubt whether the Arabs are a handsome race. How is it that, now and then', Sykes wonders, 'amid a group of roundstomached brown-skinned little rascals, tumbling in the dust of a Fellaheen village, you will see a flaxen-haired, blue-eyed child with a face that Millais would have been glad to catch a glimpse of?' Elsewhere Sykes' puzzlement turns into disgust of these inferior people that Britain was about to rule: As far as Sykes is concerned, the inhabitants of Mosul are 'eloquent, cunning, excitable, and cowardly ... one of the most deplorable pictures one can see in the East diseased from years of foul living. ... With minds of mudlarks and the appearance of philosophers', Sykes finally releases his anger, 'they depress and disgust the observer'.[71] Such were the attitudes of the man who co-invented the map of the modern 'Middle-East', who together with his French counterpart Francois-George Picot, carved up the Ottoman Empire during World War I.

And there are many more examples. In his *Essai sur l'Inégalité des Races Humaines* published in 1853, Count Arthur de Gobineau defined 'Semites' as a white hybrid race bastardised by a mixture with 'Blacks'. Said showed that Ernest Renan in his *Histoire Générale et Système comparé des Langues* introduced a comparable classification, opposing 'Semites' to 'Aryans' and that Renan was particularly sceptical about the 'racial power' of Muslims.[72] Van der Veer has added additional material explaining how 'craniometry', the measuring of skulls and 'phrenology', a scientific method that links the size of the

---

[71] Mark Sykes, *Dar-Ul-Islam: A Record of a Journey Through Ten of the Asiatic Provinces of Turkey*, London: Bickers & Son, 1904, pp. 177–178.
[72] Said, *Orientalism*, especially pp. 133 ff.

skull to individual's mental faculties, became the empirical focus of race science.[73] In England, race theorists even came up with biological explanations of foreign policy that 'explained' scientifically that the 'English Overman' was destined to rule the world due to his racial superiority.[74] 'For the first time in world history', Hobson elaborates:

the development of societies was assumed to be founded on permanent racial characteristics ... Special emphasis was placed—again for the first time in world history—on the importance of skin colour and genetic properties as a defining criterion of civilisation. ... This was now conceived of as a perma-nent hierarchy and for some, though not all, scientific racists justified the subjugation of the Other (the Yellow and Black races) by the self (the Euro-peans). In its extreme form scientific racism justified the extermination of the inferior races at worst and social apartheid at best. This racist construct rap-idly diffused into the popular imperial discourse, expressed in a seemingly never-ending set of statements issued by Imperial bureaucrats and British politicians.[75]

Nowhere did the myth of racial supremacy do more harm than in Germany after the election of the National Socialist German Worker's Party in April 1933. The idea(l) of Aryan origins and the inevitable triumph of the German *Herrenrasse* could only be fostered within a causal universe that was depleted of critical thinking. Indeed, I do not deem it too far fetched to say that Fascism is the polar opposite of a critical consciousness, because Fascism educates people to take the sur-rounding world for granted, to refrain from questioning, to accept without resistance. Hence it simulates the ultimate one-dimensional universe, a particularly devastating source for the clash regime today. In many ways the sciences fostered by the Nazis are the logical pin-nacle of the positivism of the modern human sciences. So when Nazi scholars such as Hermann Güntert, who taught Sanskrit and Iranology at the University of Kiel, pondered the objective relationship between race and language and the corrupting influence of those who are 'alien to the race',[76] they believed in the 'objective truth' of their work, in the scientific merit of their theories, in the utterly realistic representation

[73] Van der Veer, *Imperial Encounters*, pp. 145–146.
[74] See further Hannah Arendt, *The Origins of Totalitarianism*, Ohio: World Publishing Co., 1958, p. 180.
[75] Hobson, *The Eastern Origins*, p. 237.
[76] Sheldon Pollock, 'Indology, Power, and the case of Germany', in Macfie (ed.), *Orientalism*, p. 308.

of their subject matter. In other words, the work produced by German Orientalists during the Nazi period was written with serious scholarly intent, supported by empirical evidence and footnotes and grounded in Philology and History. Ultimately, the science of the Nazis merged in Josef Mengele's 'eugenics' programmes which were implemented with similar scientific exuberance.

This particularly cruel type of scientific scholarship at the service of power could only function within a social and political context depleted of intellectual (*viz.* critical) substance, because questioning the official party line meant questioning the purity of its causal systems. On the one side, the obsession of the Nazis with racial purity was a perverted extension of the entanglement of the Enlightenment with natural selection and the inevitable superiority of the 'white' race. On the other side, it also gives us an insight into how a world of causal totalities would look like. Wasn't the murder of the Jews, homosexuals, Gypsies and the physically and mentally impaired also an effort to create causal purity, an effort to be independent from the undue influence of the other? This rather important issue has been largely overlooked by theorists of Orientalism and by Said himself. The Nazis did not only find it impossible to recognise the *Herrenrasse*, without freezing the other into an unchanging object, without attributing to the Jews a set of racial characteristics that made them different from the 'truly' German nation; they attempted to thoroughly detach themselves from the corrupting impact of all 'unworthy existence'. They attempted to present to us causalities that were totally cleansed. How else could they believe in their 'manifest destiny' personified by the Führer? 'The Fascists do not view the Jews as a minority', write Adorno and Horkheimer, 'but as an opposing race, the embodiment of the negative principle. They must be exterminated to secure happiness for the world'.[77] In other words, the mass murder of the Jews, homosexuals, the Gypsies and the mentally and physically impaired were efforts to create a true and absolute genealogy; a historical tale dotted with heroic Aryan figures and racially pure personalities that would deliver us from our imperfect existence, our fallen present. The central policies of the Nazis are reflections of this effort to create causal purity, to cleanse the self from *any* impingement by the other. It started out with exclusionary laws: the 'Law on the Overcrowding of German Schools',

[77] Adorno and Horkheimer, *Dialectic of Enlightenment*, p. 168.

the 'Law on the Reconstitution of the German Civil Service', and it evolved into the policy of ghettoisation and the concentration camps which were meant to realise the territorial/spatial contraction of the other thus maximising distance to him. At the same time, the 'total state' and 'total war' functioned in order to enhance the coherence of the self. The *Endlösung*, the effort to obliterate all Jews was a culmination of these two processes. It symbolises the last ditch effort to reverse and totally negate the dialectics between the Aryan *Herrenrasse* and its Jewish other *par excellence*.

It is out of this historical constellation that we can identify yet another historical 'ideal type' populating the clash regime: the figure of the *Muselmann*. In the discourse amongst the captives in the concentration camps, the so called *Lagersprache* in German, the Muslim, as an etymological perversion termed *Muselmann* or in the plural *Muselmänner* in German, was not absent. The *Muselmann* occupied the lowest rank within the fatalistic hierarchy of the concentration camp. *Muselmänner* were 'men and women reduced to staring, listless creatures, no longer responding even to beatings, who for a few days or weeks existed, barely—and who then collapsed and were sent to the gas'.[78] The term did not denote an ethnic or political group. Rather it referred, on the one side, to a fatalistic mindset, 'to the docile acceptance of one's destiny popularly ascribed to Islam and "the East"'[79] and, on the other side, to a condition; to those 'resigned, extinguished souls who had suffered so much evil as to drift to a waking death. ... They were dead but didn't know it'.[80] His apathy differentiates the *Muselmann* from the figure of the 'savage' and the 'barbarian' who continued to threaten civilisation from without, whose existence was a reminder of a frightening past. 'At times a medical figure or an ethical category, at times a political limit or an anthropological concept', Giorgio Agamben writes, 'the *Muselmann* is an indefinite being in whom not only humanity and non-humanity, but also vegetative existence and relation, physiology and ethics, medicine and politics, and life and death continuously pass through each other'.[81] Previous to and

---

[78] Inge Clendinnen, *Reading the Holocaust*, Cambridge: Cambridge University Press, 1999, p. 35.

[79] Ibid.

[80] Elie Wiesel, 'Stay Together Always', *Newsweek*, 16 Jan. 1995, p. 58.

[81] Giorgio Agamben, *Remnants of Auschwitz: The Witness and the Archive*, Daniel Heller-Roazen (trans.), New York: Zone Books, 1999, p. 48.

after his appearance in the lexicon of the concentration camps, the *Muselmann* has had a presence in German culture. He appears in a popular children's song written by the German musician Karl Gottlieb Hering (1766–1853), which was sung in elementary schools in Germany well into the 1980s:[82]

C-a-f-f-e-e
C-a-f-f-e-e

trink nicht so viel Caffee!
Nicht für Kinder ist der Türkentrank,
schwächt die Nerven, macht dich blass und krank
Sei doch kein Muselmann,
der ihn nicht lassen kann!

C-o-f-f-e-e
C-o-f-f-e-e

don't drink so much coffee!
The Turk's drink is not for children;
it weakens the nerves and makes you pale and sick.
Don't be a Muslim
Who can't help it![83]

With Nazism, the totalitarian methodologies I have examined above and their causal fallacies come full circle. The total state, total war, the total obliteration of the Jews (or *Endlösung*), all of these manifestations of 'National Socialism' could only derive from an uncompromising belief in an absolute historical teleology that had delivered the German nation and its destiny to rule the world. In other words, the Nazis perceived themselves to be both the effect of history and its enforcer. Ultimately, the 'Third Reich' was not considered to be a random event. It was seen and portrayed as an inevitable effect of humanity's progress that made manifest the successive forms of a primordial historical intention. It was perceived to usher in a better future for humanity, the end of all clashes, in sum, a great order at the head of which Germany had positioned itself rather inevitably. 'The gigantic structure of the strictly ordered system', Eric Voegelin presaged in

---

[82] I jollily sang along during Music lessons in elementary school in Germany.

[83] See also Gil Anidjar, *The Jew, the Arab: A History of the Enemy*, Stanford: Stanford University Press, 2003, p. 142.

1938, 'spans an abyss of human nihilism, consuming itself in a search for fulfilment of reality through collective'.[84]

We have already explored the functions of historical teleology with regard to Marx, Hegel and Weber in the previous chapter. We may now extend this discussion by adding Immanuel Kant and Martin Heidegger to this list, primarily to understand why the latter sympathised with the Nazis in the immediate period after their takeover, and secondarily to enhance our understanding of the effects and functions of causality. For Kant, in clear reference to Hegel, the law of causality explicated in his 'Second Analogy', yields a deterministic principle of temporal succession. Temporal progress is subsumed under natural processes which stand under definite rules of cause and effect. Heidegger interprets this to mean that causality itself is related to temporal succession, and, even more forcefully, that 'causality *means* temporal succession'.[85] Ultimately, for Heidegger this temporal succession is not non-normative, disinterested, without 'reason' or direction. At the end of an 'unconditioned causality', lies 'transcendental freedom'. '*Freedom as a kind of causality* is related to the *possible totality of sequences of appearances in general*'.[86] In actual fact, Heidegger considers freedom to be 'nothing other than *absolute natural causality*, or ... a concept of nature that transcends all possible experience'.[87] A quick look at Heidegger's other writings shows that this ultimate freedom, which is effected by uninhibited causality, can be made actual where 'there is a community of I's, of subjects'.[88] In turn, this community could only be moulded into a totality in the 'total state' which ensures the highest form of social existence. 'The Führer-State-the one we have', he argues, 'means the accomplishment of the historical development: the actualisation of the people in Führer'.[89]

The question of the consciousness-of-the-will of a community is a problem in all democracies, which can only be resolved in a fruitful way when one recog-

---

[84] Eric Voegelin, *Political Religions*, New York: Edwin Mellin Press, 1986, p. 10.
[85] Martin Heidegger, *The Essence of Human Freedom*, Ted Sadler (trans.), London: Continuum, 2002, p. 108, emphasis added.
[86] Ibid., p. 147, emphasis in original.
[87] Ibid., p. 148, emphasis in original.
[88] Martin Heidegger, *Introduction to Metaphysics*, New Haven: Yale University Press, 2000, p. 367.
[89] Ibid., p. 247.

nizes leader's will and people's will in their essentiality. Our task today is to arrange the founding relationship of our communal being in the direction of this actuality of people and leader, where, as its actuality, the two cannot be separated. Only when the basic scheme is asserted in its essential aspect through its application, is a true leadership possible.[90]

The actuality of the situation, the realisation of Germany's manifest destiny in the people-Führer totality, the wholeness of the community, all of these Heideggerian claims would not have been expressed without the ultimate belief in the eventuality of the promise of the *Tausendjähriges Reich* which could deliver what Heidegger calls 'transcendental freedom'. Ultimately, Heidegger, Carl Schmitt and others were lured into defending the Nazi ideology because they believed in its causal grammar.

So within the cosmos of 'modernity' everything is possible, and the Nazis in Germany felt that they could make everything happen. So they rushed from conquest to conquest without a period of strategic consolidation. Now that Hegel's historical teleology had delivered Germany's mission and now that the natural world had distilled the Aryan race, the total state must hasten to accomplish the destiny that has been bestowed upon it: the all encompassing liberation of mankind. This straight road (*Autobahn*) that 'leads from the philosophical notion of totality to political totalitarianism' that Slavoj Žižek recently identified could only be taken because it was cemented by causal fallacies.[91] In the Führer, causal efficiency is maximised. *Der Führer hat immer recht*, the Leader is always right said Rudolf Hess; *In tal senso il fascismo è totalitario*, in this sense, fascism is totalitarian, Mussolini maintained. And so the infallible total state swallows the individual in order to make true its promise.

No wonder then that those who questioned this causal transmission belt delivering Germany's epochal mission intellectually (e.g. communists) or threatened its direction racially (e.g. Jews and Sinti and Roma) had to be liquidated. Mind you, to believe in and perpetuate a pure causal genealogy, we are always prompted to cleanse ourselves from the undue influence of the other, not merely 'a little bit', but totally. Alas, in modernity, this search for pure causalities has proven to be

[90] Ibid., p. 238.
[91] See Slavoj Žižek, 'Why Heidegger Made the Right Step in 1933', *International Journal of Zizek Studies*, vol. 1, no. 4, 2008, pp. 1–43.

rather persistent; it found its logical epitome in the Nazi premise that *Rassenmischung ist Völkermord*, the mixing of races is the death of nations.

The 'native' counter-discourse and the making of post-modernity

It has been argued that the Enlightenment was born in hubris, in the myth of the purity of race, and that it is out of this constellation that the idea of 'modern man' emerges. This particularly violent subject of history almost obliterated the other, not only quite literally in the many massacres colonialism and Fascism engendered, but also epistemologically. The notion of development, whether Hegelian, characterised as a law of conscious intellectual maturing, Darwinian, manifesting itself in the perfection of biological change, or 'Comtian' promising ethical improvement through the control over the material and psychological environment, minimised the West's reciprocal relation to the rest of humanity. There was a continuous effort to leave the other behind, not only in terms of historical periodisation but also scientifically. This is how the hiatus of the Enlightenment, apart from revolutionary innovations, also suggested the debasement of the western self. Belief in origins that are not interdependent, a consciousness that attempts to detach itself from the dialectics of human history, the futile effort to invent a 'liberalised' syntax that is devoid of grammatical reciprocity, that detaches the predicate from the subject, are characteristic of this self-inflicted loneliness. The repercussions of the violence of the Enlightenment will remain essential components of the clash regime and of the making of 'us' and 'them' in many ways until today.

Here, the question whether or not it has been a coincidence that the attempted 'liberalisation' of the 'West' occurred parallel to the discovery of the imaginative and signifying role played by money, is a pertinent one. Is it a coincidence, in other words, that the 'West' 'discovered' money as a means to create immediate realities during a period when it tried to rob itself of the interdependence it used to have to the rest of the world, when it became 'disenchanted' as Weber said, when it murdered such an immensely resourceful and entirely universal source of meaning such as God as Nietzsche alluded to?

Thus far, in this chapter, I have looked at disciplinary fields, their formation and function during formative periods of world history and their impact on the making of us versus them constellations. I think we can safely argue that modernity created a particularly violent syntax that we did not experience as such in Antiquity, that the clash regime as it appears to us today draws considerable sustenance from the legacies of colonialism and imperialism. But I feel I should say more about materialist constellations now and their effects on inter-group conflicts. Remember that we have been told, more systematically since the eighteenth and nineteenth centuries, that money has maximal causal efficacy, that it is a substitute for most things. 'Every man is rich or poor', Adam Smith writes, 'according to the degree in which he can afford to enjoy the necessaries, conveniences, and amusements of human life'.[92] So, comparable to words, money designates meaning to our surrounding world, e.g., the price of a scarce resource such as oil determines its value for us. Money also allocates our place in society, e.g. whether we are rich or poor. Moreover, as long as we have enough of it, money makes us believe that the distance between us and the (materialised) object is minimal. Money buys commodities, prestige and sometimes even pleasure. The capitalist has habituated us to believe in the folk tale that money makes the world turn round.

At the heart of the capitalist system, there lies the process of transaction. Transaction, quite literally, denotes the immediate transition from one action into another. A transaction 'grabs' reality, immediately turning it into something else. It must follow quite logically that a capitalist system facilitates transactions in order to arrogate to itself the highest degree of imaginative and signifying powers. A capitalist system is a causalistic tyranny; it continuously disciplines us into more and more transactions. This is the dream world of the capitalists which has delivered the nightmare of the consumer society. According to Marx:

If I long for a particular dish or want to take the mail-coach because I am not strong enough to go by foot, money fetches me the dish and the mail-coach: that is, it converts my wishes from something in the realm of imagination, translates them from their mediated, imagined or willed existence into their *sensuous*, *actual* existence—from imagination to life, from imagined being into real being. In effecting this mediation, money is the *truly creative* power.

Being the external, common *medium* and *faculty* for turning an image into reality and reality into a mere *image* (a faculty not springing from man as man or from human society as society), *money* transforms the *real essential powers of man and nature* into what are merely abstract conceits and therefore *imper-*

---

[92] Adam Smith, *The Wealth of Nations*, vol. 1, London: Dent, 1910, p. 26.

fections—into tormenting chimeras—just as it transforms *real imperfections and chimeras*—essential powers which are really impotent, which exist only in the imagination of the individual—into *real powers* and *faculties*.[93]

Marx positions the causal efficacy of money above those of nature and society. Indeed, he gives it maximum ontological potentialities, the ability to make reality, a God-like truly 'creative power'. It must follow for Marxists, that a capitalist society is a highly causal efficient society, because it can sustain its 'false consciousness' materially, because it creates its own self-fulfilling prophecies, because it endlessly perpetuates the condition it is immersed in, moulding the subject into a seemingly coherent totality. Capitalism perpetuates its own reality. Like grammar, capitalism unites disparate factors, it smoothes out difference, it envelopes and suffocates. In its effort to seek coherent causalities it becomes totalitarian. Herbert Marcuse agrees:

By virtue of the way in which it has organised its technological base, contemporary industrial society tends to be totalitarian. For totalitarian is not only a terroristic political co-ordination of society, but also non-terroristic economic-technical co-ordination which operates through the manipulation of needs by vested interests and thus precludes the emergence of an effective opposition against the whole organised by these interests. Not only a specific form of government or party rule makes for totalitarianism, but also a specific system of production and distribution which may well be compatible with a 'pluralism' of parties, newspapers, 'countervailing' forces, etc.[94]

Marcuse alerts us to the fact that capitalism exerts a totalitarian claim, that it usurps as much as it integrates. This totalitarian claim of capitalism and the societal quiescence it governs is too vast a topic to be treated appropriately within the confines of this chapter. Suffice it to say that this short excursus into the geo-politics of capitalism suggests a fourth component in our discussion of western modernity and its impact on the non-western worlds, namely that the other was not only objectified in political (Lord Hartington et al), geographical (Everest et al.) and racial (Hagenbeck et al.) terms, but also economically. From now on the other emerges as periphery, a bazaar for material exploitation. Capital turns western, and spirals out of its firmly established

---

[93] Karl Marx, 'The power of Money', in idem., *Economic and Philosophical Manuscripts of 1844*, Moscow: Foreign Languages Publishing House, 1961, p. 140, emphasis in original.

[94] Herbert Marcuse, *Towards a Critical Theory of Society*, London: Routledge, p. 2001, p. 50.

spatial locus (its core). From here it seeks out new 'economies of scale' in order to multiply globally. Like the Nazi movement or indeed today's 'global Islamist', capitalists repeat time and time again that their project claims the whole world. At least from 1492 onwards, but more violently in the eighteenth and nineteenth centuries, this outward trend manifested itself in imperial domination and colonial extension. Lord Cromer, who in 1894 declined the post of Viceroy of India and refused ten years later the position of Secretary of State for Foreign Affairs in order to become the British Consul General in Egypt, put it bluntly; 'the Englishman straining far over to hold his loved India [has to] plant a firm foot on the banks of the Nile'.[95] Thus a highly monopolistic, core-periphery dichotomy was economically realised. '[I]n order to save the 40,000,000 inhabitants of the United Kingdom from a bloody civil war', Cecil Rhodes famously concluded, 'we colonial statesmen must acquire new lands to settle the surplus population, to provide new markets for the goods produced by them in the factories and mines. The Empire', Rhodes famously warned, 'is a bread and butter question. If you want to avoid civil war, you must become imperialists'.[96]

In his enquiries into imperialism, Bukharin points to this process of 'acquiring an unheard of field for exploitation, a thing termed by the French imperialists *l'organisation d'économie mondiale* and by the German imperialists, *Organisierung der Weltwirtschaft*'.[97] This organisation of the world economy in accordance with imperial interests that Bukharin dissects, initially functioned because the imperial bureaucrats fervently believed in the possibility of the task. The imperial bureaucrats were convinced of the law of expansion. Indeed, they deemed it to be what Kipling famously referred to as the 'white man's burden' to govern the subject races. 'The fact that the "white man's burden" is either hypocrisy or racism', Arendt replies, 'has not prevented a few of the best Englishmen from shouldering the burden in earnest and making themselves the tragic and quixotic fools of imperialism'.[98] It is in this sense that I am treating imperialism as yet another outgrowth of

---

[95] From a letter Lord Cromer wrote in 1882, quoted in Arendt, *The Origins of Totalitarianism*, p. 211.

[96] Cecil Rhodes cited in Vladimir I. Lenin, *Imperialism: The Highest Stage of Capitalism*, New York: International Publishers, 1939, p. 79.

[97] Nikolai Bukharin, *Imperialism and World Economy*, London: The Merlin Press, 1972, p. 141.

[98] Arendt, *The Origins of Totalitarianism*, p. 209.

the positivism of the Enlightenment. Buoyed by the discourse of their age and the groundbreaking discoveries of their contemporaries, the imperial bureaucrats exhibited a total belief in their cause; they were convinced that a single, global empire was necessary and possible. Thus, economic hypotheses forecasting the revenue extracted from the colonies complemented biological theories of race. Whereas the latter have been largely abandoned, a quick look at contemporary models employed in the disciplines of Business Administration and Economics shows that the former continue to have an impact. Both disciplines are almost entirely dependent on quantification, modelling and other formulaic analyses. The if-then-proposition, under heavy fire in Sociology, Political 'Science', even in Mathematics for the followers of Pascal, continues to be at the heart of both of them. This may explain why economists believe that they have built a relatively successful social science, even after the post-Lehman Brothers crash of the global economy in 2008. In the material world, causal systems and their underlying promises continue to convey a sense of optimism. They continue to promise us the possibility of a better tomorrow.

This pervasive belief in causal totalities, in the possibility to bring about universal change single-handedly, was questioned when the 'West' was reminded of the continued presence of the other, when the natives took up arms and fought their way back into the western discourse and its corresponding consciousness which had attempted, unsuccessfully in the end, to subdue their presence. In many ways, the anti-colonial struggles reconnected the 'West' to the world. The dialectics of world history, always there in real terms yet not recognised by the imperial functionaries as such, returned with a vengeance. On the one side, it made it much harder to imagine a detached history when the slumber was disturbed by daily news about yet another upheaval in Mumbai, in Algiers, in Cairo, in Kabul, in Baghdad. On the other side, it was much more difficult to indulge in the material luxury extracted from the colonies that was so conducive to creating local quasi-realities, individual safe-havens that were devoid of global substance. At the end of this project, once the period of imperial indulgence was over, the imperialist lost his belief in the causal vigour that the imperial project had imbued in him. From now on history appears as coincidental; causes and effects appear detached:

Modern generations should not mistake the character of the British expansion in India. The Government was never involved as a principal in the Indian conflict ... The East India Company was a trading organisation. Its Directors were men of business. They wanted dividends, not wars, and grudged every penny spent on troops and annexations. But the turmoil in the great sub-continent compelled them against their will and their judgment to take control of more and more territory, till in the end, and almost by accident, they established an empire no less solid and certainly more peaceful than that of their Mogul predecessors. To call this process "Imperialist expansion" is nonsense, if by that is meant the deliberate acquisition of political power. Of India it has been well said that the British empire was acquired in a fit of absence of mind.[99]

This attempt of Churchill to convince his readers that the imperial project was not effected consciously, that it was not precipitated or at least accompanied by systematic political planning, indicates its demise. In other words, it is the end of the belief in the possibility (or causal efficacy) of the imperial project that signals the end of traditional imperialism. In 1947, the Congress Party in India had taken over from the British and in the same year as Churchill's book was published (1957), Britain granted independence to the Federation of Malaya, which in 1963 together with Singapore, Sarawak and British North Borneo joined to form Malaysia (in 1965 Singapore left the union). In 1951, the Iranian Prime Minister Mohammad Mossadegh nationalised the Anglo-Iranian Oil Company out of which British Petroleum emerged, and in 1956 Gamal-Abdal Nassir nationalised the Suez Canal. Everywhere on the globe the European imperial powers were on the retreat. This slow and violent process of de-colonisation couched in the native counter-discourse to the imperial project revealed the irrationality of the imperial claim. With the reinvigorated presence of the native other, the 'West' is stripped of its artificially applied historical veneer. Its imagined totality turns out to be entirely relative, interpenetrated. This is what the inevitable interconnectedness of the material, social and natural worlds does. It constantly reminds us that causes and effects are reciprocal, that they occur in a densely networked arena, that our relations to each other are mutual, dialectical and interdependent. Conversely, causal totalities yield causal incest, which is why they turn out to be genealogically unsustainable.

The dichotomies informing the clash regime with violent vigour in the colonised worlds are related to this struggle against the imperial project. The native's whisper of despair turned into a battle cry for

---

[99] Winston S. Churchill, *A History of the English-Speaking Peoples*, vol. 3, London: Cassel and Company, 1957, p. 182.

liberation when she turned the truth requirement of modernity against the 'West' itself. Indeed, the '*post*-modern' consciousness of the 'West' emerged when the 'modernist intellectual who typically spoke with the confidence of standing at the cutting edge of time and of being able to speak for others',[100] was reminded that there exists a potent counter-discourse, that the western view of the world was entirely myopic. Jacques Derrida, Pierre Bourdieu and Jean-Paul Sartre in Algeria (and later Michel Foucault in Iran), saw with their own eyes that western modernity never really muted the 'natives'. The objectification of the East was an illusion. It did not have total causal efficacy as the discourse of Orientalism implies. The natives retained their power to write their own history. Once it challenged, politically, ontologically, epistemologically, what Jürgen Habermas terms 'the project of modernity', the slumber of the West turned into its nightmare.[101] Suddenly, the 'West' was forced to accept a new reality that was more intimate (i.e. due to the reappearance of the other), and therefore more unsettling. It was due to the re-appearance of the native counter-discourse, in short, that the meaning of the West and by implication the East was debunked, that the spatial compartmentalisation of the world was relocated. It was the opposition to colonialism that made the 'new' era possible. It was this struggle that questioned the causal syntax of the Enlightenment and it was this circular interdependency that delivered the discourse of post-modernity in Europe.

At the same time, by engaging in the necessary resistance, the native counter-discourse itself experimented with an impossibility: the return to an 'authentic' identity that is cleansed of the undue influence of the other. To that end, the native discourse too played with causalities that are unreal and charged with mythical content. That does not mean that this discourse was merely reactionary. It means that the anti-colonial resistance movements were signified within the inescapable dialectics of the imperial age, despite the protestations of authenticity which suggested detachment. By using the term dialectic, I am emphasising that the anti-colonial resistance engendered a truly productive counter-discourse that was not determined by the colonial reality 'all the way

[100] Andreas Huyssen, *After the Great Divide: Modernism, Mass Culture, Post-modernism*, Bloomington: Indiana University Press, 1986, p. 220.
[101] See Jürgen Habermas, 'Modernity versus Postmodernity', *New German Critique*, vol. 22, 1981, pp. 3–14.

down' and that it had an effect on the meaning and future of the concept of the 'West'. To be more precise, the 'post' in the term post-modernity would not be there without this counter-discourse, without Fanon, Jose Marti, Mohandas Gandhi, Nelson Mandela and other central figures of the anti-colonial struggles who in many ways transcended, discursively and in practical political terms, the vicissitudes of the imperial systems enveloping their societies. This is yet another example of the reciprocity intrinsic to history. Coloniser and colonised, master and slave, civilised and savage: even in the most violent attempts to detach the self from the other, an entirely social and interdependent dialectic, which remains unresolved and hence neutral, reveals itself.

If independence was the aim, the natives didn't have a choice of course. Their causal syntax was the only device to challenge the status quo. The many theorists and activists of the anti-imperial resistance movements had to speak and write in causal terms in order to convey the urgency of the task, i.e. the resistance to imperial exploitation. If modernisation means 'changing customs and various consumptions patterns of a material nature from old to new'; if European civilisation wants the African to believe 'that he has been wild in order to create the temptation in him to become civilised', it must follow quite logically that he should return to his own self as a means to salvage it from the undue influence of the other. This is what Ali Shariati prescribed for Iranians in the 1970s and what he termed *bazgasht be khishtan* or 'return to the self'. According to him, it was this quest for 'authenticity' that explains why 'in the East, in Asia and Africa, resistance movements against prejudice appeared among the indigenous intellectuals'.[102] I think in terms of political effectiveness he was right: the battles against real and perceived imperial hegemony necessitated effectively coherent ideologies that were efficient enough to convey the immediacy of the task. On this issue Frantz Fanon, one of Shariati's main intellectual interlocutors, is explicit:

So long as the uncertainty of colonialism continues, the national cause goes on progressing, and becomes the cause of each and all. The plans for liberation are sketched out; already they include the whole country. During this period spontaneity is king, and initiative is localised. ... Each man or woman brings

---

[102] Ali Shariati, 'Civilisation and Modernisation', in Lloyd Ridgeon (ed.), *Religion and Politics in Modern Iran: A Reader*, London: I. B. Tauris, 2005, p. 192.

the nation to life by his or her action, and is pledged to ensure its triumph in their locality. *We are dealing with a strategy of immediacy which is both radical and totalitarian*: the aim and the program of each locally constituted group is local liberation. If the nation is everywhere, then she is here. One step further, and only here is she to be found. Tactics are mistaken for strategy. The art of politics is simply transformed into the art of war; the political militant is the rebel. To fight the war and to take part in politics: the two things become one and the same.[103]

Fanon prescribes a total anti-colonial struggle that transcends both locality and individual agency. The colonial subject is persuaded to enter this battle without compromise. 'This people that has lost its birthright', he states, 'will now proceed in an atmosphere of solemnity to cleanse and purify the face of the nation'.[104] Thus, the nation becomes the locus of a new totality, a solid in-group which is strong enough to tolerate even those 'who by their activities and by their complicity with the occupier have dishonoured their country. ... All this is evocative of a confraternity, a church, and a mystical body to belief at one and the same time'. Ultimately, this unity simulates 'maximal effectiveness'. In this way, the native is coded to 'die for the "cause"'.[105]

Dying for the cause is the ultimate sacrifice that any causal system that is sustained by a totalitarian methodology, prescribes. It indicates to the other the maximal effectiveness of the ideology holding the in-group together. It is a historical luxury to live in a country or cultural reality that does not demand martyrdom for a higher cause. The Islamic worlds indulged in this luxury for a long time before the anti-colonial battles, once again, prescribed death for 'higher' ideals. How did it come to that? What syntactical order emerged within the discourses of Islam? Let me share a few thoughts on these questions in the following paragraphs.

Orders of Islam and the deceptive promise of 'homo Islamicus'

In the nineteenth century, imperial bureaucrats promised that they would end competition, that western man—they were quite virulently

---

[103] Franz Fanon, 'Spontaneity: Its Strengths and Weaknesses', in Castle (ed.), *Postcolonial Discourses*, pp. 16–17, emphasis added.
[104] Ibid., p. 17.
[105] Ibid.

gender specific—spearheaded the inevitable march of humanity into the end of history, the promised land of universal liberty. They were convinced that they could defeat the barbarian other once for all or to educate him to be a little bit more like us. That subject of history called (western) 'man', a particularly violent concoction of western modernity, emerges from his self-inflicted loneliness psychologically scared, yet pathologically functional. The Enlightenment may have blurred his eyesight but he could still see the presence of the native, and the new march of the 'barbarians' out of which there emerged new promises, new positivisms, and novel ideologies that suggested that everything is possible. The Islamic worlds especially, never really a stranger to outward expansion, reinvigorated their political consciousness in order to escape the imperial reality enveloping them. Their quest for a 'parallel ontology', a being that attempts to escape the modernist mould inscribed into the western discourse, was utopian of course (because nobody can escape the determinations of time). But this did not dent the belief that it was possible nonetheless. Indeed, the oppressive imperial reality made it necessary to believe in the immanence of change that can shatter the status quo and (re)establish what is perceived to be the ideal human community, *Madinat al-nabi*, the utopia of the perfect state of the *umma*.

I have argued in the last chapter that the discourse of Islam established a part of its syntactical order when its early narrators made ontology, that is the study and science of 'being' or existence (*wujud*), central to their philosophy, or *falsafa* in Arabic. In close dialogue with the Aristotelian tradition, classical philosophers of Islam (*falasifa*) such as Ibn Sina, Ibn Arabi, al-Kindi, Ibn Rushd, Farabi, and others employed complex methods explaining how 'truth conditions' can be rationalised through the study of language, judgement, nature, syllogisms, deductions and inductions. *Falsafa* was considered to lead to the knowledge of all existing things qua existent *(ashya' al-maujudah bi ma hiya maujudah)* and philosophy itself was deemed to be the art (*sind'ah*) of arts and the science (*ilm*) of sciences. What came surreptitiously into existence in the writings of these philosophers, in short, were nothing less than the intellectual archives of the Islamic worlds. In the following paragraphs, I will continue to focus on these ideas in order to a) establish the nuances within the interpretations of Islam marshalled and b) in order to show that the 'Islamist' paradigms that emerged in the nineteenth century have led to an epistemological break with cataclysmic political consequences. Of course, I am not claiming to present a comprehensive analysis here. Delving deeper into the narratives of the early signifiers of Islamic philosophy must be the purpose of a future project. But I think it is important to show that long before the modern University erected disciplinary boundaries producing a cadre of 'specialists', these thinkers were engaged in inter-disciplinary studies; not at least in order to compare their dialectical approach to the methodologies of contemporary Islamists. All of the classical philosophers of Islam under scrutiny here were polymaths, both poets and scientists, engaged in theology and mysticism, interested in God as much as in the empirical worlds. Yet despite their wide-ranging studies, they did not advance a concrete concept of Islam that could signify a monologue within the *umma* or that would organise Muslims within a militant, coherently formulated ideology. Theirs was an *a priori* Islam almost entirely depleted of identity politics or a concrete and dichotomous notion of self and other. The historical circumstances they were writing in, the presence of functioning Islamic polities, the absence of a direct threat to their 'Muslim identity', did not merit, or require them to write in a stridently ideological mode. The violence exercised over the Islamic worlds during the colonial period changed all that.

For the classical philosophers, in many ways up until Ibn Khaldun (1332–1406), reality is not exhausted by explaining what offers itself to immediate knowledge and perception. The understanding of the surrounding world must also include an aspect of future potentiality, a utopia wherein the discrepancy between the present and the future opens up. This is why in the philosophy of Farabi and especially in Ibn Sina's intricate *danish-namaha-ye alai* (Treatise on Knowledge), philosophy takes on a forward-looking modality adequate to this idea of the capacity for change towards the transcendental object as indicated in the last chapter. In the words of Ibn Sina: the contingent existent (*mumkin al-wujud*) is always relative to the necessary being (*wajib al-wujud*).[106] Within such a dialectic, one is alerted to criticise the present in order to bridge the gap between the ontology surrounding the individual and the transcendental promise, without, however, forcing a total causality upon this process. In the writings of Abu'l-Hassan Amiri, a contemporary (and critic) of Ibn Sina, this critical premise is particularly apparent:

[106] See further Nasr with Aminrazavi (eds), *An Anthology*, pp. 196. ff.

Finally, it is incumbent on the masters of all three disciplines [tradition, theology and jurisprudence] that not one of them be induced by his pride in himself and his profession to belittle the others, and that he not be induced by vanity about his expertise in his own discipline to plunge into areas which are not his own. Rather, he should make a point of consigning the work of each discipline to those who are masters of it, granting in full to those who are knowledgeable and pre-eminent in it all the respect and honour that they merit. Nor should he contest what is required by the unbiased intellect out of love of following previous decisions (*taqlid*), especially those of someone whose infallibility is unattested; for truth is not known by the man, but rather by itself, and only then is it known who has attained it and who has missed it. He should also follow the advice of the glorious Imam 'Ali b. Talib when he says "Knowledge is bountiful, so take the best of everything"; this is the point of God's statement'. Therefore give good tidings to my servants who hear advice and follow the best thereof; such are those whom God guides, and such are men of understanding [Quran, 39:18].[107]

The position of the early Muslim philosopher at the boundaries of the empirical world surrounding him, and the transcendental object termed 'Allah', engendered the simultaneous emergence of two fundamental narratives of Islam which, despite their seeming antagonism, concur that science as such is a necessary but not a sufficient guarantee of the supreme truth, *viz.* God. The first of these, the one which was most famously espoused by Farabi and Ibn Sina is the non-separation between what can be observed and what has been revealed, between the 'real' world surrounding the individual and the transcendental world awaiting her, which results in the constitution of a syntax in which the individual can 'sense' (yet not comprehend) the presence of God. The second, the one that is more prominent in the Hanbali tradition and its interpretation by Ibn Taymiya (1263–1328), leads to an inverse syntax. It advocates detachment of God, the Quran and the hadith (compilation of the Prophets words and deeds) from the Muslim perception and intellect. Despite this apparent syntactical antagonism, however, they both create a discourse that does not usurp the totally other, *viz.* God. For both Ibn Sina and Ibn Taymiya, intellectu-

---

[107] Ibid., p. 159. In the copy of the Quran used in this study the verse is translated as follows: 'Those who listen to different speeches and preaching [regarding religions and rites] and follow the best among the variety, those are the one whom Allah has guided and they are indeed Men of Wisdom'. See *The Holy Quran*, 4th edition, Tahereh Saffarzadeh (trans.), Tehran: Sooreh Mehr, 2002.

alism and science could never really grasp or coincide with the futuristic potentiality onto which God is projected. Other influential figures whose philosophy has been positioned in between Ibn Sina and Ibn Taymiya, such as al-Ghazzali (1058–1111), similarly emphasise caution when it comes to explaining what is not immediately accessible to the senses. According to al-Ghazzali, rigorous proof is only superior where the object is sufficiently observable to deduce verifiable laws. When this is not so, as with regard to the attributes of God and the probability of the afterlife, philosophers are advised to refrain from making speculations.

So the horizon of the classical philosophers of Islam is the creative imperative proclaimed by Allah in the Quran; 'Be! And it comes into existence' (*kun fayakun*). Just as in the Bible God's command 'let there be light' was a wholly creative imperative *ex nihilo*, in the Quran the act of creation *fiat lux* is expressed in surah 36:82: 'Verily, when He decides to create somebody, something or some event, He only commands to it stating: "Be!" and immediately it comes to existence [*kun fayakun*]'. 'Creation is related to an act which at the same time bestows existence and knows all things in principle' explains Hossein Nasr. 'Therefore, not only does God utter the word *kun* (Be!) but also the spiritual root (*malakut*)'.[108] In other words, for the classical philosophers the constitutive term 'Be' appears as an ontological promise, a spiritual realisation, a contemplative opportunity, a 'utopia' at the same time as it denotes the domain of godly revelation and essence which is, by definition, out of reach to human beings. 'Be' denotes both utopia, something that can be strived for and dystopia, something that can never really be attained fully. As such the godly realm retains its necessary otherness which induces in the philosopher a constant desire to narrow the gap between that other and the self.

Even the Mutazilites, those most ardent defenders of rationalism and objective science who emerged during the latter part of the first century of the Islamic calendar, retained a critical distance to the domain claimed by God, despite their efforts to approximate that realm. On the one side, 'the approach of the Mu'tazillah [Mutazilites], in fact, consisted of the use of a kind of logical and rational method for understanding the basic doctrines of the Islamic faith. Obviously, the first

---

[108] Seyyed Hossein Nasr, *Islam and the Plight of Modern Man*, London: Longman, 1975, p. 70

condition for such an approach is belief in the freedom, independence, and validity of reason'.[109] On the other side, the Mutazilites also accepted that God is beyond the reach of such rationalisation because He/She is apart from space and time. Out of the five divine principles of the Mutazilites expressed by Abu al-Husayn al Khayyat, the two most important are, respectively, *al-tawhid* (divine unity) and *al-adl* (divine justice).[110] Both of them denote the absoluteness of God. From this perspective, positioning Him/Her within a causal syntax in order to explain His/Her essence is considered to be futile.

Of course, I do not suggest that Muslim philosophers constituted a single group professing a common ontological reality for the *umma*. Rather the contrary. At the time when Islam was written, signified, paradigmatically invented, it emerged as a polymorphous and pluralistic phenomenon. Akhbaris vs. Usulis, Asharites vs. Mutazilites, Kalam vs. Falsafah, Mashasha'i vs. Ishraqi, Urafa vs. Irfani, Sunni, Shia, Shafi'i, Maliki, Hanafi, Hanbali, etc., from the early days, immediately after the death of Muhammad, Islam became a highly contested property. The dispute at the Saqifah assembly (June 632), which has been readily abused to signify the narratives of the Sunnis and the Shia, exemplifies the movements within the discourse of Islam, movements, one must immediately note, that are fixated towards a common property, that is Muhammad, the Quran and Allah which signify the Islamicity of the discourse of Islam in the first place. Where some of today's Muslim clerics and 'neo-Orientalists' go wrong is in homogenising Muslims as a single group with a uniform political mission. 'Muslim politics, while aspiring to *umma*-wide universals, derives its force and significance from the specific contexts, times, and localities in which it takes place'.[111] The story of Islam as it was written throughout history corroborates this argument expressed by Eickelman and Piscatori.

Neither do I mean to suggest that the early philosophers of Islam implied that scientific progress or causal inference should be restricted of course. Yet for them science was important primarily to explain the

---

[109] Murtada Mutahhari, *An Introuction to 'Ilm al-Kalam*, vol. II, no. 2, 'Ali Quli Qara'I (trans.), Tehran, 1985. Available at http://www.al-Islam.org/al-tawhid/kalam.htm /Last accessed 12 Jul. 2008.

[110] See further M. Saeed Sheikh, *Islamic Philosophy*, London: The Octagon Press, 1962, pp. 5 ff.

[111] Dale F. Eickelman and James Piscatori, *Muslim Politics*, Princeton: Princeton University Press, 1996, p. 163.

empirical worlds, the here and now, that which is immediately observable by the senses. The unity of being, i.e. the existence of God or *wahdat al-wujud* in the words of Ibn Arabi, creates an insatiable desire to know. But at the end, God could not be questioned without extinguishing that desire. Hence science and progress were functional in a different place than God, the domain of whom remained a field of unending possibilities. This explains why despite their access to the 'hard sciences' the classical Muslim philosophers doubted why they retained an imaginative orientation that was strong enough to continuously transcend the present limits of their reality. Even Ibn Khaldun (1332–1406) in his seminal *Muqqadimah* pierced his systematic inquiries into world history and the growth and demise of civilisations with the note of caution that 'God knows better'.[112] The point I am making is that this particular ordering of Islam emerged not around a single proposition suggesting a unified and unchanging mission, but rather, was made up of different propositions that were held together by reference to an entirely abstract exterior unit, i.e. Allah. Since God continued to be out of reach, since he remained unexplainable by language, since God was thus by implication not usurped by the syntax of the discourse of Islam, he retained transcendental properties. Until today, the discourse of Islam has not subdued God; it has not transferred God out of His/Her transcendental shelter. This is a part of the explanation, I think, why in Muslim societies God continues to exist.

Thus, it must follow that the Islamic discourse is 'younger' than the death of God, which was so central to the making of the 'West', certainly from the nineteenth century onwards. This does not mean that the discourse of Islam has been continuously retroactive. Rather, it explains why even under the pressures of western modernity, many Muslims have retained their infinite mobilisation towards the absolute otherness of God. On this intellectual issue there has not been a compromise, which is why in Muslim societies Islam has retained its ideological promise. Repeatedly, Muslims have set out to reclaim a future-oriented interpretation of the revelation attributed to Muhammad, a worldview and historical consciousness that is not devoid of principled utopian faith. For its adherents, this utopian future opens up fables with

---

[112] See Ibn Khaldun, *The Muqaddimah: An Introduction to History*, Franz Rosenthal (trans.), N.J. Dawood (ed.), with an introduction by Bruce Lawrence, Princeton: Princeton University Press, 2004.

fantastic figures and gnomic personalities that transcend both the empirical world and the artificial confinement within national histories. It imagines the ultimate *umma* encapsulated in the idea of the rule of Muhammad over the city state of Medina (*Madinat al-nabi*), and ultimately, birth of the ideal 'homo Islamicus', who would seal the genealogy of human kind towards his 'inevitable' transcendental fate. This individual appears in Farabi in the tenth century:

[He] holds the most perfect rank of humanity and has reached the highest degree of felicity. ... He is the man who knows every action by which felicity can be reached. This is the first condition for being a ruler. Moreover, he should be a good orator and able to rouse [other people's] imagination by well chosen words. He should be able to lead people well along the right path to felicity and to the actions by which felicity is reached.

This is the sovereign over whom no other human being has any sovereignty whatsoever; he is the Imam; he is the first sovereign of the excellent city, he is the sovereign of the excellent nation, and the sovereign of the universal state (the *oikumene*).[113]

A comparable 'ideal man', the *Übermensch* of Islamic mythology, reappears in the political tracts of Ali Shariati, who wrote within the Shia-Islamic context and amidst the revolutionary upheaval in 1970s Iran, i.e. ten centuries after Farabi. According to Shariati, the ultimate homo Islamicus, who would emerge out of the depth of the Muslim masses:

holds the swords of Caesar in his hand and he has the heart of Jesus in his breast. He thinks with the brain of Socrates and loves God with the heart of Hallaj [a Persian Sufi executed on charges of heresy in 922 AD] ... Like the Buddha, he is delivered from the dungeon of pleasure-seeking and egoism; Like Lao Tse, he reflects on the profundity of his primordial nature; ... [l]ike Spartacus, he is a rebel against slave owners ... and like Moses, he is the messenger of jihad and deliverance.[114]

It becomes clearer now why many Muslims could not content themselves with the detachment of God from the individual in western

---

[113] Abu Nasr Farabi, 'The Perfect State (Mabadi ara ahl al-madinat al-fadilah)', in Nasr with Aminrazavi (eds), *An Anthology of Philosophy in Persia*, pp. 129–130.

[114] Ali Shariati, *On the Sociology of Islam: Lectures by Ali Shariati*, Hamid Algar (trans.), Berkeley: Mizan Press, 1979, p. 122. Similarly, Shariati idealised the persona of Fatima, the daughter of Muhammad, the wife of Ali and the mother of Imam Hussein who was killed at the much-fabled Battle of Karbala in 680.

modernity, why they quarrel with it over the significance of the transcendental realm. The marginalisation of God in the modern universe
has not only taken away a common Judeo-Christian-Islamic reference
point; it makes it difficult to believe in *Madinat al-fadilah* (the perfect
state). The assumed purity of the western discourse, which is significantly inflated by its pronounced atheistic rationality, does not only
make it rather more difficult to find a common field where the western
and Islamic discourse could engage each other intellectually. It disqualifies the transcendental realm *a priori*; it threatens to obliterate the syntax of a theo-philosophical language, and not only the syntax of the
Quran, but also that of contemporary Islamic utopias which promise
the re-enactment of the justice ascribed to the period of the *rashidun*
and *salaf*, the compatriots of Muhammad and the first three generations of Muslims. The discourse of Islam could not accommodate the
separation of man from God or Muhammad. If it would lose its signifiers, it would cease to be Islamic. So the 'master-discourse' of Islam, by
necessity of its manifold constitution, has repeatedly imagined a utopian order that was rendered Islamic by necessity. Today, such 'Islamutopia' continue to allow for ideological fables and mythical imagery.
Islamutopia imagine that they travel with the very language of the
Quran and the hadith and that they may finally become a part of that
fantastic transcendental project of the *umma*. Conversely, the absence
of God threads Islamutopia, desiccates faith, contests the very plausibility of theodicy. It threatens to change the Islamic calendar from 1457
(1388 in Iran) to 2010 *CE*, the presumably Common Era. It prescribes
a particular virulent counter-reality to Islamutopia that many Muslims
have continuously tried to escape from. A futile endeavour maybe, but
nonetheless an ongoing journey embarked on by many contemporary,
so called 'Islamists' as I will argue in the following paragraphs.

I have suggested that the battle against western imperialism in the
nineteenth century reinvigorated the propensity to thrust forward
towards a future potentiality, but turned it into an ideological war that
was increasingly devoid of critical substance. In many ways, the tendency towards unification and a rather more stringent interpretation
of an Islam was already apparent in the writings of Ibn Taymiya
(1263–1328) and the followers of the Hanbali tradition. '[T]hose who
traced their intellectual ancestry to Ibn Hanbal', Hourani notes, 'were
united in their attempt to maintain what they regarded as the true
Islamic teaching, that of those who adhered strictly to God's revelation

through the Prophet Muhammad'.[115] In a comparable vein, Sami Zubaida recounts the identification of Ibn Hanbal (780–856) as the 'prototype of the "fundamentalist" *alim*, a literalist in scripture ... rejecting all elements of reason—even qiyas—philosophy and theology as innovation (*bid'a*) and impious meddling in what does not concern the believer'.[116]

The followers of Ibn Hanbal were largely opposed to the dialectical reasoning (*kalam*) and the philosophical tradition of Islamic thought presented by Farabi, Ibn Sina, Ibn Rushd and Ibn Arabi. In the thirteenth century, amidst the chaos incurred by the Mongol invasions of the caliphate and the unstable rule of the Mamlukes, Ibn Taymiya emerged as the most prominent and systematic interpreter of the Hanbali tradition. In his writings, especially his *Statecraft in Accordance with the Sharia* (*al-syasa al-shariya*) the sunna of the prophet and the Quran itself are detached from dialectical interpretation. According to Ibn Taymiya, the Quran represents a coherent totality; its essence remains unattainable despite what some of the Mutazilite philosophers and Sufis promised. The Quran was deemed to be the uncreated word of God (*al-Quran kalam Allah ghair makhluq*), so it demands total, i.e. literal obedience. In this sense, Ibn Taymiya offered a rather more stringent politico-judicious interpretation of Islam that was meant to unify the 'Islamic nation' around the *sharia*: 'Unity is a sign of divine clemency', he argued, 'discord is a punishment of God'.[117]

The power of Ibn Taymiya's discourse, which benefitted from his encyclopaedic knowledge of the different schools of Islam, explains his success in refuting some of the ideas expressed by luminaries such as Ibn Sina and Farabi. In his inquiries into modern Islamic political thought, Hamid Enayat notes that it is the chaos incurred by the Mongol invasions which explains Ibn Taymiya's advocacy of strong governance. Muslims should organise themselves, if necessary, under the sovereignty of 'an unjust ruler' which would be better than there being no state at all. He also places Ibn Taymiya's political narrative in the

---

[115] Albert Hourani, *A History of the Arab Peoples*, London: Faber and Faber, 1991, p. 179. See further idem., *Arabic Thought in the Liberal Age 1798–1939*, Cambridge: Cambridge University Press, 1983, pp. 18 ff.

[116] Sami Zubaida, *Law and Power in the Islamic World*, London: I.B. Tauris, 2003, p. 81.

[117] Quoted in Albert Hourani, *A History of the Arab Peoples*, London: Faber and Faber, 1991, p. 180.

tradition of 'Sunni exponents of the theory of the Caliphate' as it developed between the eleventh and fourteenth centuries.[118] I am not entirely convinced that the Sunni-Shia reference point is useful here and that Ibn Taymiya is indeed an example of some sort of 'Sunni realism'. What I am rather more confident to point out is that in Ibn Taymiya, we find a politico-judicious movement towards the sovereignty of Islam and Muslim rule that was born out of crisis. It is not the relatively secure world of Farabi and Ibn Sina that we are dealing with here; it is secure because Islam in itself was not deemed to be at threat *tout court*. Ibn Taymiya lived during a period in which it seemed that Islamicate civilisation may be obliterated in its entirety. The Mongols had sacked Baghdad and the Caliphate ceased to exist. It is the battle with this threat that Ibn Taymiya had to accept, out of fear, not out of luxury. It is his fear to lose the master signifier which explains his immense efforts to reorder the discourse of Islam along a set of politico-judicious rules. It is the will to preserve the Islamicity of the discourse of Islam that explains the urgency in his political treatise, *al-syasa al-shariya* and the multi-volume *fatawa*, the many religious verdicts and legal opinions that he authored. Ibn Taymiya attempted to construct a similarly robust Leviathan as Thomas Hobbes tried amidst the English Civil War in the seventeenth century, in order to safeguard the continuity and authority of Islam against both external threats (e.g. the Crusaders) and internal discord (e.g. Shia, Sufis, and the 'illegitimate' Mongol rulers in Baghdad). He must have felt that the metaphysics of the classical philosophers of Islam, which he studied extensively, were not conducive to the political situation that he faced. Thus, he advocated a politico-judicious discourse that he deemed powerful enough to entice the *umma* to change their historical reality: to rise up against the Mongols who only pretended to be Muslims, but who did not rule according to the sharia.

Ibn Taymiya presents a discourse of Islam that simulates a very strategic quasi-reality: the unaffectedness of Islam by the determinations of history, in his case the devastating invasion of the Muslim heartland by the Mongols. By stressing the fundamental literality of the Quran and the Sunna, Ibn Taymiya produces a discourse of Islam that is

[118] Hamid Enayat, *Modern Islamic Political Thought: The Response of the Shi'i and Sunni Muslims to the Twentieth Century*, London: Macmillan, 1982, p. 12.

meant to escape the vicissitudes of history. What Ibn Taymiya tries to eliminate is any usurpation of his literalist reading of Islam and to present a theory of the Islamic state that is easily digestible, untainted by the intellectual complexities of Avicennian theory. Islam appears here as 'purified'. The identity of the 'real Muslims' is delineated, on the one side, from the Mongols, despite their official acceptance of Islam. On the other side, Ibn Taymiya's Islam also rejects the Shia and Sufis who were reprimanded for 'contaminating' the purity of the message of Mohammed from within. With Ibn Taymiya, *fitna* turns into a cardinal mistake, an irrationality that the *umma* could not afford anymore. The real enemies of Muslims, according to this perspective, are not only the infidels who threaten *dar al-Islam* from without, but the heretics and apostates that were tearing the unity of Islam apart from within the *umma* itself. It is this reality of internal strife and the threat of external conquest that Ibn Taymiya battles with. Hence, his efforts to unify the discourse of Islam behind the ultimate Islamic state or caliph, which would reinvigorate the purity of the rule of the *salaf*, the pious compatriots of Muhammad. And that is also the reason why his emphasis on the importance of an Islamic Leviathan and on the unity of the *umma* is comparable not only to Hobbes, but also to the *vali-e faqih*, the supreme jurisprudent that is at the heart of Ayatollah Khomeini's theory of the state, the very state that rules in Iran in the name of the 'Shia' imamate since 1979.

One should be careful not to stretch the link between Ibn Taymiya and Ayatollah Khomeini's 'Shia realism' too far, not only because they signified their discourse within very different historical contexts and periods, but also because Ibn Taymiya used the Hanbali tradition as his primary reference point, while the *vali-e faqih* in Khomeini's theory of state is conceptualised with reference to the Shia paradigm of the imamate. But the emphasis on the politico-judicious sovereignty allocated to the ultimate Islamic state and the prescription to unify the *umma* behind it, is comparable. The enemy discourse that both Ibn Taymiya and Khomeini tried to ward off is that discourse that attempts to divorce Islam from power and by extension from the political arena. Both Ibn Taymiya and Ayatollah Khomeini are entirely convinced that *din wa dawla* (religion and politics) have to merge radically in order to signify the sovereignty of Islam over the *umma* and to combat corrupt rulers, in the case of Khomeini the monarchy of the shah. Hence the urgency in their narratives and their ideological potency.

No wonder then that Ibn Taymiya functioned as a point of reference for many political movements in the Islamic worlds, for instance the '*Muwahiddun*' or Unitarians (referred to as 'Wahhabis' by their critics) who engineered the creation of Saudi Arabia in the eighteenth century and a host of twentieth century thinkers and activists who were busy forging a unitarian ideology out of Islam, which would be strong enough to 'sanctify' the sovereignty of a particular movement and to mobilise the Muslim masses against 'corrupt' or 'impious' rulers at the same time.[119] Yet it would be too simplistic, and ultimately naive, to hold Ibn Taymiya responsible for the politics of Al Qaeda and contemporary 'jihadists' simply because he and Muhammad ibn Abd al-Wahhab are referred to repeatedly in the proclamations and political tracts of Osama bin-Laden and Ayman al-Zawahiri. What seems to be rather more reasonable to argue is that the political activism and the discourse of Ibn Taymiya are taken up selectively by Al Qaeda type movements in order to legitimate their call for a clash of civilisations. Ultimately, the ideologues of Al Qaeda seem to be fascinated by Ibn Taymiya's idea that there is a very concrete and direct definition of Islam in the Quran and the Sunna. Suddenly, Islamutopia does not reveal itself as a place that is remote. It is a place the *umma* could easily venture to, if it would only return to the original message of Islam and divorce itself from the interpretive premises of Avicennian theory. For the ideologues of Al Qaeda, this possibility of a concrete Islam that could be transferred to the here and now opens up a field of unending ideological opportunities.

What is important to add here is that in the discourse of Islam at least since 1258, a whole historical memory of conquest and resistance, within different political contexts and enunciated according to different traditions, signified more vigorously the imagination of an internal-external division. With Ibn Taymiya, Islam functions both as a rigorous political programme to ward off external conquest and as an 'ideological' device suitable to delineate the '*umma*' from a whole range of unwanted others: Shia, Christians, Mongols, Sufis, Jews. The colonial period added a new dynamic to the making of the Islamic self and its corresponding others. The discourse of Islam as political ideology or 'Islamism' that emerged in the nineteenth century positions the

---

[119] On the Wahhabi movement, see also Hamid Algar, *Wahhabism: A Critical Essay*, North Haledon, NJ: Islamic Publications International, 2002.

'West' firmly within its syntax. The etymological structure ascribed to the term (i.e. Islam plus 'ism') reveals that it was constituted by a dual process: the reinterpretation of the meaning of Islam on the one side and the overbearing pressures of western modernity on the other. In turn, this dual orientation can also be discerned from the writings and biographies of their early promoters, from Rifa 'A Badawi Rafi al-Tahtawi (1801–1873), Ali 'Abd al-Raziq (1888–1966) to Sayyid Jamal ad-Din al-Afghani (also Asadabadi, 1838–1897) and Mohammed Abduh (1849–1905). All of these early narrators of the so called 'Islamic revival' wrote in relation to the 'West', not at least because all of them spent some time in European capitals.

Let me elaborate on some of their ideas and their implication for the clash regime today. The aforementioned Afghani, who was born into a Shia community in Asadabad, Iran around 1838, is widely considered to be one of the intellectual forefathers of the emergent 'Islamist' paradigms of the nineteenth and twentieth centuries.[120] Afghani experienced Britain as a colonial power during his travels through India and Afghanistan. In order to legitimate his political agenda, Afghani broke up the monopoly of the *ulema* (clerics) on the interpretation of Islamic law (the textual interpretation or *tafsir*) and jurisprudence (*fiqh*). Instead, he adhered to and advocated individual interpretation or *ijtihad* of both the Quran and the hadith.

Afghani shared with the imperial functionaries of Europe an almost blind faith in the possibility of his task, i.e. the global pan-Islamic resurgence. Malise Ruthven describes him as a 'man of action before he was a thinker [and] a born intriguer and polemicist'.[121] The resemblance with Cecil Rhodes could not be more striking. Much like Rhodes, Afghani was a very capable 'norm entrepreneur', who engineered a viable agenda fostering a basis for political action. In order to resist European imperialism, he urged allegiance to the Ottoman state, whose leader Abdul-Hamid II co-opted his ideas as a means to legitimate his domestic rule and mobilise the populace against western

---

[120] Al-Afghani's life and political thought are convincingly chronicled and interpreted in Nikki R. Keddie, *An Islamic Response to Imperialism: The Political and Religious Writings of Sayyid Jamal ad-Din al-Afghani*, Berkeley: University of California Press, 1983; Elie Kedouri, *Afghani and 'Abduh: An Essay on Religious Unbelief and Political Activism in Modern Islam*, London: Frank Cass, 1966; Hourani, *Arabic Thought*, pp. 103–129.

[121] Malise Ruthven, *Islam in the World*, London: Penguin, 1984, p. 302.

forces; he supported the Tobacco Revolts in Iran (1891) against the concession of exclusive tobacco rights to Major G. Talbot by the Qajar state; and he came to London upon invitation of the poet, writer and pro-Orabi activist Wilfrid Blunt (1840–1922) to encourage the British to leave Egypt.[122] Despite this anti-imperial activism, however, his discourse was not depleted of the 'reflexive' momentum of the classical philosophers of Islam. With Afghani, the interdependence of Islam and western modernity is acknowledged, because his discourse retained the interdependent syntax that is characteristic of the 'Avicennian' tradition:

A science is needed to be the comprehensive soul for all the sciences, so that it can preserve their existence, apply each of them in its proper place, and become the cause of progress of each one of those sciences. The science that has the position of a comprehensive soul and the rank of a preserving force is the science of *falsafa* or philosophy, because its subject is universal. It is philosophy that shows man human prerequisites. It shows the sciences what is necessary. It employs each of the sciences in its proper place. ... The Ottoman government and the Khedive of Egypt have opened up schools for the teaching of the new sciences for a period of sixty years and until now they have not received any benefits from those sciences.[123]

The first generation carrying the Islamic 'revival', certainly Muhammad Abduh (see below) and Afghani, did not 'trim' their discourse of Islam to the degree that it was devoid of philosophical content. This is one of the valuable insights that come out of Roxanne Euben's theoretically sophisticated study of Islamic 'fundamentalisms'. Euben shows, that the rationalist premise retained its centrality to their discourse and that philosophy and science were deemed to be central to their 'true' Islam.[124] In this way Islam and the 'West' were considered to be mutually constitutive, intertwined and interdependent; joined at

---

[122] See further Basssam Tibi, *Arab Nationalism. Between Islam and the Nation-State*, 3rd edition, Macmillan: London 1997, p. 93. See also Farzin Vahdat, 'Critical Theory and the Islamic Encounter with Modernity', in Michael J. Thompson (ed.), *Islam and the West: Critical Perspectives on Modernity*, Oxford: Rowman & Littlefield, 2003, pp. 123–138.

[123] Sayyid Jamal ad-Din al-Afghani, 'Lecture on Teaching and Learning', in Keddie, *An Islamic Response to Imperialism*, p. 104.

[124] Roxanne L. Euben, *Enemy in the Mirror: Islamic Fundamentalism and The Limits of Modern Rationalism*, Princeton: Princeton University Press, 1999, pp. 98 ff.

the hip through a common interest in rationality and science. Abduh and Afghani acknowledged this. They knew that they could not detach themselves from the western other *in toto*, even if they wanted to. As Abu-Rhabi indicates: 'the *nahdah* ['Renaissance'] phenomenon is based on a complex epistemological structure which has both Islamic and Western components'.[125] Since the Islamic world was at the receiving end of imperialism, the re-signification of the discourse of Islam was a consciously dialectical process. I don't think it can be reduced to a mere reaction to imperialism as the discourse of *Orientalism* implies. It had both an 'endogenous' (Islamic) and an 'exogenous' (western modernity/imperialism) dynamic, thesis and antithesis, hegemony and resistance engaged each other.[126]

The ideas of Afghani were taken up by one of his students at al-Azhar, the aforementioned Muhammad Abduh. Abduh became a judge in the Egyptian courts and was appointed 'Grand Mufti' of the country in 1899. He was a keen follower of the *kalam* philosophy of Ibn Sina and Farabi and reintroduced them to the curriculum of the al-Azhar as a part of his lectures on logic, despite strident opposition by the orthodox clergy.[127] By returning to the 'original' Islam of the pre-Umayyad period and a rational understanding of the Quran and the hadith, Abduh also argued, a synthesis between Islam and manifestations of western modernity (especially the sciences) was achievable. This would lead man 'to investigate the secrets of existence, summoning him to respect established truths and to depend on them in his moral life and conduct'.[128]

---

[125] Ibrahim M. Abu-Rabi, *Intellectual Origins of Islamic Resurgence in the Modern Arab World*, Albany, NY: State University of New York Press, 1996, p. 8.

[126] For a biographical and historical approach to Afghani and other political thinkers of Islamic modernity see Ali Rahnema (ed.), *Pioneers of Islamic Revival*, London: Zed Books, 1994. For a bibliographic overview see Yvonne Haddad and John L. Esposito, *The Islamic Revival Since 1988: A Critical Survey and Bibliography*, London: Greenwood, 1997. For an innovative critique of the mainstream literature on Islam(ism) and politics with a particular emphasis on Islamism in Egypt see especially Salwa Ismail, *Rethinking Islamist Politics: Culture, the State and Islamism*, London: I.B. Tauris, 2006.

[127] M. M. Sharif (ed.), *A History of Muslim Philosophy: With Short Accounts of Other Disciplines and The Modern Renaissance in Muslim Lands*, vol. 2, Wiesbaden, Germany: Otto Harassowitz, 1966, p. 1496.

[128] Muhammad Rashid Rida, *Tarikh al-ustadh al-imam al-shaykh Muhammad*

In his writings, Abduh is rather more theoretically and philosophically accomplished than Afghani. He did not only emphasise the political vigour of Islam, his discourse is less 'urgent', more subtle, tampered more consistently by the critical dialectics of Farabi and Ibn Sina. It was the former who cautioned that in each analysis it is problematic to draw a universal judgement from the perception of particulars.[129] By enmeshing different variables and linking them to such a conclusion with causal claim, one should be aware that this type of argumentation seriously contracts the space between understanding and explanation which is opened up by the subject matter. In particular in his politico-scientific writings, Farabi repeatedly cautions that with regard to the political world one must be careful not to link a cause and its effects together in such a way that they may be said to express the continuity of a singular historical process that is inevitable and overbearingly deterministic. Farabi's writings on politics were not anti-causal. He was not against explanation per se. But from the methodical notes enveloping his writings, a critical disposition towards arguments following an easy-going if-then logic can be discerned. From the perspective of Farabi, a method that is rendered unambiguously causal is deceptive. One has to capture the complexity of the political worlds not to narrow it down. From this perspective, political theory can never be teleological. The political sciences can never be equal in structure and system to the methodical claims of the natural sciences which operate according to different rules.

This Farabian hesitance to force an uninhibited causal imperative on his discourse of Islam is apparent in the way Abduh conceptualises the western other. Like Afghani he does not detach Islam from the West or the determinations of modernity, not out of capitulation, but because of his conviction in the inevitable dialectics of history that would not deliver an epistemology that is cleansed of interdependence and co-constitution. For Abduh, both Islam and the West were inevitably affected by their historical interaction, peaceful and violent:

'*Abduh*, vol. 1, Cairo: al-Manar, 1931, p. II. Quoted in Hourani, *A History of the Arab Peoples*, p. 308.

[129] Abu Nasr Farabi, 'Reconciliation of the Two Sages Spiritual Plato and Aristotle (kitab al-jam 'bayn ra'yay al-hakimayn, Aflatun al-ilahi wa Aristu)', in Seyyed Hossein Nasr with Mehdi Aminrazavi (eds), *An Anthology of Philosophy in Persia*, vol. 1, Oxford: Oxford University Press, 1999, p. 113.

The religious leaders of the West successfully aroused their peoples to make havoc of the eastern world and to seize the sovereignty over those nations on what they believed to be their prescriptive right to tyrannise over masses of men. They came in great numbers of all sorts of men, estimated in millions, many settling in Muslim territory as residents. There were periods of truce in which the angry fires abated and quieter tampers prevailed, when there was even time to take a look at the surrounding culture, pick up something from the medley of ideas and react to what was to be seen and heard. ... By God's will they acquired some experience of refined culture and went off to their own territories thrilled with what they had gained from their wars—not to mention the great gains the travellers gathered in the lands of Andalusia by intercourse with its learned and polished society, whence they returned to their own peoples to taste the sweet fruits they had reaped. From that time on, there began to be much more traffic in ideas.[130]

Of course, there is a particular bias towards the *umma* here, a cognitive bias that does not yield denial of the other, however. Abduh is setting out a dialectic of history that was meant to explain the inevitable bonds between Islam and the West that the imperialists were so adamant to deny. This approach to history was intrinsic to the philosophical approach to Islam that he adopted. Philosophies of Islam are not closed systems, they do not yield a totalitarian syntax, and they are certainly not revolutionary. Abduh and Afghani could indulge in the luxury of signifying a rather less urgent Islam because the caliphate was not abolished yet. The formal authority of Islam was still there. It functioned as an institutionalised, politico-judicious reality despite the imperial penetrations Muslim-majority societies were grappling with. The discourse of Abduh and Afghani established itself within this hybrid historical context which was different from the political realities facing Qutb, al-Banna, Khomeini or Mawdudi that I will discuss at a later stage. Ultimately, both Abduh and Afghani responded to and challenged the imperial reality enveloping them, with idioms and syntactic devices that were consciously dialectical, steeped in Islamic philosophy and the determinations of their age.

The preceding analysis implies that with the *nahda* there emerges a West as the significant other of a dominant discourse of Islam. The

---

[130] Muhammad Abduh, 'Islam, Reason, and Civilisation', in John J. Donohue and John L. Esposito (eds), *Islam in Transition: Muslim Perspectives*, 2nd edition, Oxford: Oxford University Press, 2007, pp. 22–23. See further Muhammad Abdu, *Al-A'mal al-Kamilah lil-Imam Muhammad 'Abduh* (The Complete Works of Imam Muhammad 'Abduh), Muhammad 'Imarah (ed.), Beirut: al-Mu'assassah al-'Arabiyyah lil-Dirasat wa al-Nashr, 1972–1974.

colonial reality forced Abduh and Afghani to position a 'West' into their writings and speeches in order to signify what Islam was and what it was not. At the same time, there did not emerge a thoroughly anti-western attitude in Afghani and Abduh. I have argued in the previous chapter that despite their supersessionist claims, early discourses of Islam could never really detach themselves entirely from the Judeo-Christian tradition because Abraham and Jesus are central to the Islamic prophecy. Within a constellation where Abraham, Jesus and Moses are a part of being Muslim, self and other could and did clash politically but never in 'ethnocentric' detachment, which is why the syntax of Islam has not lent itself to systematically racist theories. In the activism and writings of Afghani and Abduh, the western other is severely criticised but at the same time interdependence with this other is acknowledged. Their Islam was permeated by Avicennian philosophy and in that it was more 'indulgent' and less urgent than the 'post-Caliphatic Islamism' that developed with Rachid Ridha (1865–1935). The political field that opens up under the label 'post-Caliphatic Islam-ism' is structured according to state-centred approaches to political power and socio-cultural organisation and it is articulated within the confines of 'national' or area specific politics. It does not so much refer to a historical period, but a discursive syntax. Inspired by his mentors, Abduh and Afghani, but not engaged in a comparable dialogue with western modernity, Ridha was a proponent of a rather more doctrinal reinterpretation of Muslim politics inspired by the aforementioned ideas of Ibn Taymiya and the Hanbali tradition. His most consequential move was his support to the *Muwahiddun* in central Arabia and the ambitions of the movement's leader Abdul Aziz ibn Saud. The activism and legal tracts of Ridha were central to defending the new movement against allegations of 'unorthodoxy' and to legitimate the *Muwahid-dun*'s conquest of the Hejaz and the holy cities of Mecca and Medina which led to the foundation of the Saudi Arabian nation-state.

I will elaborate on the impact of those developments on the making of new Islams in the next chapter. Suffice it to say at this stage that in the early-twentieth century, and more exponentially after the abolish-ment of the Caliphate in 1924, there emerged a strong current in the Islamic worlds that accentuated fundamental differences between 'Islam' and the 'West'. In the discourse of 'post-caliphatic Islamists', the western other is pushed away rather more forcefully, not only in order to ward off imperial intrusions, but also in order to purify the Muslim self; to re-orient the *umma* towards Islamutopia and its promises of a new Islamic sovereignty. For many Muslims the end of the caliphate was traumatic; it indicated that Islam had lost its functionality, its theo-political promise. Post-caliphatic Islamisms were formulated as an answer to the political void thus created. They are sympathetic to the power of the state, they are not geared towards the metaphysics of Islam, and they are primarily ideological. They disseminate into the field of the clash regime a new dimension: the phenomenon of the van-guard Islamist who arrogates to himself the sovereign right to suspend the order of things for the sake of a particular ideological agenda. Of course, no 'Islamism' denotes a coherent movement. Islamism is not a term that can be readily used to abstract from differences within the Muslim worlds or to signify a global conspiracy against the West. There is no unified headquarter, that would organise an Islamist army. Rather, 'Islamism' is the term that has been invented in order to denote political movements and their discourses that are a product of very particular political circumstances in Muslim majority societies.

Today, it is even more apparent that the Islamist logic is expressed within the confines of the nation-state and with reference to particular political projects. Hamas, for example, is resisting US foreign policies because of that country's unrelenting support of Israel, but it is limiting its activities primarily to the occupied Palestinian territories and it is not calling for a 'global jihad'. The Justice and Development Party of the Turkish Prime Minister Recep Tayyip Erdogan is inspired by Otto-man legacies and intends to address some of the injustices created by Kemalism, for instance the headscarf ban in the public sector and the intrusions into politics by the military establishment. The Kuwaiti, Egyptian and Jordanian branches of the Muslim Brotherhood partici-pate in national elections whenever the ruling elites allow them to. The Islamic revolution in Iran had very distinct features and has not been replicated in the same way and with the same symbols elsewhere. Hez-bollah has increasingly repositioned itself within the national politics of Lebanon and the same applies to the 'Shia-nationalist' parties gov-erning Iraq. Before its brutal suppression by the Algerian state, the *Front Islamique du Salut* (FIS, Islamic Salvation Front) portrayed itself as the heir of the anti-colonial battles in the country. These Islamist movements by and large accept the nation-state as an organisational principle of the international system which re-inscribes the authority of national governments into the global order. Their primary aim is to usurp the national sovereignty expressed therein, rather than to advocate a Unitarian pan-Islamic caliphate/state. What has been called 'Islamism' in the twentieth century, is in short yet another manifestation of the multiplicity of Islam. Islamism is certainly not an emblem of the political uniformity of the *umma*.

3

THE ANGER OF NATIONS

Es entsteht ein eigenes allgemeines Behagen, wenn man einer Nation ihre Geschichte auf einer geistreichen Weise wieder zur Erinnerung bringt; sie erfreut sich der Tugenden ihrer Vorfahren und belächelt die Mängel derselben, welche sie längst überwunden zu haben glaubt. Teilnahme und Beifall kann daher einer solchen Darstellung nicht fehlen und ich hatte mich in diesem Sinne einer vielfachen Wirkung zu erfreuen.

[A strange satisfaction is generally felt, when a writer felicitously recalls a nation's history to its recollection; men rejoice in the virtues of their ancestors, and smile at the failings, which they believe they themselves have long since got rid of. Such a delineation never fails to meet with sympathy and applause, and in this respect I enjoyed an envied influence.]

Johann Wolfgang von Goethe

International relations, the nation-state and its sovereignties

I suggested in the first part of chapter one that at least since Hegel, there has developed a central discourse in and about the 'West' that is concerned with the end of history. If the 'Owl of Minerva' finally descended in the Occident, as Hegel promised, the end of history and the end of the last 'man' was deemed possible. This grand idea of an end of history emerged out of the belief in the positively euphoric vision of the Occident's supreme evolution, itself a product of the methodical trust in the effectiveness of historical development that was central to the perspective of the Enlightenment.

The Hegelian methodology, albeit not all-encompassing, became a major pillar of Enlightenment thought and particularly of the human sciences which have been continuously concerned with scientific evolution and perfection, especially from the eighteenth century onwards. From then on the (European) human sciences continued to speculate about the transcendental, but instead of pursuing the utopia of God, they accentuate the utopia of science. The individual, society, the nation, the natural world replaced God as an object of enquiry. Yet since God has been considered the only way to make sense of death, to extend the self into the otherworldly, the modern mentality thus affected, posits a pathological fear of demise and physical ends. In short, western modernity entails an element of fear: the fear of finitude. 'When it was possible to believe, really believe, in heaven and hell', Daniel Bell argues, 'then some of the fear of death could be tempered or controlled; without such belief, there is only the total annihilation of the self'.[1] Bell agrees that at least since Hegel, the 'West' is obsessed with its final decline. To escape it, its lifeline had to be extended, if necessary by infusing it with the fresh blood of other civilisations that retained their idealistic youthfulness. 'Now there is only this life, and the assertion of self becomes possible—for some even necessary—in the domination over others'.[2] On this issue there is widespread agreement in the literature, from 'right' to 'left'. Bell employs a cultural/ sociological methodology, Hardt and Negri a historical materialist one. For the former it is inevitable that the 'West' will return to God, for the latter the post-modern condition is characterised by 'Multitudes' that eventually will merge and overcome the status quo. Despite their disparate methodological starting point and conclusions, all three authors agree that there emerged a particularly virulent tendency to extend the life of 'western civilisation' in the domination of others:[3]

The European political tradition could pretend to cast its politics over the entire world, paradoxically, because it conceived of Europe as a finite horizon,

---

[1] Daniel Bell, *The End of Ideology: On the Exhaustion of Political Ideas in the Fifties*, 2nd new edition of revised edition, Cambridge, MA: Harvard University Press, 2000, p. 400.

[2] Ibid., p. 401.

[3] On Hardt and Negri's argument and the 'Muslim multitudes' see further Arshin Adib-Moghaddam, 'Islamutopia, (Post)modernity and the Multitude', in Patrick Hayden and Chamsy el-Ojeili (eds), *Globalisation and Utopia: Critical essays*, London: Palgrave, 2009, pp. 137–155.

as "the West", where sun set, *finis terrae*. Europe had to escape its own finitude. Spatial elements are always present in Europe's own self-definition, at times in expansive terms and at others in conflictual, tragic, and obsessive ones, from Homer's Aegean to Columbus's Atlantic. ... Geopolitical space has thus become a trajectory, a directed movement of destiny over foreign territories defined by the dominant imperial classes. Thus was born the national and imperialist *Grossraum*.[4]

To Hardt and Negri, expansion is inherent in the idea of the 'West'. 'Post-colonial' theorists have established, and the present study has tapped into their findings, that the imperial culture thus constituted is not unstructured or unsystematic. It is reflected in the discourse and institutional artefacts that the imperial projects informed. At least since the eighteenth century onwards, a whole new terminology designating regions was created in accordance with the interests of the imperial functionaries. Beyond it, there developed corresponding disciplines with a 'scientific' agenda, i.e. Political Science, Geo-politics, Geography, Area Studies and International Relations (IR) at a later stage. These disciplines were meant to systematically charter the world in order to make sense of it, to compartmentalise it, to make it available, analysable, and controllable. Imperial functionaries had to know where to go in order to get there or to learn to effectively control what they had already conquered. The difference to spatial compartmentalisations in the classical and middle ages was, that the emerging disciplinary apparatus was highly systematised, that it developed an internal coherence that embedded and extended the causal principle scientifically. Said and others have linked these discourse-knowledge-power mutations to the Eurocentric mapping of the world that I touched upon in the last chapter explaining why we continue to deal with a phenomenon called the 'Middle East'.[5] It was the American naval

---

[4] Michael Hardt and Antonio Negri, *Multitude: War and Democracy in the Age of Empire*, London: Penguin, 2004, p. 313.

[5] On the invented delineation of the Middle East see Pinar Bilgin, 'Inventing Middle Easts: The Making of Regions Through Security Discourses', in Bjørn Olav Utvik and Knut S. Vikør (eds), *The Middle East in a Globalised World. Papers from the Fourth Nordic Conference on Middle Eastern Studies, Oslo 1998*, London: Hurst, 2000, pp. 10–37; Roderic H. Davison, 'Where is the Middle East?', in Richard Nolte (ed.), *The Modern Middle East*, New York: Columbia University Press, 1963, pp. 13–29; Ghassan Salamé, 'The Middle East: Elusive Security, Indefinable Region', *Security Dialogue*, vol. 25, no. 1 (1994), pp. 17–35; Bassam Tibi, *Conflict and War in the Middle East. From*

officer Alfred Thayer Mahan who introduced the term in an article published in the British *National Review* in 1902.[6] The geographical delimitation catered to the strategic interest of the British Empire and thus focused upon Aden, India and the Gulf area. Thereafter, the 'Middle East' was popularised by the *Times* of London where part of Mahan's article was published. Valentine Chirol, a *Times* correspondent who built a formidable career as an eminent 'Orientalist' in Europe and the United States, subsequently began publishing a series of articles dealing with the 'Middle Eastern Question' centring around India as the strategic heartland of the British Empire, which were compiled and subsequently republished as a book in 1903 titled *The Middle East Question or Some Problems of Indian Defence*. With shifting colonial and 'strategic interests', the delineation of the 'Middle East' changed as well. When Winston Churchill was British Colonial Minister, the term referred to the area between the Bosphorus and the borders of India, and when the colonial focus shifted towards Egypt after the Second World War, that country was considered to be the centre of the 'Middle East'. The borders of the 'region' thus shifted with the strategic interests of external powers, i.e. Great Britain and, after the Second World War, increasingly the United States. Objectively, the 'Middle East' does not exist of course.

The spatial bias of the human sciences disperses into the field of the clash regime yet another binary that is constitutive of its us-versus-them logic, that is the binary of the 'west and the rest' which in turn morphs into a 'west *against* the rest' dichotomy with Huntington.[7] This binary imagines for the 'West' a favourable environment in which the other is a designated place, a desired object with limited subjective agency. There emerges out of this environment an indulgence to write,

---

Interstate War to New Security, second edition, London: Macmillan, 1998, pp. 43–60.

[6] On Mahan see P.A. Crowl, 'Mahan: The Naval Historian', in Peter Paret (ed.), *Makers of Modern Strategy*. Princeton: Princeton University Press, 1986, pp. 444–447; Alfred Thayer Mahan, 'A Twentieth Century Outlook', *Harper's Monthly*, 1897; Akire Iriye, 'The second clash: Huntington, Mahan, and civilization', *Harvard International Review*, vol. 19, no. 2, 1997, pp. 44–70.

[7] For an introduction see Stuart Hall, 'The West and the Rest: Discourse and Power', in Tania Des Gupta (ed.), *Race and Racialisation: Essential Readings*, Toronto: Canadian Scholars Press, 2007, pp. 56–60.

think, and decide on behalf of those other people who are only marginally represented. Indeed, any acknowledgement of the other beyond this 'quasi-reality' is utterly dangerous because it reminds the self of the 'interdependent' ontology of the object, the agency of the other, her subjective existence beyond our cognitive inventions. This dents the possibility of control. The other suddenly appears 'bigger' than previously thought. At this point, one is reminded that one's own rootedness in history cannot be overcome, that we are not ageless. Suddenly, discontinuities appear. The imperialist stops believing in the causal efficacy to bring about universal changes; the Nazi is disenchanted with his race and commits suicide; Nietzsche proclaims (and laments) the death of God; Foucault the death of man; the white man crumbles under his burden. But only just until on the horizon, new universalities appear, new promises of a better tomorrow, new crusades, a new struggle, and yet another novel end of history for humankind.

One of the central reasons why proclamations about an impending 'end of history' (Hegel, Weber, Fukuyama etc) or the inevitable 'end of ideology' (Daniel Bell) have proven to be premature is that today, we all continue to exist within one of the most salient products of modernity—the nation-state. How can history end, when the nation-state continues to be the most potent carrier of national memories, which are physically and ideologically expressed in our museums, institutions, flags, national anthems etc.? How can the clash mentality be overcome, if the nation-state, by definition, needs to be filled with meaning, a mission, a will, authority or a *raison d'état* or *raison d'être*? Note that these terms are anthropomorphic, i.e. they ascribe human attributes to the otherwise lifeless body of the nation-state. A useful way of achieving a better understanding of the impact of such processes of 'individualisation' on the clash regime, is to focus on the sectarian nature of the contemporary international system and its constituent units (i.e. the nation-states); to show, in other words, how this system accentuates difference, signifies war and legitimates violence. This shall be the topic of the following paragraphs.

The modern nation-state continues to be one of the central incubators of the myth of some clash of civilisations. That the nation-state and its corresponding nationalisms exacerbate inter-group conflicts should not seem strange to those readers familiar with the genealogy of 'nation-building' in Europe. At least since the eighteenth century, there developed in Europe a dominant discourse that represented the state as more than a functional institution to organise the relationship between the aristocracy, the church and the 'nation'. In the writings of Johann Gottlieb Fichte (1762–1814), Hegel, Johann Gottfried von Herder (1744–1803), Giuseppe Mazzini (1805–72), John Stuart Mill (1806–1873), Leopold von Ranke (1795–1886) and others, the state is conceptualised as a normative concept, as a polity that is destined to fulfil a higher mission. It was during this period, in other words, that the idea(l) of the liberal state and its universal mission to export 'justice' and civilisation was born:

A civilised government cannot help having barbarous neighbours: when it has, it cannot always content itself with a defensive position, one of mere resistance to aggression. After a longer or shorter interval of forbearance, it either finds itself obliged to conquer them, or to assert so much authority over them, and so break their spirit, that they gradually sink into a state of dependence upon itself: and when that time arrives, they are indeed no longer formidable to it, but it has had so much to do with setting up and pulling down their governments, and they have grown so accustomed to lean on it, that it has become morally responsible for all evil it allows them to do. This is the history of the relations of the British government with the native States of India.[8]

For Mill, that most ardent social critic of mid-Victorian Britain, the just cause of the British Empire to civilise other nations justifies the means, in this case to conquer 'barbarous neighbours' or 'to break their spirit' until they 'gradually sink into a state of dependence'. We have already established that the ideas of nation, people, civilisation and racial superiority are never very far apart. The idea of nation-hood exacerbates divisions. It is, by definition, exclusionary because it presupposes and engenders belief in difference. The idea of racial distinction is merely one manifestation of this belief in seemingly distinct identities setting us apart from others. But Mill's mode of argumentation is not reliant on the issue of race, at least not explicitly. What Mill defends is the suspension of the 'national' sovereignty of the other, i.e. uncivilised nations. He is denying them the opportunity to turn the sovereignty principle on Europe itself. In this sense, national sovereignty was deemed a prerogative of the civilised nations of Europe. 'To suppose that the same international customs, and the same rules of international morality, can obtain between one civilised nation and

[8] John Stuart Mill, *Dissertations and Discussions: Political, Philosophical and Historical*, vol. 3, London: Longmans, Green, Reader, and Dyer, 1867, pp. 168–169.

another, and between civilised nations and barbarians', Mill argues, 'is a grave error, and one which no statesmen can fall into, however it may be with those who, from a safe and unresponsible position, criticise statesmen. ... The only moral laws for the relation between a civilised and a barbarous government', Mill concludes, 'are the universal rules of morality between man and man'.[9] If the 'British nation' was the carrier of a higher cause, it was obliged to enforce its values globally, if necessary by force. This is the central premise of the modern 'liberal-crusader state' that is the product of European imperialisms in the eighteenth and nineteenth centuries. It arrogates to itself the mission to export liberty and freedom to those less fortunate peoples, who are presumed to suffer under the yoke of their own backwardness.[10]

So the concerted attack on the sovereignty of the multitudes is a function of the metaphysical mystification of the 'Westphalian' nation-state. In Europe, the nation-state emerged as a normative invention filled with a Hegelian *Geist*, spirit or consciousness. According to Hegel, the 'nation state (*das Volk als Staat*) is the spirit in its substantial rationality and immediate actuality, and is therefore the absolute power on earth'. While he acknowledges that 'each state is consequently a sovereign and independent entity in relation to others', he also notes that for 'any people at a low level of culture' this principle of mutual respect is not applicable because the 'question even arises of how far this people can be regarded as a state'. Moreover, according to Hegel the 'religious viewpoint (as in former times with the Jewish and Mohammedan nations (*Völkern*) may further entail a higher opposition which precludes that universal identity that recognition requires'.[11]

Thus, at the time when the modern principle of national sovereignty was signified, there was a tendency to immediately reserve it for relations between European, or 'civilised' nations. 'We are more enlightened and more powerful than the Arabs', writes Alexis de Tocqueville in his *Second Letter on Algeria*. 'In the time of the fall of the Roman Empire, we saw reign at the same time barbaric laws to which the

---

[9] Ibid., p. 167

[10] On the utility of 'significant others' for the discursive construction of Europe's collective identity formation, see also Iver B. Neumann, *Uses of the Other: 'The East' in European Identity Formation*, Minneapolis: University of Minnesota Press, 1999.

[11] G.W.F. Hegel, 'From Elements of the Philosophy of Right', in Brown, Nardin, Rengger (eds), *International Relations in Political Thought*, p. 471.

Barbar was submitted and Roman laws to which the Roman was submitted'.[12] Even in the writings of Hugo Grotius (1583–1645), represented by many IR theorists today as the forefather of international law, there is this tendency to confine principles and norms to a particular civilisational habitat, in his case Christianity. 'Throughout the Christian world', he argues, 'I observed a lack of restraint in relation to war, such as even barbarous races should be ashamed of'.[13] The object here is the 'Christian world' and Grotius and his followers were conscious that their normative constructions were meant to pacify relations between what was considered to be the civilised nations of Europe. For Grotius, this exclusive *jus publicum Europaeum* was very functional to legitimate imperial expansion.[14] 'Hence it is plain, because it has to be admitted', the German Professor of Law at the University of Halle Christian von Wolff (1679–1754) writes, 'that what has been approved by the more civilised nations *is* the law of nations'.[15] David Hume (1711–1776) referred to the 'fate of Europe', Jean-Jacques Rousseau (1712–1778) to the future 'commonwealth of Europe', and Adam Smith dwelled on Great Britain's economic transactions with other European kingdoms such as Portugal. For all these canonical writers, by the necessity of the cultural habitat they were accustomed to, and the conflicts they were immersed in, international relations meant interactions between European countries. International law was thought to be primarily applicable to Europe and re-definable when it came to relations with others. Consequently, there emerged a

---

[12] Alexis de Tocqueville, 'Second Letter on Algeria', reprinted in Michael J. Thompson (ed.), *Islam and the West: Critical Perspectives on Modernity*, Oxford: Rowman & Littlefield, 2003, p. 147.

[13] Hugo Grotius, 'From *The Law of War and Peace*', in Brown, Nardin and Rengger (eds), *International Relations in Political Thought*, p. 333.

[14] See further Anthony Angie, *Imperialism, Sovereignty and the Making of International Law*, Cambridge: Cambridge University Press, 2005. On Grotius see Richard Tuck, *The Rights of War and Peace: Political Thought and the International Order from Grotius to Kant*, Oxford: Oxford University Press, 2001, chapter 3 and Karma Nabulsi, 'Conceptions of Justice in War: From Grotius to Modern Times', in Richard Sorabji and David Rodin (eds), *The Ethics of War: Shared Problems in Different Traditions*, Aldershot: Ashgate, 2006, pp. 44–60.

[15] Christian von Wolff, 'From *The Law of Nations Treated According to a Scientific Method*', in Brown, Nardin and Rengger (eds), *International Relations in Political Thought*, p. 366, emphasis added.

'bifurcated international order: an horizontal international law for relations between European states and a hierarchical imperial law for relations between European and non-European peoples' as Terry Nardin recently argued.[16] Inevitably, the norms of *jus ad bellum* (justice in going to war) and *jus in bello* (justice in the conduct of war) have been practically *and* theoretically amenable to such notions of what is just and normatively defensible in the first place. 'I do not understand this squeamishness about the use of gas', said Winston Churchill symptomatically in 1919 when he was Secretary of State at the War Office. 'I am strongly in favour of using poisoned gas against uncivilised tribes'. The uncivilised tribes that Churchill refers to were the Arab and Kurdish movements that resisted the British occupation of what became to be known as Iraq. 'It is not necessary to use only the most deadly gasses', Churchill continued, 'gasses can be used which cause great inconvenience and would spread a lively terror and yet would leave no serious permanent effects on most of those affected'.[17] For Churchill, then, creating 'terror' was a viable policy tool to subdue the anti-colonial movement in Iraq which was deemed to be driven by 'uncivilised tribes', rather than real people, a whole range of Arab and Kurdish nationalists and oppositional clerics with real political agendas and grievances against their colonial masters.

Although I have cited examples from different authors who were immersed in very different politico-cultural constellations, they accurately describe that the discourse of race, civilisation and sovereignty were connected in the *zeitgeist* of modernity and its imperial outgrowth. Hypocrisy and double standards were inscribed not only in the way international politics were studied and represented, but also in the way foreign policy decisions were made. Only a minority of thinkers understood that advocating a universal order lacks moral authority if it is not based on mutually agreed, 'cosmopolitan' norms. From the trajectory of European political theories and at a later stage in the discipline of International Relations, the eighteenth century German philosopher Immanuel Kant (1724–1804) emerged as one of the most

[16] Terry Nardin, 'Theorising the international rule of law', *Review of International Studies*, vol. 34, no. 3, Jul. 2008, p. 388.
[17] Winston Churchill, 'War Office Departmental Minute, Churchill Papers, 12 May 1919. Available at http://globalresearch.ca/articles/CHU407A.html [Last accessed 12 May 2009].

prominent theoreticians of such 'idealistic' theories that purported a rather more critical attitude towards the plight of the colonialised other:

If we compare with this ultimate end the *inhospitable* conduct of the civilised states of our continent, especially the commercial states, the injustice which they display in *visiting* foreign countries and peoples (which in their case is the same as *conquering* them) seems appallingly great. America, the negro countries, the Spice Islands, the Cape, etc. were looked upon at the time of their discovery as ownerless territories; for the native inhabitants were counted as nothing. In East India (Hindustan), foreign troops were brought in under the pretext of merely setting up trading posts. This led to oppression of the natives, incitement of the various Indian states to widespread wars, famine, insurrection, treachery and the whole litany of evils which can afflict the human race.[18]

And yet even Kant, who continues to be a focal point of many 'idealist' or 'cosmopolitan' political theories until today, could not escape the consensus of his time.[19] It is symptomatic for the *zeitgeist* enveloping him, that in his *Observations on the Feeling of the Beautiful and the Sublime* (1764) he endorses some of the racist views expressed by the aforementioned David Hume. Thus, the categorical inferiority of 'the Negro' expressed by the Scot receives its 'transcendental' authority with the Prussian:

The Negroes of Africa have by nature no feeling that rises above the trifling. Mr. Hume challenges anyone to cite a single example in which a Negro has shown talents, and asserts that among the hundreds of thousands of blacks who are transported elsewhere from their countries, although many of them have even been set free, still not a single one was ever found who presented anything great in art or science or any other praiseworthy quality, even though among the whites some continually rise aloft from the lowest rabble, and through superior gifts earn respect in the world. So fundamental is the difference between these two races of man, and it appears to be as great in regard to mental capacities as in colour. The religion of fetishes so widespread among them is perhaps a sort of idolatry that sinks as deeply into the trifling as appears to be possible to human nature. A bird's feather, a cow's horn, a conch shell, or any other common object, as soon as it becomes consecrated by a few

[18] Immanuel Kant, 'From Perpetual Peace', in Brown, Nardin and Rengger (eds), *International Relations in Political Thought*, 2003, p. 442.

[19] On the Kantian ideas of 'cosmopolitanism' and 'perpetual peace' and their potential significance for contemporary politics, see among others James Bohman and Matthias Lutz-Bachmann (eds), *Perpetual Peace: Essays on Kant's Cosmopolitan Ideal*, Cambridge, MA: MIT Press, 1997.

words, is an object of veneration and of invocation in swearing oaths. The blacks are very vain but in the Negro's way, and so talkative that they must be driven apart from each other by thrashings.[20]

In his lectures on 'Physical Geography' in the latter phase of the 'critical investigations', Kant argues that people who live in 'temperate' climatic conditions such as in Europe are more 'perfect' and developed than those in hot countries.[21] Kant's 'transcendental idealism' did not merely bring about a paradigmatic revolution in modern philosophy then. It also led to a 'scientific' conceptualisation of race. This theory of race, which emphasised that whites are objectively superior to non-whites, made a decisive contribution to the field of 'physical geography'.[22] Authoritative mixing of political geography and degrees of development are linked here to a new type of scientific racism that could only emerge out of a distinctively positivistic methodology. The point I am re-emphasising is that many canonical authors of (international) political theories writing during the Enlightenment, were not cosmopolitan well wishers who were looking for a rather more inclusive dialogue among cultures. Rather, they were intoxicated by the euphoria of their age, they objectified difference; they were utterly convinced that their methodological prejudice against the lesser, non-European peoples can be scientifically justified, even measured.[23]

Let me interrogate this discussion about discourse, power and (mis) representation with a question now: is it not impossible to escape from hegemonic subjectivities which are engrained in our universities and written all over the archives that we research? Is it not impossible to imagine an 'other' beyond the discursive shackles we put on him? In

---

[20] Immanuel Kant, 'Of National Characteristics, so far as they depend upon the distinct feeling of the beautiful and the sublime', in idem, *Observations on the Feeling of the Beautiful and the Sublime*, John T. Goldthwait (trans.), Berkeley: University of California Press, 2004, pp. 110–111.

[21] See further Emmanuel Chukwudi Eze, 'The Colour of Reason: The Idea of Race in Kant's Anthropology', in idem. (ed.), *Postcolonial African Philosophy: A Critical Reader*, Oxford: Blackwell, 1997, pp. 103–140; ibid., *Race and the Enlightenment: A Reader*, Oxford: Blackwell, 1997.

[22] Ibid., *Achieving our Humanity: The idea of the Postracial Future*, London: Routledge, 2001.

[23] See further Susan E. Babbit and Sue Campbell (eds), *Racism and Philosophy*, Ithaca: Cornell University Press, 1999; Bernard Boxil (ed.), *Race and Racism*, Oxford: Oxford University Press, 2001; Julie K. Ward and Tommy L. Lott (eds), *Philosophers on Race: Critical Essays*, Oxford: Blackwell, 2002.

Orientalism, Edward Said says yes. According to him, the hegemony of Orientalism is inescapable; it seriously constrains our ability to achieve a rather more 'empathetic' understanding of the other. Even if we do not agree with this gloomy assessment in total, there is enough evidence today that seems to corroborate the pessimism of Said. Despite nascent counter-discourses of a 'subaltern' kind that Said himself acknowledged in his later writings, major disciplines in the social sciences have not effected methodological/epistemological inclusiveness. The increasingly popular field of International Relations (or 'International Studies') is a case in point. A recent survey of this discipline serves as an entry into a discussion of the political economy that underpins its 'ethnocentric' academic culture:

If hegemony means that most of the resources (richest universities and private foundations in the world), most authors in the top ranked journals (76 percent in 12 peer reviewed journals), and top universities (16 of the top 20) come, overwhelmingly, from the United States, then, yes, American IR is hegemonic. U.S. scholars are recognised more often as the "most influential" scholars in the discipline by their peers in the United States but also in the rest of the world ...[24]

In other words, the prominence and influence of US scholars is affected by the political economy of the field, i.e. the academic and industrial production of IR in the United States. This US-centric infrastructure has created a particularly 'white', almost coherently 'western' discipline. It is not only that the editorial boards of the leading IR journals are primarily staffed by scholars residing in North America (and a few in Western Europe).[25] 'International' theories themselves are almost entirely written from a 'Euro/Americo-centric' perspective. The

---

[24] Richard Jordan, Daniel Maliniak, Amy Oakes, Susan Peterson and Michael J. Tierney, *One Discipline or Many? TRIPP Survey of International Relations Faculty in Ten Countries*, Institute for the Theory and Practice of International Relations, College of William and Mary, Williamsburg, Virginia, 2009.

[25] Ibid. See further Steve Smith, 'The United States and the Discipline of International Relations: "Hegemonic country, hegemonic discipline"', *International Studies Review*, vol. 4, no. 2, Summer 2002, pp. 67–85; Robert Crawford and Darryl Jarvis (eds), *International Relations: Still an American Social Science? Towards Diversity in International Thought*, Albany, NY: State University of New York Press, 2001; K. J. Holsti, *The Dividing Discipline: Hegemony and Diversity in International Theory*, London: Allen and Unwin, 1985.

two most powerful paradigms, Liberalism, with its Idealist underbelly, and Realism, are very different with regard to their theoretical and methodological rules, but related to the same epistemological field; their theoretical premises and the terms and concepts they employ are firmly rooted in the Euro-American experience of world politics. The very language of IR, e.g. rational choice, anarchy, balance-of-power, security community, national-interest, liberal, Westphalian nation-state etc., signify cultural, political and socio-economic conditions prevalent in eighteenth/nineteenth/twentieth century Europe. Naturally, they denote the realities during the time and at the place these theories were invented in. Even the seemingly universal 'state of nature' that Hobbes explained, and which has been used (some would say 'abused) by 'political realists' to denote the 'perennial state of anarchy' of the international system, is entirely populated by beasts and predators that exist in a western habitat. The Iranian cheetah, the Indian Tiger and the poisonous snakes of the Arabian Desert are absent from it. Unsurprisingly then, contemporary controversies in the field are primarily driven by the competition between Europeans and Americans, who wrangle for dominance over the western heritage of the discipline which is taken for granted:

If international relations is an American social science, this is due to a large extent to the contributions of European-born and European-educated scholars, including the author of 'An American Social Science' [Stanley Hoffman] himself. If asked to name the truly great figures in the academic field of international relations, I would mention Sir Alfred Zimmern, E.H. Carr, Quincy Wright, Hans J. Morgenthau, Karl Deutsch, and possibly also Arnold Toynbee, Arnold Wolfers, and Raymond Aron. Only one of them was born and educated in the United States.[26]

[26] Norman D. Palmer, 'The Study of International Relations in the United States: Perspective of Half a Century', *International Studies Quarterly*, vol. 24, no. 3, Sept. 1980, pp. 347–348. See further Miles Kahler, 'Inventing International Relations: International Relations Theory after 1945', in Michael W. Doyle and G. John Ikenberry (eds), *New Thinking in International Relations Theory*, London: Westview, 1997, pp. 20–53; Steve Smith, 'The Discipline of International Relations: Still and American Social Science?', *British Journal of Politics and International Relations*, vol. 2, no. 3, 2000, pp. 374–402; Ole Waever, 'The Sociology of a not so International Discipline: American and European Developments in International Relations', *International Organization*, vol. 52, no. 4, Autumn 1998, pp. 687–727.

The discipline of International Relations, ever since it was invented and institutionalised in the early-twentieth century with a professorship at the University of Wales at Aberystwyth, has internalised a good deal of its biases and exclusionary methodologies. This 'self-confidence of IR' is criticised, because it 'is rooted to some extent in a general sense of progress and achievement that enables the almost triumphal embrace of what is seen as an expansion of European or Western civilisation'.[27] In other words, via a discipline called IR, the constructed ontology of the international system that is based on western perceptions of it, has developed a 'quasi objective' status which is taken to be thoroughly 'realistic' by its adherents. 'We have to bring off the Copernican revolution', writes Kenneth Waltz, the founder of 'neo-realist' international theory. 'A theory has explanatory and predictive power' he adds.[28] And since it is always 'written in terms of the great powers of an era', power being quantified entirely in materialist terms, it does not make sense 'to construct a theory of international politics based on Malaysia and Costa Rica'.[29] It goes without saying that from the perspective of Waltz power is uni-directional. It always moves from the core to the periphery.

Realist IR theories, including Waltz's amended 'systemic' version, depart from the notion that the international system is 'anarchic', that there is no institution beyond the nation-state that could effectively mitigate conflict. In a recent study, Booth and Wheeler have reemphasised that the element of Hobbesian fear, anarchy, uncertainty and mistrust has been pivotal to the canon of the discipline of IR; essential to the writings of John Herz and Hans Morgenthau in the United States, the British historian Herbert Butterfield and 'second-generation realists' such as John J. Mearsheimer and the aforementioned Kenneth Waltz.[30] Via a particular interpretation of Hobbes, political realism

---

[27] Branwen Gruffydd Jones (ed.), *Decolonising International Relations*, Plymouth: Rowman & Littlefield, 2006, p. 7.

[28] Kenneth N. Waltz, 'Reductionist and Systemic Theories', in Robert O. Keohane (ed.), *Neorealism and its Critics*, New York: Columbia University Press, 1985, p. 57. See further his *Theory of International Politics*, New York: McGraw-Hill, 1979.

[29] Waltz, 'Reductionist and Systemic Theories', in Keohane (ed.), *Neorealism*, p. 61.

[30] Ken Booth and Nicholas J. Wheeler, *The Security Dilemma: Fear, Cooperation and Trust in World Politics*, London: Palgrave, 2008, especially pp. 21 ff.

represents the international system as the ultimate other to be feared and tamed. This international other, the 'foreign' in foreign policy, makes possible the fundamental distinction between the internal and external, us and them. In the absence of a concept such as the international system, the nation-state fails to formulate its boundaries. The international becomes the field of the possible to be tamed. The international system as other appears as that which organises the boundary of our artificial identity and which festers a particular kind of desire: the desire to explore and conquest the cunning world out there. From this perspective, foreign policy becomes both a boundary-producing practice 'central to the production and reproduction of the identity in whose name it operates' as Campbell notes,[31] and a boundary-extending practice that continuously externalises the sovereignty of the nation-state into the international, the ultimate realm of possibility.

Such an understanding of the international as a desired object links up with a famous Marxist caveat: 'The bourgeoisie', Marx and Engels famously state, 'compels all nations, on pain of extinction, to adopt the bourgeois mode of production; it compels them to introduce what it calls civilisation into their midst, i.e. to become bourgeois themselves. In one word it creates the world after its own image'.[32] Hannah Arendt places Hobbes at the juncture of the 'so-called accumulation of capital which gave birth to the bourgeoisie' and the imperial conquests of modernity.[33] According to her, 'Hobbes was the true, though never fully recognised, philosopher of the bourgeoisie because he realised that acquisition of wealth conceived as a never-ending process can be guaranteed only by the seizure of political power, for the accumulating process must sooner or later force open all existing territorial limits'.[34]

Arendt points to a very particular form of historical isomorphism that emerges out of the modern conceptualisation of power that accentuates the necessity of conquest beyond territorial boundaries. She identifies, via Marx and Engels, both the bourgeoisie and Hobbes as instigators of this quest for sameness, the quintessential attribute of

---

[31] David Campbell, *Writing Security: United States Foreign Policy and the Politics of Identity*, Manchester: Manchester University Press, 1992, p. 68.

[32] Karl Marx and Friedrich Engels, *Manifesto of the Communist Party*, London: Verso, 1998, p. 40.

[33] Hannah Arendt, *The Origins of Totalitarianism*, Ohio: World Publishing Co., 1958, p. 190.

[34] Ibid., p. 195.

any ordered system. In other words, Arendt points to the dangers of the bourgeois sovereignty that was signified by Hobbes. From this perspective, creating world orders means destroying counter-realities, counter-identities, annihilating otherness. Foreign policy becomes an effort to reduce multiplicity, to dispel those other people that question the way the modern individual thinks, speaks and acts. Once the other is turned modern (*viz*. bourgeois), he loses the characteristics that make him different in the first place. In this sense, the 'realist' fulcrum of the discipline of International Relations is particularly modern and by implication, Arendt would add, overtly 'bourgeois'. Is it thus inevitable that Hobbes returns as the philosopher of power and sovereignty in that deepest discursive plateau of contemporary international theories?[35]

The egregious omissions of modern IR theories such as neo-realism have not been scrupulously exposed by scholarship yet, which is not at least due to the self-perpetuating academic culture of the discipline. Even the caesura of the field after the demise of 'bipolarity', the idea that everything in the international system evolved around the Cold War between the United States and the Soviet Union, has not brought about radical change, despite some salutary movements into alternative directions spearheaded by scholars such as Richard K. Ashley, Robert Cox, Richard Jackson and David Campbell. So most critical IR scholars continue to point out that the 'historiographical turn' that has only recently become a subject, is only recognised as such by a handful of authors in Europe. More dramatically, sensitive issues such as the 'white supremacy' constraining the discipline, are 'not generally discussed either as a historical identity of the American state or an ideo-

---

[35] Even nuanced internationalisms at the heart of 'happy' Globalisation theories encapsulated in the metaphor of the 'global village', or Hardt and Negri's 'Multitude' stand accused of this desire for sameness, for grand paradigms that reduce the peoples of the world to the smallest common denominator encapsulated in the cultures exported by the 'western core'. From this perspective, social networking sites such as Facebook, the Internet, MTV, CNN, multinational companies, mass produced global 'icons' such as Britney Spears, Justin Timberlake or Paris Hilton have also a ready-made political function. They are elements of a larger politico-cultural machinery that compels others to turn into people who think and act a little bit more like 'we' do. If the other does not yield to this pressure, the right-wing continuously caution, he needs to be segregated or 'equalised' through violence, if necessary.

logical commitment on which the "interdiscipline" of international relations is founded'.[36] Even as perceptive a theorist as Alexander Wendt, who has emerged as one of the most prominent proponents of 'constructivist' international theory, differentiates merely between 'Hobbesian', 'Lockean' and 'Kantian' forms of anarchy. He is not taking into consideration that Ibn Khaldun, Sun Tzu or Simon Bolivar had very different conceptions of the nature of conflict between collective entities, groups, nations or other.[37] It is true, despite some critical movements within the field, that a 'genuinely "post-western" critical international theory would interrogate not only the positivist methodology of IR but also the concomitant assumptions of western cultural distinctiveness and superiority which are constitutive of the discipline'.[38]

If the story would end here, it would be rather harmless. It is not only that the 'knowledge produced out of such a field is inadequate even to its own clientele', as Tarak Barkawi and my colleague at SOAS, Mark Laffey rightly observe.[39] It is not merely that the 'nascent cosmopolitan culture of today, like the international society which it helps to sustain, is weighted in favour of the dominant cultures of the West', as Hedley Bull remarks.[40] An understanding of international politics that is almost entirely rooted in a western epistemology signifies, quite literally, an international system that appears different if viewed from another perspective. Ultimately, 'International Relations (IR)', as it is represented in the curricula of so many Universities today, re-inscribes a biased political culture into the international system. Thus, as a discipline, IR positions itself along the series of social sciences that proclaim a universal mandate, but turn out to be entirely relative, tied to

---

[36] Robert Vitalis, 'Birth of a Discipline', in David Long and Brian C. Schmidt (eds), *Imperialism and Internationalism in the Discipline of International Relations*, New York: State University of New York Press, 2005, p. 160.

[37] See Alexander Wendt, *Social Theory of International Politics*, Cambridge: Cambridge University Press, 1999.

[38] Giorgio Shani, 'Toward a Post-Western IR: The *Umma, Khalsa Panth*, and Critical International Relations Theory', *International Studies Review*, vol. 10, issue 4, Dec. 2008, p. 723. See also Pinar Bilgin, 'Thinking Past "Western" IR?', *Third World Quarterly*, vol. 29, no. 1, 2008, pp. 5–23.

[39] Tarak Barkawi and Mark Laffey, 'The Postcolonial Moment in Security Studies', *Review of International Studies*, vol. 32, no. 2, Apr. 2006, p. 352.

[40] Hedley Bull, *The Anarchical Society: A Study of Order in World Politics*, 2nd edition, London: Macmillan, 1995, p. 205.

a particular cultural loci, if judged from the perspective of the proclaimed 'outsiders':

IR has inherited the orientalist mentality generated through the long history of European encounters with non-European peoples and cultures. With its originary Orientalism, it has been impossible for IR to approach and understand politics, international relations, and social process in Islamic cultural zones on their own terms. When turning to the question of Islam, then, we immediately confront the cultural limits of the IR discipline: Islam is beyond IR's field of apprehension as anything other than a caricature. The discipline of IR claims boldly to understand the world and offer universal knowledge. Yet in the face of Islam, IR is paralyzed; it retreats to the apparently firm ground of old assumptions of essential difference and the barbarity of the Other ...[41]

A practical consequence follows from the Eurocentrism intrinsic to the discourse of international relations and the sovereignty principle defined by its interpreters in Europe and the United States: the culture of today's international system, reflected in multilateral institutions such as the United Nations Organisation (UNO) and 'norms of appropriate behaviour' such as prohibitions on torture or genocide, do not so much establish a just world order as to bring into play the sovereignty of the powerful vis-à-vis the weak. This type of sovereignty does not disallow a continually reinforced legitimation of war. Rather the contrary. It continues to convince us that it is not merely morally justifiable to invade other nations, but also legally defensible. This is different from earlier notions of such 'just' wars. For Thomas Aquinas (1225–1274) who followed 'Augustine's understanding of war as a consequence of sin',[42] war is justified if three conditions are met: a) it must be authorised by a sovereign authority, b) there must be a just cause, and c) the warring parties should have a rightful intention. For Grotius, it is self-defence, enforcing rights, seeking reparations and punishing wrongdoers that make a war just. In the absence of inter-governmental organisation such as the League of Nations and its successor the UNO, these antecedents to the just war theories, cultivated today by Jean-Bethke-Elshtain, Michael Walzer and others, were primarily depended on normative legitimation; wars were primarily sold as a religious/national duty or as a means to defend or extend civilisation.

---

[41] Jones (ed.), *Decolonising International Relations*, p. 9.
[42] Brown, Nardin, Rengger (eds), *International Relations in Political Thought*, p. 183.

In today's international system and the culture permeating it, all of the discriminatory functions of the just war tradition are multiplied because they adopt legal properties. The 'just' wars in Vietnam, Kosovo, Iraq (1990 and 2003), Afghanistan (2001) and elsewhere were represented as such not only from a moral standpoint, as wars to fight evil (Islamist, Arabist, Communist or other), there were systematic attempts to turn them into *legal* wars. 'Collective historically constructed and ongoingly reinscribed exemplars come into play when we consider war and war making in the West', acknowledges Jean Bethke-Elshtain. 'Thus war entices us in part, because we continue to locate ourselves inside its prototypical emblems and identities—the just war fighter, the heroine of the home front, the country united and the like'.[43] Elshtain refers here to the immense identity inducing powers of war. War creates a reality in which we are more easily forced to declare which side we are actually on—'you are either with us or against us' in George W. Bush's oft-cited words. Alas, Elshtain herself felt compelled to reify that ancient binary which reappeared with intense vigour after the terrorist attacks on New York and the Pentagon in September 2001. Symptomatic for the politics of the United States during the presidency of George W. Bush, she linked the 'War on Terror' to the just war principles of Augustine[44] arguing that 'ideas about the dignity of the human person are central to American democracy because they flow directly from the religiously shaped commitment of Americans'.[45] A similar link to Augustine is suggested in the aforementioned letter signed by sixty US scholars in the aftermath of 9/11. The signatories include Elshtain, Huntington and Fukuyama:

The primary moral justification for war is to protect the innocent from certain harm. Augustine, whose early fifth-century book, *The City of God* is a seminal contribution to just war thinking, argues (echoing Socrates) that it is better for the Christian as an individual to suffer harm rather than to commit it. But is the morally responsible person also required, or even permitted, to make for *other* innocent persons a commitment to non self-defense? For Augustine, and for the broader just war tradition, the answer is no. If one has compelling evi-

---

[43] Jean Bethke Elshtain, 'Feminist Themes and International Relations', in James Der Derian (ed.), *International Theory: Critical Investigations*, London: Macmillan, 1995, p. 348.

[44] Idem., *Just War Against Terror: The Burden of American Power in a Violent World*, Basic Books: New York, 2003, p. 49

[45] Ibid., p. 38.

dence that innocent people who are in no position to protect themselves will be grievously harmed unless coercive force is used to stop an aggressor, then the moral principle of love of neighbour calls us to the use of force.[46]

From this perspective, the ultimate justification of the United States' right to wage war, first in Afghanistan in 2001 and then in Iraq in 2003, is that it is meant to have an ordering effect, that it civilises international society, and that it ratifies the fundamental distinction between friend and enemy. If this society is once again threatened by 'savage barbarians' as 9/11 showed, if international politics is in a state of anarchy as theorists of IR argue, it is necessary to pacify that system in order to secure the future of civilisation.

Elshtain, Fukuyama and Huntington could have used their prominent position to promote an alternative counter-discourse in Europe and the United States which emphasises that the Judeo-Christian premise 'love thy neighbour' implies a permanent politics of anti-violence, even if the neighbour asserts him or herself through terror. They could have employed the ideas of Walter Benjamin, Jacques Derrida or Eric Santner to present sophisticated notions of an alternative 'politics of friendship' or 'redemption' in order to interrogate the awesome power of the state.[47] They could have suggested positioning the United States in lieu with a global alliance, especially with Muslim countries, that would have been strong enough to marginalise the common enemy. They could have stressed the power of diplomacy. They could have resisted the temptations of the clash regime. But they did not. Instead they chose to legitimate the politics of the day and the hegemonic discourse of the Presidency of George W. Bush. As such they are a part of a long list of scholars in North America and Europe, who have theorised the ordering effects of war. From that perspective, war is represented, not as an invented social institution that needs to be contained, but as a viable option to order domestic and international society—war as politics by other means in the words of the Prussian soldier and theorist Carl von Clausewitz (1780–1831). Once theorised

[46] 'What We're Fighting For: A Letter from America', in David Blankenhorn, Abdou Filali-Ansary, Hassan I. Mneimneh, and Alex Roberts (eds), *The Islam/West Debate: Documents from a Global Debate on Terrorism, U.S. policy, and the Middle East*, Oxford: Rowman & Littlefield, 2005, p. 27.

[47] See further Slavoj Žižek, Eric L. Santner and Kenneth Reinhard, *The Neighbor: Three Inquiries in Political Theology*, Chicago: The University of Chicago Press, 2005.

in such a manner, war is legitimated; it turns into a viable tool in the hands of states, and a dangerous narrative professing some clash between civilisations or between civilisation and barbarity. A mini-genealogy places Elshtain and Huntington next to Carl Schmitt (1888–1985), another influential thinker who subscribes to the idea that war is inevitable: 'The political enemy need not be morally evil or aesthetically ugly; he need not appear as an economic competitor, and it may even be advantageous to engage with him in business transactions', Schmitt asserted in 1932. 'But he is nevertheless, the other, the stranger; and it is sufficient for his nature that he is, in a specifically intense way, existentially something different and alien, so that in the extreme case conflicts with him are possible'.[48] It is this notion of the perennial existence and threat of the enemy that continues to have an impact on the mindset of decision-makers, not because war is a fact of nature, but because it has been represented as such throughout the centuries. In this way aggression is normalised. Killing the other continues to be accepted, nay, deemed necessary in order to secure our polis. And so war remains an irresistible consequence of the clash regime and the clash regime remains an irresistible consequence of war.

The idea that it is necessary to 'civilise' others in order to create a world in one's own image reveals a central pathology. It stems from a sense of paranoia. In other words, the indelible urge to 'liberate' others from their selves in order to superimpose a western identity on them does nothing but exemplify a sense of profound insecurity in a world that does not yield to such aspirations. I have started to argue that in both the traditional imperialist discourse and the neo-imperial one, war is presented as a necessary device to create order in a world that is deemed to be unruly and frightening. But this is not merely a utilitarian choice in order to legitimate domination. There is also an 'irrational' dimension to be considered here. Ultimately, it is also the fear of the alien world, not only power politics, that has driven Europe and the United States into recurring clashes with other nations and peoples. In short, the alleged 'anarchy' of the international system can be identified as an incubator and manifestation of a paranoiac attitude. As such, anarchy is a cognitive disposition rather than a fact of nature. It is a pathological conviction that has serious implications for world politics.

---

[48] Carl Schmitt, *The Concept of the Political*, George Schwab (trans.), Chicago: University of Chicago Press, 2007, p. 27

As Campbell and Jackson have demonstrated in their studies of US foreign policies: many decision-makers and experts of international relations have internalised the idea that the international system is a place of perennial war and destruction.[49] The disciples of the clash regime flourish within such a habitat, which explains their firm grip over the discipline of IR. No wonder then that it is out of the confined academic culture of that discipline that Huntington's clash of civilisations thesis emerged in the first place.

That the idea of anarchy and the perennial security dilemma emanating from an unruly international system is not a fact of nature, but a psychological factor can be qualified more succinctly with a short excursus into the period of the Cold War. Several scholars have established that during that imperial competition with the Soviet Union, elites in the United States displayed a particularly virulent manifestation of this pathological fear from the 'evil' and cunning world out there. From the outset, exemplified in National Security Council Memoranda 68 authored by Paul H. Nitze in April 1950, that is shortly before the war in Korea, the competition with the Soviet Union was characterised as a war 'for the survival of the free world', as a war between light and darkness, a war for civilisation.[50] From then on, the discourse delivering the 'Cold War' is entirely dependent on the element of fear. 'On the basis of mutual fear', writes the former Dean of the School of Advanced and International Studies (SAIS) at Johns Hopkins University in 1985, 'the superpowers have developed unprecedented constraints on the use of force'. It is '[b]ecause of this mutual fear', i.e. the fear of mutually assured destruction (MAD), that 'the highest prospects for moral improvement in the management of force lie not in avoiding or abolishing force but in carefully cultivating the modalities for limiting and controlling force—including nuclear force—as a rational instrument of policy'. At the same time, we are reminded that these 'prospects', i.e. the prospect for moral improvement through fear, 'do not exist for countries of the Third World', not because they are not afraid in the first place, but because they are in

[49] Campbell, *Writing Security*, Richard Jackson, *Writing the War on Terrorism: Language, Politics and Counterterrorism*, Manchester: Manchester University Press, 2005.
[50] Foreign Relations of the United States (FRUS), 1950, vol. 1, pp. 234–292, declassified in 1975. See also Chomsky, *Deterring Democracy*, pp. 10 ff.

the throes of 'a new barbarism ... One can only hope', we are alerted, 'that with the growing interdependence of relations among modernised and less-developed countries, some of the restraints [induced by fear] that have emerged among the former will spill over to the latter'.[51] Such pronounced emphasis on the element of fear can be found in the writings of a range of central strategists of US foreign policy, especially those with a 'realist' agenda. The following paragraph extracted from an article written towards the end of the Cold War by the former US Ambassador to the Soviet Union and the godfather of 'containment theory', George Kennan, serves as yet another example:

And the weapons race [between the United States and the Soviet Union] is not all there is *in this imperfect world that needs to be contained*. There are many other sources of instability and trouble. There are local danger spots scattered about in the Third World. ... [I]f we are going to talk about containment in the context of 1985, then I think we can no longer apply that term just to the Soviet Union, and particularly not to a view of the Soviet Union drawn too extensively from the image of the Stalin era, or, in some instances, from the even more misleading image of our Nazi opponents in the last great war. ... [B]eyond that, we are going to have to recognise that a large proportion of the sources of our troubles and dangers lies outside the Soviet challenge, such as it is, and some of it even *within ourselves*. And for these reasons we are going to have to develop a wider concept of what containment means—a concept more closely linked to *the totality of the problems of Western civilisation* at this juncture in world history—a concept, in other words, more responsive to the problems of our own time—than the one I so light-heartedly brought to expression, hacking away at my typewriter there in the north-west corner of that War College building in December of 1946.[52]

Fear of the 'imperfect world', 'the problems of Western civilisation': are not the theory of anarchy in international relations, containment policies, pre-emption doctrines, symptoms of this paranoia that the world out there continuously threatens the existence of the 'West' in general and the United States in particular? Where could the element of trust, which has only recently been theorised by IR scholars, come

---

[51] Robert E. Osgood, 'Force in International Relations: The Moral Issues', in Kenneth W. Thompson (ed.), *Ethics and International Relations Vol. 2*, Oxford: Transaction, 1985, p. 54.

[52] George F. Kennan, 'The Origins of Containment', in Terry L. Deibel and John Lewis Gaddis (eds), *Containment: Concept and Policy Volume One*, Washington DC: National Defence University Press, 1986, pp. 30–31, emphases added.

from, if not from a discourse that is not hampered by fear?[53] Note that (neo)realist theories even infer a negative meaning to the term 'security' as threats to survival that require radical counterstrategies. This is a semantic misrepresentation of course. The term security, originally referring to trust, partnership or community, is reserved for conflict, mistrust, confrontation and essentially *insecurity*. As such, security is not conceived of as an opportunity to build trust. Rather, security in the (neo)realist sense suggests that human relations, and by extension international relations, are inevitably conflict ridden, trapped in the 'Hobbesian' world of self-help anarchy. These elements of fear and mistrust that are engrained in the discipline of IR have seriously marginalised the theorisation of trust and communitarianism, especially in mainstream US scholarship on world politics.[54]

In a recent study of US nationalism, Anatol Lieven links the culture of insecurity permeating the discourses in the country to the desire of the 'old "core" Protestant populations in the small towns and countryside over the new Catholic and Jewish populations of the great cities, and hostility to "aliens" in general'.[55] Others have related such attitudes of vulnerability to the colonial history of the country; to the early period when the Anglo-Americans who settled on the Atlantic Coast feared that the Catholic French and their 'Jesuit indoctrinated Indian allies' are encircling them with a 'ring of forts and rivers';[56] to the burning of Washington DC during the War of 1812; to the territorial challenge by Mexican troops in 1846; or to more recent events, chief amongst them the Japanese attack on Pearl Harbour in December 1941 and the terrorist attacks on New York and the Pentagon in September 2001. What binds these disparate events together is the fear of demise that they have engendered amongst influential strata of US society. In the opinion of Sigmund Freud, the 'fear of death makes its

---

[53] See Booth and Wheeler, *The Security Dilemma*.

[54] See further Bill McSweeney, *Security, Identity and Interests. A Sociology of International Relations*, Cambridge: Cambridge University Press, 1999, especially pp. 37–44; Helga Haftendorn, 'The Security Puzzle: Theory-Building and Discipline Building in International Security', *International Studies Quarterly*, vol. 35, no. 1, 1991, pp. 3–17.

[55] Anatol Lieven, *America Right or Wrong: An Anatomy of American Nationalism*, Oxford: Oxford University Press, 2004, p. 130.

[56] Alan K. Henrikson, 'Mental Maps' in Hogan and Paterson (eds), *Explaining the History of American Foreign Relations*, p. 184.

appearance under two conditions ... namely, as a reaction to an external danger and as an internal process'.[57] During successive periods of crisis, powerful political elites in the United States have felt compelled to control both sources of fear, the internal societal dimension (self) and the external dimensions (other) impinging on the former in order to assert the power of the state.

Moreover, recent studies by Richard Jackson, Mark Salter and Stephen Chan show how tropes such as evil, barbarian and civilisation were reified during the Cold War and continue to be functional in the discourse of the 'war on terror'.[58] [I]f now we have a War on Evil', writes Chan, 'we had an Evil Empire during part of the Cold War—as the Soviet Union was stigmatised in the soundbite politics of the United States'.[59] Jackson argues that comparing the 'War on Terror' with the Cold War after the attacks on the Pentagon and New York City in September 2001, was meant to suggest a dramatic scenario: 'the terrible and fearful danger posed by terrorism, the likely presence of terrorist "moles" in American society and the necessity of building up American military power to protect the American way of life'.[60] Zulaika and Douglass draw comparable conclusions in their study of the representation of terrorist violence in the United States and Europe: 'If for centuries the alienated and repressed part of humanity kept reappearing in the Occidental collective imagination in the dreadful forms of the Wild Man', they write in 1996, 'currently the Terrorist appears to be the epitome of such savagery for the western psyche'.[61]

Today, the fight within has been institutionalised with the Department of Homeland Security. It is also exemplified in surveillance laws such as the USA PATRIOT Act after 9/11, in 'neo-McCarthyism', in the systematic limitation of civil liberties during crisis situations. The fight against external threats, on the other side, manifests itself in the effort to project political and communicative power globally in order

[57] Sigmund Freud, 'The Ego and the Id', in Peter Gay (ed.), *The Freud Reader*, London: Vintage, 1995, p. 658.
[58] See Jackson, *Writing the War on Terrorism*; Mark B. Salter, *Barbarians and Civilisation in International Relations*, London: Pluto, 2002.
[59] Stephen Chan, *Out of Evil: New International Politics and Old Doctrines of War*, London: I.B. Tauris, 2005, p. 11.
[60] Jackson, *Writing the War on Terrorism*, 2005, p. 47.
[61] Joseph Zulaika and William A. Douglass, *Terror and Taboo: The Follies, Fables, and Faces of Terrorism*, London: Routledge, 1996, p. 157.

to compel all nations, on pain of extinction of their cultural peculiarities, to adopt an Americo-centric, 'western' world-view and style of living, to create sameness on a global scale. Scholars of 'globalisation' have theorised this power to subsume and penetrate in paradigmatic form. They define 'globalisation' as a 'process whereby many social relations become relatively delinked from territorial geography, so that human lives are increasingly played out in the world *as a single place*'.[62] The very fact that this theory has been invented 'here' indicates that it is taken for granted that it is primarily the western core that is deemed to be the agent of this globalising world. Globalisation theory, in short, reveals itself as yet another effort to signify *and* universalise a 'western' experience. The global village thus envisaged is guarded by 'our' gatekeepers or their token representatives. It turns out to be a 'white' country club with fortified boundaries: Mexicans, Arabs, Africans, non-yielding Muslims and coloured people are asked to submit to its rules, or to keep out.[63]

Crime and punishment in an 'Americanised' world order

I feel that I may have opened myself up to a lot of criticism especially by those rather more empirically spirited readers who are on the outlook for 'hard factors'. I have provided a mere sketch of how the invention of the nation-state, its assigned sovereignties and disciplinary representation has created the 'international political culture' that is contemporaneous and how the international psychology thus induced continues to feed into the clash regime that concerns us here. Let me pass directly now to more empirical/practical examples about the way power, knowledge and discourse are intertwined within this constellation.

Merum imperium

Thus far, I think we can safely argue that in the current international system, justice is not detached from power. The legitimacy of going to

[62] Jan Aart Scholte, 'The Globalisation of World Politics' in John Baylis and Steve Smith (eds), *The Globalisation of World Politics: An Introduction*, Oxford: Oxford University Press, 2001, pp. 14–15, emphasis added.

[63] For critical views on globalisation theory, see Marina Della Giusta, Uma S. Kambhampati and Robert Hunter Wade (eds), *Critical Perspectives on Globalisation*, Edward Elgar: Cheltenham, 2006.

war can be negotiated and sometimes bought,[64] and there are few 'cosmopolitan' norms that are shared by all (or even a majority) of the nation-states. Such an international system is likely to produce 'just' wars that are more amenable to the interests of the hegemon who arrogates to himself the right to punish those who deviate from the order, or *merum imperium* as the Romans used to call it. This hegemonic role can never be effective if it is not confirmed and legitimated, or socially engineered as constructivist IR theorists argue.[65] Whereas the imperial wars in the eighteenth, nineteenth and early twentieth centuries were justified almost entirely on the basis of civilisational/racial norms, the emergence of the 'international system' after the First World War granted an additional, legal dimension to the legitimation of war. National sovereignty, the monopoly of legitimate violence over a defined territory, was transformed into international sovereignty, the oligopoly of the powerful over the rest. 'International society' and its prevalent culture, far from rescuing the weak from conflict, rationalises their subjugation. The international system since its inception in the twentieth century has served the purpose to produce clashes that are presented as morally and legally 'rational'.

The second point that I have made in this chapter is that International Relations, as a discipline written almost entirely in the United States and western Europe, translates this rationality of war by means of discourse. Many prominent IR departments, especially in the United States, are staffed with former members of government or embedded

---

[64] On 'bribing' at the UN, see Ilyana Kuziemko and Eric Werker, 'How Much is a Seat on the Security Council Worth?: Foreign Aid and Bribery at the United Nations', *Journal of Political Economy*, vol. 114, no. 51, 2006, pp. 905–930.

[65] See Emanuel Adler, 'Seizing the Middle Ground: Constructivism in World Politics', *European Journal of International Relations*, vol. 3, no. 3, 1997, pp. 319–363; Ronald L. Jepperson, Alexander Wendt, and Peter J. Katzenstein, 'Norms, Identity, and Culture in National Security', in Peter J. Katzenstein (ed.), *The Culture of National Security. Norms and Identity in World Politics*, New York: Columbia University Press, 1996, pp. 33–75; Yosef Lapid and Friedrich Kratochwil (eds), *The Return of Culture and Identity in IR Theory*, London: Lynne Rienner, 1996; John Gerard Ruggie, 'What Makes the World Hang Together? Neo-utilitarianism and the Social Constructivist Challenge', *International Organization*, vol. 52, no. 4, 1998, pp. 855–885; and Wendt, *Social Theory of International Politics*, especially chapters one and two.

'consultants' of the state who are particularly fond of parsimonious, easily digestible paradigms with 'predictive power' such as (neo)realism. 'Although the policy community exercised less and less influence on the course of international relations research in the 1980s', the political economy of the field is criticised, 'foundations, through the patterns of their funding, could still shift incentives, particularly for younger scholars'.[66] Consequently, 'security studies' received large-scale funding in the 1980s and indeed after the terrorist attacks on the United States in 2001 and onwards. The state was and continues to be rather reluctant to relinquish its influence over a discipline that has a profound impact on the way we study and rationalise war and peace.

Neither is it surprising that the discipline of IR gained such prominence in the United States. The spatial organisation of the world was very necessary for the European immigrants who rationalised their colonial project with ideas of expansion and 'transcendental sovereignty', the godly ordained, universal mission to promote justice.[67] As Gilles Deleuze and Claire Parnet convincingly argue, the 'becoming' of the United States is 'geographical', not at least because 'American literature operates according to geographical lines: the flight towards the West, the discovery that the true East is in the West, the sense of the frontiers as something to cross, to push back, to go beyond'.[68] 'The cause of America is in a great measure the cause of all mankind', writes Thomas Paine (1737–1809) in his pamphlet *Common Sense*, which was an immediate bestseller when it was published during the American Revolution. In Herman Melville's (1819–1891) *Moby Dick*, this heroic mission to transcend boundaries is represented by Ahab whose effort to subjugate nature (symbolised by Moby-Dick, the 'great white whale') is thwarted. And as Ahab's ship the *Pequod* sinks at the end, so too does the raft carrying Mark Twain's Tom Sawyer and Huckleberry Finn (1835–1910) succumb to higher forces. What remains is the mythic image of the 'unconquered', the sea, the river, the 'unchartered terri-

---

[66] Kahler, 'Inventing International Relations: International Relations Theory after 1945', in Doyle and Ikenberry (eds), *New Thinking in International Relations*, p. 38.

[67] See also Richard W. van Alstyne, *The Rising American Empire*, New York: Norton, 1974.

[68] Gilles Deleuze and Claire Parnet, 'On the Superiority of Anglo-American Literature', in idem., *Dialogues II*, Hugh Tomlinson, Barbara Habberjam and Eliott Ross Albert (trans.), London: Continuum, 2006, pp. 27–28.

tory', until, of course, the next 'tragic hero' embarks on the journey to experience them. Both Twain and Melville (and other novelists such as Nathaniel Hawthorne) were very critical of the idea that America was somehow exceptional, that it could transcend any boundary, that it was destined to create a world in its own image. 'The free can't conquer but to save', 'America Right or Wrong', in the 1840s Melville parodied the attitudes permeating his country with refreshingly ironic vigour:

And we Americans are the peculiar, chosen people—the Israel of our time; we bear the ark of the liberties of the world. Seventy years ago we escaped from thrall; and, besides our first birthright—embracing one continent on earth— God has given to us, for a future inheritance, the broad domains of the political pagans, that shall yet come and lie down under the shade of our ark, without bloody hands being lifted. ... Long enough have we been sceptics with regard to ourselves, and doubted whether, indeed, the political Messiah had come. But he has come in *us*, if we would but give utterance to his promptings. And let us always remember that with ourselves, almost for the first time in the history of the earth, national selflessness is unbounded philanthropy; for we cannot do a good to America, but we give almost to the world.[69]

Whereas American culture continued to produce eloquent and outspoken dissent, successive US governments adhered to and reemphasised the idea that America is exceptional. 'I always consider the settlement of America with reverence and wonder', writes John Adams eleven years before the Declaration of Independence in 1776, adding that he sees it 'as the opening of a grand scene in Providence for the illumination of the ignorant, and the emancipation of the slavish part of mankind all over the earth'.[70] Successive generations of US decision-makers understood that their self-proclaimed mission to export the idea(l) of America opens up a varied tool box to legitimate hegemony. In this regard, they inherited the mantle of the European imperialists that we have already laid out. In the United States, as in Europe earlier, the imperial discourse was reliant on a rather nonchalant and crude self-designation based on (white) America's presumed racial and civilisational superiority. Such inherited, quintessentially European attitude is exemplified in the following speech by Republican Senator Albert

---

[69] Herman Melville, *White Jacket*, in *Redburn, White Jacket, Moby Dick*, New York: The Library of America, 1983, p. 506.
[70] Quoted in James Chace, *The Consequences of the Peace: The New Internationalism and American Foreign Policy*, Oxford: Oxford University Press, 1992, pp. 170–171.

Beveridge (1862–1927) in front of the US Senate in 1900. I think it serves as an adequate signpost to deepen our discussion of the political functionality of racism for the white-American narrative in the following paragraphs:

The Philippines are ours forever, 'territory belonging to the United States', as the Constitution calls them. And just beyond the Philippines are China's illimitable markets. We will not retreat from either. We will not repudiate our duty in the archipelago. We will not abandon our opportunity in the Orient. We will not renounce our part in the mission of our race, trustee, under God, of the civilisation of the world. We will move forward to our work, not howling our regrets like slaves whipped to their burdens, but with gratitude for a task worthy of our strength, and thanksgiving to Almighty God that He has marked us as His chosen people, henceforth to lead in the regeneration of the world. ... Mr. President, this question is deeper than any question of party politics; deeper than any question of the isolated policy of our country even; deeper even than any question of constitutional power. It is elemental. It is racial. God has been preparing the English-speaking and Teutonic peoples for a thousand years for nothing but vain and idle self-contemplation and self-admiration. No! He has made us the master organisers of the world ...[71]

The ideas of Beveridge about what it means to be American are not exceptional, of course. They did not develop in isolation. They travelled from Europe where 'ethnological' race theories were professionalised at least from the eighteenth century onwards as discussed in the last chapters. The functionality of racism during the Philippine-American War (1899–1903), that puts the quote of Beveridge into its historical context, is picked up by Roxanne Lynn Doty in her study about the politics of representation in 'North-South' relations. According to her, what was being engineered during this period 'was a "Western bond" ... The differences between European powers and the United States could be overcome by this "Western bond", which accentuated the differences between the West and the non-West'.[72] To that end, Filipinos were likened to the 'Negro', the 'Chinaman', the 'Indian', 'Mohammedan' and other 'coloured' and 'spotted' peoples deemed 'uncivilised' and racially 'inferior'.[73]

---

[71] *Congressional Record*, 56th Congress, 1st session, 1900, 33, pt. 1, pp. 704; 710–711.

[72] Roxanne Lynn Doty, *Imperial Encounters: The Politics of Representation in North-South Relations*, London: University of Minnesota Press, 1996, p. 33.

[73] Ibid., p. 43.

Doty refers to the 'eugenic' ordering of the Philippine-American War in accordance with the penumbra of racism. Moving one step further, we can establish that racism functioned as an ordering device for international and *domestic* society. The primitive emphasis on the purity of blood legitimated not only the systematic subjugation of the African-American community in America itself (after all slavery was written into the constitution of the United States). It was not only the 'Negro' other who was placed out of the realm of the law.[74] Being white secured a distinct form of politico-judicious sovereignty and privilege that was meant to structure both the domestic and international realm in favour of America's immigrant elites from Europe.

So the geography of racism that ordered the national narrative in America at least since the eighteenth century was exported and reified through the thematic of white supremacy, which indicates the truly functional 'bio-power' that racism unleashes, not only within the regimented contours of the nation, but also in the rather more unstructured body of the international system. The creation of a colony in the west coast of Africa in 1822 by white Americans organised in the 'American Colonization Society' out of which the nation-state of Liberia emerged in 1847, is a very obvious example of that systematic dispersion of racism into the international realm.[75] In this case, racism does not function as a means to subsume the 'other' under a narrative of civilisational superiority, there is no room for partial conversion. The creation of Liberia exemplifies a form of 'exclusive racism', which does not allow for any compromise. Every strategy to civilise the other is doomed. She has to be segregated not only by social class, but geographically, not only in enclaves but beyond visibility. Exclusive racism makes the

---

[74] The culture of lynching, that is the extrajudicial killing of individuals, was an inevitable outgrowth of this constellation. The numbers are intensely contested, but studies have shown that in '1899, an average of two African-Americans a week were put to death' by raging white mobs. 'By the 1950s, more than four thousand lynchings had occurred in the United States of America'. Bud Schultz and Ruth Schultz, *The Price of Dissent: Testimonies to Political Repression in America*, Berkeley: University of California Press, 2001, pp. 121–122.

[75] See also Elliott P. Skinner, 'Ethnicity and Race as Factors in the Formation of United States Foreign Policy', in Michael P. Hamilton (ed.), *American Character and Foreign Policy*, Grand Rapids, MI: William B. Eerdmans, 1986, p. 120.

'other' invisible. So the deportations of freed slaves, lauded by Thomas Jefferson as 'the most desirable measure',[76] were thought to be necessary in order to 'move the Negroes beyond the pale of the white men'.[77] Deporting the 'Negroes' was deemed inevitable because 'they infest the suburbs of the towns and cities, where they become the depositories of stolen goods'.[78] 'Everything connected with their condition, including their colour, is against them', noted another supporter of the Colonization Society. '[N]or is there much prospect that their state can ever be greatly ameliorated, why they shall continue among us'.[79]

I have already mentioned that the appearance of blood consciousness in the United States, in its oneiric, yet fastidiously planned geographical realisation, was inherited from Europe. There was no American exceptionality involved in this regard. There was even a blueprint for the creation of Liberia: the making of Sierra Leone by British colonialists was also 'rationalised' in racial terms, precipitated by the deportation of 'London's black poor', both Africans and Asians from 1787 onwards. This is not the place to provide an exhaustive geography of the spatial dynamics of European race theories, from Sierra Leone, Liberia to the 'white Australia policy', Apartheid and right-wing Zionism in Israel. The point that I am reemphasising here is that at least since the eighteenth century, the idea of racial superiority was continuously inscribed into the American narrative, that it became co-constitutive of the country's self-perception and that the theory of racial superiority expanded outwards from eighteenth-century Europe. John H. Smyth, the US Minister to Liberia from 1878–1881 makes this 'bio-lineage' rather explicit:

Race allegiance is compatible with patriotism, with love of the land that gave us birth. ... Though we are part of this great national whole, we are a distinct

---

[76] Quoted in Henry Nobel Sherwood, 'The Formation of the American Colonization Society', *The Journal of Negro History*, vol. 2, no. 3, Jul. 1917, p. 210.

[77] Ibid., p. 211.

[78] Ibid., p. 213.

[79] Ibid. A similar belief in the racial superiority of white Americans was explicit in Haiti. It was during the Wilson Presidency, according to one author, when rebelling Haitians, privately referred to as 'real niggers' and 'coons', were killed 'for sheer sport'. Constance G. Anthony, 'American Democratic Interventionism: Romancing the Iconic Woodrow Wilson', *International Studies Perspectives*, vol. 9, no. 3, Aug. 2008, p. 249.

and separate part, an alien part racially, and destined to be so by the immutable law of race pride, which is possessed by our white fellow citizens, if not by
us. The sentiments, the something stronger than sentiment which makes an
English-American proud of his connection with La Belle France, and a Ger-
man-American fondly attached to the memories of the Fatherland, and all
European races of their Aryan descent, has something that partakes of the
moral sublime.[80]

Here, America is positioned squarely within an imagined genealogy
of 'European races' and the mythical idea of 'Aryan' purity. A prominent early analysis of the linkages between Europe and America came
from Alexis de Tocqueville (1805–1859) in his *Democracy in America*
(1835, 1840). Toqueville argues that America is a direct product of
Europe, save the progressive changes in politics and society that the
competition between European aristocracy and democracy brought
about. Because this element of 'class competition' was lacking in
America, democracy within the country tends '*to change without
developing*'.[81] His argument that the country is a cruder copy of the
European original indicates that for Tocqueville, America was politically static, that American society did not go through the domestic
upheavals and conflicts that gave European societies their critical edge.
According to him, it also shows more clearly that America adopted a
missionary zeal that was even more 'righteous' than the one developed
by imperial strategists in Europe. American society, according to Tocqueville, was born of religious norms that were accepted without contestation. America, in other words, did not contend itself with the mandate
of racial and/or civilisational superiority to legitimate conquest.

As a French aristocrat, Tocqueville was generally sceptical about
democratic forms of governance and his criticism of America is not
unrelated to this attitude.[82] But his observation that the country
equipped itself explicitly with the mandate of the (Christian) God is
pertinent. For Tocqueville, this explains why democracies such as
America waged war with an all-out force that left no room for diplo-

[80] Skinner, 'Ethnicity and Race as Factors in the Formation of United States
Foreign Policy', in Hamilton (ed.), *American Character and Foreign Policy*,
p. 121.
[81] Hayden White, *Metahistory: The Historical Imagination in Nineteenth Century Europe*, Baltimore: Johns Hopkins Press, 1973, p. 209, emphasis in
original.
[82] Ibid., p. 211.

macy or negotiations.[83] In short, for America, conquest has a powerful religious connotation that makes it that much harder to resist its lure. On this point, Tocqueville was not wrong. George W. Bush's pronouncement that it was God who instructed him to invade Iraq may be taken as a contemporary example of this pervasive attitude. The well-documented political and cultural impact of North American evangelicals on the politics of the country is yet another.[84]

I have argued in the last chapter that power and sovereignty are defined as transcendental when they emerge out of totalising systems that claim maximum causal efficacy. Some of the most dominant western discourses between the eighteenth and the early-twentieth century, certainly nationalism and imperialism, have invariable functioned to legitimate domination. The ontology of the contemporary international system, as taught in the discipline of IR, emerged out of this ideological habitat. It was engineered on the premise that the leading nations, positioned within a discursive formation called the 'West', have the moral duty to rescue humanity from disaster. The United States, to the envy of many 'classical imperialists' in Europe, emerged as the enforcer of this right to pre-empt in order to 'pacify'. As Theodore Roosevelt put it in 1904:

All that this country desires is to see the neighbouring countries stable, orderly, and prosperous. Any country whose people conduct themselves well can count upon our hearty friendship. If a nation shows that it knows how to act with reasonable efficiency and decency in social and political matters, if it keeps order and pays its obligations, it need fear no interference from the United States. Chronic wrongdoing, or an impotence which results in a general loosening of the ties of civilised society, may in America, as elsewhere, ultimately require intervention by some civilised nation, and in the Western Hemisphere the adherence of the United States to the Monroe Doctrine may force the United States, however reluctantly, in flagrant cases of such wrongdoing or impotence, to the exercise of an international police power.[85]

---

[83] See further Marcus Cunliffe, 'Formative Events from Columbus to World War I', in Hamilton (ed.), *American Character and Foreign Policy*, pp. 10 ff.

[84] See further John J. Mearsheimer and Stephen M. Walt, *The Israel Lobby and US Foreign Policy*, London: Penguin, 2007, especially pp. 132 ff.; Lawrence Davidson, 'Christian Zionism as a Representation of American Manifest Destiny', *Critique: Critical Middle Eastern Studies*, vol. 14, no. 2, Summer 2005, pp. 157–169; Peter Singer, *The President of Good and Evil: Taking George W. Bush Seriously*, London: Granta, 2004, especially pp. 90 ff;

[85] *Congressional Record*, 58th Congress, 3rd session, 1904, 39, pt.1, p. 19.

Within this Americo-centric discourse, war is merely one signpost of a universal mission to engineer a world order that is amenable to the interest of the ruling classes in America, which is not bound to geographic delimitation. The international system in its entirety is perceived to be the place to achieve this aim. By the necessity of this global mission, the United States is turned into a vehicle of supreme justice and US society is coded in order to silently bear the brunt of this awesome self-perception. During and after the intervention of the country in World War I, Woodrow Wilson emerged as the archetypal 'internationalist' expressing this vision to create a 'world remade in America's image and therefore permanently at peace'.[86] In January 1918, ignoring both his French and British allies, Wilson put forward his Fourteen Points, a peace settlement with Germany which advocated global free trade and universal, liberal democracy, that is norms and values that were considered to be quintessentially American and reflective of the country's moral high-ground. The fourteenth point suggested a 'general association of nations', that could sustain the sovereignty of their constituent nation-states.[87] This idea was developed by Wilson into the League of Nations which was created in 1920.

Conventional wisdom tells the student of international law and diplomacy that the League of Nations provided the first step towards managing international conflict. But this argument can be interrogated with an alternative one. Far from providing a blue print to 'pacify' world politics, international law also distributes legal authority to making war. The League, for the first time in human history, made it possible to 'legalise' hegemonic wars globally. From now on, justice was not merely morally constituted; it could be legally defined. In other words, and quite irrespective of the intention of their sponsors, the League and the UN, which was established in 1945, made it possible to make a legal case for war on top of a moral one. In such an international system, 'justice' is turned into a double-edged-sword: the sovereignty of the weak can be pierced more facilely.[88]

---

[86] Andrew J. Bacevich, *The New American Militarism: How Americans Are Seduced by War*, Oxford: Oxford University Press, 2005, p. 10.

[87] *Congressional Record*, 65th Congress, 2nd session, 1918, 56, pt. 1, p. 691.

[88] See further Casper Sylvest, '"Our passion for legality": International Law and Imperialism in Late Nineteenth-Century Britain', *Review of International Studies*, vol. 34, no. 3, Jul. 2008, pp. 403–423. Christian Reus-Smit, 'Liberal Hierarchy and the License to Use Force', *Review of International*

There is no suggestion here that organisations such as the League of Nations or the UN were deliberately created in order to make conflict more easily justifiable. Neither do I mean to imply that a world without international law is likely to be more pacified than our current order. What I am saying is that such multilateral organisations make it easier to produce 'just wars' because they continue to make aggression possible, that in its current form, the international system and its legal mechanisms are imperfect and susceptible to dangerous manipulation. The UN is not a pacifist organisation, neither is it democratic of course, given that the five permanent members of the Security Council (Britain, China, France, Russia and the United States) retain their authority to veto any resolution that conflicts with their national interests. It is this very obvious hierarchy inscribed into the UN and provisions such as the 'right of self-defence' (Article 51 of the UN charter) that have, repeatedly, turned the organisation into a forum to legalise aggression. Today, we are more easily swayed into battling the other by the 'rational' lawyer than the hysterical propagandist. Governments are aware of that. So their decision to engage in the politics of multilateral institutions such as the UN is primarily determined by their interest to sell a war to both civil society and the 'international community'. The production of 'legal wars' makes the propagandist less vulnerable because it covers his hysteria with legalistic codewords. Today, he does not punish at will or out of rage; he punishes according to laws that are rendered 'just'.

The First Persian Gulf War (1991) is a recent example that shows how war is legally and morally engineered within such a system. The moral case was straight forward: The world was told that order in the international system could only be delivered by 'American strength and will—the strength and will to lead a unipolar world, unashamedly laying down the rules of world order and being prepared to enforce it'.[89] When Iraq was defeated, President Bush Sr. told the US Congress in his

---

Studies, vol. 31, no. 1, 2005, pp. 71–92; Helen M. Kinsella, 'Discourse of Difference: Civilians, Combatants, and Compliance with the Laws of War', *Review of International Studies*, vol. 31, no. 1, 2005, pp. 163–185; Jean Cohen, 'Whose Sovereignty? Empire versus International Law', *Ethics and International Affairs*, vol. 18, no. 1, 2004/2005, pp. 1–24.

[89] Charles Krauthammer, 'The Unipolar Moment', *Foreign Affairs*, vol. 70, no. 1, 1991, p. 33.

1991 State of the Union address, we 'will have sent an enduring warning to any dictator or despot, present or future, who contemplates outlaw aggression'. America, he envisioned, had to burden the share of delivering the 'new world order', because '[a]mong the nations of the world, only the United States has had both the moral standing, and the means to back it up. We are the only nation on earth', Bush pointed out, 'that could assemble the forces of peace'.[90] At first sight, and once we juxtapose it to the declaration of war proclaimed by Woodrow Wilson in April 1917, President Bush's plea for a 'new' world order appears to be as old as the idea of American 'internationalism' itself. According to Wilson:

It is a fearful thing to lead this great peaceful people into war, into the most terrible and disastrous of all wars, civilisation itself seeming to be in the balance. But the right is more precious than peace, and we shall fight for the things we have always carried nearest our hearts,—for democracy, for the right of those who submit to authority to have a voice in their own Governments, for the rights and liberties of small nations, for a universal dominion of right by such a concert of free peoples as shall bring peace and safety to all nations and make the world itself at last free. To such a task we can dedicate our lives and our fortunes, everything that we are and everything that we have, with the pride of those who know that the day has come when America is privileged to spend her blood and her might for the principles that gave her birth and happiness and the peace which she has treasured. God helping her, she can do no other.[91]

The moralistic tenor of this passage is comparable to the emphasis on the exceptionality of the United States expressed by Bush Senior (the early foreign policy speeches of Barack Obama are also moralistic, if by far more intellectually sophisticated). But if we focus on the international context enveloping both leaders, the difference I am alluding to becomes clearer. Whereas Wilson was entirely dependent on America's moral authority transmitted by the US military, itself sustained by the country's economic power, Bush's moral mandate was enriched, even legally constituted by the laws and statutes permeating the international system. Whereas the former could only claim legitimacy on normative grounds, the latter successfully made a legal case for it.

[90] Quoted in Michael T. Klare, 'The Pentagon's New Paradigm', in Micah L. Sifry and Christopher Cerf (eds), *The Gulf War Reader. History, Documents, Opinions*, New York: Times Books, 1991, p. 468.
[91] *New York Times*, 3 Apr. 1917.

The Second Gulf War is central to the study of contemporary international relations because for the first time in its history, the international system as we know it conveyed a near-unanimous mandate to wage war on one of its members.[92] The war was the archetypal 'just' war, because justice was not merely normatively asserted but legally constituted. For four decades, the Cold War between the Soviet Union and the US prevented this. With the fall of the Berlin Wall, the demise of the Warsaw Pact and the disintegration of the Soviet Union, international political culture shifted in favour of the United States. IR theorists writing in the neo-realist tradition theorised this new situation subsuming it under the label 'uni-polarity'.[93] In other words, it was believed that the United States was the only remaining globally dominant *pole* within the international system. And as indicated earlier, for Francis Fukuyama, who was a staunch supporter of the two invasions of Iraq and until recently an ardent promoter of the 'neoconservative' agenda, the new constellation signified 'not just the end of the Cold War, or the passing of a particular period of postwar history', it indicated something much more momentous. For Fukuyama, the United States had brought about 'the end of history as such: that is, the end point of mankind's historical evolution and the universalisation of Western liberal democracy as the final form of human government'.[94]

So the end of the Cold War ushered into a period of immense transitory euphoria. The exuberance was socially constituted in that it was the international community that empowered the US to enact its role as global Leviathan. Pushing the dictator of Iraq out of Kuwait and reconstituting the status quo were considered just and legitimate causes for war. War was legalised by successive UN resolutions. America's new world order norm was turned into an internationally accepted 'norm of appropriate behaviour' defining the benchmark for dissent in the post-Cold war international system. The impression was created that deviation from the rules and norms of appropriate behaviour enshrined in the international political culture of the 'new' global system, will only be tolerated to the extent that US interests are not

---

[92] See also Campbell, *Writing Security*, and idem. *Politics Without Principle: Sovereignty, Ethics, and the Narratives of the Gulf War*, London: Lynne Rienner, 1993.

[93] See for instance Birthe Hanse, *Unipolarity and the Middle East*, Richmond, Surrey: Curzon, 2000.

[94] Francis Fukuyama, 'The End of History', *The National Interest*, no. 16, Summer 1989, p. 4.

compromised.[95] 'A UN bedtime story', Jean Baudrilliard wrote at that time:

the UN awoke (or was awakened) from its glass coffin (the building in New York). As the coffin fell and was shattered (at the same time as the Eastern bloc), she spat out the apple and revived, as fresh as a rose, only to find at once the waiting Prince Charming: the Gulf War, also fresh from the arms of the cold war after a long period of mourning. No doubt together they will give birth to a New World Order, or else end up like two ghosts locked in vampiric embrace.[96]

So the contemporary international system has become a permanent vehicle for relations of hegemony and for multifarious techniques of domination. We do not wage imperial wars anymore, we do not colonise, we make legal wars; killing people can now be justified in the court of law. In today's world order, international law is the precondition that makes killing acceptable; it extends the sovereignty of the Leviathan rather than contracting it. With regard to the First Gulf War, this legally constituted mandate to kill, bestowed upon the Bush Sr. Administration by the 'international community', certainly re-invoked the euphoria of American hegemony, especially amongst the emerging neoconservative caste of the political elites in the country. With this mandate, the idea of a new world order entirely under American tutelage was thought to be finally realisable.[97] I have argued most recently in *Iran in World Politics* that it was this exuberant attitude that lent itself to manipulation by the neoconservative networks surrounding George W. Bush's administration, especially after the terrorist attacks on the country in September 2001.[98] Irving Kristol, one of the most influential ideologues of US neoconservatism, exclaims this pervasive attitude. According to him:

[F]or a great power, the 'national interest' is not a geographical term, except for fairly prosaic matters like trade and environmental regulation. A smaller

[95] See also William Pfaff, 'More Likely a New World Disorder', in Sifry and Cerf (eds), *The Gulf War Reader*, p. 487.
[96] Jean Baudrillard, *The Gulf War Did Not Take Place*, Bloomington: Indiana University Press, 1995, p. 46.
[97] For instance Charles Krauthammer, 'Bless our Pax Americana', *The Washington Post*, 22 Mar. 1991; Joshua Muravchik, 'At Last, Pax Americana', *New York Times*, 24 Jan. 1991.
[98] See further my, *Iran in World Politics: The Question of the Islamic Republic*, New York: Columbia University Press, 2008, especially chapter three.

nation might appropriately feel that its national interest begins and ends at its borders, so that its foreign policy is almost always in a defensive mode. A larger nation has more extensive interests. ... And large nations, whose identity is ideological, like the Soviet Union of yesteryear and the United States of today, inevitably have ideological interests in addition to more material concerns. ... Suddenly, after two decades during which 'imperial decline' and 'imperial overstretch' were the academic and journalistic watchwords, the United States emerges as uniquely powerful. ... With power come responsibilities, whether sought or not, whether welcome or not. And it is a fact that if you have the kind of power we now have, either you will find opportunities to use it, or the world will discover them for you.[99]

Successive US administrations have acted upon this understanding of the international system as a place to maximise the country's (inter) national interest and to extend its sovereignty. Indeed, as touched upon earlier, 'political realists'—neo, offensive, defensive, neo-classical—prescribe that states should follow that strategy in order to attain or sustain an exalted 'power position'.[100] Hence, domination is inscribed both into the statutes of the international system and the way they are studied and represented. What, in effect, does it mean when the former US Secretary of State Cordell Hull wrote in his diaries that the victor nations of the Second World War (i.e. the USA, Soviet Union, United Kingdom, China and France) should have the ultimate responsibility for the maintenance of international security and peace?[101] It means that these countries can ratify the basic distinction between friend and enemy. And so it is that the US state and its allies have repeatedly arrogated to themselves both the moral claim and the legal authority to

---

[99] Irving Kristol, 'The Neoconservative Persuasion', in Irwin Stelzer (ed.), *Neoconservatism*, London: Atlantic, 2004, pp. 36–37.

[100] For a review of the core components of political (neo) realist theory see among others Joseph M. Grieco, 'Realist International Theory and the Study of World Politics', in Michael W. Doyle and G. John Ikenberry (eds), *New Thinking in International Relations Theory*, Oxford: Westview, 1997, pp. 163–201; Robert O. Keohane (ed.), *Neorealism and its Critics*, New York: Columbia UP, 1986; John A. Vasquez, *The Power of Power Politics: From Classical Realism to Neotraditionalism*, Cambridge: Cambridge University Press, 1999.

[101] See Cordell Hull, *The Memoirs of Cordell Hull, Vol. 2*, New York: Macmillan, 1948, especially pp. 1649–1652. Hull was an ardent Wilsonian. He organised the Dumbarton Oaks Conference in 1945 during which world representatives devised the United Nations Charter. He also won the Noble Peace Price.

order the international system. It should not come as a surprise then that they clash with the proclaimed 'bad guys' or 'pariah' (literally non-native) states that are perceived to threaten this self-perception. Ultimately, not unlike racism within the domestic realm, the contemporary international system fragments and creates caesuras within the continuum of humanity. It subdivides nations into those who are powerful and those who are subordinated. The strong dominate the weak, kill or be killed, us or them—the contemporary international system presents itself as a particularly sophisticated form of social Darwinism. No wonder then that it continues to signify ongoing clashes between its constituent units and their imagined 'civilisations'.

Let me divert this discussion into another direction now. Within such an international system, war is about two things; it is not simply about 'just' wars, it is also about punishment as a means to assert one's own national and/or civilisational superiority. The US invasion of Iraq in 2003 is a case in point. It seems to me that this war was not merely about conquering Iraqi oil fields.[102] The United States and its allies do not need to formally occupy a country in order to tap into its oil wealth, as their sound relationship with Saudi Arabia and the other Gulf monarchies shows. In my opinion, the Iraq War (and the war in Afghanistan) was also about punishment, about setting yet another example for those who attempted to question the status quo in September 2001 through terror. It was also about penetrating deep into the Muslim world in order to democratise it from within. 'The rise of a free and self-governing Iraq', George W. Bush proclaimed a few months after the invasion of the country, 'will deny terrorists a base of operation, discredit their narrow ideology, and *give momentum to reformers across the region*. This will be a decisive blow to terrorism *at the heart of its power*, and a victory for the security of America and the civilized world'.[103] Hence, the civilisation-barbarism binary returns. For Norman Podhoretz, one of the many proponents of neoconservative ideology, the occasion was even more momentous. He expected war to 'bring about the long-delayed reform and modernisation of

---

[102] This argument was made most forcefully by Michael Klare. See his 'Deciphering the Bush Administration's Motives', in Micah L. Sifry and Christopher Cerf (eds), *The Iraq War Reader: History, Documents, Opinions*, London: Simon and Schuster, 2003, pp. 392–402.

[103] 'Remarks by the President on Iraq and the War on Terror', *United States Army War College*, Carlisle, Pennsylvania, 24 May 2004.

Islam',[104] a prescription for a 'bio-war', a struggle for the 'hearts and minds' of Muslims, that was echoed by the former Director of the CIA, James Woolsey:

America and the western world are at war with 'fascist' Middle East governments and totalitarian Islamists. The freedoms we stand for are loathed and our vulnerable systems under attack. Liberty and security will be in conflict as we line up behind the new march of democracy.

Thus the War on Terror was transplanted into Afghanistan and Iraq, not only militarily but also discursively; hard power carried by the military caste and bio-power spearheaded by the media, think tanks pundits, 'organic intellectuals', embedded academics, radically merge in the 'war on terror'. And once again, as I have indicated with the Freudian excursion above, this new war, that is signified and practiced in global terms, has both an internal and an external dimension. It is not only the 'other' that is assaulted but also dissident elements threatening the presumed coherence within the in-group. This interpenetration of the internal/external dimensions of the War on Terror indicates that, in actual fact, it is *not* some clash of civilisations. Rather it is a clash between a right-wing coterie on the one side and its enemies on the other: Christian, Jew, Oriental, Muslim, American, Hindu or any other individual or group that resists for that matter:

This is about the war we are in, whom it is with, *how we have to fight it inside our own countries and how we have to fight it abroad*. The war is, essentially, similar to the Cold War. This is the origin of the phrase World War IV, which Professor Eliot Cohen came up with in America shortly after September 11 2001, to characterise the parallels between this war and what he called World War III—the Cold War.[105]

In the absence of a direct threat to the United States, in the absence of weapons of mass destruction, or of any other 'security' reason to go to war, the invasion of Iraq was also a 'bio-war', a struggle over identity, a battle with racial connotations. Almost by necessity, it was not merely based on the ideologically orthodox notion of 'civilisational superiority', but on top of that on the more primitive sentiment of race. I am writing 'almost by necessity' because without a direct threat

[104] Norman Podhoretz, 'How to Win World War IV', *Commentary*, 113, Feb. 2002.
[105] James Woolsey, 'At War for Freedom', *The Observer*, 20 Jul. 2003, emphasis added.

emanating from Iraq, the state was obliged to use race, couched in the age-old language of the fight between civilisation and barbarity, in order to exercise its sovereign power, in order to oblige US soldiers to pull the trigger in the name of patriotism, the 'free world', an imagined 'West'. So statements after 11 September 2001 by Tony Blair, George W. Bush, former Vice President Dick Cheney, former Attorney General John Ashcroft and others designating the new enemy as 'a group of barbarians', dichotomisations of world politics into the freedom loving 'civilised world' versus the 'evil savages', were not coincidental.[106] They were necessary components in the technology of power unleashed on the peoples of Iraq (and Afghanistan) after the terrorist attacks on the United States in September 2001. In other words, in contemporary world politics racism, far from being muted, reveals itself as a latent instrument that continues to contribute to the functionality of power. Internally, by the practice of racial profiling, the detention of 'well over 5000 ... Arabs and Muslims ... since September 11',[107] the 'discriminatory treatment, illegal harassment, and unconstitutional imprisonment' of mainly Muslim nationalities by the US Immigration and Naturalisation services;[108] and externally, through the War on Terror in the third worlds. Indeed, racist discourse has always commanded a grammar with interchangeable referents (Jews, African-Americans, Latinos, the Japanese after Pearl Harbor, the Vietnamese, Arabs, etc.) and interchangeable signifiers (kike, nigger, caffer, greaser, Jap, gook, hadji, etc.). 'From the viewpoint of racism', Deleuze and Guattari write, 'there is no exterior, there are no people on the outside. There are only people who should be like us and whose crime is not to be'.[109] Creating sameness is the ultimate aim of racism.

---

[106] 'President urges readiness and patience: Remarks by the President, Secretary of State Colin Powell and Attorney General John Ashcroft at Camp David, Thurmont, MD', *White House News and Policies*, 15 Sept. 2001. See further Jackson, *Writing the War on Terrorism*, 2005 and Corinna Mullin, *Constructing Political Islam as the New Other: America and its Post-War on Terror Politics*, London: I.B. Tauris, forthcoming, 2010.

[107] Chrystie Flournoy Swiney, 'Racial Profiling of Arabs and Muslims in the US: Historical, Empirical and Legal Analysis Applied to the War on Terrorism', *Muslim World Journal of Human Rights*, vol. 3, issue 1, 2006, p. 4.

[108] Ali Mazrui, 'Islam and the United States: Streams of Convergence, Strands of Divergence', *Third World Quarterly*, vol. 25, no. 5, 2004, p. 806.

[109] Gilles Deleuze and Felix Guattari, *A Thousand Plateaus: Capitalism and*

Dungeons of the 'new' world order

The functionality of a racist discourse as an instrument of power can be explained further in relation to the torture at Abu Ghraib.[110] At Abu Ghraib all the discriminatory effects of modernity merged to create a sophisticated torture system. I consider it a 'modern' effect because the rationalisation of punishment was central to the system of torture at the prison complex. The violence thus perpetuated was not arbitrary. Rather, it was calculated and supervised. For instance, interrogators were very conscious 'not to leave marks on the body' of the victims.[111] Furthermore, a report by the British medical journal *The Lancet*, established in August 2004, that US military doctors and medics were 'complicit' in the torture of Iraqi detainees and faked death certificates to try and cover up homicides. 'The medical system collaborated with designing and implementing psychologically and physically coercive interrogations', writes the author, University of Minnesota professor Steven Miles. 'Army officials stated that a physician and a psychiatrist helped design, approve, and monitor interrogations'.[112]

At Abu Ghraib, torture and science worked hand in hand. In his report dated March 2004, US Army Major General Antonio M. Taguba found that 'between October and December 2003 at the Abu Ghraib Confinement Facility (BCCF) numerous incidents of sadistic, blatant, and wanton criminal abuses were inflicted on several detainees', which he classifies as 'systemic and illegal abuse', perpetrated by 'several members of the military police guard force'.[113] More specifically, the abuse included:

Schizophrenia, vol. 2, Brian Massumi (trans.), London: Athlone, 1988, p. 178.

[110] Parts of the following sections are taken from my 'Abu Ghraib and Insaniyat', *Monthly Review*, vol. 59, no. 7, Dec. 2007, pp. 20–36.

[111] 'No Blood, No Foul: Soldiers Accounts of Detainee Abuse in Iraq', *Human Rights Watch*, vol. 18, no. 3 (G), Jul. 2006, p. 30. Also available at http://hrw.org/reports/2006/us0706/ [Last accessed 14 Aug. 2007].

[112] The report is available at http://www.thelancet.com/journal/vol364/iss9435/full/llan.364.9435.review_and_opinion.30574.1. See also Sandro Contenta, 'US Doctors Tied to Prisoner Abuse Faked Death Certificates, Report Says; Helped Design Torture at Abu Ghraib', *Toronto Star*, 20 Aug. 2004.

[113] 'The Taguba Report: Article 15–6 Investigation of the 800th Military Police Brigade, March 2004', in Karen J. Greenberg and Joshua L. Dratel (eds), *The Torture Papers: The Road to Abu Ghraib*, Cambridge: Cambridge

Punching, slapping, and kicking detainees; jumping on their naked feet ...
Forcibly arranging detainees in various sexually explicit positions for photo-
graphing ... Forcing naked male detainees to wear women's underwear ...
Forcing groups of male detainees to masturbate themselves while being photo-
graphed and videotaped ... Arranging naked male detainees in a pile and then
jumping on them ... Positioning a naked detainee on a MRE Box, with a sandbag on his head, and attaching wires to his fingers, toes, and penis to stimulate
electric torture ... Placing a dog chain or strap around a naked detainee's neck
and having a female soldier pose for a picture ... A male MP guard having sex
with a female detainee ... Taking photographs of dead Iraqi detainees ...[114]

From the outset of the war in Iraq in 2003, the 'shock and awe'
campaign was meant to display a show not of measure or even-hand-
edness, but of excess. In this kind of dialectic between the punisher and
his victim, an extreme form of neo-imperial logic ruled: superiority had
to be displayed violently and with unadulterated physical force. At
Abu Ghraib, it was not enough to humiliate the victim; it was not
enough to physically demonstrate absolute power to the body of the
subject, to break her. The power of the punisher had to be engrained
in the very memory of the victim and, by extension, in the consciousness of the occupied nation and culture that was at the receiving end
of the Leviathan's wrath. This type of power had both racist and licentious connotations. It is power that is motivated by desire; power that
is total in its ambition; the type of 'macho' power that feminises its
object in order to function properly.[115]

University Press, 2005, p. 416. Also available at http://news.findlaw.com/
hdocs/docs/iraq/tagubarpt.html [Last accessed 18 Aug. 2007]. See also
Mark Danner, *Torture and Truth: America, Abu Ghraib, and the War on
Terror*, London: Granta, 2004; Jennifer K. Harbury, *Truth, Torture and the
American Way: The History and Consequences of US Involvement in Tor-
ture*, Boston: Beacon Press, 2005; and Jeremy Brecher, Jill Cutler and
Brendan Smith (eds), *In the Name of Democracy: American War Crimes in
Iraq and Beyond*, New York: Metropolitan 2005.

[114] 'The Taguba Report', in Greenberg and Dratel (eds), p. 416.

[115] This 'macho attitude' permeating the war in Iraq was adequately captured
by Joseph Massad in the immediate aftermath of the Abu Ghraib scandal:

'While Western Orientalist accounts never tire of speaking of sexism and
women's oppression in the Arab World, including the Western horror at
"honour crimes", it might be time to address the rampant Western misogyny which disdains all that is feminine and posits women as the terrain of
male conquest. It should not be forgotten that in America, not in the Mus-

Within such a power constellation, the Leviathan claimed absolute rule: the Iraqi society was rendered helpless; the army was dissolved, institutional structures were demolished, history was erased. Only the oil ministry was deemed valuable enough to be guarded. Without the existence of institutional constrains that could challenge what happens on the ground, the Leviathan's power was multiplied. The Bush administration claimed, and for a short period assumed, the status of prosecutor, jury, judge and defence-lawyer all in one. The torture at Abu Ghraib is indicative of this constellation, indicative of the licentious desire and racism that underpinned the discourse of the global War on Terror. For a short, yet decisive moment, the Bush administration made the international system it wanted to supervise subordinate to the sovereign right to punish anyone it deemed threatening to its global mandate, including the citizens of the United States. Crucially, the laws of that international system did not contain the country's ability to exercise its powers. Consider this account of a US soldier who was questioned by *Human Rights Watch*:

A few more weeks of this, and a group of us went to the colonel there and told him we were uneasy about … this type of abuse, or just the treatment. … And within a couple hours a team of two JAG officers, JAG lawyers, came and gave

---

lim World, between 40 per cent and 60 per cent of women killed, are killed by their husbands and boyfriends … It is with this misogyny as background, that the US military understood well that American male sexual prowess, usually reserved for American women, should be put to military use in imperial conquests. In such a strategy, Iraqis are posited by American supermasculine fighter-bomber pilots as women and feminised men to be penetrated by the missiles and bombs ejected from American warplanes. By feminising the enemy as the object of penetration (real and imagined), American imperial military culture supermasculinises not only its own male soldiers, but also its female soldiers who can partake in the feminisation of Iraqi men'.

Josep Massad, 'Imperial Mementos', *Al-Ahram Weekly*, Issue No. 691, 20–26 May 2004. Available at http://weekly.ahram.org.eg/2004/691/op2.htm [Last accessed 25 Aug. 2007]. On the linkage between imperialism and desire see also Edward Said, *Orientalism: Western Conceptions of the Orient*, London: Penguin, 1995, especially pp. 187 ff. or Robert C. Young, 'Colonialism and the Desiring Machine', in Gregory Castle (ed.), *Postcolonial Discourses: An Anthology*, Oxford: Blackwell, 2001, pp. 74–98 and Joseph Massad, *Desiring Arabs*, Chicago: The University of Chicago Press, 2007.

us a couple of hours slide show on why this is necessary, why this is legal, they're enemy combatants, they're not POWs, and so we can do all this stuff to them and so forth. ... Some of the slides were about the laws of war, the Geneva Convention, but it was kind of a starting-off point for them to kind of spout-off, you know: why we don't have to follow these Geneva Convention articles and so forth. Like, you know, inhumane and degrading treatment, well, this specifically relates to POWs so we don't have to do this. So basically we can do inhumane and degrading treatment.

And then they went on to the actual treatment itself, what we were doing, what we'd signed off on and those type of things: cold water and nudity, strobe lights, loud music—that's not inhumane because they're able to rebound from it. And they claim no lasting mental effects or physical marks or anything, or permanent damage of any kind, so it's not inhumane. And then there was also [discussion about] degrading [treatment]. Like what's more degrading than being thrown completely naked in the middle of a mud pile, with everybody looking at you and spraying water on you ... I felt they were really kind of patronising us and blowing smoke and just treating us like children. Like "Well it's OK". [They] just came and said whatever they had to say to patch it up and continue with the war.[116]

Thus, the torture at Abu Ghraib was 'legalised' at the same time as life outside the confines of the prison complex was rendered anarchic. A similar process can be discerned in relation to the detainees at Guantanamo. In 2003, the US Justice Department sent a legal memorandum to the Pentagon, indicating that federal laws prohibiting maiming, slapping, assault, poking or shoving detainees were not applicable to military interrogators who questioned Al Qaeda personnel because the legal authority of the President as 'Commander in Chief' supersedes these statutes. The eighty-one-page memo, which was declassified in April 2008, also 'legalised' the use of mind-altering drugs that do not have 'an extreme effect' that could lead to 'a profound disruption of the senses or personality'.[117] So in the War on Terror, power and law merged to create a sophisticated, legally legitimated system of torture, which was—via rendition flights to third countries—effectively globalised. The former British Foreign Minister Robin Cook, who resigned from his post as Leader of the House of Commons and Lord

[116] 'No Blood, No Foul: Soldiers Accounts of Detainee Abuse in Iraq', *Human Rights Watch*, pp. 14–15.
[117] Dan Eggen and Josh White, 'Memo: Laws Didn't Apply to Interrogators: Justice Department Official in 2003 said President's Wartime Authority Trumped Many Statutes', *The Washington Post*, 2 Apr. 2008, p. A01.

President of the Council in March 2003 in protest against the Iraq War, was one of the few establishment figures in the United Kingdom (another one was Clare Short at a later stage), who was adamant to bring the situation to the attention of a wider public and to point out the complicity of the Bush administration in the global torture system that it was administering:

The techniques which were authorised included hooding detainees, stripping them naked, intimidating them with dogs and keeping them in stress positions. Those same techniques have now surfaced in different islands of the new Rumsfeld Gulag, from Guantanamo to Abu Ghraib to Kabul. It is simply inconceivable that such common practices could appear on different sides of the globe without central approval and direction.[118]

But let us return to the Iraq War and the way it was presented to the public. Ultimately, the legitimation of the conflict as a part of the War on Terror represented Iraq as an ally of bin-Laden, which explains why US soldiers marked some of their bombs with messages such as 'with love from Ground Zero', or 'in the name of the New York Fire Brigade'. That the link between Al Qaeda and Iraq was bogus was obvious to most serious observers of the rather secular Iraqi-Ba'thist state. Yet it took the US Defence Department four years to establish, what most of them knew, i.e. that Saddam Hussein's regime was not cooperating with Al Qaeda before the invasion. Ironically, the report's release came on the same day when then Vice President Cheney, appearing on a radio program, repeated his allegation that Al Qaeda was operating inside Iraq 'before we ever launched' the war, under the direction of Abu Musab al-Zarqawi, who was killed in June 2006.[119] The report, in a recently declassified section, shows that it was Douglas Feith, then US Undersecretary of Defence, who asserted in a briefing given to Cheney's chief of staff in September 2002, that the relationship between Iraq and Al Qaeda was 'mature' and 'symbiotic', marked by shared interests and evidenced by cooperation across ten categories, including training, financing and logistics.[120] Thus, Iraqis were labelled 'terrorists' in

---

[118] Robin Cook, 'George Bush's contempt for international law damages both America and Britain', *The Independent*, 26 Jun. 2004, p. 45.

[119] See R. Jeffrey Smith, 'Hussein's Pre-war Ties with al-Qaeda Discounted: Pentagon Report Says Contacts Were Limited', *The Washington Post*, 6 Apr. 2007. Available at http://www.washingtonpost.com/wp-dyn/content/article/2007/04/05/AR2007040502263.html [Last accessed 27 Aug. 2007].

[120] Ibid. The declassified report and documents are available at http://www.

the discursive build up to the war in order to maximise the power of the US Army before, during and after the invasion, to make it easier for US soldiers 'to pull the trigger'. It is within this constellation that some of them were introjected with racist hate, with 'bio-power' that made Abu Ghraib possible. Consciously, through the myth of Iraqi complicity in 9/11, and unconsciously through the constant emphasis on the 'Islamic threat' in the mass media of the country, many US soldiers were coded to loathe their victims, the natives who were thought to be complicit in the attack on the American homeland, the Muslim enemy who had to be broken, the 'barbarians' who had to be punished for their abomination, the black hordes who were threatening the walls of the polis.[121] 'I think part of the problem is the blatant racism against the Arabs', stated a US soldier pertinently. 'When you have an enemy you kind of have to demonise them a little bit like that in order to make yourself capable of pulling a trigger'.[122] 'Predisposition + opportunity', General Taguba established later, '= criminal behaviour'.[123] Taguba also concluded that,

Soldiers were immersed in the Islamic culture, a culture that many were encountering for a first time. Clearly there are major differences in worship and beliefs, and there is the association of Muslims with terrorism. All these causes exaggerate differences and create misperceptions that can lead to fear or devaluation of a people.[124]

The racist attitudes thus unleashed, made possible the kind of sexual humiliation and torture the Iraqi prisoners had to endure. Ultimately, in the dark corners of the Abu Ghraib prison complex, the *Muselmann*, that exceptional being who had endured the horrors of the Holocaust, returns, ironically, to the heart of his cultural homeland after his presence in the concentration camps of central and eastern Europe. Gilbert

---

dodig.osd.mil/fo/Foia/ERR/Part2–07–Intel-04.pdf [Last accessed 27 Aug. 2007].

[121] See also Emran Qureshi and Michael A. Sells (eds), *The New Crusades: Constructing the Muslim Enemy*, New York: Columbia University Press, 2003; Edward Said, *Covering Islam: How the Media and the Experts Determine how we see the World*, London: Vintage, 1997.

[122] 'No Blood, No Foul: Soldiers Accounts of Detainee Abuse in Iraq', *Human Rights Watch*, p. 34.

[123] 'The Taguba Report', in Greenberg and Dratel (eds), *The Torture Papers*, p. 449.

[124] Ibid., p. 448.

Achcar was the first to render the link between the plight of the *Muselmann* and the war on terror explicit. He points to the invention of the 'unlawful combatants' by Donald Rumsfeld which Achcar defines as a '"civilised" equivalent under the "rule of law" of what *Untermenschen* (subhumans) were for the Nazi state'.[125] To establish such a discursive link does not mean that the systematic brutality of the Nazi state is in any way or scope comparable to the abominations of the War on Terror, I think. But it does mean, from a metahistorical perspective, that every act of cruelty perpetuated by the state, or elements of it, is not an isolated incident, but precipitated and enveloped by a particular politico-cultural constellation and the discourses permeating it. Have we really managed to flush out racism from the political consciousness of the elites governing us? Would we have thought that Abu Ghraib could be possible in our contemporary age? Can we draw a strict *cognitive* boundary between traditional fascism and the neo-fascist attitudes of some individuals on the extreme right-wing in neoconservative circles in the United States? Today, overt racism is one of the most veiled cognitive dispositions in the western world, which makes it that much more difficult to detect its articulation. In the aftermath of 9/11, however, it came to the fore for a very short but decisive period in the many writings and opinion pieces of influential neoconservative ideologues. I found Michael Ledeen representative of this strand of 'ultra-neoconservative thinking' that is ultimately racist. On the issue of western superiority, Ledeen is unmistakeably brutish:

Now we know better, and our enemies will soon see the evidence in their own streets, deserts, and mountain redoubts. We have rediscovered the roots of our national character, which are an unshakeable confidence in the rightness of our mission, deep religious conviction, and a unique ability to come together to prevail against frightening obstacles. Once we have defeated the latest incarnation of servitude-this time wrapped in a religious mantle-we must remind ourselves of what we are, and the magnitude of our task. Next time, we must not listen to leaders who delight us with fables of peace and who tell us we are not worthy of our high calling. *Next time, we must dismiss those who tell us that all people are the same, all cultures are of equal worth*, all values are relative, and all judgments are to be avoided. Silvio Berlusconi was right: We've accomplished more than our enemies, and the overwhelming majority of mankind knows it.[126]

---

[125] Gilbert Achcar, *The Clash of Barbarisms: The Making of the New World Disorder*, London: Paradigm, 2006, p. 86.
[126] Michael Ledeen, 'Rediscovering American Character', *National Review*

For yesterday's fascist and today's ultra-neoconservative, there is a pronounced racial difference between us and them, an insurmountable distinction that segregates the economically, culturally and racially developed 'West' from those unfortunate people beyond this confine. So I don't think that my emphasis on a cognitive link between fascism and the attitude displayed by Michael Ledeen is shrill or too far-fetched. Ledeen himself has expressed his fascination for aspects of Mussolini and his regime which he researched for his PhD and subsequent publications co-written by Italian writers with ultra-rightwing sympathies.[127] It seems to me entirely plausible that the myth of a 'global Islamic threat' advocated by many networked neoconservatives surrounding the White House has been compared to 'the classic anti-Semitic belief in a "cosmopolitan" Jewish conspiracy to gain political power through a centralised and unified network'.[128]

A quick look through the pages of David Frum and Richard Perle's angry book *An End to Evil: How to Win the War Against Terror* corroborates that criticism further. Whereas Ledeen has been influential as a consultant surrounding the White House and as an armchair ideologue endowed with 'Freedom Chairs' at the American Enterprise Institute and the Foundation for Defence of Democracies, Frum and Perle are more directly immersed in politics. The former served as a special assistant to George W. Bush and coined the phrase 'axis of evil' designating Iraq, Iran and North Korea and identifying these countries as central theatres for the War on Terror. Richard Perle, on the other side, served for the Reagan administration as an assistant Secretary of Defense and worked on the Defense Board Advisory Committee between 1987 and 2004. He was Chairman of the Board during the immediate build-up to the invasion of Iraq from 2001 to 2003 under the George W. Bush administration.

Frum and Perle's book is both a manifesto for imperial war making and an indictment of the timidity of political discourse in the United

---

Online, 10 Oct. 2001. Available at http://www.aei.org/news/filter.,newsID. 13236/news_detail.asp [Last accessed 14 Apr. 2003].

[127] See further John Laughland, 'Flirting with Fascism: Neocon theorist Michael Ledeen draws more from Italian fascism than from the American right', *The American Conservative*, 30 Jun. 2003. Available at http://www. amconmag.com/article/2003/jun/30/00013/ [Last accessed 12 Mar. 2009].

[128] Neil MacMaster, 'Islamophobia in France and the "Algerian Problem"', in Qureshi and Sells, *The New Crusades*, p. 288.

States. While many are too politically correct to say so, they point out, the real enemy of the United States *is* Islam. 'We sometimes wonder', Frum and Perle write, 'how the war on terror escaped being called the war on You-know-who. ... [A]ll the available evidence indicates that militant Islam commands wide support, and even wider sympathy, amongst Muslims world wide, including Muslim minorities in the West'.[129] Consequently, all Muslims must be considered dangerous, untrustworthy and prone to brutality. They have to be policed, confined, supervised, and bullied into submission, if necessary through violence. 'A world at peace; a world governed by law; a world in which all people are free to find their own destinies', the authors argue, '[t]hat dream has not yet come true, it will not come true soon, but if it ever does come true, it will be brought into being by American armed might'.[130] This armed might of America should be exercised primarily in the Muslim worlds. No wonder then that one astute political theorist likened this type of discourse to a new kind of 'anti-Semitism' that substitutes violence against Jews with the subjugation of Muslims. The comparison seems entirely plausible to me:

Once it was another set of Semites who could not be trusted, whose primary loyalties lay elsewhere, who needed to be given a clear message about what was expected of them. Once, at the end of the nineteenth century, it was the Jewish anarchist and the Jewish communist who were portrayed as agents of global terror. Now it is Muslims who are involved in shadowy global conspiracies, Muslims who have 'fellow travellers'. The old language of anti-Semitism has found another target.[131]

Ledeen, Frum and Perle are frequent clash disciples, because they emerge from the depth of a vast political culture filled with hate and violence. On several occasions, I have pointed towards the connections between racism and imperialism in the western discourse. I have also alluded to the centrality of racism and imperialism for the making and persistence of the clash regime, yesterday and today. Ledeen, Frum and Perle must be considered contemporary disciples of the clash regime, exactly because their type of thinking about the other has historic precedence.

---

[129] David Frum and Richard Perle, *An End to Evil: How to Win the War Against Terror*, New York: Ballantine Books, 2004, pp. 34–35

[130] Ibid., p. 239.

[131] Anne Norton, *Leo Strauss and the Politics of American Empire*, London: Yale University Press, 2004, p. 212.

When we talk about a cultural constellation as structural as the clash regime, we must always connect the dots that qualify our argument, resisting the temptation, at the same time, to inflate them into a dogmatic scheme that would strangle to oblivion opposing discourses. And the linkages between the old imperial order and our present predicament are many. So we find that the current counterinsurgency manual distributed to the US Army commends T.E. Lawrence ('Lawrence of Arabia'), the very man who is deplored by many Arabs and Muslims because he co-instigated the revolts against the Ottoman Empire in the name of Arab unity, and then stepped back and couldn't do anything when Britain and France carved up what was left of the Ottoman Empire amongst themselves. In the manual, it is stated that Lawrence's 'experiences in the Arab revolt [against the Ottoman Empire] made him a hero and also provide some insights for today'. The manual also points to the importance of native collaborators under the revealing heading 'The host nation doing something tolerably is normally better than us doing it well'. The US Army should draw the lessons from the Vietnam War, it is pointed out, when 'in some things', according to General Creighton Abrams, the US Commander in Vietnam in 1971, 'we helped too much. And we *retarded* the Vietnamese by doing it. *We* can't run this thing. ... *They've* got to run it. The nearer we get to that the better off *they* are and the better off *we* are'. The critical reader is immediately struck by the emphasis (in the original) on the pronouns *they* and *we*. It establishes the syntactical structure setting the fundamental boundary between us (occupier) and them (the natives). Once that boundary is established *they* can exercise what *we* tell them ideally via an armada of native informants and friendly politicians. 'Do not try to do too much with your own hands', Lawrence is quoted in the manual. 'Better the Arabs do it tolerably than that you do it perfectly. It is their war, and you are to help them, not to win it for them'.[132] Lawrence, Frum, Perle and Ledeen, imperialism and the war on terror, Arabs and Arabs, Muslims and Muslims, natives and natives, the imperial functionaries have changed, the language of imperialism has morphed, the discourse of power is more sophisticated, but the object of (neo)imperialism remains the same.

[132] *Counterinsurgency*, Headquarters: Department of the Army, Dec. 2006. Available at http://www.usgcoin.org/library/doctrine/COIN-FM3–24.pdf [Last accessed 26 Dec. 2009].

A far more insidious 'bio-political' sub-plot of the 'war on terror' is discernable once we engage more systematically with the wider ideological excesses of contemporary neoconservatism in the United States, an aggressive, occasionally fascist ideology that American society will have to deal with for quite some time to come. It was Seymour Hersh, the investigative journalist of *The New Yorker*, who made the link between neoconservative ideology and racism explicit. Hersh revealed that the attitude that 'Arabs are particularly vulnerable to sexual humiliation became a talking point among pro-war Washington conservatives in the months before the March 2003 invasion of Iraq'.[133] Hersh argued further, that US neoconservatives learned of such 'vulnerability' from a book entitled *The Arab Mind* authored by the Israeli cultural anthropologist Raphael Patai in 1973. The following paragraph gives an impression about the mode of argumentation throughout Patai's book:

As far as the traditional Arab sex mores can be observed without penetrating into the secrets of the bedchamber, the impression is gained that they are the product of severe repressions. The avoidances observed in public between men and women, the existence of two separate societies, male and female, each with its own customs, language, and religious obligation, and many other factors indicate, even to the psychologically untrained observer, behaviour patterns developed in response to early repression.[134]

Patai then moves on to discuss Arab 'child-rearing practices', and the sexual hospitality of 'various Arab tribes' in the nineteenth century, whose men wore 'loincloth and walk about without any covering on the head', and whose women wore 'no clothing above the waist'.[135] Surprisingly (or maybe not), according to an academic quoted by Hersh, this book became 'the bible of the neo-cons on Arab behaviour'. Hence, in the discussions of the 'neo-cons', two themes emerged: 'one, that Arabs only understand force and, two, that the biggest weakness of Arabs is shame and humiliation'. In turn, such ideas about the way Arabs can be broken found their way into the so called *Pride-*

---

[133] Seymour M. Hersh, 'The Gray Zone: How a secret Pentagon program came to Abu Ghraib', *The New Yorker*, 24 May 2004. Available at http://www.newyorker.com/archive/2004/05/24/040524fa_fact?printable=true [Last accessed 27 Jul. 2007].

[134] Raphael Patai, *The Arab Mind*, revised edition, New York: Charles Scribner's Sons, 1983, p. 128.

[135] Ibid., pp. 133–134.

and-Ego-down-Approach, a particularly subjugating form of psychological torture 'legitimately' exerted by US interrogators in order to 'break' their detainees:

The government consultant said that there may have been a serious goal, in the beginning, behind the sexual humiliation and the posed photographs. It was thought that some prisoners would do anything—including spying on their associates—to avoid dissemination of the shameful photos to family and friends. The government consultant said, 'I was told that the purpose of the photographs was to create an army of informants, people you could insert back in the population'. The idea was that they would be motivated by fear of exposure, and gather information about pending insurgency action, the consultant said. If so, it wasn't effective; the insurgency continued to grow.[136]

I am conscious that one has to be very careful with sources which remain unnamed, especially when they are cited by journalists. But I have decided to use this material, because in this specific case there is enough independent evidence to support the type of racist attitude I am alluding to. Consider this account of Brigadier General Janis L. Karpinski given during an interview conducted at Camp Doha on 15 February 2004:

It became sport. ... [E]ven saying this makes me feel sick to my stomach, but, they were enjoying what they were doing and the MPs who saw this opportunity—seized the opportunity. ... I would imagine ... it went something like this—in the DFAC or when they were sitting around the Internet Café. 'Oh yeah, you should see what we do to the prisoners sometime'. 'Can I come over and watch?' 'Oh yeah. How about Thursday'. And because we had a clerk over there who was thoroughly enjoying all of this sport, and the pictures anyway, and she was the girlfriend of the guy who was one of the kingpins in this. We had a guy from the maintenance who must have been one of the invited participants and—these are bad people. That was the first time I knew that they would do such a thing as to bring a dog handler in there to use for interrogation.[137]

Even more insidious examples include incidents when detainees were referred to as 'Jihad Jerry', 'Gus', 'Shitboy', 'one of the three wise

[136] Hersh, 'The Gray Zone'. See also Trish Schuh, 'Racism and Religious Desecration as US policy: Islamophobia a retrospective', *Counterpunch*, 6/7 May 2006. Available at http://www.counterpunch.org/schuch05062006.html [Last accessed 15 May 2006].
[137] The Taguba Report (Annex)', in Greenberg and Dratel (eds), *The Torture Papers*, pp. 530–531.

223

men',[138] or when they were told to 'curse' Islam.[139] Moreover at Abu Ghraib, loyalty to Islam was turned into an expedient vehicle to extract 'critical intelligence' from detainees through psychological torture. In a Memorandum, dated 20 November 2003, for instance, a 'request for exception to CJTF [Combined Joint Taskforce]-7 Interrogation and Counter Resistance Policy' was made (essentially, a measure to extend the legal 'boundaries' for the interrogations). The 'subject' in this particular case was a Syrian male and an 'admitted foreign fighter who came to commit Jihad against Coalition Forces in Iraq' and who was 'captured in an attempted IED attack in Baghdad'.[140] The detainee is thought to be 'at the point where he is resigned to the hope that Allah will see him through this episode in his life, therefore he feels no need to speak with interrogators'. He thus has to be 'put in a position where he will feel that the only option to get out of jail is to speak with interrogators'.[141] To that end:

[i]nterrogators will reinforce the fact that we have attempted to help him time and time again and that they are now putting it in Allah's hands. Interrogators will at maximum throw tables, chairs, invade his personal space and continuously yell at the detainee. Interrogators will not physically touch or harm the detainee ... If the detainee has not broken yet, interrogators will move into the segregation phase of the approach. ... During transportation, the Fear up Harsh approach will be continued, highlighting the Allah factor. ... MP working dogs will be present and barking during this phase. Detainee will be strip searched by guards with the empty sandbag over his head for the safety of himself, prison guards, interrogators and other prisoners. Interrogators will wait outside the room while detainee is strip searched. Interrogators will watch from a distance while detainee is placed in the segregation cell. Detainee will be put on the adjusted sleep schedule ... for 72 hours. Interrogations will be conducted continuously during this 72 hour period. The approaches which will be used during this phase will include, fear up harsh, pride and ego down, silence and loud music. Stress positions will also be used in accordance with CJTF-7 IROE in order to intensify this approach.[142]

This passage links up with many arguments I have made thus far: the technical language provides an example for the type of 'scientific

---

[138] 'Ibid., p. 472.
[139] Ibid., p. 524. For more graphic examples see p. 522 or p. 504.
[140] Ibid., p. 466.
[141] Ibid.
[142] Ibid., p. 467.

torture' I have mentioned at the beginning of this section; the aim 'to break the detainee' exemplifies the licentious character of bio-power that can only be unleashed in a situation where an invading army wilfully creates anarchy; and the fact that dogs were employed and the constant reference to 'the Allah factor' further elaborates on the type of racism that is at stake here.

Sceptics may argue that what I have said thus far is confined to the combat situation in Iraq, to the abominations intrinsic to war. But such criticism undervalues the effect of discourse on practice. The point I am making is that the Iraq War was enveloped by a discourse with racist connotations that affected the way US soldiers perceived their counterpart. Aggression towards the other was justified by many spokespersons of the politico-cultural field in the United States. I have mentioned the trenchant writings of bestselling author Anne Coulter in my other books and there are many other examples beyond the ones already cited:[143] from a surprisingly Islamophobic book titled *The Everlasting Hatred: The Roots of Jihad* written by the best-selling author and influential Christian-Zionist activist Hal Lindsey, to the bizarre reaction of radio presenter Don Imus to the news of the crash of an Iranian civilian airliner and the deaths of its passengers.[144]

As a result of this massive upsurge of anti-Islamic sentiments, Muslims are not simply judged anymore. Their presence calls for management strategies; they have been turned into a police matter. A rather immediate effect of this securitisation of Muslim communities has been that government takes Muslims permanently into account and that society is placed in a state of perpetual alert, because of their alleged potencies to disrupt our everyday life. 'There is no escaping the unfortunate fact', Daniel Pipes writes, 'that Muslim visitors [to the United States] must undergo additional background checks. Mosques require a scrutiny beyond that applied to churches and temples'.[145] Such surveillance of Muslims should not stop here. Pipes also supports the supervision of universities. To that end, his internet portal 'Campus Watch' publishes 'reports' about professors who are thought to harbour anti-American or anti-Israeli sentiments. Ironically, when it comes to Islam, the cacophony of the rightwing is echoed by the erudite, left-

[143] See Adib-Moghaddam, *Iran in World Politics*, part 3.
[144] See further, Lieven, *America Right or Wrong*, pp. 167ff.
[145] Daniel Pipes, 'The Enemy Within', *New York Post*, 24 Jan. 2003.

leaning literary critic. For Christopher Hitchens, for instance, punitive measures should be spread even more widely:

Liberal reluctance to confront this sheer horror is the result, I think, of a deep reticence about some furtive concept of 'race'. It is subconsciously assumed that a critique of political Islam is an attack on people with brown skins. One notes in passing that any such concession implicitly denies or negates Islam's claim to be a universal religion. Indeed, some of its own exponents certainly do speak as if they think of it as a tribal property. And, at any rate, in practice, so it is. The fascistic subculture that has taken root in Britain and that lives by violence and hatred is composed of two main elements. One is a refugee phenomenon, made up of shady exiles from the Middle East and Asia who are exploiting London's traditional hospitality, and one is the projection of an immigrant group that has its origins in a particularly backward and reactionary part of Pakistan. ... In Britain, in the 21st century, there are now honour killings, forced marriages, clerically mandated wife-beatings, incest in all but name, and the adoption of apparel for females that one cannot be sure is chosen by them but which is claimed as an issue of (of all things) free expression. This would be bad enough on its own and if it were confined to the Muslim 'community' alone. But, of course, such a toxin cannot be confined, and the votaries of theocracy now claim the God-given right to slaughter females at random for nothing more than their perceived immodesty. The least we can do, confronted by such radical evil, is to look it in the eye (something it strives to avoid) and call it by its right name. For a start, it is the female victims of this tyranny who are 'disenfranchised', while something rather worse than 'disenfranchisement' awaits those who dare to disagree.[146]

Academics and journalists function as complicit narrators of the type of racism at stake here.[147] Consider a symposium organised by the American Enterprise Institute in March 2006. At this occasion, Pierre Rehov, a French filmmaker, Nancy Kobrin, an affiliated professor to the University of Haifa, Peter Raddatz, a German 'scholar' of Islamic Studies and the co-author of the 'Encyclopaedia of Islam' and Gudrun Eussner, a journalist specializing in mass communication, political science, and Iranian philology, pondered the 'Muslim rape epidemic that is sweeping Europe and over many other nations host to immigrants from the Islamic world'. In the written introduction to the symposium, the organisers state that the 'direct connection between the rapes and

[146] Christopher Hitchens, 'Don't Mince Words: The London car bomb plot was designed to kill women', *Slate.com*, 2 July 2007.
[147] On the link between culture and anti-muslim and anti-Arab prejudice see also Douglas Little, *American Orientalism: The United States and the Middle East Since 1945*, London: I.B. Tauris, 2002.

Islam is irrefutable, as Muslims are significantly overrepresented among convicted rapists and rape suspects. The Muslim perpetrators themselves boast that their crime is justified', it is claimed, 'since their victims were, among other things, not properly veiled'.[148] Of course, there is no supporting material given, no court proceedings, not even a single statement. Instead, one of the participants offers following 'explanation':

[Islam's] biologistic 'thinking' demands the 'pure' man as the real human dominating the 'impure' woman as a lower form, rather close to some animal-like existence. Therefore, sexuality cannot be sublimated and has to serve— aside from ramifications into homo-, paedo- and sodo-variants—a basic double function: fertilising and punishing.[149]

Citing a book by Temple Grandin and Catherine Johnson entitled *Animals in Translation: Using the Mysteries of Autism to Decode Animal Behavior*, another participant links the behaviour of 'Arab Muslim boys' to that of dogs:

In my work on Islamic suicide terrorism, I have noted that the rage is really against the prenatal Muslim mother, misdirected to the infidels who represent her in the jihadi mind's eye. Interestingly enough, Grandin also notes that 'humans have neotenised dogs: without realising it, humans have bred dogs to stay immature for their entire lives'. (p. 86) I would substitute the word 'bred' for concepts like child-rearing practices, etc. And raise the question as can it be that Arab Muslim boys turned rapists have been 'neotenised', that is raised to stay immature for their entire lives?[150]

Suddenly, now that we have delved into the vulgar and disturbing discourse enveloping it, I found it easier to explain the types of torture exercised at Abu Ghraib and Guantanamo, for if film-makers and scholars seriously discuss how the behaviour of Arab-Muslim men can be linked to that of dogs, it is that much easier to explain why US soldiers could participate in denigrating their captives. If highly educated 'experts', invited by a prominent US think tank that hosts influential neoconservative strategists, quite 'academically' dehumanise 'Arab-Muslims', one should not be surprised about the residues of racism that are inscribed in some of our institutions. In this sense, the tortur-

---

[148] 'Symposium: To Rape an Unveiled Woman', *FrontPageMagazine.com*, 7 Mar. 2006.
[149] Ibid.
[150] Ibid.

ers at Abu Ghraib are themselves victims of an overarching cultural constellation that is impervious to the plight of the other. During the War on Terror, this culture of racism resurfaced once again, and at Abu Ghraib it added yet another regrettable document to the archives of human atrocities against each other.

I could go on giving more and more examples of the violence perpetuated during the Presidency of George W. Bush. Of course, there is no suggestion in all of this, that there have not been any opposing voices. The election of the current US President Barack Obama itself is the outcome of a protest movement against the neoconservative current in US politics, against the excesses of the Bush administration, against the narrative of an unending global War on Terror. Moreover, it should not be forgotten that one of the reasons why there is so much published material available on the torture at Abu Ghraib and Guantanamo Bay is because US society has empowered itself to guarantee a degree of transparency in the political process of the country, that is in the face of the most resourceful state in the world. The fact that the US is a democracy made the preceding documentation of the Bush Administration's policies possible in the first place. Indeed, at the time of writing, the Obama administration released four Justice Department memos on CIA 'interrogations' mostly intact, in response to a public records request from the American Civil Liberties Union and other groups, despite strident objections by the security community of the country. At the same time, President Obama granted legal immunity to CIA officials who followed Justice Department guidelines in carrying out water-boarding, the near-drowning technique of prisoners, and other 'interrogation' methods of terror suspects following the 9/11 attacks, whilst leaving it open if those lawyers who made a legal case for torture should be prosecuted.[151]

---

[151] President Obama also issued a series of executive orders that closed the 'black site' secret prisons and halted the use of 'enhanced interrogation techniques' that had been used there. He also committed himself to close the prison at Guantánamo within a year, which he has not followed up on at the time of writing. See further Mark Danner, 'The Red Cross Torture Report: What it means', *New York Review of Books*, vol. 56. no. 7, Apr. 2009. Available at http://www.nybooks.com/articles/22614 [Last accessed 29 Apr. 2009]. The declassified documents show that CIA interrogators used water-boarding at least eighty-three times in August 2002 against Abu Zubaydah, a suspected Al Qaeda operative and 183 times in March 2003 against Khalid Sheikh Mohammed, another suspected leader of Al Qaeda.

Yet the topic of the last paragraphs was not if and how US civil society affects the foreign policies of the state and the ethical and moral standards of the country's intelligence services, a topic worth exploring more systematically. Rather, I wanted to show how a particular racist discourse, which gained impetus in the aftermath of the terrorist attacks on 11 September 2001, made possible the torture at Abu Ghraib and how the events there cannot be detached from the salient components feeding into the clash regime today. Alas, to speak freely against anti-muslim sentiments—or even to admit their pernicious existence—is so alien to a historical narrative that has erased the abominations of racism from its archives, and so extraneous to the mainstream of academia which treats racism as a peripheral area of enquiry, that it is bound to make little headway for a long time.[152] Do students study racism as a core component of their IR module, in their Political Science course, in Middle Eastern studies? The majority of them do not.[153] Does the topic of racism occupy a prominent place in our syllabi? Not so much. No wonder then that there is a vast space populated by caricatures of the other, which we have yet to conquer and to redraw empathetically.

The first step into that direction is to resist the lure of the current political culture that is obsessed with the alleged 'Muslim' threat. Why, asks the security conscious reader, if it is in the name of Islam that cities all over the world are attacked? First, because subsuming the act of a few into the vast spaces of the discursive formations claimed by Islam does not yield analytical and factual value. How far would have our understanding of the Irish Republican Army got if we had looked at

[152] For notable exceptions, see Richard Jackson, 'Language, policy and the construction of a torture culture in the war on terrorism', *Review of International Studies*, vol. 33, no. 3, July 2007, pp. 353–371; Alex Belamy, 'No Pain, No Gain? Torture and Ethics in the War on Terror', *International Affairs*, vol. 82, no. 1, 2006, pp. 121–148; Achcar, *The Clash of Barbarisms*, 2006.

[153] Sankaran Krishna accuses IR of collective 'amnesia' when it comes to issues such as racism. See idem. 'Race, Amnesia, and the Education of International Relations', in Gruffydd Jones (ed.), *Decolonising International Relations*, pp. 89–108. See further Geeta Chowdhry and Shirin M. Rai, 'The Geographies of Exclusion and the Politics of Inclusion: Race-based exclusions in the teaching of international relations', *International Studies Perspectives*, vol. 10, no. 1, Feb. 2009, pp. 84–91.

what the Pope and Catholicism says about the legitimacy of armed insurgency?

It is simply wrong to argue that in the 'historical imagination of many Muslims and Arabs, bin-Laden represents nothing short of the new incarnation of Saladin' and to derive from this that the 'House of Islam's war for world mastery is a traditional, indeed venerable, quest that is far from over'.[154] Such line of argumentation buys into the propaganda of Al Qaeda type movements. Prof. Karsh seems to accept the myth that bin-Laden is acting in the name of 'many' Muslims. Alleging such kind of global 'Muslim' conspiracy implicitly fortifies the constitutive powers of the violent agenda of Al Qaeda and other movements who must feel quite honoured and exalted to be compared to Saladin by a senior academic. I am using the term constitutive consciously here, because the fear of this minority called 'Al Qaeda' has affected not only domestic politics in the United Kingdom, France, Germany, the United States, Australia and elsewhere, it has led to the suspension of hard earned civil liberties. In the aftermath of 9/11, Jonathan Steele, a contributor to *The Guardian* even went so far as to liken New York City to Brezhnev's Moscow. To him, the city had become a 'sad place' that had lost its 'worldwide reputation for loud voices and strongly expressed opinions'. It was now 'tip-toeing around in whispers' and it seemed to be in the grip of 'a stifling conformity which muzzles public discourse on US foreign policy, the war on terrorism and Israel'.[155] In this way, the obsession with Al Qaeda and the ensuing hype around the war on terror had the regrettable effect to subdue one of the most vibrant, and cosmopolitan cities of the world.

If we believe with Herbert Marcuse that 'free society' requires freeing ourselves from any form of meta-narrative, economics, politics, history, the state etc.,[156] freedom from bin-Laden means liberating ourselves from the 'quasi-Islamist' discourse attached to him. But many writers, journalists, liberals, neoconservatives, right-wing parties etc. are busy doing the opposite. They are helping to morph disparate

---

[154] Efraim Karsh, *Islamic Imperialism: A History*, London: Yale University Press, 2006, p. 234.

[155] Jonathan Steele, 'New York is starting to feel like Brezhnev's Moscow, Public debate in America has now become a question of loyalty', *The Guardian*, 16 May 2002.

[156] Herbert Marcuse, *Towards A Critical Theory of Society*, vol. 2, Douglas Kellner (ed.), London: Routledge, 2001, p. 51.

issues into a supposedly global Islamic conspiracy. By doing so, they are contributing to the recruitment targets of self-proclaimed 'jihadi groups'. It is immensely conducive to Al Qaeda's struggle that the Danish newspaper *Jyllands-Posten* published cartoons of the Prophet Muhammad that were deemed derogatory by many Muslims. It is very useful that during that period Martin Henriksen, a spokesmen of the ultra rightwing Danish Popular Party (DPP), stepped in front of the camera to designate Islam as a 'terrorist movement' taking pride in the fact that 'criticising Islam is the official policy of [his] party'.[157] The Al Qaeda recruiter who preys on disenfranchised Somali immigrants in London, Paris, Rome and Madrid must be very pleased that the best-selling Italian novelist Oriana Fallaci complains about Somali Muslims leaving 'yellow streaks of urine that profaned the millenary marbles of the Baptistery' in Florence. 'Good Heavens!' she writes in one of three short books written after 9–11. 'They really take long shots, these sons of Allah, wondering if Muslim men will one day 'sh[...] in the Sistine Chapel'.[158]

There are, of course, less vulgar examples of such instances of anti-Islamic utterance such as the global proclamation against 'Islamic totalitarianism', which was drafted after the cartoon controversy by a range of authors and writers, including Hirsi Magan Ali and Salman Rushdie. Here, the obsession with bin-Laden has had the power to create strange bedfellows. 'After having overcome fascism, Nazism, and Stalinism', these self-conscious liberals concur wholeheartedly with such staunchly (neo)conservative figures as Margaret Thatcher, John Woolsey and Norman Podhoretz, 'the world now faces a new global threat: Islamism'.[159] So the erudite, liberal writer converges with the networked, right-wing (neo)conservative when it comes to castigating some Islam. Ultimately, their different ideological persuasions do not prevent them to agree on the idea that there is a coherent and virulent 'Islamist' threat out there. Of course they do not realise it, but they

---

[157] Available at http://www.dailystar.com.lb/article.asp?edition_id=10&categ_id=2&article_id=22175 [Last accessed 12 Jan. 2007].

[158] Margaret Talbot, 'The Agitator: Oriana Fallaci directs her fury toward Islam', *The New Yorker*, 5 Jun. 2006.

[159] An English version of the letter was posted on the webpage of the *Jillands-Posten* newspaper which published the cartoons that sparked the worldwide protests by many Muslims. Available at http://www.jp.dk/indland/artikel:aid=3585740/ [Last accessed 8 May 2006].

share this delusion with the ardent Al Qaeda propagandist who is equally adamant to globalise his agenda. 'We also stress to honest Muslims that they should move, incite, and mobilise the [Islamic] nation', demands bin-Laden himself.[160] They do not need to. These self-designated liberals and right-wing activists are doing their job perfectly well. Together with the wars in Iraq and in Afghanistan their sweeping campaigns against 'Islamic totalitarianism' have extended Al Qaeda's sway over a small group of disillusioned minorities in Europe, feeding into the 'home grown terrorism' we are dealing with today.

A serious consequence of this mode of confrontation is that it makes it difficult to individualise the political formation of terrorism, that it complicates threading the narratives constituting it, dissecting the mindsets sustaining it and deconstructing the ideas legitimating it. In other words, by conflating a politico-ideological movement such as Al Qaeda with some Islam (or even Islamism) as a whole, it is that much harder to penetrate the syntactical 'epicentre' of terrorism, the thick layer of normative constructions, rhetorical practices, textual representations, power symbols, and imagery which envelope the terrorist nucleus. These have to be disentangled and spread out for critical investigation rather than enmeshed into unitary categories. It should become obvious that such an endeavour cannot be pursued from 'within' the state as British, German and French politicians repeatedly request. Rather the contrary. In order to break terrorism up, in order to decipher its codes and penetrate the ideology producing it, abstractions such as 'Muslim', 'Islam', 'British', 'Asian', all of them problematic and alas part and parcel of the contemporary discourse, must be interrogated from 'without', from a dispassionate, non-governmental vantage point, a position that is the exact opposite of the embedded informants' advocated by many politicians today. Engendering discourse that works against nihilistic violence, in short, asks for societal emancipation from the politics of the state, not encroachment by it.

Avicennian dialecticians and Qutbian Islamists

For all the efforts to subsume the globe under the ironclad narrative of one imagined civilisation (Americo-centric, Anglo-centric, Franco-

---

[160] *BBC Monitoring*, 12 Feb. 2003.

centric etc.), there continuously appears, at the other extremity of the world, a collective discourse entirely devoted to another order, to another form of sovereignty, to other categories. I have started to argue in the last chapter that in the Islamist imagination this order is a newly devised 'original Islam' that is located in the period of the *rashidun*, the righteous compatriots of Muhammad.

Orientalists have argued that in the discourse of Islam there has been, from the outset, a political dynamic. Bernard Lewis alludes to this when he says that during 'Muhammad's lifetime, the Muslims became at once a political and a religious community, with the prophet as head of state'.[161] This has not been disputed by historians of Islam. But Lewis and Maxime Rodinson, are wrong to imply at the same time that Matthew 23:21—'render unto Caesar the things which are Caesar's; and unto God the things which are God's'—means that the early Christian community was apolitical, that Jesus 'wanted to teach men to achieve their salvation and nothing else', as the latter argues.[162] This was not the only message. In the same Gospel, Jesus says that he has not come to bring peace, but a sword. Jesus was certainly not a violent individual, but to assume that the gospels do not contain a political potentiality or that Jesus' resistance did not lend itself to ideological manipulation is historically incorrect. Indeed, the very fact that the 'Kingdom of God' was not realised during his lifetime created the political dynamism that transmuted Christianity into a global phenomenon. The messianic promise translated into both a spiritual and political utopia. It is an obvious hypocrisy to ascribe a political rationality only to movements and belief-systems other than 'ours'. It is also a deceptive strategy to silence some of the grievances of the other side. Once we consult critical theory, a rather more convincing interpretation of the early community around Jesus emerges. 'One must take early Christianity more seriously than most people do, in order to be impressed by the almost unbelievable radicalism of this small group of people' Erich Fromm writes. The early Christians lived:

in a small part of the Roman Empire at the height of its power and glory. ... Yet this small group of Palestinian Jews carried the conviction that this power-

[161] Bernard Lewis, *The Crisis of Islam: Holy War and Unholy Terror*, London: Phoenix, 2003, p. 4.
[162] Maxime Rodinson, *Muhammad: Prophet of Islam*, London: I.B. Tauris, 2002, p. xvi.

ful world would soon collapse. Realistically, to be sure, they were mistaken; as a result of the failure of Jesus' reappearance, Jesus' death and resurrection are interpreted in the gospels as constituting the beginning of the new eon, and after Constantine an attempt was made to shift the mediating role of Jesus to the papal church. Finally, for all practical purposes the church became the substitute—in fact, though not in theory—for the new eon.[163]

Until the discourse of the Enlightenment, the image of Jesus as the leader of one of the greatest resistance movements in human history was rather salient. He was also the most prominent example for martyrdom in the cause of god. Ever since he was crucified, 'the worship of death, the *Einverständnis mit dem Tode* had held sway over civilisation: death as reward, as entrance into life, prerequisite of happiness and salvation'. It is true, as Herbert Marcuse writes, that this idea has lost its ideological power, that it does not threaten the status quo, that its message is weaker than the promise of modernity, that 'it helps, again and again, to prevent and "contain" revolution'.[164] But surely this is not because the discourse of Christianity is essentially apolitical, but an effect of its theological reengineering. One could mention here the Council of Ephesus in 431 'which condemned millennialism and expurgated works of earlier church fathers thought to be tainted with the doctrine'.[165] And, of course, the secularising premise of the reformation that merged with the perspective of western modernity. It was this re-signification of the discourse of Christianity that gave birth to the 'apolitical Christ' (and the idea that he must have had white skin and blue eyes). The process of secularisation 'replaced religious values by secular values ... an otherworldly by and inner-worldly orientation ... and the primacy of the religious institutions by that of the political and economic ones'[166] Before this caesura, 'at least from the second half of the Middle ages onward', Foucault argues, 'the Bible was the great form for the articulation of religious moral, and political protests against the power of kings and the despotism of the church'. Reference

---

[163] Erich Fromm, *To Have or to Be?*, London: Continuum, 2005, p. 46.
[164] Marcuse, *Towards a Critical Theory of Society*, p. 173.
[165] Malise Ruthven, *Fundamentalism: The Search for Meaning*, Oxford: Oxford University Press, 2004, p. 14.
[166] Wolfgang Schluchter, *Religion and America*, Mary Douglas and Steven M. Tipton (eds), Boston: Beacon Press, 1982. Here quoted from idem., 'The future of religion', in Alexander and Seidman (eds), *Culture and Society*, p. 250.

to the Bible 'functioned ... as a protest, a critique, and an oppositional discourse'. In the Middle Ages, Jerusalem was not only 'always a protest against all the Babylons that had come back to life'. It was 'a protest against eternal Rome, against the Rome of the Caesars, against the Rome that shed the blood of the innocent in the circus'.[167] Indeed, was it not after the beheading of his friend, relative and baptiser John at the hands of King Herod that Jesus began teaching the message that got John the Baptist arrested in the first place? 'Repent' he warned from now on 'for the Kingdom of God is at hand' (Matthew, 4:17). Ultimately then, it was a political event that propelled Jesus into adopting the responsibility of leadership of this group of Palestinian Jews.

The Quran like the Bible and the Torah has been repeatedly turned into the weapon of insurrection and revolt; its syntax provides enough flexibility to signify political action. In this regard, it is not different from other religions. There is a dialectic in the discourse of Islam between *din* and *dawlah*. The former denotes the transcendental realm, the latter the centrality of politics and governance. As Hamid Dabashi notes, the Quran itself:

consists of two major parts, each at narrative and normative odd with the other. The 114 *surahs* or chapters of the Qur'an are divided into those revealed in Mecca between 610 and 622 (or ten years before the commencement of the Islamic calendar until the prophet's migration from Mecca to Medina), and those revealed in Medina between 622 and 632 (or from year 1 on the Islamic calendar to year 10). The Meccan *surahs* correspond to the rising crescendo of the Prophet's mission and are revolutionary and destabilising in their moral defiance of injustice and tyranny, as he brings the Meccan pariahs and the downtrodden together around his insurrectionary revelations. The Medinan *surahs*, on the contrary, are the record of the prophet's consolidating his power in Medina and the establishing of his political community. Between the Meccan and the Medinan chapters of the Qur'an, the moral uprising of a revolutionary movement and the political consolidation of power, there is thus a narrative and normative tension.[168]

The phrase *Islam din wa dawlah* indicates that discursive formations of Islam entail a political connotation. It does not tell us whether such politics is weighted in favour of the state or in support of resistance to

[167] Michel Foucault, *Society Must be Defended: Lectures at the Collège de France*, David Macey (trans.), London: Penguin, 2004, p. 71.
[168] Hamid Dabashi, *Islamic Liberation Theology: Resisting the Empire*, Routledge: London, 2008, p. 188.

it. The Quran, by necessity of its political syntax, has repeatedly signified narratives that were either conducive to combating the state/
caliphate, or to legitimate it.

This contraction and expansion of an Islam either as a theory of
governance or as a theory of resistance is reflected in the politics of the
umma after the death of Muhammad. Following the death of the
Prophet in 632, there emerged three successive forms of caliphatic
authority: First, 'Muhammadian', characterised by the rule of the
'rashidun' or righteous caliphs Abu Bakr (r. 632–634), Umar ibn al-
Khattab (r. 634–644), Usman ibn Affan (r. 644–656) and Ali ibn Talib
(r. 656–661). The rashidun, unlike later rulers, could legitimate their
authority through their immediate association or familial ties with the
Prophet. This 'Muhammadian' mandate was substituted by the hereditary and monarchic authority claimed by the Umayyad caliphs (661–
750). It was during their rule that the political competition within the
umma became more divisive, and when Shia discourses were formulated more forcefully, especially after the killing of Muhammad's
grandson Hussein by the forces of the Umayyad caliph Yazid (r. 680–
683) at the Battle of Karbala in 680. In 749–750, the Umayyad
caliphate was overthrown by the Abbasids, whose authority was
expressed in dynastic terms and who established themselves in Baghdad, until the Mongol invasion in 1258.

So from the outset, there was an immense competition over Islam,
over its political message, theological content and transcendental
promise, an ongoing battle over Muhammad, the Quran, the knowledge thereof and its dispersal into society by powerful authorities. The
early history of the *umma* also indicates that Islam has never really
functioned as solely a theory of state. It was always also enacted within
society, within the shelter of the mosque, practised by Muslims in their
everyday lives. What has been called Islam has to be conceived of as a
discursive field open to both the politics of the state, and the politics of
resistance, to both societal organisation and revolt. It should be
remembered that three out of the four rashidun—Umar, Usman and
Ali—the second, third and fourth Caliphs were killed by Islamic coun-
ter-movements and not by non-Muslims. Indeed, the Quran itself
entails a rich political theology that accentuates the rise and fall of
empires. The ascendancy of Moses despite the might of the Pharaoh,
the revolt of Muhammad against the 'pagan' Meccan tribes or the success of the other prophets against the worldly powers of the day, the

Quran, rather comparable to the Bible, puts particular emphasis on the viability of political opposition and the empowerment of, what we would call today, the disadvantaged strata of society. It delivers a syntax that has signified, repeatedly, an anti-foundational discourse that accentuates the plight of the *mostazafan* (oppressors) against the *mostakbaran* (oppressors). In the recent literature about Muslim politics, this anti-foundational functionality of Islam is increasingly acknowledged: 'The fancy footwork of belated and blind ideologues notwithstanding', writes Dabashi with regard to the politics of Islam today, 'the ordinary Muslims in the streets of Tehran, Cairo, Peshawar, or Ramallah, whether or not they even consciously recognise themselves as believing Muslims, are the sole source of revolutionary energy and aspiration'.[169] 'As long as there are Muslims', writes Salman Sayyid in a comparable vein, 'the promise and fear of Islamism will remain, for in the end, for us Muslims, Islam is another name for the hope of something better...'.[170] Dabashi and Sayyid place central importance on Islam not as a sacrosanct ideology, but as a kind of critical explosive which humankind can throw into oppressive orders in order to blast them out of their consensual mode and thus awaken the spirit of the subjugated multitudes. They profess, in short, that in the face of every state-centred Islam, every form of Islamic imperialism, there is an anti-hegemonic discourse that claims an equally 'Islamic' legitimacy.

So comparable to other discursive formations that are directed towards the transcendental, the discourse of Islam has a political momentum inscribed to it. Islam has not only been the Islam of the caliphs or monarchs; there are many versions of Islam that were opposed to the state, and not only within the 'Shia' discourse as it is too often assumed, but also in 'Sunni' political thought. Authority within this formation, the authority of the Shia Imams, the authority of the caliphs, the authority of the Ayatollahs, Mullahs, Sheikhs and Muftis today, has been recurrently challenged. Indeed, like Isaac Deutscher's (1907–1967) 'non-Jewish Jew', we can refer to a list of seemingly 'non-Muslim Muslims' who gained their notoriety out of their revolt against the sovereignty of such authorities. They too adopted, entirely self-consciously, a position at the margins of society in order

---

[169] Ibid., p. 142.
[170] S. Sayyid, *A Fundamental Fear: Eurocentrism and the Emergence of Islamism*, London: Zed, 1997, p. 160.

to achieve radical goals. They too expressed their dissatisfaction with the politics of identity opting for a universal, humanistic message. Their escape to the utopia of God was a statement against a theocratic order on earth. The primary difference between the non-Jewish Jew and the non-Muslim Muslim is that the latter's history has not been written yet. The non-Muslim Muslim is an orphan of history, whereas the non-Jewish Jew has been privileged culturally and intellectually. The anti-foundational, critical merit of the non-Muslim Muslim are buried in the archives of the Islamic worlds, carefully guarded by the ruling classes who are terrified by the disruptive potencies that their histories may unleash. One would have to refer to Mansur al-Hallaj, the ninth century radical Sufi (Islamic mystique) who was executed for heresy because of his self-identification with God and who vilified caliphatic power, choosing to surround himself with the most radical elements of society; Hafiz, whose odes on wine drinking and against doctrinal authority guaranteed him the eternal wrath of the orthodox clergy; Jalal ad-Din Balkhi (Rumi), whose 'school of love' enticed the human spirit towards transcending otherness and who was equally critical of the ruling strata of society; Ibn Arabi who was condemned as a heretic for having claimed to have seen the Prophet Muhammad and who stressed the equality of all individuals before God; Sohra-vardi, the theoretician of the 'school of illumination' or *ishraq* who was executed because of his radical ideas; Mullah Sadra, the founder of transcendental theosophy who was ostracised from his home town Shiraz; the aforementioned Ali Shariati, Iran's archetypal revolutionary intellectual who died in London under suspicious circumstances just before Ayatollah Khomeini's return to Tehran in 1978; or Hashem Aghajari, a war veteran and lecturer of history at Tehran University who was sentenced to death for blasphemy and apostasy in 2002 after criticising the authority of the Shia clergy (the sentence was eventually suspended). I am aware that I am abstracting from disparate historical contexts and individual biographies here, but it is accurate to say that all of these mystiques, philosophers, poets and intellectuals have expressed an anti-foundational rationality that was at odds with the status quo confronting them.

No wonder then that during the rapturous period of colonialism, the 'ideological' promise of the Quranic syntax and its vivid political theology has proven to be irresistible to the 'Islamist' project. What emerged with Abduh and Afghani in the late nineteenth century was yet another intense competition about and over the political message of Islam. We have established in the last chapter that the writings of Abduh and Afghani do not express so much a metaphysical discourse of Islam as an anti-imperial message. With the student of Abduh, Rachid Ridha, there emerges a 'post-Caliphatic' discourse that became the source of rather more state-centred interpretations of the Islamic corpus. Here Islam functions as a political necessity in order to accentuate the authority of the state and to prove the futility of western intrusions into the geographical and discursive territories of the re-signified *umma*.

Whereas Abduh and Afghani experimented with different notions of Islamic governance during a period when Islamic polities were still in existence, the situation radically changed with the abolition of the caliphate in 1924 and the ensuing dominance of secular-nationalist governments in Turkey, Iran, Egypt and elsewhere in the Islamic worlds. The 'Khalifat' movement that was established in British India in 1919 and which garnered support in many countries, not only failed to resurrect the idea of the caliphate, it enflamed the confessional politics in south-central Asia and elsewhere even further. The demise of the idea of the caliphate during this period is reflected in the shifting terminology of Muslim activists. Here, Ridha has been identified as the first prominent 'Islamist' who blurred the boundaries between the Islamic state, a new idea, and the Islamic caliphate. Enayat notes that in his writings Ridha uses the phrase *al-khilafat al-Islamiyyah* (Islamic caliphate) interchangeably with the term *ad-dawlah* (state) or *al-hukumat al-Islamiyyah* (Islamic state of government).[171] This is indicative of the readjustments that the political realities required. Ridha thought that it would be impossible to resurrect the caliphate out of the ruins of the Ottoman Empire, but that it would be politically viable and necessary to establish an Islamic state in the meantime. According to Esposito:

[T]he political realities of the post-World War I period pushed Rid[h]a toward a more conservative and anti-western position [than Afghani and Abduh]. While maintaining the transnational Islamic ideal and identity of Muslims, he pragmatically and reluctantly accepted the reality of modern states and nation-

---

[171] Hamid Enayat, *Modern Islamic Political Thought: The Response of the Shi'i and Sunni Muslims to the Twentieth Century*, London: Macmillan, 1982, p. 77.

alism, though he would subordinate them to membership and solidarity in the broader Islamic community.[172]

Esposito is right to point out that Ridha was by far more suspicious of the European powers surrounding him than his mentor Abduh. Ridha did not engage in a comparable dialogue with the canons of western modernity, not at least because the demise of the caliphate required a rather more pro-active political syntax and an urgent refutation of western imperialisms. It becomes apparent, once again, that all discourses of Islam always appear intimately close to the culture and age penetrating them. If there are ninety-nine names for and attributes of God as a famous Hadith attributed to Muhammad stipulates, and if these attributes are merely 'mothers' which give birth, in a grand dialectical act of recreation to all the rest as Ibn Arabi writes, then the meaning of Islam itself is fluctuating, at least within the confines of those godly attributes, and by far beyond in Ibn Arabi's idea of Islam. So apart from Islam's 'supreme signifier', which finds its expression in the transcendental immanence of Allah, the fundamental codes of the many discourses of Islam, those constituting its syntax, language, norms of appropriate behaviour, ideologies, disciplines, are entirely dependent on the *zeitgeist* of the day and age in question. It is true, as Aziz al-Azmeh notes, that 'there are as many Islams as there are situations that sustain it'.[173]

In the discourse of the 'neo-Islamists', at least since Sayyid Qutb (1906–1966), but more forcefully in the publications of the ideologues of Al Qaeda, this ingrained interdependence between Islam and its significant others is negated. It is exactly because of the danger of being subsumed into the western temporality that some of Islam's most active twentieth century thinkers and writers—Qutb, Abu-l-Ala Mawdudi (1903–1979), Hassan al-Banna (1906–1949) and others—were engaged in the grand project to solidify ideas that not only discriminate one polity from another, but also mobilise ideological passions in order to simulate authenticity. One important contemporary debate about the emergence of such Islamisms emphasises this 'essentialist' re-interpretation. Both Euben and Salwa Ismail have focused on this issue, especially with regard to the inference of Muslim superiority in

---

[172] John L. Esposito, *The Islamic Threat: Myth or Reality*, 3rd edition, Oxford: Oxford University Press, 1999, p. 61.

[173] Aziz al-Azmeh, *Islams and Modernities*, London: Verso, 1996, p. I.

the writings of Sayyid Qutb.[174] Of course, the difficulty with trying to create a 'truly independent' Islamic collective order is that it exacerbates ideological polarisation more than it enables dialogue and empathy. The previous chapters discussed how and why an ideological Islam emerged in resistance to European imperialisms, how and why it was fostered by Abduh and Afghani in order to legitimate political action. The following paragraphs will elaborate further why the Islamist discourse has been politicised even more rigorously in the twentieth century in response to the imperial challenge of the 'West' and the authoritarianism of the post-colonial state and how and why it continues to affect, even pervert Muslim perceptions of the other at the time of writing.

The political syntax of the neo-Islamist conceptualisation of Islam can be dissected more closely once we compare it with the discourse of the classical philosophers. One of the reasons why Farabi and Ibn Sina have not been resurrected to signify Muslim politics today is because for the purpose of insurrection and revolution, their theories are too 'conservative', too philosophical, too methodical, too ordered. Classical Islamic philosophy does not lend itself to revolution. It cannot be turned into building blocks of a system of thought that maximises distance between the self and the other. It is not useful to simulate insurmountable dichotomies. It is not conducive to affecting a historical rupture. It does not lend itself to a 'clash of civilisations'.

The great utopia of a new temporality that 'neo-Islamists' imagine can only be reached by simulating maximal causal efficacy. No wonder then that Ibn Sina's caution that the here and now 'is not actually existent at all, in relation to time itself, otherwise the continuity of time is disrupted [which is] impossible' does not seem useful to that agenda.[175] If the passage of time can not be interrupted, how could the *umma* overcome western (post)modernity which is contemporaneous with it? If, as Farabi says, the 'excellent universal state will arise only when all the nations in it co-operate for the purpose of reaching felic-

---

[174] Roxanne L. Euben, *Enemy in the Mirror: Islamic Fundamentalism and the Limits of Modern Rationalism*, Princeton: Princeton University Press, 1999, p. 51; Salwa Ismail, *Rethinking Islamist Politics: Culture, the State and Islamism*, London: I.B. Tauris, 2003, p. 40.

[175] Ibn Sina, 'The Healing: On time (al-Shifa)', in Seyyed Hossein Nasr with Mehdi Aminrazavi (eds), *An Anthology of Philosophy in Persia*, vol. 1, Oxford: Oxford University Press, 1999, p. 245.

ity', how can the neo-Islamist assert his seemingly autonomous identity over the rest of the world in general and the West in particular?[176] The difference I am alluding to becomes apparent in the following section which I have taken out of one of Osama bin-Laden's speeches and which I found particularly pertinent because of the strident structure delivering his argument: 'I say the West's occupation of our country is old, yet new, and that the confrontation and conflict between us and them started centuries ago', bin-Laden proclaims in a typical vein:

This confrontation and conflict will go on because the conflict between right and falsehood will continue until Judgement Day. Such a confrontation is good for both countries and peoples. God says: 'If God did not drive some back by means of others, the earth would be completely corrupt ...' [Quran, 2:251] Those who interpret the Quran say that this verse means that had the believers not fought the infidels, the latter would have defeated the believers and the earth would have been corrupted by their ill deeds. So, pay attention to the importance of conflict.[177]

Here, an impressive amount of arbitrary inventions is pressed into the mould of an argument that is ultimately aggressive and deterministic. The entire structure of it conveys urgency; it easily flows from one presumed cause to the other. Hence the current standoff between Al Qaeda and the United States (i.e. the effect) is linked to the Crusades, Quranic ordinances and generally to a seemingly readily available epistemology of conflict and difference (these are considered to be the causes). In this sense, the argument of bin-Laden is typically modern. It is geared to the modern consciousness, that believes in the teleology of history and the deceptively causal promise contained therein. For its addressees, the message appears immediately appealing because bin-Laden's discourse is built around 'narrow' causalities. In this way, bin-Laden smoothes over complexities. He makes sense of the world and our position in it in a deceptively easy manner. Like cocaine or 'speed', bin-Laden intoxicates his recipient with the idea that everything is possible. Caught in the 'flash' of such an intoxicating discourse, 'we' think 'we' understand. Suddenly disparate incidents in

[176] Abu Nasr Farabi, 'The Perfect State (Mabadi ara ahl al-madinat al-fadilah)', in Nasr with Aminrazavi (eds.), *An Anthology of Philosophy in Persia*, p. 126.
[177] Bruce Lawrence (ed.), *Messages to the World: The Statements of Osama bin Laden*, James Howarth (trans.), London: Verso, 2005, p. 217, emphasis added.

'our' life can be explained in a coherent way, suddenly 'we' believe in this struggle, suddenly 'we' are ready to die and kill for it. Only the sober mind can resist the lure of this positivistic flash and since the discourse of Islam proscribes any kind of intoxication that blurs reason, bin-Laden and his followers are deviant in more than one way. The difference to the discourse of Farabi could not be more striking: 'Do not be deceived by the fact that there are many people with emaciated opinions', Farabi warns:

for a group that follows one opinion and adheres to a leader who guides them regarding the matter they agree on are of the rank of one mind. But, as we already mentioned, the one mind may err with regard to the same thing, especially if this mind does not reflect frequently on the opinion to which it adheres and does not consider it with an examining and critical eye. Acceptance of a thing at face value or negligence in inquiry about it may veil, blind, and elude a mind.[178]

This is as much as to say that without reflection (or criticism) human inventions are more easily accepted as seemingly 'true' and 'natural' verities, when they are, in actual fact, deceptive. The critical consciousness of Farabi escapes the modern consciousness of bin-Laden. For the latter identity is pronounced, the Islamicity of the narrative is constantly accentuated. At the same time, differences are rendered unbridgeable, essential and eternal. Typically, such rigorous causal structure is achieved through the employment of binaries: infidel versus Muslim, Islam versus the West, us versus them. Consider as another textual example, this passage taken from the foreword of Sayyid Qutb to Sayyid Abul Hasan's influential book *Islam and the World: The Rise and Decline of Muslims and its Effects on Mankind*, which was originally published in 1950:

[T]his work is not only a refreshing example of religious and social research but also of how history can be recorded and interpreted from the wider *Islamic view point*. ... For quite some time, we in the East have, unfortunately, become accustomed to borrowing from the West not only its products but also the techniques of recording history used by its scholars with all their imperfections and shortcomings. This in spite of the fact that it has now been proved that

[178] Abu Nasr Farabi, 'Reconciliation of the two sages Spiritual Plato and Aristotle (kitab al-jam 'bayn ra'yay al-hakimayn, Aflatun al-ilahi wa Aristu)', in Seyyed Hossein Nasr and Mehdi Aminrazavi (eds), *An Anthology of Philosophy in Persia*, vol. 1, Oxford: Oxford University Press, 1999, p. 113.

their methods of approach and treatment are usually inadequate and not in keeping with historical veracity. The fact that they apprehend life from a specific and narrow point of view often leads them to draw the wrong conclusions.[179]

Here we find a precursor to the syntactical structure adopted by bin-Laden, although the argument is expressed with more nuances and less aggressive vigour. Qutb imprisons the vast differences of western peoples in terms 'they' and 'them' notably during a period when Europe was recovering from the ruptures of the Second World War. At the same time, he is not only reducing the East to the Islamic world and hence undervaluing the presence of other Asiatic peoples, but he is also inventing a unitary 'Islamic gaze' and by that allowing himself to articulate this 'Islamic' viewpoint to the reader.

Some of the rather more shrill studies about Qutb have identified him as the archetypal fundamentalist, a label that Euben attaches to him as well, despite her nuanced analysis of his life and theories. But Qutb advocates the contrary to a fundamentalist reading of the Quran. Qutb imagines for Islam a new environment, which is explicitly political. To many of the ordinances expressed in the Quran, he suddenly offers a new context, which establishes a viable ideology, a political manifesto thought to be suitable to combat, on the one side, the 'corrupt' and 'unjust' rule of the Egyptian state, especially after Qutb's split with Nassir's Free Officers Movement from 1954 onwards, and, on the other side, the politico-cultural 'harassment' of Islam by the 'West'. The discourse of Qutb is not fundamentalist, not literalist. It is inventive, not retroactive. His discourse is forward looking as the titles of his major books, *al-mustaqbal li hadha al-din* (The future is for this religion) and *ma'alim fi al-tariq* (Signposts along the way) indicate. The discourse of Qutb is meant to signify the competition over power in Egypt, especially after his incarceration and his experiences of death and torture in the jails of Nassir's autocracy. Qutb used his prison years to advocate total opposition to the political and cultural situation not only in Egypt, but also throughout the Islamic world, which was thought to be caught up in the evils of the *jahiliya*, the pre-Islamic 'age of ignorance' in Arabia. His discourse constitutes the politico-

---

[179] Sayyid Qutb, 'Foreword', in Sayyid Abul Hasan 'Ali Nadwi, *Islam and the World: The Rise and Decline of Muslims and its Effect on Mankind*, Leicester: UK Islamic Academy, 2005, pp. ix–x, emphasis added.

cultural field, defined in terms of geographical and historical boundaries, in which the present *jahiliya* can be juxtaposed to the ideal state of the *umma*—the ultimate state of perfection that he takes the liberty to author.

For Qutb, the sovereignty of God is deemed absolute and primarily political rather than philosophical. 'So what is Islam', he asks. 'Islam is a revolutionary concept and a way of life, which seeks to change the prevalent social order and remould it according to its own vision'. Suddenly, Muslims are not placed within an ontological order that is metaphysical; they are turned into a revolutionary vanguard. 'Based on this definition, the word "Muslim" becomes the name of an international revolutionary party that Islam seeks to form in order to put its revolutionary programme into effect'.[180] Suddenly, it is not the active intellect or reason 'without which our state would be the state of wild beasts, of children and lunatics' as Razi writes that yields universal progress.[181] It is only through offensive jihad, which 'seeks to replace the dominance of non-Islamic systems' that progress can be attained. It is not the quest for happiness that is central to some of Farabi's most canonical writings. The ultimate goal for Qutb is 'world revolution for the simple reason that any revolutionary ideology, which is humanity specific and seeking universal welfare, cannot reduce itself to a particular state or nation'.[182] The ideology thus signified, and which we can describe as 'Qutbian', is weighed towards politics. Jihad, *umma*, *ijtihad*, *jahilliya*, the central terminology of the discursive formation of Islam is interpreted politically, almost entirely divorced, in essence and meaning, of its original metaphysical habitat. So ideologically virulent was his agenda, carried forward by the institutionalised power of the Muslim Brotherhood or *al-ikhwan al Muslimin* in Arabic, that Nassir ordered his execution in 1966 on the trumped up charges that he masterminded a plot to have him and other officials assassinated.

A quick look at the writings of the early philosophers shows that the terms 'Muslim' and 'Islam' are not central at all to their syntactical

---

[180] Sayyid Qutb, 'The Essence of Jihad', in Albert J. Bergesen (ed.), *The Sayyid Qutb Reader: Selected Writings on Politics, Religion, and Society*, London: Routledge, 2008, p. 59.

[181] Abu Bakr Muhammad Zakariyya Razi, 'Spiritual Physick (al-Tibb al-ruhani)', in Nasr with Aminrazavi (eds), *An Anthology of Philosophy in Persia Vol. I*, p. 355.

[182] Qutb in Bergesen (ed.), *The Sayyid Qutb Reader*, p. 64.

order, that the Islamic collective was taken as a given. Conversely, Qutb was busy defining the meaning of Islam and being Muslim at every twist and turn of his discourse. Ibn Sina and Farabi did not have to define themselves, their 'Muslim-ness' was undisputed, the order they lived in was considered to be Islamic, and their identity was not a scarce resource that needed to be proclaimed loudly. Neo-Islamists such as Qutb, on the other side, were born into a cultural and political habitat that was politically violent and culturally reactionary. The neo-Islamist is in many ways, an orphan of Islam. His genealogy was interrupted by the violence of the West. Now he is trying to find his ancestral 'authenticity' via an overtly pronounced rebellion against the very genealogy that delivered him. At the end of this 'biological' struggle, he hopes to find his true, archetypal 'Muslim' identity.

What I have said thus far implies that at least since the invention of Islamism in the nineteenth century a counter-discourse has emerged, which positions itself in two locations. Horizontally, against authoritarian states within the Islamic worlds and 'vertically' against hierarchical world orders. In other words, in this new signification of the meaning of Islam and the collective *umma*, autocracy within the Islamic worlds and 'imperialism' are the primary targets. This Islamist narrative yields a very different Islam from the one imagined by the classical philosophers, which we can describe as 'Avicennian'. The Quran itself did not change, but the interpretation of it did. What shifted was the discursive formation of Islam.

For Ibn Sina, Farabi, Ghazali, Ibn Taymiya, Ibn Hanbal, Ibn Arabi, Ibn Khaldun, Ibn Rushd and others, the 'West' was not a topic at all, because the 'West' (as a discursive formation as discussed) was not invented yet. Obviously, neither did they have to juxtapose 'Islamic governance' with communism and/or liberal democracy as Qutb, al-Banna, Mawdudi, Khomeini and others did. The point I am making is that until the slow demise of the grand Islamic polities from the nineteenth century onwards, Ottoman in Turkey and the Arab worlds, Qajar in Persia and Mogul in South Asia (and perhaps even earlier), the prevalent discourse of Islam was rather different, in its rituals, syntax, terminology, methods, than the one which emerged thereafter and which continues to be written today. Even the Mongol invasion that tempted Ibn Taymiya into a rather more stringent politico-judicious signification of an Islam did not yield a major epistemological break. The rupture incurred by the violence of the colonial order changed that. Suddenly, a new discourse emerges which is populated by different objects: the West, modernity, interstate-war, capitalism, welfare, secularism and other modern factors.

In the Qutbian mode, Islam's political rationale or *dawlah* usurps its transcendental premise or *din*. The prototypical Qutbian is primarily zoon politikon, not homo Islamicus. The latter represents the *Endziel* of his deliberations. There he hopes to find Islamutopia, one of the last remaining utopias of humankind. In the meantime, he feels compelled to fight for an Islamic ontology that is as autonomous as possible. I have argued in *The International Politics of the Persian Gulf* that in Muslim-majority societies the period since the ending of the 'age of empires' and the emergence of new nation-states had been too short for the emergence of symbiotic political identities and effective governmental bureaucracies to sustain them. Identity had become a 'scarce resource' and influential Muslim thinkers and activists confronted the 'West' as a means to forge a new 'Islamic' self-understanding for the transnational *umma*.[183] By necessity then, Islamism challenges the overbearing presence of the western other. But this creates a dilemma. In order to cleanse Islam from the West, the discourse thus created has to place the western other within its syntax. How else can it signify difference? In this act of comparison and juxtaposition, a dialectical process is engendered, which does not yield total autonomy, but interdependence.

Indeed, the methodologies of contemporary discourses of Islam remain almost entirely dependent on the western other. The difference is that in the 'Avicennian mode' this is consciously acknowledged, whereas in the 'Qutbian mode' it is suppressed. And yet, in the Qutbian grammar, subject (the *umma*) and object (the West) remain intertwined. Without the object the Islamist could not exist in the first place. For Qutb, Islam has to 'play the role of the leader of mankind' because 'Western civilisation is unable to present any healthy values for guidance'.[184] For Hasan al-Banna, 'Islam is the antithesis of secular Western democracy because the 'Western way of life ... has remained

[183] On state building in the region see further my, *The International Politics of the Persian Gulf*, especially chapter 2 and Betty Anderson, 'The Duality of National Identity in the Middle East: A critical review', *Critique: Critical Middle Eastern Studies*, vol. 11, no. 2, Fall 2002, pp. 229–250.

[184] Bergesen (ed.), *The Sayyid Qutb Reader*, p. 35.

incapable of offering to men's minds a flicker of light, a ray of hope, a rain of faith, or of providing anxious persons the smallest path towards rest and tranquillity'.[185] In Abu-l-Ala Mawdudi's writings, the 'Kingdom of God', that can only be brought about in the Islamic state, is the 'very antithesis of secular Western democracy' which is thought to be entirely dependent on the 'sovereignty of the people. ... This is not the case in Islam. On this count, Islam has no trace of Western democracy'. Rather the contrary. Islam 'altogether repudiates the philosophy of popular sovereignty and rears its polity on the foundations of the sovereignty of God and the vicegerency (*khilafa*) of man'.[186] In all of this, an imagined and highly politicised Islam is juxtaposed to an equally imagined and essentialised western other. It must be the shadow of the West, in other words, that the Islamist sees when he performs his *asr* prayer in the twilight of the Oriental sun.

Islamutopia and the battle for the umma

I have argued that Islamisms advocate authenticity; they define autonomy as a virtue. This epistemological break from previous notions of Islam has a number of implications. First, it denotes a new relationship between an Islamism and the other, particularly the 'West'. For Qutb, the 'West' has nothing to offer to Islam, the future order had to be

[185] Hasan al-Banna, 'The New Renaissance', in Donohue and Esposoito (eds), *Islam in Transition*, p. 60. The Brotherhood played a pivotal role in mobilising volunteers to fence off Zionist aspirations of statehood in Palestine (Hamas is an offspring of the Brotherhood). Moreover, the organisation's institutional structure, encompassing schools, hospitals, companies and factories, empowered the Brotherhood to conduct a violent campaign against the Egyptian monarchy and Jewish and British interests in the country. As a consequence, Prime Minister Nuqrashi Pasha ordered the disbanding of the Brotherhood on 8 December 1948, less than three weeks before his assassination by the Ikhwan. Two months later, on 12 February 1949, al-Banna himself was assassinated by government agents.

[186] Abu-l-Ala Mawdudi, 'Political Theory of Islam', Donohue and Esposoito (eds), *Islam in Transition*, p. 264. Most of Mawdudi's theoretical ideas and political activism were developed in British ruled India between 1937 and 1941. He established the *Jama'at-e Islami* in 1941. Translated into Arabic by Ali Nedvi, Mawdudi's most prominent works—*Jihad in Islam*, *Islam and Jahiliyya* and *The Principles of Islamic Government*—reached a considerable audience in Muslim circles both in southern Asia and beyond.

thoroughly Islamic; it had to be cleansed of any undue influence of the other. With the emergence of Al Qaeda, the discourse of Qutb is abused to further an agenda that would realise this goal, not through education and intellectual activism as both al-Banna and Qutb advocated, but through unmitigated violence. For the ideologues of Al Qaeda, the West is the source of all evil in the world. Bin-Laden and Zawahiri say: 'To kill the American and their allies—civilians and military—is an individual duty incumbent upon every Muslim in all countries, in order to liberate the al-Aqsa Mosque and the Holy Mosque from their grip, so that their armies leave all the territory of Islam'.[187] The political sovereignty that Al Qaeda claims, the will to power that bin-Laden and Zawahiri express are not qualified either theologically or philosophically. Apart from scattered references to the Quran, the discourse of Al Qaeda is almost entirely devoid of authoritative substance. This type of discourse works for Al Qaeda because it liberates its leaders from any kind of intellectual engagement with the traditions of Islam or the precedence attributed to Muhammad. It liberates bin-Laden and Zawahiri from any kind of regulatory context, from the syntax of the Quran, from the authority of the Mullah, Muftis and Islamic judges. It is in this way that the indiscriminate killing of civilians, prohibited in all authoritative schools of Islam, can be decreed without any doubt.

Secondly, within the discourse of Al Qaeda, one is alerted to purify the Quran and *hadiths* from the 'distortions' brought about by neoplatonic philosophy and logic, Iranian (Persian) mythology and metaphorism, Jewish scripture and Christian theology. From this perspective, one is compelled to organise oneself in the 'ultimate' Islamic state because everything surrounding us is *jahiliya*, The urgent need to establish the Islamic state par excellence legitimates total, offensive *jihad*, against both 'the hypocrites' within the community—'apostate' rulers who stand in the way of creating God's laws—and the 'infidels' (*kafir*) harassing Islam from 'the West'. These themes find their particular, totalitarian interpretation in the agenda of Muhammad 'Abd al-Salam Faraj (see his *al-farida al-gha'iba*, The Absent Commandment), Ayman al-Zawahiri (former leader of the Egyptian *Jihad* which in 1998 merged with bin-Ladin's organisation to establish the 'International Front for Fighting Jews and Crusaders') and bin-Laden himself.

---

[187] 'The World Islamic Front (February 23 1998)', in Lawrence (ed.), *Messages to the World*, p. 61.

Partly because of political expediency, partly because of their marginalisation in the various domestic political contexts, these individuals and scattered groups at the fringes of the contemporary neo-Islamist spectrum do not limit themselves to relatively confined opposition anymore. They do not seek to reform Muslim societies through political education as Qutb and al-Banna advocated. They are engaged in a 'horizontal war'—a struggle against Muslim states and societies which are perceived to have deviated from the true path of 'Muhammadian Islam'—and a 'vertical war'—an ongoing struggle against US foreign policies.[188] Perceptive authors with an alternative conceptualisation of Islam, such as Mohammed Arkoun, have identified the self-fulfilling prophecy of the discourse thus ensued:

> Modern Islamic discourse has accentuated the doctrinal rigidity of representations of Islam 'applicable to all times and in all places' and reduced them to the socially-controlled performance of identificatory rites. Unfortunately, contemporary Islamic and political studies have added their scientific weight to the corroboration of this static and ahistorical perspective.[189]

Arkoun pays particular attention to the 'neo-Islamist' mode of argumentation, which is almost entirely reliant on artificial binaries. He points to the invention of an Islam that is juxtaposed to an equally invented caricature of 'America', the 'West' or the 'infidels'. As such Islamism engenders a polarised world-view, permeated by seemingly inconceivable dualities: *jahiliya* vs. *the* Islamic order, the righteous *umma* vs. the infidels, *din* (true religion) vs. *kufr* (impiety) or the rightly guided prophets (*salaf*) vs. the polytheist (*mushriukkun*) or

---

[188] The *Jama'at al Takfir wa al Hijra* ('The Society of Excommunication and Holy Fight') founded in Egypt after a split with the Muslim Brotherhood in 1967 by Sheikh Shukri Ahmad Mustafa, for instance, advocated armed struggle against both state and society (the same as the Egyptian *al-Jihad*). The Islamic Liberation Organisation (ILO) established in the early 1970s and led by Salih Siriyya, on the other side, focused its activities exclusively on combating the state. It was another neo-fundamentalist grouping, the *Munazzamat al-Jihad* ('The Holy War Organisation'), however, that was responsible for the assassination of President Anwar Sadat of Egypt on 6 October 1981. Prior to the assassination (in the late 1970s), the founders of the *Takfir* and ILO were both executed in a nation-wide crackdown of militant Islamist movements.

[189] Mohammed Arkoun, 'Islam, Europe, the West: Meanings-at-stake and the will-to-power', in Andrew Rippin (ed.), *Defining Islam: A Reader*, London: Equinox, 2007, p. 256.

pagans (*wataniyun*). In its totalitarian manifestation, currently termed 'Al Qaeda', neo-Islamism is divorced from the original discourse of Islam, because it is depleted of metaphysics, transcendentalism and philosophy. The discourse of Al Qaeda is not even post-Islamic; it is counter-Islamic. God is turned into commander in chief, the *umma* into his guerrilla force, and the young disillusioned convert into his executioner. Islam reduced to *dawlah* contradicts the *din wa dawlah* dialectic lived and preached by Muhammad. Thus, the Quranic revelation loses its transcendental essence. Indeed, it *has* to be cleansed from intellectualism and spirituality in order to function as an ideological device. Al Qaeda cannot afford the metaphysics of Islam, the discourse of Ibn Sina and Farabi is not functional when it comes to waging war. The latter's journey of purification demanded a sophisticated intellectual jihad; Al Qaeda's jihad is thoroughly militaristic; bin Laden and Zawahiri are soldiers and propagandists rather than religious scholars or political philosophers. Their idea of political leadership was exemplified in the 'Islamic Emirate of Afghanistan', one of the most reactionary and totalitarian polities in the history of the Islamic world, which was governed by the self-proclaimed 'Taliban' until the invasion of the country by the United States in 2001.

Al Qaeda type groups claim the total reassertion of the objectivity of *sharia* law, the all-encompassing sovereignty of their selective adoption of Quranic verses, without any concessions to the current passage of time. The perfect world of Al Qaeda is a world without others, without westerners, Shiites, reformist Muslims, etc. There is nothing in the other that Al Qaeda wants. Their terror missions are strategic only in the sense that they are meant to bring about that ultimate order depleted of any otherness. Their alliance with the CIA during the Afghan struggle against the Soviet Union was only strategic in the sense that it was meant to help the movement to take another step towards establishing that ultimate order. This is why it is misleading to describe their terror missions as suicidal. Rather they are *homicidal*, they are meant to destroy as much of the 'corrupt' world surrounding them as possible. The victims of Al Qaeda are the causalities in their fight for an autonomous temporality. In this specific sense, the ideology of Al Qaeda is entirely comparable to the ideology of the Nazis and its insatiable quest for sameness that I discussed in the last chapter. Both movements are premised on the idea that it is necessary to thoroughly detach their followers from the corrupting impact of all 'unworthy existence'. Both attempt to foster political orders that are totally cleansed of any impingement by others.

For Al Qaeda and their sympathisers, the battle with the West and 'apostate Muslims' is not negotiable. 'There can be no dialogue with the occupiers except with weapons', says bin-Laden.[190] This inability to compromise, by necessity of the totalitarian ideology espoused, not only explains why Al Qaeda has failed to garner structural support throughout the Islamic worlds, why it continues to operate on the fringes, why it does not command a global army of 'jihadists' as it is too often alleged in the international media, it also indicates yet another internal-external transgression that debunks the civilisational division assumed by the Huntingtonian clash divide. Al Qaeda wages total war against the 'West' *and* 'apostate Muslims' in order to create a true and absolute genealogy; a mythical tale dotted with heroic figures and 'authenticated' personalities that would deliver Muslims from their 'imperfect' existence, from their fallen present. The central policies of Al Qaeda are reflections of this effort to create causal purity. So I believe that my description of their ideology as totalitarian is warranted. Total war: 'we call on everyone who believes in God and wants reward to comply with His will and to kill the Americans ... and whichever devil's supporters are allied with them';[191] total history: 'I say that the West's occupation of our country is old, yet new ... This confrontation and conflict will go on because the conflict between right and falsehood will continue until Judgment Day;'[192] a total state (through total war): the attacks on Washington and New York constitute 'a great step forward along the road towards uniting Muslims under the banner of monotheism in order to establish the rightly guided Caliphate';[193] and total positivism: 'we reiterate the importance of high morale and caution against false rumours, defeatism, uncertainty, and discouragement'.[194] All of this delivers the pathology of an imagined clash of civilisations in bin-Laden's mind. Of course, this

[190] Lawrence (ed.), *Messages to the World*, p. 217.

[191] Ibid., p. 61.

[192] Ibid., p. 217.

[193] Thomas Hegghammer, 'Al-Qaida Statements 2003–2004—A Compilation of Translated Texts by Usama bin Ladin and Ayman al-Zawahiri', *FFI Rapport—2005/01428*, Norwegian Defence Research Establishment, 24 Jun. 2005, p. 21

[194] *BBC Monitoring*, 12 Feb. 2003.

pathology—upon closer inspection—appears as delusional as its professional 'theorisation' by bin-Laden's counterparts in the 'West':

I say that there is no doubt about this. This [Clash of Civilisations] is a very
clear matter, proven in the Qur'an and the traditions of the Prophet, and any
true believer who claims to be faithful shouldn't doubt these truths, no matter
what anybody says about them. What goes for us is whatever is found in the
Book of God and the *hadith* of the Prophet. But the Jews and America have
come up with a fairytale that they transmit to the Muslims, and they've unfortunately been followed by the local rulers [of the Muslims] and a lot of people
who are close to them, by using 'world peace' as an excuse. That is a fairytale
that has no substance whatsoever![195]

In all of this, in grammar and syntax, Al Qaeda is totalitarian. The
element of a systematic theorisation of race, which is absent despite
derogatory designations of Hindus, Jews and Shiites (typically termed
'Persians'), would make it almost synonymous with Nazism. 'The Nazi
State', Foucault says, 'makes the field of the life it manages, protects,
guarantees, and cultivates in biological terms absolutely coextensive
with the sovereign right to kill anyone, meaning not only other people,
but also its own people'.[196] Al Qaeda is similarly nihilistic, save the
biological component. It too kills its 'own' people, in Iraq, Afghanistan, Pakistan, the World Trade Centre in New York, Tavistock Square
in London and elsewhere. The 'value' of the crisis thus created is that
it cleanses, that it promises to overturn everything that is corrupt,
bringing to the end the all-encompassing age of ignorance. 'So, pay
attention to the importance of conflict', says bin-Laden.[197] Like Hitler,
bin-Laden puts *all* existing orders under threat. The difference is, of
course, that the latter does not have the strategic and ideological capa-
bilities at hand to follow up on his promises. Al Qaeda, for all the huff
and puff that its discourse creates, has been an ideological incubator
for marginal groups. Certainly, bin-Laden does not have a mass following that he would need for a war with global consequences.

I have argued that one of the reasons why Al Qaeda's ideology has
not been espoused by mainstream Islamist movements is because of its
anti-intellectual nature, its legitimation of unconstrained violence and
its anti-diplomatic agenda. For the current leadership of the Muslim
Brotherhood, Hamas, Hezbollah, or the Islamic state in Iran, ideologis-

---

[195] Lawrence (ed.), *Messages to the World*, pp. 124–125.
[196] Foucault, *Society Must be Defended*, p. 260.
[197] Lawrence (ed.), *Messages to the World*, p. 217.

ing an Islam functions in order to mediate politics to receptive constituencies. An Islam that has to be signified in a nuanced way in order to legitimate the respective political agenda under conditions that are intensely competitive, i.e. within a context in which there are other movements and ideologies vying for the attention of society. The metaphysics of Islam are not suppressed. Rather, they are rationalised in order to accentuate the incorruptibility of the respective movement and its ability to mediate between the utopian yearnings of society and the transcendental claim of the Islamic state/movement. An Islam that is consciously made here to function on the 'boundaries between heaven and earth', which is the exact phrase that Michel Foucault used in order to explain the Islamic Revolution in Iran in 1979.[198] Foucault was amongst the few intellectuals in western Europe who understood what was happening in the country and who was thus far ahead of his contemporaries and some of his detractors today.[199] He understood, to be more precise, that in Iran, an Islam that attempted to claim a dual orientation: one ontological, engaged with the here and now, with politics, economics, society and other worldly matters, the other utopian, a drama of the otherworldly:

For anyone who did not look for the 'underlying reasons' for the movement in Iran was but attentive to the way in which it was experienced, for anyone who tried to understand what was going on in the heads of these men and women when they were risking their lives, one thing was striking. They inscribed their humiliations, their hatred for the regime, and their resolve to overthrow it at the bounds of heaven and earth, in an envisioned history that was religious just as much as it was political. They confronted the Pahlavis, in a contest where everyone's life was on the line, but where it was also a question of millennial sacrifices and promises. So that the famous demonstrations, which played such an important role, could at the same time respond in an effective way to the threat from the army (to the extent of paralysing it), follow the rhythm of religious ceremonies, and appeal to a timeless drama in which the secular power is always accused.[200]

---

[198] Michel Foucault, 'Useless to revolt?', in idem., *Power: Essential Works of Foucault, 1954–1984, Vol. 3*, James D. Faubion (ed.), Robert Hurley et. al. (trans.), London: Penguin, 1997, pp. 449–453.

[199] See Janet Afary and Kevin B. Anderson, *Foucault and the Iranian Revolution: Gender and the Seductions of Islamism*, Chicago: University of Chicago Press, 2005.

[200] Foucault, 'Useless to Revolt', p. 450.

Heaven and earth, political and religious, ceremonial dramas and secular power, Foucault understood that in the Iranian case, these forces were not assembled in order to stand in opposition to each other, the Qutbian and the Avicennian tradition were not rendered dichotomous. Rather, they were made to function in a dialectical relationship, they were co-constitutive: Islamism and Islamutopia worked hand in hand to deliver the Islamic Republic. Foucault understood that the dialectics emerging out of the revolutionary process might not yield to a Hegelian, final reconciliation of opposites. The Islamic Revolution was spiritual and empirical, religious and secular, western and eastern, progressive and nativist, modern and fundamentalist, revolutionary and reactionary, progressive and retroactive. The first stamps printed by the Islamic Republic depicted Mossadegh and Qutb, al-e Ahmad and Shariati, nationalists and Islamists. The current 'Supreme Leader' of the Iranian state and successor of Khomeini, Ayatollah Ali Khamenei is a keen student of the poetry of Muhammad Iqbal. At the same time, he appreciates the political doctrines of Sayyid Qutb, whose major works he translated into Persian. What I am trying to indicate with these examples is that the project of the Islamic Republic of Iran cannot be satisfactorily subsumed under a particular label, Islamic, nationalist, modern, fundamentalist or other. The Islamic Republic is a particularly hybrid project. It has ushered into a post-modern Islamicity and a post-Islamist modernity in Iran and, to a certain degree, beyond. The fact that Foucault underestimated the authoritarian moment of the revolutionary movement should not distract from his ability to discern and emancipate the utopian yearnings of the Iranian multitudes, over the opportunistic take-over of the state by the Khomeinist factions.

The hybridity of the Islamic Republic indicates that the dialectic between Islam and western (post)modernity has remained unresolved, that their interrelationship has created a parallel temporality that is not moving towards synthesis by necessity of the supremacy of one system over the other. We are not in Hegel's world here. A dialectic between the 'West' and Islam is ongoing in Iran. We have not reached an endpoint; Iranians are still plotting their project. At this very moment, the Islamic Republic conceals both a metaphysics of government expressed by a vibrant civil society and a politics of religion monopolised by the state, that is constantly evolving. In the imagination of its makers, the Islamic revolution would situate itself, ideally, as an effort of fantastic reconciliation, in the vast vacuum created by the absence of the prophets and the Shia Imams, separating the promised land of God and the ontological reality which men, banned from paradise, have erected for themselves. In essence, the Islamicised revolution has been an effort to bridge the gap between the here and now, on the one side and God on the other. In the political theory devised by Khomeini, the *vali-e faqih*, the Supreme Jurisprudent who sits on top of the intricate constitutional framework in Iran, is conceptualised, politically and theologically, as that link between the people and the transcendental. Hence also the centrality of the *imam-e zaman*, the *vali-e asr* (the Lord of the Age) or Mahdi in Shia mythology that was so dominant in Ali Shariati's characterisation of revolution as a 'revolt against history' (that in turn fascinated even sceptical observers such as Salman Rushdie).[201] The pious Twelver-Shia is convinced that the Imam Mahdi will return from occultation to establish the just rule of God on earth and if he is not pious, but a shrewd political leader, he recognises the potent political utility of this idea. The Mahdi appears as that missing link between the here and now and the ultimate other, that is God. Within such metaphysics of time, the reality surrounding many Iranian revolutionaries, that here and now, had been relative to the otherworldly reality awaiting them.[202] This explains their willingness to sacrifice themselves in the street battles against the army of the Shah and the invading battle units of Saddam Hussein's Iraq during the First Gulf War (1980–1988). For them, the Islamic Revolution created a feeling of vertigo, a sense of romantic exaltation, and arrogance towards the passing passage of time. Revolutions, like the music of Wagner or the poetry of Rumi, do that to the human mind. They are particularly intoxicating, especially when couched in powerful religious symbols as in the Iranian case.[203] So the Iranian revolutionaries reached out to heaven, only to experience the intense disappointment that the unavailability of God inevitably wrought upon their project. What is the left is the hardcore politics of the revolution, depleted of the spiritual essence that Foucault detected in the utopian consciousness of the masses.

---

[201] On Salman Rushdie and Islam see further Ian Almond, *The New Orientalists: Postmodern Representations of Islam from Foucault to Baudrillard*, London: I.B. Tauris, 2007, pp. 94–109.

[202] This orientation towards god and the relativity of the presence in the here and now is expressed in Article 2 of the Iranian Constitution.

[203] See further, my, *Iran in World Politics*, parts 1 and 5.

The revolution in Iran is the contemporary example *par excellence* for the way an Islam is reconfigured in order to function as a movement towards Islamutopia, the transcendental epicentre of the *umma*. This indelible progression towards a future, presumably 'just' order was central to the writings of many contemporary 'manufacturers' of Islamicised discourses. Muhammad Iqbal, for instance, whose writings and activism had a decisive impact on the creation of Pakistan in 1947, refers to this political lag between reality and utopia by saying that Islam 'demands loyalty to God, not to thrones'.[204] Here, God exemplifies Islamutopia, the thrones the oppressive status quo that needs to be overturned to narrow the gap to the former, the political rationale being to mobilise the Muslim masses in British India. A comparable promise of a future utopia can be discerned from the writings of Ali Shariati in 1970s Iran. According to him: 'God is infinite, everlasting and absolute. Thus humankind's journey towards Him is perpetual and eternal; there is no pause'.[205] This is as much as to say that the ideal society can only be engineered through perpetual mobilisation, in this case, through revolutionary action against the dictatorship of the Shah and the containment of western imperialism. The Islamic order moves towards Islamutopia as an experiment, as an inadequate step. There is an implicit understanding that the totality of the politico-religious experience can only be attained elsewhere. As such, in the dialectic between *din*, the transcendental utopia (or Islamutopia) and *dawlah*, the politics happening here and now, the latter is prompted to catch up with the former. In summary: exactly because Islamutopia is rendered unattainable, the discrepancy between the ontological reality encompassing society and that utopian promise encapsulated by God lends itself rather ideally to resistance to the status quo, in terms of both domestic dissent against authoritarian states and internationally, against real or perceived 'unjust' orders. Narrowing this space between reality and utopia creates a major dynamic for revolt.

The utopia of a better tomorrow and the unsatisfactory reality of today are in a dialectical relationship to each other. Revolutions simulate how the former could look like, but they cannot escape the deter-

---

[204] Muhammad Iqbal. 'The Principle of Movement in the Structure of Islam', in Kurzman (ed.), *Liberal Islam: a Sourcebook*, Oxford: Oxford University Press, 1998, p. 256.

[205] Ali Shariati, 'Humanity and Islam', in Charles Kurzman (ed.), *Liberal Islam*, p. 189.

minations of the temporal sequence they are born into, not even through repression and violence as Iran's right-wing must have realised by now. 'In order to bend the temporal order into a religious shape', the contemporary Iranian philosopher Soroush suggests, 'one should understand what religion is all about. This understanding is obtained by acquiring religious knowledge which is *always time bound*'.[206] In the Iranian case, this means that the imagined rebirth of Islamutopia has been concomitant with the penetrating presence of western modernity, as I have argued. Both the West and an Islam are present in contemporary Iran by necessity of their temporal cross-fertilisation in Iranian history. This interpenetration can be discerned from the terminology and constitutional structure of Iran, which entail both modern (western) ideas/institutions *and* Islamic ordinances. This is most obvious in the very concept of the Islamic Republic, but it is also obvious from other central terms and constitutional organs of the Iranian polity:

Term/Institution	'Modern' (ontological)	'Islamic' (Islamutopia)
Hesballah	Hesb (i.e. party)	Allah (i.e. god)
Vali-e Faqih/Rahbar-e Enqelab (Currently Ayatollah Ali Khamenei)	Rahbar (i.e. leader), Enqelab (i.e. revolution)	Vali-e Faqih (i.e. Supreme Jurisprudent of Islamic law)
Daneshjuan-e musal-manan-e piramun-e khatt-e imam	Daneshjuan (i.e. Students) Khatt (i.e. political line)	Musalmanan (i.e. Muslims) Imam (i.e. religious leader, Khomeini/ Khamenei)
Majlis-e khobregan-e rahbari	Majlis (Assembly)	Khobregan (Islamic legal experts or *mojtaheds*)

A lot has been written about the seemingly retroactive and fundamentalist nature of the revolution in Iran. But one of the reasons why Ayatollah Khomeini was criticised by many Shia religious authorities

---

[206] Abdolkarim Soroush, *Reason, Freedom, and Democracy in Islam: Essential Writings of Abdolkarim Soroush*, Mahmoud Sadri and Ahmad Sadri (trans. and ed.), Oxford: Oxford University Press, 2000, p. 33, emphasis added.

(sources of emulation) was exactly because he departed from the quietist tradition of Shiism, much in the same way that Qutb constructed a version of Islam that was rather more amenable to politico-ideological mobilisation than the orthodox Sunni canon. The difference is, of course, that once Khomeini usurped the Iranian nation-state, he was operating within the confines of its bureaucracy and linkages to the international system, especially after the invasion by Saddam Hussein in 1980. Conversely, Qutb could afford to imagine an Islamic construct that was entirely detached from any impingement by the other. Once in power, Khomeini the statesman had to be pragmatic. He was forced to realise that it was impossible to escape the determinations of his age. So political vilification of his imagined 'West' and the United States as the 'Great Satan' did not mean that he was 'anti-modern'. In fact, he was very willing to ameliorate ideas developed in Europe in order to strengthen his political agenda and to construct an Islamic state that would be viable and enduring. On the necessity to master the politics of the day, Khomeini was explicit:

A mojtahed [Islamic legal scholar] should be fully aware of his time. It is not acceptable that he should say that he will not express an opinion regarding political issues. Familiarity with the methods of dealing with the tricks and deceits of the culture governing the world, the possession of an economic understanding and knowledge ... familiarity with policies and even politicians ... An authoritative interpreter should possess the intelligence and shrewdness necessary for managing and safeguarding a great Islamic or even a non-Islamic society. He should in addition to possessing piety and sincerity, and asceticism befitting a mojtahed, be a skilful manager.[207]

Khomeini was a child of his time, and a product of the political cultures enveloping Iran and the wider Muslim worlds during that particular historical juncture. He was shot through with both the Avicennian and Qutbian notions of Islam. The political thought and practice of Khomeini was affected by philosophy and Islamism, Avicenna and Qutb, Iqbal and Mawdudi. He was certainly not a fundamentalist who would advocate a literalist reading of the Quran. If anything, he was not considered to be fundamentalist enough by some segments of the *ulema* (clergy) in the country. Indeed, in 1989 Kho-

---

[207] 'Message addressed by Khomeini to the instructors and students of religious seminaries', 22 February 1989. Reprinted in Lloyd Ridgeon (ed.), *Religion and Politics in Modern Iran: A Reader*, London: I.B. Tauris, 2005, pp. 199–200.

meini was reprimanded by a group of ultra-orthodox clerics for writing a letter to then Soviet leader Mikhail Gorbachev urging him to consider the philosophy of Ibn Sina, Ibn Arabi. Mullah Sadra, and Sohravardi. Communism was in its dying days, Khomeini observed, and Gorbachev would do well to resist the 'materialism of the West' and consider 'the Islamic world-view' instead. In an open letter addressed to Khomeini, his reference to these mystics and philosophers was heavily criticised by the orthodox clergy:

You have not referred Mr. Gorbachev to the truth of the holy Qur'an, but have asked him to read [the works of] the condemned heretic Avicenna, the Sunni pantheist and arch-mystic Ibn al-Arabi, the works of Sohravardi who was executed by the Muslims for his ideological deviations, and the writing of Mollah Sadra, who was exiled to the village of Kahak near Qom because of his intellectual deviations. ... [W]e fail to understand why you refer the gentleman to deviant philosophers and mystics for the study of Islam. Are there not sufficient reasons in the Qur'an to prove the existence of God and the explain the principles and precepts of religion? Does it mean that the leaders of Islam are unable to explain the truth of the Qur'an without resorting to philosophy and mysticism? You know that both Greek philosophy and Indian mysticism existed long before the advent of either the Prophet Muhammad or Moses and Jesus. If philosophy and mysticism were sufficient to guide mankind, then was there and need for the Almighty to grace us with the mission of the prophets?[208]

In his reply to this letter, Khomeini remained unrepentant:

This old father of yours has suffered more from stupid reactionary Mullahs than anyone else. When theology meant no interference in politics, stupidity became a virtue. If a clergyman was able, and aware of what was going on [in the world around him], they searched for a plot behind it. You were considered more pious if you walked in a clumsy way. Learning foreign languages was blasphemy, philosophy and mysticism were considered to be sin and infidelity. In the Feiziyeh my young son Mostafa drank water from a jar. Since I was teaching philosophy, my son was considered to be religiously impure, so they washed the jar to purify it afterwards. Had this trend continued, I have no doubt the clergy and seminaries would have trodden the same path as the Christian Church did in the Middle Ages.[209]

All of this does not mean that the Islamic Republic, in its entirety, has displayed the intellectual resources to divorce itself from a totalitarian

---

[208] Quoted in Baqer Moin, *Khomeini: Life of the Ayatollah*, London: I.B. Tauris, 1999, p. 275.
[209] Ibid., p. 276.

reading of Islam. What I am saying is that the original formulation of
the revolution expressed the romantic rejection of authority, the critical
consciousness that is willing to operate in a perpetual state of suspended
judgement. Turning this anti-foundational consciousness of the revolutionaries into a foundation for the Islamic Republic was Khomeini's
singularly historic genius and some would say betrayal. Since then,
Iran's state has repeatedly turned towards violence against its people
when it felt that this consciousness has to be subdued ideologically in
order to reify the power of the state. Yet the Iranian example also
shows that utopian yearnings can never really be muted entirely, nothing can ever be solely ideological or 'Islamist'. People continue to enact
utopia in Iran. The ideals of the revolution continue to have an impact
on the politics of the country. Once the utopia of 'freedom' is uttered,
it is impossible to flush it out in its entirety. Ultimately, the power of
the Islamicised discourse in Iran depends upon the legitimacy of the
political system that rules in its name. If this system is rejected by the
multitudes, if the intense dialectic between state and society does not
continuously yield results in favour of the latter, Islamism in Iran will
only survive by the force of the bayonet.

So the post-revolutionary Iranian state has continuously engineered
a discourse of Islam and what it means to be 'Iranian'. More fundamentally, it has attempted to create a new type of sovereignty that has
both an ontological and a transcendental claim. This discourse is different from Al Qaeda's understanding of the ultimate Islamic polity.
Whereas the Islamic Revolution, as much as Hamas, the 'Iraqi Mahdi
army', the Muslim Brotherhood or the Lebanese Hezbollah, is produced within the nation-state, Al Qaeda type groups claim the total
reassertion of the objectivity of the *umma*, the all-encompassing sovereignty of their particularistic interpretation of the early days of the
Muslim community, without major concessions to the nation-state
system. For the Taliban-al Qaeda alliance, Afghanistan had been reduced
to the status of an 'Emirate', rather than a state, without an official
capital or a constitution and without a definition of Afghan nation-
hood. Mullah Omar did not take up a position as head of state but
declared himself *amir al-momenin* (commander of the faithful) staying
in Kandahar rather than choosing to travel to the Afghan capital
Kabul. The concept of the nation-state, central to the politics in Egypt,
Turkey, Palestine, Lebanon, Iraq, Iran and elsewhere, are resolutely
rejected, as in Ayman al-Zawahiri's July 2005 letter to Abu-Musab al-

Zarqawi where he celebrated the latter's battle against polytheism, secularists, detractors and inferiors in Iraq anticipating the establishment of a pan-Islamic caliphate that would follow the 'pure way of the Prophet, and the sublime goal that the Prophet left to his companions'.[210] In the absence of that ultimate caliphate, believing in the totalitarian message demands huddling together with one's fellow believers and accepting a sect like existence within a loose, transnationally stratified brotherhood.

Conversely, in the Iranian case, the frail nation-state is elevated to the highest level of political authority. In a revealing decree in January 1988, Ayatollah Khomeini declared that an Islamic government (by implication Iran) has the right to overrule Islamic ordinances if it would be in the interest (*maslahat*) of the *umma* and the state. Khomeini announced that the legitimacy of the government was 'derived from the absolute domination of the Prophet of God'. This was 'the most important of God's ordinances (*ahkam-e elahi*)' and was hence superior to 'all ordinances that were derived or directly commanded by Allah'.[211] In other words, if it was in the interest of the state and the *umma*, major Islamic pillars (even prayer, fasting and the pilgrimage to Mecca) could be annulled—the Islamic state can 'suspend Islam' if the politics of the moment demands it.

To move all of this into a different direction: If the Quran can be said to have a theory of truth that is immediately relevant to the current state of humankind, as contemporary 'Avicennian' thinkers such as Nasr Hamid Abu Zayd, Muhammad Arkoun, Hossein Nasr or Abdol-Karim Soroush argue, it appears to us within the mystique of the prevailing reality which itself is always a product of social change.[212]

---

[210] 'Zawahiri's July letter to Zarqawi', 13 Oct. 2005. Available at http://www. dni.gov/letter_in_english.doc [Last accessed 12 Aug. 2006].

[211] See Khomeini's letter to then President (and current 'Leader of the Revolution'), Ali Khamenei published in *Keyhan*, 8 Jan. 1988. See also Asghar Schirazi, *The Constitution of Iran: Politics and the State in the Islamic Republic*, John O' Kane (trans.), London: I.B. Tauris, 1997, pp. 64–65.

[212] See Nasr Hamid Abu Zayd, *Reformation of Islamic Thought: A Critical Historical Analysis*, Amsterdam: Amsterdam University Press, 2006 and idem. *Rethinking the Qur'an: Towards a Humanistic Hermeneutics*, Utrecht: Humanistics University Press, 2004. On translated introductory readings and guidance for further research of 'liberal' Islamic writings see Kurzman (ed.), *Liberal Islam*; Donohue and Esposito, *Islam in Transition*.

Ultimately, each age reinterprets Islam, not because the Quran changes, but because there *has never been* a fixed and nontrivial object as Islam independent of a historical/discursive context, or the hundreds of millions of Muslims and non-Muslims who have read the scriptures and who came up with their own interpretations. True, at least two of Islam's central tenets, *tawhid*, or the oneness of god and the *shahada*, *la ilaha illa Allah wa-Muhammad rasul Allah* (there is no god but god and Muhammad is his prophet), do push the *umma* towards conformity. But this conformity is spiritual above anything else manifesting itself in the yearly pilgrimage of millions of people from different races and social classes during the *haj*. On the political, social and economic level, however, there is no such uniformity, no a-historical sacred canopy that has the powers to veil everything beneath it. Otherwise, the ontological status of Malcolm X would have been the same as bin-Laden's today. Islam has never been a singular system, or a coherent cultural and political threat. Since Muhammad, it has engendered both a potent utopian alternative and an ontological, transnational space where different spiritual, cultural, religious, socio-economic and political narratives extract themselves, some of them violent, some of them imperialistic and some of the largely pacifist. It must follow that there has never been such a thing as an Islamic civilisation that would clash with some 'West' in actual, strategic terms or even culturally.

Despite the shift towards a more rigid and totalitarian register since the early twentieth century, some latent, contemporary discourses of Islam remain closely tied to their original utopia and, beyond that, in the line of critical thinking that we could spawn from Farabi, Ibn Sina, al Kindi and Ibn Rushd to German idealist philosophy in the Kantian tradition and Anglo-American romanticism. Such discourses of Islam continue to articulate a radical 'criticism of hegemony', whatever the impediments that politics is seen to place in the way of any functional, inclusive articulation of this movement. Ultimately, they are irreconcilable with the *fiqh*-oriented Islam upheld by the orthodox clergy on the one side and the totalitarian ideology espoused by Al Qaeda type movements on the other. But simply because pluralistic articulations of Islam are suppressed by the politics of the day, does not mean that they do not exist or that they are not a part of the political cultures permeating the contemporary Islamic worlds. What Raymond William Baker termed the 'new Islamists' in a study of their intellectual and political fortunes in Egypt, must be analytically appreciated as the newest manifestation

263

of the adaptability of Islamicised inventions, this time in vibrant cross-fertilisation with the demands of democracy and social justice.[213]

At this point of time, much that has been subjugated in the invention of 'post-colonial' nation-states, much that has been erased or glossed over when Arab, Turkish and Persian nationalisms engineered their own myths and narrations, is in the process of being questioned. One of the primary agents of the 'critical turn' I am referring to is the continued search for Islamutopia—one of the oldest universalities of humankind. Understanding how this Islamutopia links up with other critical narratives with a universal outreach—or indeed the 'Multitude' that Hardt and Negri ponder—requires a deep understanding of the discursive formations of Islam. Through such an effort, which is primarily intellectual, the Muslim multitude is repositioned within the epistemology of humanity where its genealogy is rooted. This perspective not only 'avoids the limitations of dichotomous views of East and West, or North and South' as Bryan S. Turner argues.[214] Such an engagement captures Islam's normative momentum in history. It appreciates that Islamutopia holds great enigmas for its agents. It acknowledges that its core motive is the flight or *hegra* to the 'certitude' of the perfect 'Islamopolis' or *Madinat al-nabi*. It values that this ancient motive has taken on special powers in relation to western (post)modernity. It understands, in short, that Islamutopia opens up the possibility of hope at the most profound level of human imagination: the transcendence of the mundane human order and the anticipation of a just order instead. We may disagree, but this is why the believer in such utopias laughs at us. As far as she is concerned, she is part of a grand, fantastic project that we are struggling to comprehend, to our own detriment.

---

[213] See Raymond William Baker, *Islam Without Fear: Egypt and the New Islamists*, Cambridge, MA: Harvard University Press, 2003.

[214] Bryan S. Turner, 'From Orientalism to Global Sociology', in idem. *Orientalism, Postmodernism and Globalism*, London: Routledge, 1994, p. 104.

4

US AND THEM

THE ART OF ENGAGEMENT

As to my homeland it is not Khurasan, nor any other place in the East or the West, and as to my creed I am neither a Jew, nor a Zoroastrian, not even a Muslim as this term is generally understood.

Mowlana Jalal ad-Din Balkhi (Rumi)

The Clash regime today

Every regime has its *arcanum dominationis*, its secret of power, and it is here that I have attempted to challenge the clash regime. The perspective that I have taken throughout this book is to find out how ideas became what they are, to examine them before they became 'real' and before they claimed factual validity. To that end, this study has positioned itself within the realms of anthropology, philosophy, history, geography, methodology, sociology, politics, international studies and semiotics and, more explicitly, among the theoretical layers enveloping and connecting these fields. Of course, I had to take as my starting point whatever terms and definitions are already given. But I hope this study made it clear that this does not imply that analysis has to be subdued to preconceived meanings. I have tried to pick up concepts such as Islamism, Orient, Occident and the West, simulate their perspicuity, only to reassess and question their presumed coherence, acknowledging that the meaning of such dubious totalisations cannot be divorced from their discursive settings and from strategies of ideological engineering. To put it simply: these terms are utterly value-laden and intransigently complex. They are shot through with myths, inventions and outright lies. Thus, one must be sceptical of accounts attempting to capture such complex transcendental and ideational systems we have conveniently called 'Islam(ism)' and the 'West'. I hope that this study has made a contribution to the growing literature that accepts that their plurality cannot be confined to a set of singular formulas, that despite the 'ancient' efforts to unify their essence, such confessional identities are always affected by inventions of the human mind and thus subject to processes of social engineering.

At the same time, I am aware that this study has had to accept and grapple with a central contradiction. While it is normatively important and analytically correct to dissect and challenge the discourses informing the clash regime, it is intellectually naive to assume that truculent notions of 'Islam(ism)' and the 'West' have lost their plausibility, for instance as ingredients of exclusionary ideologies carried by right-wing movements. Since the us-versus-them logic permeating the clash regime today has been continuously inscribed in the archives of world history by a whole range of prominent orators, theoreticians, historians, grammarians, polemicists and politicians, it continues to claim quasi-objective validity. Of course, my perusal of the ideas of canonical thinkers here and there does not claim to appropriate their oeuvre, not even in the slightest. I have focused and highlighted the rather more problematic aspects of their writings in order to stress the reasons why they have not managed to forge a theoretical incentive and normative momentum that could signify a common fate for humanity; that even in Weber, Hegel, Kant and Husserl, we find traces of the rapturous politics of identity; that any universalist agenda, once stripped of its superficial promises of inclusivity, retains its exclusionary fulcrum. I believe that my rather more pronounced focus on the western discourse has been necessary and valid because today and in the past, the violence of this discourse, both in terms of the quantity of the people maimed and killed in its name and in terms of the quality of the dissemination of its message via media channels and academia, is a strong indicator of its ferocity and penetration which need to be accounted for analytically.

At the same time, I retain my emphasis on the argument that the clash regime is a social formation, that the clashing discourses here and there have created a common field, that discourses of Islam are com-

US AND THEM: THE ART OF ENGAGEMENT

plicit in our current predicament. In other words: it is out of the unresolved, historically engineered sources of discursive dissonance between
us and them that the clash regime extracts its power from today. There
is a clash regime present within society because a) humanity has not
come up with a potent counter-regime that could signify a common
fate for all of us and b) because throughout history there have been
influential social actors who have been sufficiently endowed with
authoritative powers via institutions and disciplines which have effectively disseminated and formalised their exclusionary definitions of self
and other. Today, the clash regime functions not only because society
has recourse to an immense array of clash-conducive memories, but
because of powerful individuals who reify a clash mentality; a disposition that signals that 'we' and 'they' have been on a collision course
throughout history. Indeed, many of the books and tracts of the clash
disciples are 'canonical' and are taught and passed on in our class-
rooms. Without this regular co-constitution, the clash regime would
not be contemporaneous in the first place. Hence, it has structural
properties; it is continuously reproduced, objectified in formal and
informal institutions, internalised by society and introjected into our
very consciousness. Ultimately, the one-dimensional clash mentality
thus engendered reveals itself as one of the most salient dispositions of
humankind.

Today, the clash regime multiplies itself in the networked spaces of
the Internet and travels effortlessly along the ethers of a technologi-
cally globalised world. So at the time of writing, in Afghanistan, the
Taliban send multimedia messages to Afghan mobiles, showing clips of
roadside bombs and suicide operations that kill and maim US and
NATO soldiers who are typically depicted as 'infidel invaders'. On the
other side, in the United States, twenty-eight million copies of the
insidiously anti-muslim propaganda film *Obsession: Radical Islam's
War Against the West* were distributed to newspaper subscribers in the
contested states of the Presidential election of 2008. The movie has its
own website and was widely disseminated during David Horowitz's
'Islamo-Fascism Awareness Week' held on campuses all over the United
States. It describes 'radical Islam' as a threat to 'western civilisation',
quite comparable to the menace of Nazi Germany.[1]

[1] See Isabel Macdonald, 'The Anti-muslim Smear Machine Strikes Again?',
CommonDreams.org, 11 Oct. 2008.

267

Indeed, one of the reasons why the clash regime is so functional today is that it is a part of globalisation. 'Al Qaeda resembles less the centralised command structures of twentieth-century revolutionary parties', one observer points out, 'than the cellular structures of drug cartels and the flattened networks of virtual business corporations'.[2] According to another author, the 'jihad achieves globalisation within a landscape of purely accidental relations separated as if by a vast abyss from a politics of control linked to causes and intention'.[3] In other words, after the terrorist attacks on the United States in September 2001, globalisation also means that the barriers of geographical space and the security associated with them are further blurred, which in turn indicates that political violence travels rather more effortlessly. While the likelihood of thermonuclear confrontation during the Cold War provided a calculable threat, transnational networks such as Al Qaeda strike out of the opaque spaces of a globalised world system, and do not react towards deterrence or any form of missile defence system for that matter. This globalisation of violence means that '[s] tates no longer have a monopoly on the means of mass destruction: more people died in the attacks on the World Trade Centre and the Pentagon than in the Japanese attack on Pearl Harbour in 1941'.[4] In short, today, the disciples of the clash regime have exponentially more instruments at their hands to cause mass deaths and destruction.

Secondly, the clash regime continues to find a prominent place in academia and the international media. Reading Bernard Lewis, who popularised the phrase 'clash of civilisations' in an article published in the *Atlantic Monthly* in 1990, we are alerted that the stakes involved far transcend 'the level of issues and policies and the governments that pursue them'.[5] The clash of civilisations, he famously maintained, is 'the perhaps irrational but surely historic reaction of an ancient rival against our Judeo-Christian heritage, our secular present, and the

[2] John Gray, *Al Qaeda and What It Means to be Modern*, London: Faber and Faber, 2003, p. 76.
[3] Faisal Devji, *Landscapes of the Jihad: Militancy, Morality, Modernity*, London: Hurst, 2005, p. 20.
[4] Robert O. Keohane, 'The Globalisation of Violence, Theories of World Politics and "The Liberalism of Fear"'. Available at http://www.ssrc.org/sept11/essays/keohane.htm [Last accessed 14 Mar. 2003].
[5] Bernard Lewis, 'The Roots of Muslim Rage', *Atlantic Monthly*, Sept. 1990, p. 60.

worldwide importance of both'.[6] In a recent interview with *Foreign Policy*, Lewis re-emphasised his oft-cited prediction:

I certainly think there is something in the 'clash of civilisations'. What brought Islam and Christendom into conflict was not so much their differences as their resemblances. There are many religions in the world, but almost all of them are regional, local, ethnic, or whatever you choose to call it. Christianity and Islam are the only religions that claim universal truth. Christians and Muslims are the only people who claim they are the fortunate recipients of God's final message to humanity, which it is their duty not to keep selfishly to them-selves—like the Jews or the Hindus or the Buddhists—but to bring to the rest of mankind, removing whatever obstacles there may be in the way. So, we have two religions with a similar self-perception, a similar historical back-ground, living side by side, and conflict becomes inevitable.[7]

And we know by now about Samuel Huntington's essay published in *Foreign Affairs* in 1993, which has become one of the most promi-nent papers in recent history. Huntington famously suggested that 'the paramount axis of world politics will be the relations between "the West and the Rest"' adding that 'a central focus of conflict for the immediate future will be between the West and several Islamic-Confu-cian states'.[8] Many scholars have taken 9/11 to be an empirical indica-tor of his forecast despite of the fact that Huntington himself doubted that it corroborates his thesis. 'It would have been unlike Samuel P. Huntington to say "I told you so" after 9/11', writes Prof. Fouad Ajami in the *New York Times* in 2008. 'Those 19 young Arabs who struck America on 9/11 were to give Huntington more of history's compliance than he could ever have imagined'.[9]

Thirdly, the style of writing and editorial policies of some influential media conglomerates is also a part of the cultural apparatus sustaining the clash regime today. 'The planned construction of over 180 mosques in Germany', one reads in the German magazine *Der Spiegel* sympto-matically, 'is mobilising right-wing xenophobes but also an increasing number of leftist critics. They fear the Muslim places of worship will

---

[6] Ibid.

[7] 'Seven Questions: Bernard Lewis on the two biggest myths about Islam', *Foreign Policy*, Aug. 2008. Available at http://www.foreignpolicy.com/story/cms.php?story_id=4455 [Last accessed 21 Oct. 2008].

[8] Samuel P. Huntington, 'The Clash of Civilisations?', *Foreign Affairs*, vol. 72, no. 3, 1993, pp. 48–49.

[9] Fouad Ajami, 'The Clash', *New York Times*, 6 Jan. 2008.

facilitate the establishment of a completely parallel society'.[10] Such media reports not only suggest an artificial difference and distance between Islam and Europe, and, by implication, between Muslims and the societies they live in and contribute to on a daily basis; they also exemplify a conscious effort to link Muslims with societal division, even secession. Without wanting to commit a great deal of space to this form of journalistic discrimination, which would need another book to study, let me add that the mainstream German media, including *Der Spiegel*, tends to be rather tardy in their responses to attacks against minorities in the country. The delayed and rather muted reaction to the brutal murder of Marwa al-Sherbini in July 2009 serves as an example. Al-Sherbini, a thirty-one year old Egyptian-Muslim woman who was pregnant at the time of her killing, had filed a complaint after the defendant verbally abused her at a playground in the southeastern German town of Dresden calling her a 'terrorist' amongst other things.[11] Invited to the courtroom for an appeal hearing, the defendant, who emigrated from Germany from Russia, attacked al-Sherbini with a knife stabbing her eighteen times. As her husband Elwi Ali-Okaz tried to save her, he was not only stabbed by him, but shot by a police officer who mistook Ali-Okaz for the attacker.

Even if we agree that such obviously racist attacks continue to be tragic exceptions, there is considerable room to criticise, on the one side, the late reaction of the German government and the media including *Der Spiegel*, which only responded more directly to the murder after protests in Egypt and Turkey; and, on the other side, the residue of xenophobic anti-immigrant attitudes in Germany. A recent, wide-ranging study commissioned by the Friedrich Ebert Stiftung and conducted by academics of the University of Leipzig indicates that aversion to foreigners (*Ausländerfeindlichkeit*) is widespread (26 per cent amongst the respondents).[12] Yet in the reports about the murder of al-

---

[10] Jochen Bölsche, 'Domes and Minarets? Not in my Backyard Say an Increasing Number of Germans', *Spiegel Online*, 16 Jul. 2008. Available at http://www.spiegel.de/international/germany/0,1518,565146,00.html [Last accessed 24 Jul. 2008].

[11] Kate Connolly and Jack Shencker, 'The Headscarf Martyr: Murder in German Court Sparks Egyptian Fury', *The Guardian*, 7 Jul. 2009, p. 17.

[12] Oliver Decker, Katharina Rothe, Elmar Brähler, *Ein Blick in die Mitte—Zur Entstehung rechtsextremer und demokratischer Einstellungen*, Berlin: Friedrich Ebert Stiftung, 2008. Available at http://www.fes.de/rechtsextremis-

Sherbini, there was scarce reference to such subliminal bias. The linkage seems obvious enough and one would have hoped that the German media would seize the opportunity to spearhead a campaign accentuating an inescapable, yet suppressed reality; that Germany is a multicultural country and that the meaning of Germany has to be reinterpreted accordingly. Instead, the media discourse in the country retains the discursive bias towards the supposed 'other', for instance in designations of immigrants as *Ausländer* or foreigner. The correct term in German would be *Minoritäten* or *Minderheiten* (minorities), a term that would emancipate them from their 'otherness' acknowledging the reality that they are a part of German society. Xenophobia and racism fester particularly well in a discursive continuum with various undisturbed myths about the 'other'. If there is no constant interference and resistance, especially by the media, counter-dominant ideas threaten to be subordinated to the cacophony of the resurgent right-wing, in Germany and elsewhere in Europe.

Of course, there is no suggestion here, that *Der Spiegel*, which continues to be the leading investigative magazine in Germany, is part of a conspiracy to demonise minorities in the country or Muslims specifically. But what I am saying is that the many articles about a supposedly latent 'Muslim menace'—demographic, cultural, political—that we read almost on a daily basis, are part of a larger cultural constellation that is negatively biased towards 'Islam', and everything it is supposed to stand for. In the case of *Der Spiegel*, this was particularly apparent during the editorship of Stefan Aust between 1994 and 2008. In the case of the highly influential Axel Springer group, which publishes a range of daily newspapers and magazines in Germany and beyond, it can be discerned directly from the editorial guidelines. All of Axel Springer's many outfits have to adhere to the company's five socio-political preambles written in 1967, amended in 1990 following the reunification of Germany and supplemented in 2001. These set the general parameters of the editorial policy pursued: 1. To uphold liberty and law in Germany which is defined as a country belonging to the 'Western' family of nations, and to further the unification of Europe; 2. To promote reconciliation of Jews and Germans and support the

---

mus/inhalt/studie.htm [Last accessed 12 Jun. 2009]. See further Kai Hafez, *Islam and the West in the Mass Media: Fragmented Images in a Globalising World*, Cresskill, NJ: Hampton Press, 2000.

vital rights of the State of Israel; 3. To support the Transatlantic Alliance and solidarity with the United States of America in the common values of free nations; 4. To reject all forms of political extremism; 5. To uphold the principles of a free social market economy.[13]

Fourthly, bestselling authors such as Christopher Hitchens and Martin Amis have also joined the chorus. Both talk and write with a particularly angry virulence about Muslims. The former is a passionate supporter of the war in Iraq and 'regime change' in Iran and the latter demands that Muslims should 'suffer until they get their house in order', that they should be banned from travelling, deported, and strip-searched. 'Discriminatory stuff, until it hurts the whole community and they start getting tough with their children'.[14] Writers, journalists, academics, right-wing politicians, think tank functionaries and media pundits—in each and every corner of society you will find influential individuals warning us about the Islamic threat from without and the dangers of the Muslim presence within.[15] A list of a few 'ideal types' of the different strata of society I am alluding to proves the point.

The Pulitzer Prize winning journalist (Charles Krauthammer) says:

On September 11, American foreign policy acquired seriousness. It also acquired a new organising principle: We have an enemy, radical Islam; it is a global opponent of worldwide reach, armed with an idea, and with the tactics, weapons, and ruthlessness necessary to take on the world's hegemon; and its defeat is our supreme national objective, as overriding a necessity as were the defeats of fascism and Soviet communism.[16]

The Conservative politician (Margaret Thatcher) proclaims:

Islamic extremism today like bolshevism in the past, is an armed doctrine. It is an aggressive ideology promoted by fanatical, well armed devotees.

---

[13] In accordance with those 'articles of association' *Axel Springer* is the only German publishing house, which refused to publish the advertising campaign of the German Left Party led by Oskar Lafontaine and Gregor Gysi in 2005. Apart from its principally anti-war stance, it has been one of the principle aims of *Die Linke* in Germany to defuse the 'Muslim threat' thesis in Germany's political discourse.

[14] Quoted in *The Independent* (Extra Section), 29 Jan. 2008, p. 3.

[15] See further Jocelyne Cesari, *When Islam and Democracy Meet: Muslims in Europe and in the United States*, London: Palgrave, 2004, p. 3.

[16] Charles Krauthammer, 'The Real New World Order: The American and the Islamic Challenge', *The Weekly Standard*, 7:9, 12 Nov. 2001. Available at http://www.weeklystandard.com/Content/Public/Articles/000/000/000/456zfygd.asp [Last accessed 6 May 2006].

And, like communism, it requires an all-embracing long-term strategy to defeat it.[17]

The theoretician of the 'new left' (Perry Anderson) concurs:

Since Muhammad clearly enjoins *jihad* against infidels in Holy Places, latter-day Salafism—notwithstanding every effort of Western, or pro-Western, commentators to euphemise the Prophet's words—is on sound scriptural grounds, embarrassing though this undoubtedly is to the moderate majority of Muslims. The result is a ready, though not inexhaustible, supply of young, fanatical fighters against 'global unbelief', who have made a reality of the clash of civilisations in the Middle East—there being virtually no point of contact between their vision of the world and that of the Western intruders into it.[18]

And the networked writer and blogger (Andrew Sullivan) states:

This is why this coming conflict is indeed as momentous and as grave as the last major conflicts, against Nazism and Communism, and why it is not hyperbole to see it in those epic terms. What is at stake is yet another battle against a religion that is succumbing to the temptation Jesus refused in the desert—to rule by force. The difference is that this conflict is against a more formidable enemy than Nazism or Communism.[19]

This study has repeatedly embraced the idea that resistance to the clash regime is necessary. But at the same time I have to concede that it is doubtful that any counter-regime would persuade the hardcore disciples of the clash. It will not persuade Susanne Winter, a lawyer and a member of Austria's right-wing Freedom Party who recently called the Prophet Mohammed a 'child abuser' and warned that Austria faces an 'Islamic [*sic*] immigration tsunami'.[20] Neither would her fellow countryman Klaus Emmerich, a veteran TV pundit who declared after the election of Barack Obama in the United States that he 'would not want the western world to be directed by a black man' because 'blacks aren't as politically civilised', repent.[21] One is equally

---

[17] Margaret Thatcher, 'Islamism is the new Bolshevism', *The Guardian*, 12 Feb. 2002.

[18] Perry Anderson, 'Jottings on the Conjuncture', *New Left Review*, vol. 48, November-December 2007. Available at http://www.newleftreview.org/?view=2695 [Last accessed 12 Jan. 2009]

[19] Andrew Sullivan, 'This is a Religious War', *New York Times*, 7 Oct. 2001.

[20] Tony Paterson, 'Anger in Austria after politician brands Mohamed a "child abuser"', *The Independent*, 16 Jan. 2008.

[21] Mark Mazower, 'Prejudice in Europe is more than skin deep', *The Financial Times*, 16 Nov. 2008.

unlikely to persuade Michael Burleigh or Melanie Philips, two 'icons' of the conservative press in Britain who have repeatedly expressed their profound anger about the supposedly real and present 'Islamist' challenge to 'western' civilisation.[22] Or would we expect that the current Prime Minister of Israel, Benyamin Netanyahu, would change his mind about the inevitability of the clash of civilisations? He seems to be entirely serious when he writes that the 'soldiers of militant Islam and Pan-Arabism do not hate the West because of Israel; they hate Israel because of the West'.[23] For these clash disciples, their imagined 'Islam' will continue to be the antithetical system *par excellence* and the Muslim next door will be presented to us as the 'social antichrist' who could potentially plot and scheme to disrupt our civilised order.

I am equally convinced that this study will not persuade Ayman al-Zawahiri, who concurs with the clash of civilisation ideas when he declares that the 'crusaders and the Jews do not understand but the

---

[22] See Michael Burleigh, *Sacred Causes: Religion and Politics from the European Dictators to Al-Qaeda*, London: Harper, 2006; Melanie Philips, *Londonistan*, London: Encounter, 2006. Another author with similar attitudes describes the situation as follows:

'It bears repeating: An Islamified Europe would be as great a threat to the United States today as a Nazified Europe would have been to the United States in the 1940s. Even before Pearl Harbor, Franklin Roosevelt understood that a Nazi-dominated Europe would be more than a fearsome military and industrial threat; it would be a civilisational threat. Now we face another civilisational threat in insurgent Islam'.

Tony Brinkley, *The West's Last Chance: Will We Win the Clash of Civilisations?*, Washington DC: Regnery, 2005, p. 185. A comparable belief in the clash idea and its political functionality can be found in the writings of many Israeli historians who do not subscribe to—or who have departed from the theses of the country's 'new historians'. See, most recently, Benny Morris', *1948: The First Arab-Israeli War*, Yale: Yale University Press, 2008. Morris depicts the war as a part of the global struggle between the Islamic east and the west. On this topic see further Jonathan Cook, *Israel and the Clash of Civilisations: Iraq, Iran and the Plan to remake the Middle East*, London: Pluto, 2008.

[23] Benjamin Netanyahu, *Fighting Terrorism: How Democracies Can Defeat Domestic and International Terrorism*, New York: Farrar, Straus, and Giroux, 1995, p. 87.

language of killing and blood';[24] or members of the *Hizb ut-Tahrir* for that matter who ponder *The Inevitability of the Clash of Civilisations* in one of their publications. Writers of the ultra-rightwing Iranian newspaper *Jomhuri-ye Eslami* appear to be equally adamant when they pontificate that the:

degenerated and immoral theory of 'War Among Civilisations' theorised and advocated by Samuel Huntington, is now the bedrock and [theoretical] substructure for plans and strategies of the government of the little Bush. It is this same depraved and corrupt theory that has urged the junior Bush to speak of the need for the outbreak of another 'crusade' in this day and age, and which has placed the American President—at the age of fictitious and imaginary rule of democracy in the world today—on top of the list of criminals and blood-suckers of history …[25]

No, I doubt that we can persuade them. Today, the discourses constituting the clash regime perform indispensable political functions for their agents. An important methodological lesson that I have drawn from its trans-historical and transnational composure is that any critique of the clash regime must account for culture and counter-culture, containment and stabilisation, salience and flexibility, conservatism and upheaval, reification and change. As I have tried to demonstrate in the previous chapters, in most areas of practice and discourse, the clash regime has not been hegemonic. Nonetheless, this study has also demonstrated why it has not departed from the archives of human history. Indeed today, by far more than in Antiquity, reification of clash conducive ideas is rather strong. Hence, to present a viable argument for contemporary critical theory and politics, trends of both reification and contestation must be analysed. It is not a matter of determining whether one affirms or negates the clash regime, whether one ignores it, or whether one emphasises its relevance or denies its effects on society, international politics, the media and international public discourse

---

[24] 'Al-Qaeda's Statement: Full Text', *BBCNews.com*, 21 May 2003. Available at http://news.BBC.co.uk/go/pr/fr/2/hi/mddle_east/3047903.stm [Last accessed 22 Feb. 2008]. At the time of writing, another high ranking member of Al Qaeda, namely Abu Yahya al-Libi has warned the Saudi government about pursuing its 'dialogue amongst religions' initiative. 'No moderation', he proclaimed. 'No rapprochement, no cooperation between us and other religions'. See 'Al-Qaeda warns against closer ties between religions', *Agence France Press* (AFP), 23 May 2008.

[25] *Jomhuri-ye Eslami*, 22 June 2002, p. 1

in advance; but to account for the fact that it is out there, to discover how it got there, to continuously provide a critical analysis of the institutions, norms and ideologies that perpetuate its exclusionary logic.

My methodological conclusions would be incomplete were I not to reemphasise that the clash regime is surprisingly mimetic; that its disciples share methodological, psychological and syntactical affinities in the way they propagate and institutionalise their agenda, without necessarily being aware of their fraternal bond. The clash regime is a vast cultural artefact constituted by many social agents, norms, networks and ideologies. Within this system, individuals, groups and institutions are entirely linked to each other subjectively. Bin-Laden is dependent on his imagined West to legitimate his terrorist strategy. Michael Ledeen could not propagate a global war on 'Islamo-fascism' without Al Qaeda. Ayman al-Zawahiri needs to vilify the United States and the 'West' more generally in order to question the status quo in the wider Islamic worlds. To highly dissimilar degrees and with highly different outcomes, bin-Laden and Ledeen tap into the archives of the clash regime and its supermarket of exclusionary ideas thus positioning themselves within its one-dimensional universe. As such, the clash regime refers to an inter-subjective system that is hybrid and sociopathic. It is hybrid because there is no formal—psychological, syntactical and methodological—boundary between the clash disciples. They speak the same language with two accents. And it is sociopathic because its constituent agents seem autonomous, but only because they attempt to artificially isolate their selves from any impingement by the other, so that all they allow themselves to know about them is their 'otherness'. Having defined their identities and interests in terms of the categories bequeathed upon them by their inevitable interaction with the other, they have become a social group, albeit a traumatised one that does not perceive itself as such.[26] This social group, with its implicit inter-subjective dependencies, is widespread. Its transnational geography is highlighted in the 'innumerability' of the structural components of the clash regime, in the fact that they are both one and many, that they emanate from innumerable loci in human history and practice. So the clash regime refers to an unquantifiable multiplicity. Its

[26] On the psychoanalytic category of a 'regressed group' see further Fred C. Alford, *Group Psychology and Political Theory*, New Haven: Yale University Press, 1994, especially pp. 87 ff.

vastness puts the few examples that I could sketch in this study into perspective.

The clash regime is utterly indiscriminate. It continuously informs and signifies a permanent battle within groups and between societies. The clash regime operates horizontally and vertically: Al Qaeda kills both Muslims and other individuals in the United States, East Asia and Europe; Christian-Zionists in the United States are as opposed to 'Muslims' as to 'East-coast' liberals and left-leaning European intellectuals; the current President of Iran Mahmoud Ahmadinejad invites the former 'Grand Wizard' of the Ku Klux Klan (KKK) David Duke, a member of a white supremacist, anti-immigrant group called 'American Springs' George Kadar, staunchly atheist friends of the holocaust denying British historian David Irving such as Lady Michelle Renouf, members of German neo-Nazi parties such as the *NPD* and adherents to the ultra-orthodox anti-Zionist Jewish group Neturei Karta, to a conference in the capitol of the Islamic Republic, Tehran; Alexander Baron, a contemporary British writer with sympathies for the fascist British National Party (BNP) laments the influence of the 'organised homosexual movement' in an article published by the 'Islamic Party of Britain'.[27] In fact, you will find that homophobia is a regrettably pervasive transnational pathology that is shared by today's disciples of the clash regime, both here and over there, undoubtedly because homosexuality challenges and questions their fascistically ordered world all the way to the rules and norms governing their sexuality.

The tendency to delineate what is conjoined, to artificially detach what is interdependent and to try to centrifuge what is hybrid is not only prevalent in social and political studies, but also in the natural sciences. Today, the logic of the clash regime animates the so called 'hard sciences' as well. There rages a particularly pertinent debate between human geographers, conservation biologists and biogeographers about the battle between 'native' and 'non-native' or 'alien' species in our habitat. Daniel Simberloff, director of the 'Institute for Biological Invasions' at the University of Tennessee in Knoxville, for instance, argues that non-native species threaten the natural environment of the United States with unprecedented ferocity. According to

---

[27] See http://www.islamicparty.com/commonsense/36movement.htm [Last accessed 10 Mar. 2009]. This Alexander Baron should not to be confused with the author and screenwriter who passed away in 1999.

him, 'extinctions of both island and continental species have both been demonstrated and judged by the public to be harmful. Although more public attention has been focused on non-native animals than non-native plants', he continues, 'the latter more often cause ecosystemwide impacts'. In order to meet this clear and imminent threat, he calls for '[i]ncreased regulation of introduction of non-native species' noting that 'invasion biologists have recently developed methods that greatly aid prediction of which introduced species will harm the environment and thus enable more efficient regulation'.[28]

A counter-argument to the case of surveillance, regulation and confinement of 'non-native species' is made by Charles Warren. Warren points to the potentially harmful social impact of a discourse that employs value-laden terms such as native, alien, pure or integrity. He draws attention to 'bioxenophic' studies that could fester anti-alien sentiments in the natural sciences. According to him, terms such as 'Rhodobashing', designating conservationists' battle for controlling rhododendron (a genus of flowering plants), are uncomfortably close to racist terms such as 'Paki-bashing'. He concludes that the reference to race, population levels or genetic identities invites charges of 'eco-fascism':[29]

A desire to preserve the native species may be positively represented as an expression of ecological patriotism but, just as patriotism can slide into racism, so discourses about the 'righteousness' of native species can all too easily bleed into the claims made by racists and xenophobic nationalists. Through such discursive overlap, political ideology has invaded the realm of vegetative politics; alien species are branded as second-class citizens, and well-intentioned ecology is tarred with the brush of jingoism. ... Strong conceptual and empirical continuities link ecological nativism with Nazi/neo-Nazi ideas, most tellingly in the horticulture of Nazi Germany ... [R]acists and fascists (including Hitler) have sometimes legitimated their arguments by drawing on conservation discourses about the threats posed by alien species.[30]

---

[28] Daniel Simberloff, 'Non-native species *Do* threaten the natural environment!' *Journal of Agricultural and Environmental Ethics*, vol. 18, no. 6, Dec. 2005, p. 595.

[29] Charles R. Warren, 'Perspectives on the "alien" versus "native" species debate: a critique of concepts, language and practice', *Progress in Human Geography*, vol. 31, no. 4, 2007, p. 436. For a recent response see Christopher D. Preston, 'The terms "native" and "alien"—a biogeographical perspective', *Progress in Human Geography*, vol. 33, no. 4, 2009, pp. 1–10.

[30] Warren, 'Perspectives on the "alien" versus "native" species debate', pp. 435–436.

The political issue that is criticised here is the quest for 'purity' and insulation, which echoes the anti-immigrant discourse of many pundits and right-wing politicians. I believe that critics of the native-non-native divide are right on that account. Consider the attitudes of the aforementioned Daniel Pipes, who became a board member of the United States Institute for Peace in April 2003 on the recommendation of George W. Bush. When Pipes laments that 'West European societies are unprepared for the massive immigration of brown-skinned peoples cooking strange foods and not exactly maintaining Germanic standards of hygiene', he is calling for nothing else than confinement and racial segregation. When he warns Europeans that 'Muslim immigrants bring with them a chauvinism that augurs badly for their integration into the mainstream of the European societies' and that 'the Rushdie affair was merely a prelude to further troubles' because ultimately 'Iranian zealots threaten more within the gates of Vienna than outside them', he is essentially calling for a 'species framework strategy' that would rescue Europe from the 'Muslim invaders' threatening the continent from within.[31]

Unsurprisingly, once it had been transplanted into the realm of the policy world, the native non-native binary informs very particular historical narratives that further such problematic notions of self and other. A report submitted to the US Congress in 1999, for instance, speaks of the invasion of the United States by 'notorious' non-native plants such as the 'Russian thistle' and infective pests caused by the 'gipsy moths, Japanese beetles, Asian long-horned beetles, fire ants, Africanized honeybees and zebra mussels'. Among the measures proposed to control and prevent those sources of pests and disease, is a 'bounty system' which would ensure that an 'animal or plant is killed and removed from the population'.[32] In a follow up report presented to the US Congress in 2003, the geo-politics of the native-non-native binary is historicised: 'For the first few centuries after the arrival of Europeans in North America', it is stated, 'plants and animals of many species were sent between the two land masses'. The white settlers did not consciously allow for any import of harmful 'non-native' species.

[31] Daniel Pipes, 'The Muslims are coming! The Muslims are coming!', *National Review*, 19 Nov. 1990, p. 28.
[32] M. Lynne Corn, Eugene H. Buck, Jean Rawson, and Eric Fischer, 'Harmful non-native species: Issues for Congress III', Congressional Research Service Report, 8 Apr. 1999. Available at http://ncseonline.org/NLE/CRSreports/Biodiversity/biodv–26.cfm [Last accessed 24 Jul. 2009].

Rather, the 'transfer of non-natives consisted not only of *intentional* westbound species ranging from pigs to dandelions, but also *intentional* eastbound grey squirrels and tomatoes'. In the nineteenth century, the situation changed. During that period, there emerged a 'national focus' on the real and present dangers of the 'remaining non-native species crossing the Atlantic *uninvited* and often *unwelcome*'.[33]

The native-non-native, self-other divide in that report is entirely premised on the notion that American history started with the 'discovery' of the continent by the European settlers. There is no mentioning here of the smallpox epidemic that killed almost the entire native American population of the Massachusetts Bay in 1618–1619 or similar mass deaths until the first federal vaccination programme was instituted in 1832, the so called 'Indian Vaccination Act'.[34] Of course, for the Native Americans it was the arrival of the non-native Europeans that was unwelcome. It had devastating consequences exactly because of the intentional transfer of 'non-native' species and the unfamiliar viruses they carried. Moreover, the authors of the report ignore that the 'national focus' on the 'invasive non-native species' in the nineteenth century, could only emerge out of the discriminatory delimitations inscribed into the idea of 'America' and its racially whitened geographic spaces during that period in the first place. Ultimately then, the us-versus-them logic that is currently displayed in some quarters of the natural sciences and the environmental politics enveloping them, reveals residues of a biased conceptualisation of self and other, native and non-native, which is reminiscent of the intensely dualistic perspective of the racial discourse that emerged out of the period of the Enlightenment. I have discussed this passion for racial purity and genealogically cleansed identities at length in the previous chapters.

How well politics vegetates on the fertile discursive field in which the invented native-non-native binary flourishes has not been suffi-

[33] Ibid., emphasis added.

[34] This argument is laid out most prominently in Alfred Cosby's *Ecological Imperialism: the biological expansion of Europe, 900–1900*, new edition, Cambridge: Cambridge University Press, 2004. Crosby's book is too wide-ranging to be criticised satisfactorily in a footnote. But the holistic way Crosby treats seemingly coherent categories such as Caucasian, neo-European etc. is problematic. Crosby adheres to static approaches to race and identity which brings his analysis—at times—dangerously close to early twentieth century theories of racial integrity.

ciently addressed either in the natural sciences or in social and political studies. And yet the issues at stake here are acutely relevant to the politics enveloping us. Many asylum seekers have been assembled in so called 'immigration centres', highly discriminatory, supervised spaces surrounded by walls, barbwire and policed checkpoints. Wouldn't the right-wing expand measures of physical confinement to all 'non-native species', human and other, if the hybridity and trans-spatial movement of the natural worlds would allow for it?

To discuss what I have been saying in the past few paragraphs further; if anthropology (or ethnology) transplanted the myth of purity into the social and political arenas, the natural sciences have developed their own spaces of exclusion, confinement and surveillance, with the difference, that their discourse has not abandoned faith in the panacea of 'objective' science. Alas, salutary efforts by the new 'environmental romanticists' to forge multilateral cooperation against and around the threat of global warming, HIV, or space unbound influenzas caused by post-penicillin viruses such as H1N1 ('Swine Flu') or H5N1 ('Bird Flu') are seriously hampered by the identity politics that have been transferred to the natural sciences. Even studies by those researchers who have tried to get around the native-non-native divide have merely managed to introduce equally problematic methodologies based on the measurement of identity and 'genetic integrity'.[35] Behind such approaches lies a fascination with and belief in the DNA *zeitgeist*; in the manipulation, containment and engineering of nature and our bodies, which is both alarming and promising. It is promising not only because of the advancements in the treatment of terminal illnesses, especially cancer that it contributes to. But also because research into deoxyribonucleic acid (DNA) marks a scientific departure from racial and anatomical hierarchies which were central to the research of the phrenologists of the nineteenth century, the eugenic experiments of the Nazis and the haematologists of the mid-twentieth century.

Furthermore, the structure of DNA, *The Double Helix* invented by James D. Watson, and the Human Genome Project launched by the US Congress with an initial federal budget of $3 billion in 1988, does not only point to our atomised biological constitution. It also implies that

---

[35] See T. A. Jones, 'The Restoration Gene Pool Concept: Beyond the native versus non-native debate', *Restoration Ecology*, vol. 11, no. 3, 2003, pp. 281–290.

we are all made of the same stuff. If you and I are constituted of the same chemical formulas, we may be able to mitigate some of our differences on that basis. Writers such as Shirlee Taylor Haizlip in her autobiographical memoir *The Sweeter the Juice* engage with this ameliorating utopia that the de-codification of the genome promises. To Haizlip, such research shows that race is a social construction rather than a genetic reality. This is very true, but at the same time DNA research does also entail all the ingredients of a potentially dangerous dystopia. Behind it lurks one of the most central legacies of the Enlightenment project: the fascination with perfection (the mass obsession with the perfect body image is a related pathology):

> However paranoid the vision of a genetically 'purified' world, we are right to fear it when every news bulletin brings breaking research on how foetuses can be altered in the womb and genes in plants, animals and perhaps human beings can be manipulated, whether for profit or prophylaxis. Disability rights activists alert us to something real when they insist that we suffer an immeasurable loss when we value life only in terms of its functionality and flawlessness.[36]

When it comes to moving to a critical appreciation of the way the natural sciences can contribute to a new understanding of self and other, one has to start where Marcuse and the theorist of the Frankfurt School left: with criticism of the ways the human species has contributed to the destruction of the natural habitat, with a critical analysis of the ways the science of nature has contributed to the oppression of its subject. This calls for nothing short of a re-enchantment with nature, a dialectical communication between the individual and her natural habitat in which the latter acknowledges the uncontrollable trans-spatiality of the former. So construed, as a realm of interdependent particularity, nature becomes a source of resistance to totalising tendencies which are so central to the anthropocentric notions adopted from the perspective of modernity. Contemporary critical theorists put it this way: the pseudo-objective 'science' informed by an interest in control and exploitation would have to give away 'to a "metascience" whose full normative context includes reference to ethics, values, social justice, and ecology'.[37]

[36] Sarah E. Chinn, *Technology and the Logic of American Racism: A Cultural History of the Body as Evidence*, London: Continuum, 2000, p. 168.
[37] Steven Best and Douglas Kellner, *The Postmodern Turn*, London: The Guildford Press, 1997, p. 269.

I have extended my discussion of the clash regime into the natural sciences in order to give yet another example of its versatility and prevalence today. All its inter-subjective practices and theories run through its structures on a daily basis objectifying its salience in society and its impact on individual perceptions of the other. In particular, the aim to sustain the us-versus-them logic of the clash regime will gain in urgency whenever there is yet another war (e.g. Iraq, Afghanistan) or confrontation within society (e.g. the Danish cartoon controversy, Rushdie *fatwa*). During periods of conflict, the clash regime becomes the common playing field for those strata of society that have an interest in mobilising destructive passions for a particular political or socio-economic agenda, both here and over there.

As such, the clash regime is an ongoing multi-civilisational construction accentuating conflict. Its geography encompasses zones in Europe, the United States, Asia, and in other parts of the world that this study has not covered. A fundamental conclusion, a matter of fact statement, can now be made: The cultural hybridity and transnational virulence of the clash regime puts to rest ideas such as the clash of civilisations which are premised on the fiction of territoriality. The clash regime resists geography, it is de-territorial. The battles within it resemble a civil war. It is a war *within* a social system, not *between* cultural or geographical entities. It is a war between right-wing xenophobes, fundamentalist terrorists, imperialists and other clash disciples, here and there, along with their institutions and discourses which are divorced from geographic delimitations. It is a war between brothers and sisters who are fighting within a mimetic, common history that has delivered their combative language and the memories of exclusion and discrimination they are reinvigorating. It is a battle within a violent group that is pestering us to believe in their war. Beyond the imagination of its adherents, there exists no clash of civilisations. We have a fundamental choice here—to be dragged into that civil war or to resist it.

Negative dialectics: signposts of a counter-regime

Even if we are biologically coded to think in terms of self-other categories as cognitive psychologists and neuro-physiologists argue, sociologists, social psychologists and philosophers have shown that the categories we believe in are affected by the interaction between both mind and world. Nonetheless, we have been habituated to see our surrounding world as anything but a social construction. No wonder then that the battle cry goes up that one is a 'traitor', an 'irrational idealist', whenever, in a critical analysis, one is perceived to be questioning too bluntly traditions and memories. One will be castigated for questioning the sovereignty of the 'official discourse' that is not only at the heart of the 'Westphalian nation-state', but our very 'identity' as Muslims, Christians, Hindus, Argentineans, Americans, Arabs, Chinese, Turks, that many of us believe in so strenuously. Make no mistake about it, it is much easier to take sides in a particular clash situation, especially the side of the country and culture one lives in. But what we need is the opposite. Today, more than ever we need people who are willing to tip-toe between the trenches rather than to shoot from within them. Alas, amongst the mainstream, converse preferences rule. In the absence of a future-oriented alternative that would be powerful enough to question the status quo, belief in binary divisions remains rather strong. In other words, we are continuously compelled to maximise our difference to the other. As a result, totalitarian methodologies thrive, and epistemologies of difference continue to be spun. By the force of the us-versus-them dichotomisations thus created, an exponential mass of violence in the name of the 'in-group' (and converting the out-group) is repeatedly unleashed.

So do we have to despair? What are some of the prospects and ingredients for a counter-regime to the clash if its structural cohesion is as prevalent as I have claimed? What important qualification in the designation of self, other or being (ontology), have been accomplished and are needed to battle the us-versus-them logic permeating the clash regime?

It took a long time until 'postmodern' thinkers and critical theorists recognised 'being' as compromised by the interpenetration of different histories, causal systems and temporalities. Whereas in the nineteenth century, the dominant western discourse expressed a fundamental believe in the inevitability of a universal 'embrace', the twentieth century is pierced with doubt and scepticism of the (causal) efficacy and moral necessity of that project. Hence, this particular Eurocentric discourse has been in the process of losing out in its Faustian bargain with modernity (*viz. Der Untergang des Abendlandes* as Oswald Spengler observed during World War I).[38] Since then, the central conception

[38] Oswald Spengler, *The Decline of the West*, one volume edition, New York: Knopf, 1939.

of temporality itself has been in question. This is not only exemplified by the demise of 'absolute simultaneity' in the science of Max Planck, Albert Einstein and Werner Heisenberg, as Ernst Cassirer observes.[39] It is manifest in the novels of Samuel Beckett, Bertold Brecht and Franz Kafka, the philosophy of Derrida, Baudrillard, Deleuze, Guattari, Foucault, the psychology of Freud and Kierkegaard and the critical theory of the Frankfurt School. Some of their ideas have even penetrated the curricula of 'new disciplines' such as 'Middle Eastern' studies and International Relations, albeit rather slowly.[40] In this 'post-modern' oeuvre where Akbar S. Ahmed sees 'a spirit of pluralism',[41] Ziauddin Sardar the opposition to 'totalising reason',[42] and Robert Cox 'a multi-civilisational world order',[43] a consciousness convergent with the implications of physical relativity is present: the interpenetration of the time-continuum by other temporalities. Through the post-modern lens, we perceive realities in the plural; we see political entities as invented (Hobsbawm) and imagined (Anderson).[44] The Eurocentric sense of time

[39] See further Ernst Cassirer, *Substance and Function and Einstein's Theory of Relativity*, William C. and Marie C. Swabey (trans.), Chicago: Open Court, 1923, especially pp. 417 ff. and 449–456.

[40] On IR and critical theory see amongst others Richard Wyn Jones (ed.), *Critical Theory and World Politics*, London: Lynne Rienner, 2001; Andrew Linklater, *Beyond Realism and Marxism: Critical Theory and International Relations*, London: Macmillan, 1990. More recently the discipline has also experimented with Edward Said's ideas. See Shampa Biswas, 'Empire and Global Public Intellectuals: Reading Edward Said as an International Relations Theorist', *Millennium: Journal of International Studies*, vol. 36, no. 1 (2007), pp. 117–133; Geeta Chowdhry, 'Edward Said and Contrapuntal Reading: Implications for critical interventions in International Relations', *Millennium: Journal of International Studies*, vol. 36, no. 1 (2007), pp. 101–116 and Raymond Duvall and Latha Varadarajan: 'Travelling in Paradox: Edward Said and critical international relations', *Millennium: Journal of International Studies*, vol. 36, no. 1 (2007), pp. 83–99.

[41] Akbar S. Ahmed, *Postmodernism and Islam: Predicament and Promise*, London: Routledge, 1992, p. 10.

[42] Ziauddin Sardar, *Postmodernism and the Other: The New Imperialism of Western Culture*, London: Pluto Press, 1998, p. 6.

[43] Robert W. Cox, 'Thinking about Civilisations', *Review of International Studies*, vol. 26, no. 2 (2000), p. 232.

[44] See Benedict Anderson, *Imagined Communities: Reflections on the Origin and Spread of Nationalism*, new edition, London: Verso, 2006; Eric J. Hobsbawm, *Nations and Nationalism since 1780: Programme, Myth, Reality*, 2nd edition, Cambridge: Cambridge University Press, 1992; Eric J. Hobs-

as linear, universal, and uninterrupted is exposed as a fallacy. The belief in the eschatological function of history—Hegelian, Weberian, Imperial, Christian, Liberal, Neoconservative, Marxist, Positivist— loses its causal promise. Eurocentrism is exposed as an invention of the laboratories of the Enlightenment. Suddenly, (western) 'man could be erased, like a face drawn in sand at the edge of the sea':[45] The inescapable dialectics of history are giving the 'West' the burial that it deserves. From now on, the 'West' is spelled with a lower case 'w'.

Do we have to mourn this process of erosion? Do we have to stand vigil for the demise of the 'west' as we know it? Those ideas (and their agents) that are entirely dependent on ideological signification—the nation-state and a whole range of historians, journalists and politicians—do. They are compelled to do so, because their primary aim is to legitimate and extend their sovereignties, national, confessional, religious or other. As the wife of former US Vice President Dick Cheney expressed in a book revealingly entitled *Telling the Truth*, 'If we are to be successful as a culture, we cannot follow Foucault and turn away from reason and reality'. Rather the (seemingly) contrary. 'We must follow the great thinkers of the Enlightenment and find the will to live in truth ... The answer may very well determine whether we survive'.[46] The Enlightenment functions here, once again, as the 'grand signifier' of the 'west' whose differentiated inner constituencies do not necessarily yield to this kind of collectivisation anymore. The 'west' has become the fairytale to which the right-wing can always retreat in times of crisis, and where it can readopt its optimistic attitude and the corresponding belief that it can lead humanity towards universal sameness. It does not come as a surprise, thus, that Lynn Cheney (and her husband of course) were ardent supporters of the Bush administration's wars of 'liberation' in Iraq and Afghanistan.

Even in France, for long the bastion of 'deconstructive' thought, excitable politicians such as Nicolas Sarkozy (and his flamboyant foreign minister Bernard Kouchner), have reaped the benefits of the discursive shift away from the critical current that gained impetus with

---

bawm and Terence Ranger (eds), *The Invention of Tradition*, Cambridge: Cambridge University Press, 2004.

[45] Michel Foucault, *The Order of Things: An Archaeology of the Human Sciences*, London: Routledge, 2002, p. 422.

[46] Quoted in Eric Laurent, *Bush's Secret World: Religion, Big Business and Hidden Networks*, Andrew Brown (trans.), Cambridge: Polity, 2004, p. 39.

the counter-cultural movement of the 1960s. 'For Sarkozy', Alan Badiou writes, 'the evils of May 68—forty years ago—have been constantly invoked as the cause of the "current crisis of values"'.[47] So the contemporary disciples of the Enlightenment continue to enact their universal project. They continue to believe in the possibility of their cause. In the meantime, they accept the casualties of the Enlightenment project: collateral damage. 'For the Enlightenment, whatever does not conform to the rule of computation and utility is suspect', Adorno and Horkheimer warned us decades ago. 'So long as it can develop undisturbed by any outward repression, there is no holding it. ... Enlightenment is totalitarian'.[48]

And yet, neither Adorno and Horkheimer, nor Foucault was complicit in the attempted 'murder' of 'western man' in order to erase reason. They were neither 'irrational' serial killers, nor nihilists. 'In attempting to uncover the deepest strata of Western culture, Foucault introduces *The Order of Things*, 'I am *restoring* to our silent and apparently immobile soil its rifts, its instability, its flaws'.[49] Adorno and Horkheimer have a comparably reconstructive project in mind when they write that 'we had set ourselves noting less than the discovery why mankind instead of entering into a truly human condition, is sinking into a new kind of barbarism'.[50] Critical theory and 'archaeology' function here as a means to reveal interdependencies between us and them—deconstruction in order to reconstruct. The imperialist and fascist can never accept this. Neither can the guild historian. For him, history is the field where the ghosts of the past are banished, the superiority of the self is asserted, where questions are answered, where the 'truth' is presented as such. He is immersed in the *Lust of Knowing*, in Robert Irwin's eloquent words. But this lust can easily turn into licentious desire, if it is not tempered by a critical attitude, by an understanding that a 'true history of Orientalism' or even a 'truer one' can never be written from within the discipline and its discourse that produced the knowledge it operates on in the first place.[51] In short, no

[47] Alain Badiou, 'The Communist Hypothesis', *New Left Review*, vol. 49, Jan./Feb. 2008, p. 34.
[48] Theodor W. Adorno and Max Horkheimer, *Dialectic of Enlightenment*, London: Verso, 1997, p. 6.
[49] Foucault, *The Order of Things*, p. xxvi, emphasis added.
[50] Adorno and Horkheimer, *Dialectic of Enlghtement*, p. xi.
[51] Robert Irwin, *For Lust of Knowing: The Orientalists and Their Enemies*,

Orientalist can write a 'truer' history of 'Orientalism' if he is not willing to liberate himself from the particular kind of rationality enveloping him, the epistemology attached to him, the ontology penetrating him and the history fascinating him.

Such dialectical negation posits an acceptance that for every order and reality out there, there is an alternative one somewhere else on the globe. By looking at the different discourses dialectically, as composing a number of hybrid and overlapping fields one can express a critical challenge to the politics of violence inspired by the clash regime. In *Culture and Imperialism*, Edward Said introduces the term 'contrapuntality', which I found comparable to the idea of 'negative dialectics' originally conceptualised by Adorno and other members of the Frankfurt School:

If at the outset we acknowledge the massively knotted and complex histories of special but nevertheless overlapping and interconnected experiences—of women, of Westerners, of Blacks, of national states and cultures—there is no particular intellectual reason for granting each and all of them an ideal and essentially separate status. Yet we would wish to preserve what is unique about each so long as we also preserve some sense of the human community and the actual contests that contribute to its formation, and of which they are all a part.[52]

Note that Said acknowledges here that differences exist, but that they should be considered as a part of a common human experience. As a form of negative dialectic that does not yield to the final reconciliation of opposites in the Hegelian sense, contrapuntality yields a dialogical communication in which self and other, object and subject retain their independence from one another. Thus, contrapuntality opens up overlapping epistemological territories without forcing them into one universal field. Contrapuntality negates an all-encompassing logic for humankind, whether Islamic, western, modern or communist. The other is not viewed as something profoundly disturbing and alien that needs to be objectified and oppressed. Rather, subject and object are deemed inextricably intertwined. 'In its proper place, even epistemologically', Adorno explains, 'the relationship of subject and object would lie in the realisation of peace among men as between men and

London: Penguin, 2007, p. 5. See also idem., 'Lured in the East', *The Times Literary Supplement*, no. 5484, 9 May 2008, pp. 3–5.
[52] Edward Said, *Culture and Imperialism*, London: Vintage, 1993, p. 36.

their Other. Peace is the state of distinctness without domination, with the distinct participating in each other'.[53] What Adorno demands here is that the other is granted her own field to express herself. As such, negative dialectics open up spaces in which empathy with the individual as neighbour is combined with solidarity with her as a fellow human being. The distinctness of me and you signifies an indissoluble bond; it should not function as a sight for attrition and usurpation. 'One must think of the "other"', to quote from Seyla Benhabib's interpretation of Adorno, 'as that utopian longing toward the non-identical which can only be suggested as "allegory" and as "cipher"'.[54] In terms of a counter-discourse to the clash regime such an understanding of self and other supports critical research that brings out commonalities within difference. It suggests that history is revealed as 'western' history, by juxtaposing it to the presence of the east in the west as John M. Hobson did in his *The Eastern Origins of Western Civilisation*; that the 'perennial philosophy as it was formulated in the west', is expressed in the words of Rumi, Lao Tzu, Chuang Tzu, Buddha, and Lankavatara Sutra as Aldous Huxley proposes;[55] that the 'collective will' behind the French revolution is re-evaluated by relating it to the collective will that engendered the Islamic revolution in Iran, as Foucault suggests; that language and grammar are 'deconstructed' in order to reveal their ideological functions as Deleuze, Guattari and Derrida attempt; or that 'world History' is interrogated by a 'critical consciousness' as Jack Goody demands:

A more critical stance is necessary to counter the inevitably ethnocentric character of any attempt to describe the world, past or present. That means firstly being sceptical about the west's claim, indeed about any claim coming from Europe (or indeed Asia), to have invented activities and values such as democracy or freedom. Secondly, it means looking at history from the bottom up rather than from the top (or from the present) down. Thirdly, it means giving adequate weight to the non-European past. Fourthly, it requires an awareness of the fact that even the backbone of historiography, the loca-

---

[53] Theodor W. Adorno, 'Subject and Object', in *The Essential Frankfurt School Reader*, Andrew Arato and Eike Gebhardt (eds and trans.), Oxford: Basil Blackwell, 1978, p. 500.

[54] Seyla Benhabib, *Critique, Norm and Utopia: A Study of the Foundations of Critical Theory*, New York: Columbia University Press, 1986, p. 212.

[55] Aldous Huxley, *The Perennial Philosophy*, London: Chatto and Windus, 1950.

tion of events in time and space, is variable, subject to social construction, and hence to change.[56]

I am aware that those thinkers come from very different disciplinary and cultural backgrounds and that their object of analyses differ profoundly. Yet I think it is safe to say that in their writings all of them express dissatisfaction that the other continues to function as supplement. The task of their criticism lies in the affirmation of ontological overlay and epistemological interdependence. They affirm, in other words, the agency of the other; her ability to write her own history and to affect everything that is happening here. Such scholarship raises the awareness that it is beneficial to take the standpoint of the other in order to evaluate the validity claims of our own history and state of being. Out of this contrapuntal dialogue a common fate is crystallised: empathy is freed from the shackles of tribal thinking; the other emerges as a place that we can appreciatively embrace. This self-other dialectic does not yield to a Hegelian final reconciliation of opposites. It does not engender the annihilation of the 'out-group'. Rather, it yields a Platonic 'open-endedness' in which sameness can never appear; in which the usurpation of the other by the self is rendered unachievable because the impossibility of this task is finally acknowledged. At the same time, our existence is not accepted in-and-of itself. There emerges an understanding that we can never be thoroughly autonomous. But this should not mean that we have to continuously emphasise our difference, that we have to relentlessly reinvent our categories in strict juxtaposition to our significant others. This is what the fascists tried and Al Qaeda continues to endeavour and I hope I have made it clear that their project was/is futile. The opposite logic rules. If it is in the difference to the other that our own appearance emerges, if we cannot sustain our identity in total isolation, if sameness is unachievable, we are compelled to accept the other's identity as such, not at least because it is the source of our own identity in the first place.[57]

---

[56] Jack Goody, *The Theft of History*, Cambridge: Cambridge University Press, 2006, p. 13.

[57] In particular, critical feminist discourse has been very successful in signifying the interpenetration of identities without obliterating interdependent categories such as 'man' and 'woman'. See especially: Seyla Benhabib, *Situating the Self: Gender, Community and Postmodernism in Contemporary Ethics*, Cambridge: Polity Press, 1992; Judith Butler, *Gender Trouble: Feminism and the Subversion of Identity*, London: Routledge, 1990; Trinh T. Minh-ha,

The realm of freedom from thinking in dichotomies—civilisational, racial, political, religious, environmental—does not commence until the point is passed where we accept the totality of nouns—America, East, West, Islam, Muslim, Orient, Occident—in mere isolation from the movement of verbs—to think, to perceive, to believe. The difference is apparent. When Sayyid Qutb went to the United States in 1948 he must have thought the following: these are American people, doing what Americans do, which is decadent, licentious and 'primitive'.[58] He did not think instead that his perception of what he called the 'animalistic' American way of life is affected by his socialisation;[59] that he perceives this 'alien' world as such because it does not correspond to the culture he was brought up with, that his conclusions were helplessly mono-causal and one-dimensional. The Qutbian Islamist, once he imagines his autonomous history, once he believes that he may realise the grand project of distinctiveness, is condemned to profess in the totality of nouns. Viewing himself as a 'hybrid creature' would be devastating, because it would question the seemingly coherent and safe ideational territories he wants to escape to. He is entangled in a paradox of his own making. How can he escape the *jahiliya* when he declares that it is all around us?

Today, the ideological enterprises in Lebanon, Palestine, Iraq, Iran and elsewhere are putting into operation entire machinery for producing politico-cultural and socio-economic discourses concerning Islam. Not only are we compelled to speak of Islam as an all-encompassing reality, we are also confronted with a whole set of 'Islamic pop symbols' from Hamas baseball hats in Palestine to *Zam Zam* Cola in Iran. And so, in this differentiated, pluralistic space, a fundamental political process manifests itself: Arab and Muslim societies demand that 'Islam' functions—not only in the mosques, but also in the public spheres. It is inevitable thus that many of these societies find themselves embroiled with a strange *zeitgeist* permeated by seemingly contradictory ideas,

---

Women, Native, Other: Writing, Postcoloniality and Feminism, Bloomington: University of Indiana Press, 1989; and Monique Wittig, *The Straight Mind and Other Essays*, Boston: Beacon, 1992.

[58] Qutb's writings on the United States are compiled in 'Abd al-Fattah al-Khalidi (ed.), *Amrika min al-Dakhil bi-minzar Sayyid Qutb* (America from the Inside, Through the Eyes of Sayyid Qutb), Jiddah: Dar al-Manarah, 1986.

[59] Ibid., p. 104.

embodied in culturally different ideal types: coolly expedient rationality (Islam as politics) poised against the exigencies of Islamic utopianism (Islam as salvation), in the extreme cases embodied, respectively, in inhumane technocrats locked in political battles with hysterical ideologues. In many ways, a politically unattractive choice especially when the intrinsic tensions within that dialectic are not bridged.

But it is equally true to say that within this pluralistic space a counter-discourse is proliferating. It is analytically correct and normatively important to point to the millions of Muslims in Europe and 'the peoples of Arabia, Turkey, and Iran [who] are rewriting their history and re-interpreting their religious thought by using the inescapable methods and epistemology of critical reason' as Arkoun does.[60] This does not imply necessarily that Muslims are willing to bargain the transcendental claim of Allah. But it means that the understanding of Islam's sovereignty on earth has been bound back to the inherent dialectics of the Islamic revelation. In other words, the Muslim multitudes acknowledge that the authority of the Islamic discourse cannot be asserted by force; it can only be claimed when it is an act of acknowledgement. It cannot be attained by blind obedience to ordinances that are rendered a-historical and forced upon others. No just order can be asserted via the deification of power, or the sanctification of the Leader. The Ayatollah himself can merely claim to be a sign (*ayat*) of this hidden truth which is nestled in the Islamic logos. Any other claim that sanctifies his (no women Ayatollahs yet) power is hubristic, even heretical. He is, in the words of Soroush, not part of 'religion' per se, the transcendental claim of which remains constant. He is part of the ontology of Islam, which changes in accordance with religious understanding:

Numerous are those who harbour the illusion that whatever they happen to believe is the very essence of religion and religious knowledge. Massive campaigns must be launched to tear asunder these twin veils of delusion and hubris so that one may realise that one's religious belief, however immaculate, is still one's own comprehension of religion, not religion as such. Second, it must be understood that religious knowledge is not the personal knowledge of a single individual but a branch of human knowledge that has a collective and dynamic identity and that remains viable through the constant exchange, cooperation, and competition of scholars. As such, religious knowledge is replete with error, conjecture, and conviction. Error plays as much of a role in religious knowl-

[60] Arkoun, 'Islam, Europe, the West', in Rippin (ed.), *Defining Islam*, p. 263.

edge as does insight. If one deems an opinion false, even though that opinion will depart from his or her personal knowledge, it does not depart from religious knowledge as such. It is in this sense that religious knowledge changes, evolves, contracts, expands, waxes, and wanes. It is temporal and in constant commerce with other realms of human culture.[61]

Soroush self-consciously writes in the 'Avicennian' tradition of Islam. His 'theory of the contraction and expansion of religious interpretation' is positioned within the long tradition of *kalam* or Islamic theology, *usul* or applied logic in religious jurisprudence and *irfan* or the esoteric dimensions of the Islamic discourse. His theory depends on differentiating between what I called Islamutopia, on the one side and the ontology engendered by knowledge of Islam's religious essence, on the other. He does not attempt to distil an Islamic discourse which is artificially detached from the impingement of other competing ones; for him the ontology of Islam is interpenetrated, overlapping, hybrid. At the same time, he argues that Islam's religious essence reveals itself in the before and after of our temporality, that is by definition beyond our grasp. 'For, how could there be time if there is no before and after', Avicenna asks.[62] In the Avicennian conceptualisation of time, there couldn't, which is why Soroush positions God beyond the temporality (and ontology) enveloping his object, that is the *umma*.

In Soroush, there is a suspicion towards totalities. The ontology of Islam is not considered detached, it is dialectical and interdependent. Other contemporary Muslim theoreticians agree. For Tariq Ramadan, for instance, 'it is essential to remember that the corpus of the *sharia* is a human construction, and some aspects of the Qur'an and the *sunna* were revealed over time'. It is inevitable that a 'new context changes the horizon of the text, renews it, and sometimes gives it an original purport, providing responses never before imagined'.[63] But we shouldn't stop here. Taking the argument of Soroush and Ramadan one step

---

[61] Abdolkarim Soroush, *Reason, Freedom, and Democracy in Islam: Essential Writings of Abdolkarim Soroush*, Mahmoud Sadri and Ahmad Sadri (eds and trans.), Oxford: Oxford University Press, 2000, p. 34.

[62] Ibn Sina, 'The Healing: On time (al-Shifa)', in Seyyed Hossein Nasr with Mehdi Aminrazavi (eds), *An Anthology of Philosophy in Persia, Volume I*, Oxford: Oxford University Press, 1999, p. 245.

[63] Tariq Ramadan, 'The Way (Al-Sharia) of Islam', in Mehran Kamrava (ed.), *The New Voices of Islam: Reforming Politics and Modernity, A Reader*, London: I.B. Tauris, 2006, p. 72.

further we are left with an ontology of Islam that is entirely relative. If religious knowledge can never really grasp the religious essence of Islam, if ontological Islam can never really catch up with Islamutopia, the existence of everything surrounding us is in doubt.

This place of doubt depleted of safe territories that we could retreat to in times of ideational crisis, refers to the mystical world of Omar Khayyam (1048–1123). I call it mystical because for Khayyam the necessary being, that is God, mystifies the relative being, that is the individual and his/her social world. In Khayyam's world, there is doubt exactly because in relation to God, the world we are living in is disorderly, intransigently complex and not all comprehensible in its entirety. 'Whenever it is said that such and such an attribute has a necessary existence in such and such a thing', Khayyam writes, 'what is meant is that it exists in the mind and the intellect, *and not in reality*. Similarly whenever it is said that the existence of such and such an attribute is dependent upon the existence of some other attribute, what is meant is *existence in mind and the intellect*'.[64] Khayyam reveals himself here as an early 'postmodernist'. He is entirely convinced that our surrounding world is engineered because the realm of actual reality belongs to God. In other words, in his philosophy Khayyam alerts us to the fact that relative to God, the self-concocted world surrounding us appears 'unreal'. Khayyam expresses the melancholy thus ensued, the torment that the unavailability of Godly reality created in him, in his world famous quatrains:

> Since neither truth nor certitude is at hand
> Do not waste life in doubt for a fairy land
> O let us not refuse the goblet of wine
> For sober or drunk in ignorance we stand[65]

Khayyam's quatrains and philosophy serves as a measure of what Islamic poetry and art might yet bring about in this irresistibly critical mode. Khayyam expresses our alien reality, thus giving the lie to notions of Islam as a total system immune from the grim realities of historical events. In his own words:

---

[64] Umar Khayyam, 'The Necessity of Contradiction, Free Will and Determinism (Darurat al-tadadd fi'l-alam wa'l-jabr wa'l-baqa)', in Nasr with Aminrazavi, *An Anthology of Philosophy in Persia*, p. 404, emphasis added.

[65] Quoted in Mehdi Aminrazavi, 'Martin Heidegger and Omar Khayyam on the Question of "Thereness" (*Dasein*)', in Anna-Teresa Tymieniecka (ed.),

Eternity!—for it we find no key;
Nor any of us past the Veil can see.
Of Thee and me they talk behind the Veil
But when that parts, no more of Thee and me.[66]

The very failure of Khayyam to redeem himself, the fact that neither his poetry nor his 'drunkenness' can bring him closer to God, is also, paradoxically, the source of the irresistible critical merit of his poetry and philosophy. Khayyam presages that the Muslim is constantly obliged to bridge the gap between this alien world and the necessary and absolute Divinity designated as God. Yet this Islamutopia is by definition unattainable, sameness with God is the 'impossible ontology' or *mumtani al-wujud* in Ibn Sina's words. In this way, Khayyam and the Avicennian tradition establishes 'an ontology based on the "poverty" of all things before God and their reliance upon the Source of all being for their very existence'.[67] Mysticism (Sufism), poetry, the arts and philosophy become the inevitable routes to seek respite from the mundane world and to simulate closeness with God. They hold out the promise, never to be kept, of a realm of consciousness where the individual could at last find an image of perfect equilibrium, of sensuous pleasure that would rescue her from the antinomies of her present existence. As such, Islamic philosophy and poetry embody a much perfected form of ontological negation.

Let me expand this discussion now and relocate it at the same time. To my mind, the music of Wagner, Bach and Beethoven's late style express the same power of negation, the ethos of a sensuous escape from the ontological order, that the radically transcendental philosophy (and poetry) of Rumi, Khayyam, Hafiz, Saadi, and Ibn Sina embodies. I would even go one step further, following Adorno. In the aesthetic expression of utopia, the construction of dichotomous identities, whether of Orient and Occident, is minimised, because works of art with maximal aesthetic value are depleted of 'tribal identities'. This is why Rumi, Hafiz, Khayyam, Bach, Wagner, Beethoven are almost universally revered. Their art positions itself beyond categories. They

---

Islamic Philosophy and Occidental Phenomenology on the Perennial Issue of Microcosm and Macrocosm, Dordrecht: Springer, 2006, p. 281.

[66] Ibid., p. 283.

[67] Seyyed Hossein Nasr, *The Islamic Intellectual Tradition in Persia*, Mehdi Aminrazavi (ed.), London: Curzon, 1996, p. 81.

give us a glimpse into the 'Naturschöne', the naturally sublime, a sign of reconciliation between self and other.[68]

The German Marxist thinker Ernst Bloch expresses a similar belief in aesthetic reconciliation especially with regard to the mediating power of music. 'Only the musical note, that enigma of sensuousness', he writes, 'is sufficiently unencumbered by the world yet phenomenal enough to the last to return—like the metaphysical word—as a final material factor in the fulfilment of mystical self-perception, spread purely upon the golden sub-soil of the receptive human potentiality'.[69] Bloch alludes to the dual constitution of music, which has both formal properties and transcendental ones. In this, he concurs with other German thinkers such as Schopenhauer and Nietzsche who coined the term 'musical ecstasy' in his *The Birth of Tragedy*. They all agree that music is 'at once the most humanly revealing form of art and the form most resistant to description or analysis in conceptual terms'.[70] From this perspective, music both rationalises and mystifies, it has both mathematical structure and emotional power. If musical aesthetics could hitherto not negotiate between these two extremes, it is an indicator that music brings both to the fore, without reconciling them in a final, grand synthesis. There is no transcendence or unity, for what music potentially presages is a 'figuring-out *in fonte hominum et rerum* that is utopian and fermenting, in an area of intensity that is open only to music'.[71] For Bloch especially, Beethoven's compositions are anti-Hegelian, even contra-Enlightenment because they do not mimic perfect harmony. Beethoven may touch and tease the irreconcilable, but he finally keeps them apart. In this, music is the most successful of the arts 'succeeding visuality and belonging to the formally eccentric philosophy of inwardness, its ethic and metaphysics'. For Bloch, this means that '[b]oth the existence and the concept of music are only attained in conjunction with a new object-theory, with the metaphysics of divination and utopia'.[72] Thus the transformative force of music

[68] On Adorno's use of the term 'Naturschöne', see further Benhabib, *Critique, Norm and Utopia*, pp. 211 ff.
[69] Ernst Bloch, *The Principle of Hope*, vol. 1, Neville Plaice, Stephen Plaice and Paul Knight (trans.), Oxford: Basil Blackwell, 1987, p. 120.
[70] Christopher Norris, *Deconstruction and the Interests of Theory*, London: Pinter, 1988, p. 31.
[71] Bloch, *The Principle of Hope*, p. 228.
[72] Ibid., pp. 130–131.

lies in its unreconciled vigour which defies capitulation to Hegelian totalities.

Art expressed in this form is as 'trans-historical' as the clash regime which is why it is entirely equipped to battle with it at this level without prescribing tribal passions. I get emotional when I listen to Wagner, so did Hitler. The pop singer Madonna is fascinated by the poetry of Rumi, so was Ayatollah Khomeini. It is in this sense that art embodies the potentiality of change without, however, falling into the trap of Hegel's big promise that it can bring about the final reconciliation of opposites, the great myth of perfect harmony. This is art as continuous renewal that does not usher in a grand synthesis. For Adorno there is:

more pleasure in dissonance than in consonance: and this repays hedonism in due measure. What is incisive is dynamically sharpened, differentiated from itself and from the monotony of affirmativeness, and becomes an attraction. This attraction, no less than a disgust with optimistic nonsense, leads the new art into a no-man's-land that represents the inhabitable earth. ... Negation is able to transform itself into pleasure, not into what is positive.[73]

Once it is realised that the contrapuntal composition of art is not reconcilable, the Hegelian promise reveals itself as a fallacy. Here we can establish a nuance between Bloch and Adorno. Whereas the former professed in the ability of music to effectively respond to emergent social and historical configurations, the latter's negative dialectic is notably more pessimistic. For Adorno, the 'promise held out by the work of art that it will create truth by lending new shape to the conventional social forms is as necessary as it is hypocritical'. It is necessary because art unleashes irresistible transcendental powers:

That factor in a work of art which enables it to transcend reality certainly cannot be detached from style; but it does not consist of the harmony actually realised, of any doubtful unity of form and content, within and without, of individual and society; it is to be found in those features in which discrepancy appears: in the necessary failure of the passionate striving for identity.[74]

And it is hypocritical because with the advent of the modern 'culture industry', the emancipatory and redeeming forces of art are subjugated

---

[73] Theodor W. Adorno, *Aesthetic Theory*, C. Lenhardt (trans.), Gretel Adorno and Rolf Tiedemann (eds), International Library of Phenomenology and Moral Sciences, London: Routledge & Kegan Paul, 1984, pp. 66–67.

[74] Adorno and Horkheimer, *Dialectic of Enlightenment*, p. 131.

to the cult of consumption (e.g. pop shows such as the 'X Factor' or 'American Idol'). Instead of exposing itself to the intrinsic resistance of art to loose the power of negation and critique, the culture industry pushes art towards conformity with the status quo; art as commodity and 'obedience to social hierarchy. Today', Adorno writes, 'aesthetic barbarity completes what has threatened the creations of the spirit since they were gathered together as culture and neutralised'.[75] The only way the critical theorists could escape this conundrum, is to free himself from the determinations of his day and age, to seek the powers of negation, if necessary in music and literature (Becket in Adorno's case). It is true, that Adorno famously concluded that writing poetry after Auschwitz is barbaric. But this does not mean that he advocated cultural, political and social apathy. Like Khayyam, who tampered his despair by positioning himself within the realm of Islamic mysticism (if necessary by drinking a few carafes of wine), Adorno identified radical negation as the only means to prepare ourselves for the massive process of 'final displacement' that will be brought about by the messianic utopia awaiting us:

The only philosophy which can be responsibly practised in the face of despair is the attempt to contemplate all things as they would appear from the stand-point of redemption ... Perspectives must be fashioned that displace and estrange the world, reveal it to be, with its rifts and crevices, as indigent and distorted as it will appear one day in the messianic light.[76]

Critical theory reveals itself here as a prophylaxis to prepare humanity for the experience of the absolute realm of possibility, *mumtani al-wujud*, encapsulated in the 'suridealistic' encounter with God. According to Adorno, this final encounter will evaporate all residues of our superstitious belief in an 'orderly' world. As long as the poet, composer, artist, mystic, philosopher and intellectual do not despair in their effort to bridge the gap between the status quo and that utopia, they are compelled to search for the 'truth' which engenders a critical attitude towards the status quo. Here, does it matter if it is History or God which constitutes the horizon, the place towards which all meaning strife in the quest for the 'ultimate surideal', the 'end of history' or 'judgment day'? Does it matter if it is the dialectical materialism of

[75] Ibid.
[76] Theodor W. Adorno, *Minima Moralia*, E.F.N. Jephcott (trans.), London: New Left Books, 1974, p. 247.

Marx or Jesus' 'Kingdom of God', the Buddhist Nirvana or the Hindu Karma, that animates critique? It does, when the continual transformation towards a future potentiality is monopolised by the state, the party or another polity or when values such as equality, social justice and human rights are compromised. One is compelled to remind the fundamentalists on all sides—those who misunderstand the text and themselves—that if they believe in what they preach, they can relax and rest assured that at the end of all of this, it will be revealed whose utopia is the 'right' one. At the same time, for us mortals, it does not really matter which utopia inspires us, as long as it compels us to sustain a global impetus against reification, against quests for authenticity, against hegemony, against totalities, against the deification of power. As long as utopia holds out the promise of continuous transformation towards a better tomorrow, where the relation between knower and known is a dialectic potentially open for contrapuntal re-imagining, it is not something that we should be afraid of.[77]

It was Immanuel Kant who asked whether one should leave the comforting bosom of one's own rationality and venture out to discover the 'other'. After some serious critical contemplation, he remained where he departed from. Others did dare to venture further. Some of them paid a heavy price—delusion and insanity in Nietzsche's case, melancholy and despair in the case of Khayyam. Optimistically, I do believe—and in my other books, have tried to demonstrate—that today we can appreciate the archives filled with the work of eastern and western, northern and southern thinkers in a truly comparative manner. It is not at least thanks to the availability of a counter-archive to the clash regime, that we have enough knowledge at hand to free ourselves from the shackles of tribal thinking. So that the next time we read a history of the 'West' or 'Islam', we immediately ask how the 'other' is represented; if she is not abused as a supplement in order to enunciate what the 'self' stands for. Next time we attend a seminar or lecture, we should pierce the speaker with questions about the validity of categories such as race, nationality, religious confession etc. We should ask if it is analytically unproblematic to place ourselves inside such suspicious totalisations.

[77] The case for utopia has been recently revisited by Patrick Hayden and Chamsy el-Ojeili. See their edited volume, *Globalisation and Utopia: Critical essays*, London: Palgrave, 2009.

No discourse is innocent, nothing in the social world is apolitical and I hope that some of the ideas in the foregoing have indicated that all unities are dubious. Freeing oneself from their totalitarian impact is utterly rewarding. Mind you, it does shatter the infinitesimally small mosaics out of which we have created our identities. But once we pull our selves together and start the process of picking up the pieces, they will appear clearer to us; we will be able to analyse and comprehend them more easily and to reconfigure them within a wider frame than before. And so it is that we can attain a multicultural consciousness without committing any pagan betrayal of our own mosaic composition. At that stage of our intellectual journey, we may be truly liberated.

BIBLIOGRAPHY

Abduh, Muhammad, 'Islam, Reason, and Civilisation', in John J. Donohue and John L. Esposito (eds), *Islam in Transition: Muslim Perspectives*, 2nd edition, Oxford: Oxford University Press, 2007, pp. 20–23.
——— *Al-A'mal al-Kamilah lil-Imam Muhammad 'Abduh* (The Complete Works of Imam Muhammad 'Abduh), Muhammad 'Imarah (ed.), Beirut: al-Mu'assassah al-'Arabiyyah lil-Dirasat wa al-Nashr, 1972–1974.
Abu-Lughod, Ibrahim, *Arab Rediscovery of Europe: A Study in Cultural Encounters*, Princeton: Princeton University Press, 1963.
Abu-Rabi, Ibrahim M., *Intellectual Origins of Islamic Resurgence in the Modern Arab World*, Albany, NY: State University of New York Press, 1996.
Achcar, Gilbert, *The Clash of Barbarisms: The Making of the New World Disorder*, London: Paradigm, 2006.
Adam, Ian and Helen Tiffin (eds): *Past the Last Post*, Hemel Hempstead: Harvester Wheatsheaf, 1991.
Adang, Camilla, *Muslim Writers on Judaism & the Hebrew Bible: From Ibn Rabban to Ibn Hazm*, Leiden: Brill, 1997.
Adib-Moghaddam, Arshin, 'Discourse and violence: The friend-enemy conjunction in contemporary Iranian-American Relations, *Critical Studies on Terrorism*, vol. 2, no. 3, Dec. 2009, pp. 512–526.
——— 'Islamutopia, (Post)modernity and the Multitude', in Patrick Hayden and Chamsy el-Ojeili (eds), *Globalisation and Utopia: Critical essays*, London: Palgrave, 2009, pp. 137–155.
——— 'A (short) History of the Clash of Civilisations', *Cambridge Review of International Affairs*, vol. 21, no. 2, Summer 2008, pp. 217–234.
——— *Iran in World Politics: the Question of the Islamic Republic*, New York: Columbia University Press, 2008, 2010.
——— 'Abu Ghraib and Insaniyat', *Monthly Review*, vol. 59, no. 7, Dec. 2007, pp. 20–36.
——— *The International Politics of the Persian Gulf: A Cultural Genealogy*, London: Routledge, 2006, 2009.

BIBLIOGRAPHY

—— 'The Theory of Regional Security Complexes: Exploring the Options', *International Studies Journal*, issue 9, vol. 3, no. 1, Summer 2006, pp. 25–37.

—— 'Global Intifadah: September 11th and the Struggle Within Islam', *Cambridge Review of International Affairs*, vol. 15, no. 2, July 2002, pp. 203–216.

Adler, Emanuel, 'Seizing the Middle Ground: Constructivism in World Politics', *European Journal of International Relations*, vol. 3, no. 3, 1997, pp. 319–363.

Adorno, Theodor W., Max Horkheimer, *Dialectic of Enlightenment*, John Cumming (trans.), London: Verso, 1997.

—— *Aesthetic Theory*, C. Lenhardt (trans.), Gretel Adorno and Rolf Tiedemann (eds), International Library of Phenomenology and Moral Sciences, London: Routledge & Kegan Paul, 1984.

—— 'Subject and Object', in *The Essential Frankfurt School Reader*, Andrew Arato and Eike Gebhardt (eds and trans.), Oxford: Basil Blackwell, 1978, pp. 497–511.

—— *Minima Moralia*, E.F.N. Jephcott (trans.), London: New Left Books, 1974.

Afary, Janet and Kevin B. Anderson, *Foucault and the Iranian Revolution: Gender and the Seductions of Islamism*, Chicago: University of Chicago Press, 2005.

Agamben, Giorgio, *Remnants of Auschwitz: The Witness and the Archive*, Daniel Heller-Roazen (trans.), New York: Zone Books, 1999.

Ahmad, Aijaz, 'Between Orientalism and Historicism', in A.L. Macfie, (ed.), *Orientalism: A Reader*, Edinburgh: Edinburgh University Press, 2000, pp. 285–297.

—— *In Theory: Classes, Nations, Literatures*, London: Verso, 1992.

Ahmed, Akbar S., *Postmodernism and Islam: Predicament and Promise*, London: Routledge, 1992.

Al-e Ahmad, Jalal, *Plagued by the West (Gharbzadegi)*, Paul Sprachman (trans.), New York: Caravan, 1982.

Alexander, Jeffrey C. and Steven Seidman (eds), *Culture and Society: Contemporary Debates*, Cambridge: Cambridge University Press, 1990.

Alford, Fred C., *Group Psychology and Political Theory*, New Haven: Yale University Press, 1994.

Algar, Hamid, *Wahhabism: A Critical Essay*, North Haledon, NJ: Islamic Publications International, 2002.

Ali, Tariq, *The Clash of Fundamentalisms: Crusades, Jihads and Modernity*, London: Verso, 2003.

Almond, Ian, *The New Orientalists: Postmodern Representations of Islam from Foucault to Baudrillard*, London: I.B. Tauris, 2007.

Alstyne, Richard W. van, *The Rising American Empire*, New York: Norton, 1974.

Althusser, Louis, *For Marx*, Ben Brewster (trans.), London: Verso, 2005.

BIBLIOGRAPHY

Amin, Samir, *Eurocentrism*, Russell Moore (trans.), New York: Monthly Review Press, 1989.

Aminrazavi, Mehdi, 'Martin Heidegger and Omar Khayyam on the Question of "Thereness" (*Dasein*)', in Anna-Teresa Tymieniecka (ed.), *Islamic Philosophy and Occidental Phenomenology on the Perennial Issue of Microcosm and Macrocosm*, Dordrecht: Springer, 2006, pp. 277–287.

Amiri, Mojtaba, (ed.), *Theory of Clash of Civilisations: Huntington and His Critics*, Tehran: Foreign Ministry Publishing House, 1995.

Anderson, Benedict, *Imagined Communities: Reflections on the Origin and Spread of Nationalism*, new edition, London: Verso, 2006.

Anderson, Betty, 'The Duality of National Identity in the Middle East: A Critical Review', *Critique: Critical Middle Eastern Studies*, vol. 11, no. 2, Fall 2002, pp. 229–250.

Angie, Anthony, *Imperialism, Sovereignty and the Making of International Law*, Cambridge: Cambridge University Press, 2005.

Anidjar, Gil, *The Jew, the Arab: A History of the Enemy*, Stanford: Stanford University Press, 2003.

Anthony, Constance G., 'American Democratic Interventionism: Romancing the Iconic Woodrow Wilson', *International Studies Perspectives*, vol. 9, no. 3, Aug. 2008, pp. 239–253.

Arendt, Hannah, *The Origins of Totalitarianism*, Ohio: World Publishing Co., 1958.

Arkoun, Mohammed, 'Islam, Europe, the West: Meanings-at-stake and the will-to-power', in Andrew Rippin (ed.), *Defining Islam: A Reader*, London: Equinox, 2007, pp. 252–265.

Ashraf, Ahmad, 'The Appeal of Conspiracy Theories to Persians', *Interdisciplinary Journal of Middle Eastern Studies*, vol. 5, Fall 1996, pp. 57–88.

Assad, Thomas J., *Three Victorian Travellers: Burton Blunt and Doughty*, London: Routledge & Kegan Paul, 1964.

Augustine, *The Confessions*, R.S. Pine-Coffin (trans.), London: Penguin Books, 1961.

Al-Azmeh, Aziz, *Islams and Modernities*, London: Verso, 1996.

Babbit, Susan E. and Sue Campbell (eds), *Racism and Philosophy*, Ithaca: Cornell University Press, 1999.

Bacevich, Andrew J., *The New American Militarism: How Americans Are Seduced by War*, Oxford: Oxford University Press, 2005.

Badiou, Alain, *Theoretical Writings*, London: Continuum, 2006.

————— 'The Communist Hypothesis', *New Left Review*, vol. 49, Jan./Feb. 2008, pp. 29–42.

Baker, Raymond William, *Islam Without Fear: Egypt and the New Islamists*, Cambridge, MA: Harvard University Press, 2003.

Al-Banna, Hasan, 'The New Renaissance', in John J. Donohue and John L. Esposito (eds), *Islam in Transition: Muslim Perspectives*, 2nd edition, Oxford: Oxford University Press, 2007, pp. 59–63.

Baraz, Daniel, *Changing Perceptions: Late Antiquity to the Early Modern Period*, New York: Cornell University Press, 2003.

Barkawi, Tarak, *Globalisation and War*, Lanham, MD: Rowman & Littlefield, 2005.

Barkawi, Tarak and Mark Laffey, 'The postcolonial moment in security studies', *Review of International Studies*, vol. 32, no. 2, Apr. 2006, pp. 329–352.

Barrett, Paul H. and R. B. Freeman, *The Works of Charles Darwin*, vol. 22, New York: New York University Press, 1989.

Baudrillard, Jean, *The Gulf War Did Not Take Place*, Bloomington: Indiana University Press, 1995.

Bayly, C.A., *The Birth of the Modern World 1780–1914: Global Connections and Comparisons*, Oxford: Blackwell, 2004.

Belamy, Alex, 'No Pain, No Gain? Torture and Ethics in the War on Terror', *International Affairs*, vol. 82, no. 1, 2006, pp. 121–148.

Bell, Daniel, *The End of Ideology: On the Exhaustion of Political Ideas in the Fifties*, 2nd new edition of revised edition, Cambridge, MA: Harvard University Press, 2000.

Benhabib, Seyla, *Situating the Self: Gender, Community and Postmodernism in Contemporary Ethics*, Cambridge: Polity Press, 1992.

———— *Critique, Norm and Utopia: A Study of the Foundations of Critical Theory*, New York: Columbia University Press, 1986.

Benjamin, Walter, 'Theses on the Philosophy of History', in *Illuminations*, Hannah Arendt (ed.) and Harry Zohn (trans.), New York: Schocken Books, 1968.

Bergesen, Albert J. (ed.), *The Sayyid Qutb Reader: Selected Writings on Politics, Religion, and Society*, London: Routledge, 2008.

Bernal, Martin, *Black Athena: The Afroasiatic Roots of Classical Civilisation*, vol. 1: *The Fabrication of Ancient Greece 1785–1985*, London: Free Association Books, 1987.

Best, Steven and Douglas Kellner, *The Postmodern Turn*, London: The Guildford Press, 1997.

Bhaba, Homi K., *The Location of Culture*, London: Routledge, 1994.

Bilgin, Pinar, 'Thinking Past "Western" IR?', *Third World Quarterly*, vol. 29, no. 1, 2008, pp. 5–23.

———— 'Inventing Middle Easts: The Making of Regions Through Security Discourses', in Bjørn Olav Utvik and Knut S. Vikør (eds), *The Middle East in a Globalised World. Papers from the Fourth Nordic Conference on Middle Eastern Studies, Oslo 1998*, London: Hurst, 2000, pp. 10–37.

Biswas, Shampa, 'Empire and Global Public Intellectuals: Reading Edward Said as an International Relations Theorist', *Millennium: Journal of International Studies*, vol. 36, no. 1, 2007, pp. 117–133.

Bloch, Ernst, *The Principle of Hope, Vol. 1*, Neville Plaice (trans.), Stephen Plaice and Paul Knight, Oxford: Basil Blackwell, 1987.

Bohman, James and Matthias Lutz-Bachmann (eds), *Perpetual Peace: Essays on Kant's Cosmopolitan Ideal*, Cambridge, MA: MIT Press, 1997.

Booth, Ken and Nicholas J. Wheeler, *The Security Dilemma: Fear, Cooperation and Trust in World Politics*, London: Palgrave, 2008.

Booth, Ken and Tim Dunne (eds), *Worlds in Collision: Terror and the Future of Global Order*, London: Palgrave, 2002.

Boroujerdi, Mehrzad, *Iranian Intellectuals and the West: The Tormented Triumph of Nativism*, Syracuse: Syracuse University Press, 1996.

Bourdieu, Pierre, *The State Nobility: Elite Schools in the Field of Power*, Lauretta C. Clough (trans.), Cambridge: Polity Press, 1996.

Böwering, Gerhard, 'The Concept of Time in Islam', *Proceedings of the American Philosophical Society*, vol. 141, no. 1, Mar. 1997, pp. 55–66.

Boxil, Bernard (ed.), *Race and Racism*, Oxford: Oxford University Press, 2001.

Boyce, Mary, *A History of Zoroastrianism, Vol. 1: The Early Period*, Leiden: Brill, 1975.

Braudel, Fernand, *On History*, Sarah Matthews (trans.), Chicago: Chicago University Press, 1980.

Brecher, Jeremy, Jill Cutler and Brendan Smith (eds), *In the Name of Democracy: American War Crimes in Iraq and Beyond'*, New York: Metropolitan, 2005.

Brotton, Jerry, *The Renaissance Bazaar: From the Silk Road to Michelangelo*, Oxford: Oxford University Press, 2002.

Brown, Chris, Terry Nardin and Nicholas Rengger (eds), *International Relations in Political Thought: Texts from the Ancient Greeks to the First World War*, Cambridge: Cambridge University Press, 2002.

Buck-Morss, Susan, *Thinking Past Terror: Islamism and Critical Theory on the Left*, London: Verso, 2003.

―――― *Dreamworld and Catastrophe: The Passing of Mass Utopia in East and West*, Cambridge, MA: MIT Press, 2000.

Bukovansky, Mlada, *Legitimacy and Power Politics. The American and French Revolutions in International Political Culture*, Princeton: Princeton University Press, 2002.

Bukharin, Nikolai, *Imperialism and World Economy*, London: The Merlin Press, 1972.

Bull, Hedley, *The Anarchical Society: A Study of World Politics*, 2nd edition, London: Macmillan, 1995.

Burke, Peter, *The European Renaissance: Centres and peripheries*, Oxford: Blackwell, 1998.

Burleigh, Michael, *Sacred Causes: Religion and Politics from the European Dictators to Al-Qaeda*, London: Harper, 2006.

Butler, Judith, *Gender Trouble: Feminism and the Subversion of Identity*, London: Routledge, 1990.

Campbell, David, *Writing Security: United States Foreign Policy and the Politics of Identity*, Manchester: Manchester University Press, 1992.

———— *Politics Without Principle: Sovereignty, Ethics, and the Narratives of the Gulf War*, London: Lynne Rienner, 1993.

Cartledge, Paul, *The Greeks: A Portrait of Self and Others*, Oxford: Oxford University Press, 2002.

Cassirer, Ernst, *Substance and Function and Einstein's Theory of Relativity*, William C. and Marie C. Swabey (trans.), Chicago: Open Court, 1923.

Castle, Gregory (ed.), *Postcolonial Discourses: An Anthology*, Oxford: Blackwell, 2001.

Cesari, Jocelyne, *When Islam and Democracy Meet: Muslims in Europe and in the United States*, London: Palgrave, 2004.

Chace, James, *The Consequences of the Peace: The New Internationalism and American Foreign Policy*, Oxford: Oxford University Press, 1992.

Chan, Stephen, *Out of Evil: New International Politics and Old Doctrines of War*, London: I.B. Tauris, 2005.

Chejne, Anwar G., *Ibn Hazm*, Chicago: Hazi, 1982.

Chelebi, Katib, *The Balance of Truth*, Geoffrey L. Lewis (trans.), London: George Allen and Unwin Ltd., 1957.

Chinn, Sarah E., *Technology and the Logic of American Racism: A Cultural History of the Body as Evidence*, London: Continuum, 2000.

Chomsky, Noam, *Deterring Democracy*, London: Vintage, 1992.

Chowdhry, Geeta, 'Edward Said and Contrapuntal Reading: Implications for Critical Interventions in International Relations', *Millennium: Journal of International Studies*, vol. 36, no. 1, 2007, pp. 101–116.

Chowdhry Geeta and Shirin M. Rai, 'The Geographies of Exclusion and the Politics of Inclusion: Race-based Exclusions in the Teaching of International Relations', *International Studies Perspectives*, vol. 10, no. 1, Feb. 2009, pp. 84–91.

Churchill, Winston S., *A History of the English-Speaking Peoples*, vol. 3, London: Cassel and Company, 1957.

Clendinnen, Inge, *Reading the Holocaust*, Cambridge: Cambridge University Press, 1999.

Cohen, Jean, 'Whose Sovereignty? Empire versus International Law', *Ethics and International Affairs*, vol. 18, no. 1, 2004/2005, pp. 1–24.

Cole, Juan R. I., 'Invisible Occidentalism: Eighteenth-century Indo-Persian Constructions of the West', *Iranian Studies*, vol. 25, issues 3 and 4, 1992, pp. 3–16.

Coleman, John and Clark Walz (eds), *Greeks and Barbarians: Essays on the Interactions between Greeks and Non-Greeks in Antiquity and the Consequences for Eurocentrism*, Bethesda: CDL Press, 1997.

Constable, Olivia Remie (ed.), *Medieval Iberia: Readings from Christian, Muslim, and Jewish Sources*, Philadelphia: University of Pennsylvania Press, 1997.

Cook, Jonathan, *Israel and the Clash of Civilisations: Iraq, Iran and the Plan to Remake the Middle East*, London: Pluto, 2008.

BIBLIOGRAPHY

Corbey, Raymond, 'Ethnographic Showcases, 1870–1930', *Cultural Anthropology*, vol. 8, no. 3, Aug. 1993, pp. 338–369.

Cosby, Alfred, *Ecological Imperialism: The Biological Expansion of Europe, 900–1900*, new edition, Cambridge: Cambridge University Press, 2004.

Cox, Robert W., 'Thinking about Civilisations', *Review of International Studies*, vol. 26, no. 2, 2000, pp. 217–234.

Crampton, Jeremy W. and Stuart Elden (eds), *Space, Knowledge and Power: Foucault and Geography*, London: Ashgate, 2007.

Crawford, Robert and Darryl Jarvis (eds), *International Relations: Still an American Social Science? Towards Diversity in International Thought*, Albany, NY: State University New York Press, 2001.

Crooke, Alastair, *Resistance: The Essence of the Islamist Revolution*, London: Pluto, 2009.

Crowl, Philip A., 'Mahan: The Naval Historian', in Peter Paret (ed.), *Makers of Modern Strategy*. Princeton: Princeton University Press, 1986, pp. 444–447.

Cunliffe, Marcus, 'Formative Events from Columbus to World War I', in Michael P. Hamilton (ed.), *American Character and Foreign Policy*, Grand Rapids, Michigan: William B. Eerdmans, 1986, pp. 3–13.

Curzon, George Nathaniel, *Subjects of the Day: Being a Selection of Speeches and Writings*, London: George Allen & Unwin, 1915.

Dabashi, Hamid, *Islamic Liberation Theology: Resisting the Empire*, London: Routledge, 2008.

——— *Theology of Discontent: The Ideological Foundation of the Islamic Revolution in Iran*, New York: New York University Press, 1993.

Daniel, Norman, *Islam and the West: The Making of an Image*, Edinburgh: Edinburgh University Press, 1960.

Danner, Mark, 'The Red Cross Torture Report: What it Means', *New York Review of Books*, vol. 56. no. 7, Apr. 2009. Available at http://www.nybooks.com/articles/22614 [Last accessed 29 Apr. 2009].

——— *Torture and Truth: America, Abu Ghraib, and the War on Terror*, London: Granta, 2004.

Darwin, Charles, *The Origin of Species*, Ware: Wordsworth, 1998.

Davidson, Lawrence, 'Christian Zionism as a Representation of American Manifest Destiny', *Critique: Critical Middle Eastern Studies*, vol. 14, no. 2, Summer 2005, pp. 157–169.

Davison, Roderic H., 'Where is the Middle East?', in Richard Nolte (ed.), *The Modern Middle East*, New York: Columbia University Press, 1963, pp. 13–29.

Defrémery, C. and B.R. Sanguinetti, *Voyages d'Ibn Batoutah, texte arabe accompagné d'une traduction*, vol. 4, Paris: Imprimerie Nationale, 1879.

Deleuze, Gilles, *The Logic of Sense*, London: Continuum, 2004.

Deleuze, Gilles and Felix Guattari, *A Thousand Plateaus: Capitalism and Schizophrenia*, vol. 2, Brian Massumi (trans.), London: Athlone, 1988.

BIBLIOGRAPHY

Deleuze, Gilles and Claire Parnet, *Dialogues II*, Hugh Tomlinson, Barbara Habberjam and Eliott Ross Albert (trans.), London: Continuum, 2006.

Derrida, Jacques, *Margins of Philosophy*, Alan Bass (trans.), Brighton: Harvester Press, 1982.

——— *Writing and Difference*, new edition, London: Routledge, 1990.

——— *L'écriture et la différance* (Writing and Difference), Paris: Editions du Seuil, 1967.

Devji, Faisal, *Landscapes of the Jihad: Militancy, Morality, Modernity*, London: Hurst, 2005.

Al-Djawziyya, Ibn Qayyim, *Hidayat al-Hayara fi-l Radd ala-l-Yahud wa-l-Nasara* (The Guidance of the Perplexed in Answering the Jews and the Christians), Sayf al-Din al-Katib (ed.), Beirut: Manshurat Dar Maktabat al-Hayat, no date.

Donohue, John J. and John L. Esposito (eds), *Islam in Transition: Muslim Perspectives*, 2nd edition, Oxford: Oxford University Press, 2007.

Doty, Roxanne Lynn, *Imperial Encounters: The Politics of Representation in North-South Relations*, London: University of Minnesota Press, 1996.

Duvall, Raymond and Latha Varadarajan: 'Travelling in Paradox: Edward Said and Critical International Relations', *Millennium: Journal of International Studies*, vol. 36, no. 1, 2007, pp. 83–99.

Eickelman, Dale F and James Piscatori, *Muslim Politics*, Princeton: Princeton University Press, 1996.

Elshtain, Jean Bethke, 'Feminist Themes and International Relations', in James Der Derian (ed.), *International Theory: Critical Investigations*, London: Macmillan, 1995, pp. 340–360.

——— *Just War Against Terror: The Burden of American Power in a Violent World*, Basic Books: New York, 2003.

Enayat, Hamid, *Modern Islamic Political Thought*, London: Macmillan, 1982.

Engels, Frederick, 'On the History of Early Christianity' in Karl Marx and Frederick Engels (eds), *On Religion*, Moscow: Progress Publishers, 1975, pp. 275–300.

Esposito, John L., *The Islamic Threat: Myth or Reality*, 3rd edition, Oxford: Oxford University Press, 1999.

Euben, Roxanne L, *Enemy in the Mirror: Islamic Fundamentalism and the Limits of Modern Rationalism*, Princeton: Princeton University Press, 1999.

Eze, Emmanuel Chukwudi, *Achieving our Humanity: The Idea of the Postracial Future*, London: Routledge, 2001.

——— *Race and the Enlightenment: A Reader*, Oxford: Blackwell, 1997.

——— 'The Colour of Reason: The Idea of Race in Kant's Anthropology', in idem. (ed.), *Postcolonial African Philosophy: A Critical Reader*, Oxford: Blackwell, 1997.

Fabian, Johannes, *Time and the Other: How Anthropology Makes its Object*, New York: Columbia University Press, 1983.

Fadl, Khaled Abou El, *Speaking in God's Name: Islamic Law, Authority and Women*, London: One World Publications, 2003.

Fanon, Frantz, *Toward the African Revolution: Political Essays*, Haakon Chevalier (trans.), Harmondsworth: Penguin, 1970.

—— *The Wretched of the Earth*, Constance Farrington (trans.), New York: Grove Press, 1963.

Farabi, Abu Nasr, 'Paraphrase of Aristotle's Analytica Posteriora (kitab al-burhan)', in Seyyed Hossein Nasr with Mehdi Aminrazavi (eds), *An Anthology of Philosophy in Persia, Volume I*, Oxford: Oxford University Press, 1999, pp. 93–110.

—— 'Reconciliation of the Two Sages Spiritual Plato and Aristotle (kitab al-jam 'bayn ra'yay al-hakimayn, Aflatun al-ilahi wa Aristu)', in Seyyed Hossein Nasr with Mehdi Aminrazavi (eds), *An Anthology of Philosophy in Persia, Volume I*, Oxford: Oxford University Press, 1999, pp. 110–118.

—— 'The Perfect State (mabadi ara ahl al-madinat al-fadilah)', in Seyyed Hossein Nasr with Mehdi Aminrazavi (eds), *An Anthology of Philosophy in Persia, Volume I*, Oxford: Oxford University Press, 1999, pp. 119–133.

Faroqhi, Suraiya, *The Ottoman Empire and the World Around it*, London: I.B. Tauris, 2005.

Foucault, Michel, *Society Must Be Defended: Lectures at the Collège de France*, Mauro Bertani and Alessandro Fontana (eds), David Macey (trans.), London: Penguin, 2004.

—— *Power: Essential works of Foucault, Volume 3*, James D. Faubion (ed.), Rober Hurley et. al. (trans.), London: Penguin, 2002.

—— *The Order of Things: An Archaeology of the Human Sciences*, London: Routledge, 2002.

—— *The Will to Knowledge: The History of Sexuality, Volume 1*, Robert Hurley (trans.), London: Penguin, 1998.

—— *The Archaeology of Knowledge*, London: Routledge, 1989.

Frank, Andre Gunter, *ReOrient: Global Economy in the Asian Age*, Berkeley: University of California Press, 1998.

Freud, Sigmund, 'The Ego and the Id', in Peter Gay (ed.), *The Freud Reader*, London: Vintage, 1995.

Fried, Lisbeth S., 'Cyrus, the Messiah? The Historical Background to Isaihah 45:1', *The Harvard Theological Review*, vol. 95, no. 4, 2002, pp. 373–393.

Fromm, Erich, *To Have or to Be?*, London: Continuum, 2005.

Fukuyama, Francis, *The End of History and the Last Man*, New York: Free Press, 1992.

—— 'The End of History', *The National Interest*, no. 16, Summer 1989, pp. 3–18.

Fuller, Graham E. and Ian O. Lesser, *A Sense of Siege: The Geopolitics of Islam and the West*, Boulder, Co: Westview, 1995.

Gabrieli, Francesco 'Apology for Orientalism', *Diogenes*, no. 50, Summer 1965, pp. 128–136.

Gadamer, Hans-Georg, *Truth and Method*, 2nd edition, London: Continuum, 2004.

Gay, Peter (ed.), *The Freud Reader*, London: Vintage, 1995.

Gerges, Fawaz, *America and Political Islam: Clash of Cultures or Clash of Interests?* Cambridge: Cambridge University Press, 1999.

Gerli, E. Michael, *Medieval Iberia: An Encyclopedia*, London: Routledge, 2002.

Ghamari-Tabrizi, Behrooz, *Abdolkarim Soroush, Religious Politics and Democratic Reform*, London: I.B. Tauris, 2008.

Gheissari, Ali, *Iranian Intellectuals in the 20th Century*, Austin: University of Texas Press, 1998.

Gibb, Hamilton A. R., 'The Heritage of Islam in the Modern World', *International Journal of Middle East Studies*, vol. 1, no. 1, Jan. 1970, pp. 3–17.

Giusta, Marina Della, Uma S. Kambhampati and Robert Hunter Wade (eds), *Critical Perspectives on Globalisation*, Cheltenham: Edward Elgar, 2006.

Goldhammer, Kurt, *Der Mythus von Ost und West: Eine Kultur-und religionsgeschichtliche Betrachtung*, München: Ernst Reinhardt, 1962.

Goody, Jack, *The Theft of History*, Cambridge: Cambridge University Press, 2006.

——— *Islam in Europe*, Cambridge: Polity, 2004.

Gray, John, *Al Qaeda and What it Means to be Modern*, London: Faber and Faber, 2003.

Greenberg, Karen J. and Joshua L. Dratel (eds), *The Torture Papers: The Road to Abu Ghraib*, Cambridge: Cambridge University Press, 2005.

Grieco, Joseph M., 'Realist International Theory and the Study of World Politics', in Michael W. Doyle and G. John Ikenberry (eds), *New Thinking in International Relations Theory*, Oxford: Westview, 1997, pp. 163–201.

Grotius, Hugo, 'From *The Law of War and Peace*', in Chris Brown, Terry Nardin and Nicholas Rengger (eds), *International Relations in Political Thought: Texts from the Ancient Greeks to the First World War*, Cambridge: Cambridge University Press, 2002, pp. 325–334.

Grunebaum, G.E. von, *Modern Islam: The Search for Cultural Identity*, Berkeley: University of California Press, 1962.

Gurwitsch, Aron 'The Last Work of Edmund Husserl', *Philosophy and Phenomenological Research*, vol. 16, no. 3, Mar. 1956, pp. 380–399.

Habermas, Jürgen, 'Modernity versus Postmodernity', *New German Critique*, vol. 22, 1981, pp. 3–14.

Haddad, Yvonne, 'Muhammad Abduh: Pioneer of Islamic Reform', in Ali Rahnema (ed.), *Pioneers of Islamic Revival*, London: Zed, 2005, pp. 30–63.

Haddad, Yvonne and John L. Esposito, *The Islamic Revival Since 1988: A Critical Survey and Bibliography*, London: Greenwood, 1997.

Hafez, Kai, *Islam and the West in the Mass Media: Fragmented Images in a Globalising World*, Cresskill, NJ: Hampton Press, 2000.

—— (ed.), *The Islamic World and the West: An Introduction to Political Cultures and International Relations*, Leiden: Brill, 2000.

Haftendorn, Helga, 'The Security Puzzle: Theory-Building and Discipline Building in International Security', *International Studies Quarterly*, vol. 35, no. 1, 1991, pp. 3–17.

Hagenbeck, Carl, *Beasts and Men: Being Carl Hagenbeck's Experiences for Half a Century Among Wild Animals*, Hugh S. R. Elliot and A. G. Thacker (trans.), London: Longmans Green, and Co., 1912.

Hall, Edith, *Inventing the Barbarian: Greek Self-definition Through Tragedy*, Oxford: Oxford University Press, 1989.

Hall, Stuart, 'The West and the Rest: Discourse and power', in Tania Des Gupta (ed.), *Race and Racialisation: Essential Readings*, Toronto: Canadian Scholars Press, 2007, pp. 56–60.

Halliday, Fred, *Islam and the Myth of Confrontation*, London: I.B. Tauris, 1995.

Hanse, Birthe, *Unipolarity and the Middle East*, Richmond, Surrey: Curzon, 2000.

Harbury, Jennifer K., *Truth, Torture and the American Way: The History and Consequences of US Involvement in Torture*, Boston: Beacon Press, 2005.

Hardt, Michael and Antonio Negri, *Multitude: War and Democracy in the Age of Empire*, London: Penguin, 2004.

Harrison, Thomas (ed.), *Greeks and Barbarians*, Edinburgh: Edinburgh University Press, 2002.

Hartog, François, *The Mirror of Herodotus: The Representation of the Other in the Writing of History*, Janet Lloyd (trans.), Berkeley: University of California Press, 1988.

Hegel, Georg Wilhelm Friedrich, 'From Elements of the Philosophy of Right', in Chris Brown, Terry Nardin and Nicholas Rengger (eds), *International Relations in Political Thought: Texts from the Ancient Greeks to the First World War*, Cambridge: Cambridge University Press, 2002, pp. 470–475.

—— *The Philosophy of History*, New York: P.F. Collier & Son, 1902.

—— *Lectures on the Philosophy of Religion*, Peter C. Hodgson, J. Michael Stewart and HS Harris (eds), Berkeley: University of California Press, 1985.

—— *Hegel's Science of Logic*, A. V. Miller (trans.), Atlantic Highlands, NJ: Humanities Press, 1989

Hegghammer, Thomas, 'Al-Qaida Statements 2003–2004—A compilation of translated texts by Usama bin Ladin and Ayman al-Zawahiri', *FFI Rapport—2005/01428*, Norwegian Defence Research Establishment, 24 Jun. 2005.

Heidegger, Martin, *The Essence of Human Freedom*, Ted Sadler (trans.) London: Continuum, 2002.

—— *Introduction to Metaphysics*, New Heaven: Yale University Press, 2000.

Henrikson, Alan K., 'Mental Maps', in Michael J. Hogan and Thomas G. Paterson (eds), *Explaining the History of American Foreign Relations*, Cambridge: Cambridge University Press, 1991, pp. 177–192.

Herodotus, *Histories*, George Rawlinson (trans.), Ware: Wordsworth, 1996.

Hippo, Augustine of, 'From *The City of God against the Pagans*', in Chris Brown, Terry Nardin and Nicholas Rengger (eds), *International Relations in Political Thought: Texts from the Ancient Greeks to the First World War*, Cambridge: Cambridge University Press, 2002, pp. 119–135.

Hitti, Philip K., *Islam and the West: A Historical Cultural Survey*, Princeton: D. Van Nostrand Company Inc., 1962.

Hobsbawm, Eric J. *Nations and Nationalism Since 1780: Programme, Myth, Reality*, 2nd edition, Cambridge: Cambridge University Press, 1992.

——— and Terence Ranger (eds), *The Invention of Tradition*, 2nd edition, Cambridge: Cambridge University Press, 2004.

Hobson, John M., *The Eastern Origins of Western Civilisation*, Cambridge: Cambridge University Press, 2004.

Hodgson, Marshal G. S., 'The Role of Islam in World History', *International Journal of Middle East Studies*, vol. 1, no. 2, 1970, pp. 99–123.

Hogan, Michael J. and Thomas G. Paterson (eds), *Explaining the History of American Foreign Relations*, Cambridge: Cambridge University Press, 1991.

Holsti, K. J., *The Dividing Discipline: Hegemony and Diversity in International Theory*, London: Allen and Unwin, 1985.

Hourani, Albert, *A History of the Arab Peoples*, London: Faber and Faber, 1991.

——— *Islam in European Thought*, Cambridge: Cambridge University Press, 1991.

——— *Arabic Thought in the Liberal Age 1798–1939*, Cambridge: Cambridge University Press, 1983.

——— *Europe and the Middle East*, London: Macmillan, 1980.

Hourani, Albert and S. M. Stern (eds), *The Islamic City*, Oxford: Oxford University Press, 1970.

Huff, Toby E. and Wolfgang Schluchter (eds), *Max Weber and Islam*, New Brunswick: Transactions, 1999.

Hull, Cordell, *The Memoirs of Cordell Hull*, vol. 2, New York: Macmillan, 1948.

Huntington, Samuel P., *The Clash of Civilisations and the Remaking of World Order*, London: Simon & Schuster, 1997.

——— 'The Clash of Civilisations?', *Foreign Affairs*, vol. 72, no. 3 1993, pp. 22–49.

——— 'If Not Civilisations, What? Samuel Huntington Responds to His Critics', *Foreign Affairs*, vol. 72, no. 5, 1993, pp. 186–194.

Hurd, Elizabeth Shakman, 'Appropriating Islam: The Islamic Other in the Consolidation of Western Modernity', *Critique: Critical Middle Eastern Studies*, vol. 12, no. 1, Spring 2003, pp. 25–41.

BIBLIOGRAPHY

Huxley, Aldous, *The Perennial Philosophy*, London: Chatto & Windus, 1950.

Huyssen, Andreas, *After the Great Divide: Modernism, Mass Culture, Postmodernism*, Bloomington: Indiana University Press, 1986.

Iqbal, Muhammad, 'The Principle of Movement in the Structure of Islam', in Charles Kurzman (ed.), *Liberal Islam: A Sourcebook*, Oxford: Oxford University Press, 1998, pp. 255–269.

Iriye, Akire, 'The Second Clash: Huntington, Mahan, and Civilization', *Harvard International Review*, vol. 19, no. 2, 1997, pp. 44–70.

Irwin, Robert, *For Lust of Knowing: The Orientalists and Their Enemies*, London: Penguin, 2007.

Isaac, Benjamin, *The Invention of Racism in Classical Antiquity*, Princeton: Princeton University Press, 2004.

Ismail, Salwa, *Rethinking Islamist Politics: Culture, the State and Islamism*, London: I.B. Tauris, 2006.

Jackson, Richard, 'Language, Policy and the Construction of a Torture Culture in the War on Terrorism', *Review of International Studies*, vol. 33, no. 3, July 2007, pp. 353–371.

——— *Writing the War on Terrorism: Language, Politics and Counterterrorism*, Manchester: Manchester University Press, 2005.

Jay, Martin, *The Dialectical Imagination: A History of the Frankfurt School and the Institute of Social Research 1923–1950*, London: Heinemann, 1973.

Jepperson, Ronald L., Alexander Wendt, and Peter J. Katzenstein, 'Norms, Identity, and Culture in National Security', in Peter J. Katzenstein (ed.), *The Culture of National Security. Norms and Identity in World Politics*, New York: Columbia University Press, 1996, pp. 33–75.

Jones, Branwen Gruffydd (ed.), *Decolonising International Relations*, Plymouth: Rowman & Littlefield, 2006.

Jones, Richard Wyn (ed.), *Critical Theory and World Politics*, London: Lynne Rienner, 2001.

Jones, T. A., 'The Restoration Gene Pool Concept: Beyond the Native Versus Non-native Debate', *Restoration Ecology*, vol. 11, no. 3, 2003, pp. 281–290.

Jordan, Richard Daniel Maliniak, Amy Oakes, Susan Peterson and Michael J. Tierney, *One Discipline or Many? TRIPP Survey of International Relations Faculty in Ten Countries*, Institute for the Theory and Practice of International Relations, College of William and Mary, Williamsburg, Virginia, 2009.

Kabbani, Rana, *Europe's Myth of Orient*, Bloomington: Indiana University Press, 1986.

Kahler, Miles, 'Inventing International Relations: International Relations Theory after 1945', in Michael W. Doyle and G. John Ikenberry (eds), *New Thinking in International Relations Theory*, London: Westview, 1997, pp. 20–53.

Kamrava, Mehran, *Iran's Intellectual Revolution*, Cambridge: Cambridge University Press, 2008.

―――― (ed.), *The New Voices of Islam: Reforming Politics and Modernity, A Reader*, London: I.B. Tauris, 2006.

Kant, Immanuel, 'From *Perpetual Peace*', Chris Brown, Terry Nardin and Nicholas Rengger (eds), *International Relations in Political Thought: Texts from the Ancient Greeks to the First World War*, Cambridge: Cambridge University Press, 2002, pp. 432–450.

―――― *Observations on the Feeling of the Beautiful and the Sublime*, John T. Goldthwait (trans.), Berkeley: University of California Press, 2004.

Karsh, Efraim, *Islamic Imperialism: A History*, London: Yale University Press, 2006.

Kearney, R., *Dialogues with Contemporary Continental Thinkers*, Manchester: Manchester University Press, 1984.

Keddie, Nikki R., *An Islamic Response to Imperialism: The Political and Religious Writings of Sayyid Jamal ad-Din al-Afghani*, Berkeley: University of California Press, 1983.

Kedourie, Elie, *Afghani and 'Abduh: An Essay on Religious Unbelief and Political Activism in Modern Islam*, London: Frank Cass, 1966.

Kelly, Marjorie (ed.), *Islam: The Religious and Political Life of a World Community*, London: Praeger, 1984.

Kennan, George F., 'The Origins of Containment', in Terry L. Deibel and John Lewis Gaddis (eds), *Containment: Concept and Policy Volume One*, Washington DC: National Defence University Press, 1986, pp. 23–31.

Kennedy, Paul, *The Rise and Fall of the Great Powers: Economic Change and Military Conflict from 1500 to 2000*, London: Fontana, 1988.

Keohane, Robert O., (ed.), *Neorealism and its Critics*, New York: Columbia University Press, 1986.

―――― 'The Globalisation of Violence, Theories of World Politics and "The Liberalism of Fear"'.

Available at http://www.ssrc.org/sept11/essays/keohane.htm [Last accessed 14 Mar. 2003].

Kepel, Gilles, *The Roots of Radical Islam*, London: Saqi, 2005.

―――― *Jihad: The Trail of Political Islam*, London: I.B. Tauris, 2002.

―――― *Allah in the West: Islamic Movements in America and Europe*, Cambridge: Polity, 1997.

Ibn Khaldun, *The Muqaddimah: An Introduction to History*, Franz Rosenthal (trans.), N.J. Dawood (ed.), with an introduction by Bruce Lawrence, Princeton: Princeton University Press, 2004.

Al-Khalidi, Abd al-Fattah (ed.), *Amrika min al-Dakhil bi-minzar Sayyid Qutb* (America from the Inside, through the eyes of Sayyid Qutb), Jiddah: Dar al-Manarah, 1986.

Khatami, Mohammad, *Islam, Dialogue and Civil Society*, Canberra: Centre for Arab and Islamic Studies, The Australian National University, 2000.

——— 'Dialogue between East and West', in John J. Donohue and John L. Esposito (eds), *Islam in Transition: Muslim Perspectives*, 2nd edition, Oxford: Oxford University Press, 2007, pp. 366–370.

Khayyam, Umar, 'The Necessity of Contradiction, Free Will and Determinism (Darurat al-tadadd fi'l-alam wa'l-jabr wa'l-baqa)', in Seyyed Hossein Nasr with Mehdi Aminrazavi (eds), *An Anthology of Philosophy in Persia, Volume I*, Oxford: Oxford University Press, 1999, pp. 401–411.

Kinsella, Helen M., 'Discourse of Difference: Civilians, Combatants, and Compliance with the Laws of War', *Review of International Studies*, vol. 31, no. 1, 2005, pp. 163–185.

Klare, Michael T., 'The Pentagon's New Paradigm', in Micah L. Sifry and Christopher Cerf (eds), *The Gulf War Reader. History, Documents, Opinions*, New York: Times Books, 1991, pp. 466–476.

——— 'Deciphering the Bush Administration's Motives', in Micah L. Sifry and Christopher Cerf (eds), *The Iraq War Reader: History, Documents, Opinions*, London: Simon and Schuster, 2003, pp. 392–402.

Krishna, Sankaran, 'Race, Amnesia, and the Education of International Relations', in Branwen Gruffydd Jones (ed.), *Decolonising International Relations*, Plymouth: Rowman & Littlefield, 2006, pp. 89–108.

Kristol, Irving, 'The Neoconservative Persuasion', in Irwin Stelzer (ed.), *Neoconservatism*, London: Atlantic, 2004.

Kuziemko, Ilyana and Eric Werker, 'How Much is a Seat on the Security Council Worth?: Foreign Aid and Bribery at the United Nations', *Journal of Political Economy*, vol. 114, no. 51, 2006, pp. 905–930.

Laiou, Angeliki, 'The Just War of Eastern Christians and the Holy War of the Crusaders', in Richard Sorabji and David Rodin, *The Ethics of War: Shared Problems in Different Traditions*, London: Ashgate, 2006, pp. 30–43.

Lapid, Yosef and Friedrich Kratochwil (eds), *The Return of Culture and Identity in IR Theory*, London: Lynne Rienner, 1996.

Laurent, Eric, *Bush's Secret World: Religion, Big Business and Hidden Networks*, Andrew Brown (trans.), Cambridge: Polity, 2004.

Lawrence, Bruce (ed.), *Messages to the World: The Statements of Osama bin Laden*, London: Verso, 2005.

Leff, Gordon, *Medieval Thought: St. Augustine to Ockham*, Harmondsworth: Penguin, 1958.

Lenin, Vladimir I., *Imperialism: The Highest Stage of Capitalism*, New York: International Publishers, 1939.

Levinas, Emmanuel, *Difficult Freedom: Essays on Judaism*, Sean Hand (trans.), Baltimore: Johns Hopkins University Press, 1990.

——— 'Politics After!', in idem. *Beyond the Verse: Talmudic Readings and Lectures*, Bloomington: Indiana University Press, 1994.

——— *Time and the Other, and Additional Essays*, R. A. Cohen (trans.), Pittsburgh: Duquesne University Press, 1987.

Lewis, Bernard, *Western Impact and Middle Eastern Response*, Oxford: Oxford University Press, 2002.

—— *The Crisis of Islam: Holy War and Unholy Terror*, London: Phoenix, 2003.

Lewis, David Levering, *God's Crucible: Islam and the Making of Europe 570–1215*, London: W.W. Norton and Co., 2009.

Lieven, Anatol, *America Right or Wrong: An Anatomy of American National-ism*, Oxford: Oxford University Press, 2004.

Linklater, Andrew, *Beyond Realism and Marxism: Critical Theory and Inter-national Relations*, London: Macmillan, 1990.

Little, Douglas, *American Orientalism: The United States and the Middle East Since 1945*, London: I.B. Tauris, 2002.

Lockman, Zachary, *Contending Visions of the Middle East: The History and Politics of Orientalism*, Cambridge: Cambridge University Press, 2004.

Macfie, A. L., (ed.), *Orientalism: A Reader*, Edinburgh: Edinburgh University Press, 2000.

Machiavelli, Nicolò, *The Prince*, W.K. Marriott (trans.), London: Encyclopae-dia Britannica, 1952.

MacMaster, Neil 'Islamophobia in France and the "Algerian Problem"', in Emran Qureshi and Michael A. Sells (eds), *The New Crusades: Constructing the Muslim Enemy*, New York: Columbia University Press, 2003, pp. 288–313.

Marandi, Seyed Mohammad, 'The Oriental World of Lord Byron and the Ori-entalism of Literary Scholars', *Critique: Critical Middle Eastern Studies*, vol. 15, no. 3, Fall 2006, pp. 317–337.

Marcuse, Herbert, *Towards a Critical Theory of Society*, Douglas Kellner (ed.), London: Routledge, 2001.

—— *One-Dimensional Man: Studies in the Ideology of Advanced Industrial Society*, London: Routledge, 1964.

Marx, Karl and Friedrich Engels, *The Communist Manifesto*, London: Pen-guin, 2002.

—— *Manifesto of the Communist Party*, London: Verso, 1998.

Marx, Karl, *Surveys from Exile*, David Fernbach (ed.), London: Pelican, 1973.

—— *Economic and Philosophical Manuscripts of 1844*, Moscow: Foreign Languages Publishing House, 1961.

Massad, Joseph, *Desiring Arabs*, Chicago: The University of Chicago Press, 2007.

Mastnak, Tomaž, 'Europe and the Muslims: The Permanent Crusade', in Emran Qureshi and Michael A. Sells (eds), *The New Crusades: Constructing the Muslim Enemy*, New York: Columbia University Press, 2003, pp. 205–248.

Matar, Nabil, *Europe Through Arab Eyes, 1578–1727*, New York: Columbia University Press, 2009.

Matin-Asgari, Afshin, 'Islamic Studies and the Spirit of Max Weber: A Critique of Cultural Essentialism', *Critique: Critical Middle Eastern Studies*, vol. 13, no. 3, Fall 2004, pp. 293–312.

Mawdudi, Abu-l-Ala, 'Political Theory of Islam', in John J. Donohue and John L. Esposito (eds), *Islam in Transition: Muslim Perspectives*, 2nd edition, Oxford: Oxford University Press, 2007, pp. 74–77.

Mazrui, Ali, 'Islam and the United States: Streams of Convergence, Strands of Divergence', *Third World Quarterly*, vol. 25, no. 5, 2004, pp. 793–820.

—— *Cultural Forces in World Politics*, Oxford: James Currey, 1990.

Mazumdar, P.D., *The Oriental Christ*, Boston: George H. Ellis, 1883.

McClintock, Anne, *Imperial Leather: Race, Gender and Sexuality in the Colonial Contest*, London: Routledge, 1995.

McSweeney, Bill, *Security, Identity and Interests. A Sociology of International Relations*, Cambridge: Cambridge University Press, 1999.

Mearsheimer, John J. and Stephen M. Walt, *The Israel Lobby and US Foreign Policy*, London: Penguin, 2007.

Meier, Andreas (ed.), *Der politische Auftrag des Islam: Programme und Kritik zwischen Fundamentalismus und Reformen—Originalstimmen aus der islamischen Welt*, Wuppertal: Peter Hammer Verlag, 1995.

—— (ed.), *Politische Strömungen im Modernen Islam: Quellen und Kommentare* [Political Currents in modern Islam: Sources and Commentaries], Bonn: Bundeszentrale für politische Bildung, 1995.

Melville, Herman, *White Jacket*, in *Redburn, White Jacket, Moby Dick*, New York: The Library of America, 1983.

Michel, Thomas F. (ed.), *A Muslim Theologian's Response to Christianity: Ibn Taymiyya's Al-Jawab Al Sahih*, Delmar, NY: Caravan Books, 1985.

Mill, John Stuart, *Dissertations and Discussions: Political, Philosophical and Historical*, vol. 3, London: Longmans, Green, Reader, and Dyer, 1867.

Mirsepassi, Ali, *Intellectual Discourse and the Politics of Modernization: Negotiating Modernity in Iran*, Cambridge, MA: Harvard University Press, 2000.

Moin, Baqer, *Khomeini: Life of the Ayatollah*, London: I.B. Tauris, 1999.

Morgan, Michael L., *Discovering Levinas*, Cambridge: Cambridge University Press, 2007.

Moser, Brigitte (trans. and ed.), *Die Chronik des Ahmed Sinan Celebi genannt Bihisti: Eine Quelle zur Geschichte des Osmanischen Reiches unter Sultan Bayezid II*, Beiträge zur Kenntnis Südeuropas und des Nahen Orients, München: Dr. Dr. Rudolf Trofenik, 1980.

Mottahedeh, Roy P., 'The Clash of Civilisations: An Islamicist's Critique', *Harvard Middle Eastern and Islamic Review*, vol. 2, no. 1, 1995, pp. 1–26.

Mullin, Corinna, *Constructing Political Islam as the New Other: America and its Post-War on Terror Politics*, London: I.B. Tauris, forthcoming, 2010.

Muñoz, Gema Martín (ed.), *Islam, Modernism and the West. Cultural and Political Relations at the End of the Millennium*, London: I.B. Tauris, 1999.

Mutahhari, Murtada, *An Introuction to 'Ilm al-Kalam*, vol. 2, no. 2, 'Ali Quli Qara'I (trans.), Tehran, 1985. Available at http://www.al-Islam.org/al-tawhid/kalam.htm /Last accessed 12 July 2008a.

Mutman, Mahmut, 'Under the Sign of Orientalism: The West vs. Islam', *Cultural Critique*, no. 23, Winter 1992–1993, pp. 165–197.

Nabavi, Negin, *Intellectuals and the State in Iran: Politics, Discourse and the Dilemma of Authenticity*, Gainesville: University of Florida Press, 2003.

Nabulsi, Karma, 'Conceptions of Justice in War: From Grotius to Modern Times', in Richard Sorabji and David Rodin (eds), *The Ethics of War: Shared Problems in Different Traditions*, Aldershot: Ashgate, 2006, pp. 44–60.

Nadwi, Sayyed Abul Hasan 'Ali, *Islam and the World: The Rise and Decline of Muslims and its Effect on Mankind*, Leicester: UK Islamic Academy, 2005.

Nardin, Terry, 'Theorising the International Rule of Law', *Review of International Studies*, vol. 34, no. 3, Jul. 2008, pp. 385–401.

Nasr, Seyyed Hossein, *The Islamic Intellectual Tradition in Persia*, Mehdi Aminrazavi (ed.), London: Curzon, 1996.

―――― *Islam and the Plight of Modern Man*, London: Longman, 1975.

Nasr, Seyyed Hossein with Mehdi Aminrazavi (eds), *An Anthology of Philosophy in Persia*, vol. 1, Oxford: Oxford University Press, 1999.

Netanyahu, Benjamin, *Fighting Terrorism: How Democracies Can Defeat Domestic and International Terrorism*, New York: Farrar, Straus, and Giroux, 1995.

Neumann, Iver B., *Uses of the Other: 'The East' in European Identity Formation*, Minneapolis: University of Minnesota Press, 1999.

Nietzsche, Friedrich, *Das Philosophenbuch: Theoretische Studien*, Paris: Aubier-Flammarion, 1969.

Norris, Christopher, *Deconstruction and the Interests of Theory*, London: Pinter, 1988.

Norton, Anne, *Leo Strauss and the Politics of American Empire*, London: Yale University Press, 2004.

Nye, Stephen, *Letter of Resolution Concerning the Doctrine of the Trinity and the Incarnation*, London, 1690.

Osgood, Robert E., 'Force in International Relations: The Moral Issues', in Kenneth W. Thompson (ed.), *Ethics and International Relations Vol. 2*, Oxford: Transaction, 1985, pp. 49–58.

Paddison, Ronan, Chris Philo, Paul Routledge and Joanne Sharp, *Entanglements of Power: Geographies of Domination/Resistance*, London: Routledge, 1999.

Palmer, Norman D., 'The Study of International Relations in the United States: Perspective of Half a Century', *International Studies Quarterly*, vol. 24, no. 3, Sept. 1980, pp. 343–363.

Pappe, Ilan, *The Ethnic Cleansing of Palestine*, Oxford: One World, 2006.

Perlman, M., 'Notes on anti-Christian Propaganda in the Mamluk Empire', *Bulletin of the School of Oriental and African Studies*, University of London, vol. 10, no. 4, 1942, pp. 843–861.

Peters, Francis E., 'The Early Muslim Empires: Umayyads, Abbasids, Fatimids', in Marjorie Kelly (ed.), *Islam: The Religious and Political Life of a World Community*, London: Praeger, 1984.

Pfaff, William, 'More Likely a New World Disorder', in Micah L. Sifry and Christopher Cerf (eds), *The Gulf War Reader. History, Documents, Opinions*, New York: Times Books, 1991, pp. 487–491.

Philips, Melanie, *Londonistan*, London: Encounter, 2006.

Pipes, Daniel, 'The Muslims are coming! The Muslims are coming!', *National Review*, 19 Nov. 1990.

Pollock, Sheldon, 'Indology, Power, and the Case of Germany', in A.L. Macfie (ed.), *Orientalism: A Reader*, Edinburgh: Edinburgh University Press, 2000, pp. 302–323.

Preston, Christopher D., 'The Terms "Native" and "Alien"—A Biogeographical Perspective', *Progress in Human Geography*, vol. 33, no. 4, 2009, pp. 1–10.

Qureshi, Emran and Michael A. Sells (eds), *The New Crusades: Constructing the Muslim Enemy*, New York: Columbia University Press, 2003.

Qutb, Sayyid, 'The Essence of Jihad', in Albert J. Bergesen (ed.), *The Sayyid Qutb Reader: Selected Writings on Politics, Religion, and Society*, London: Routledge, 2008, pp. 59–60.

——— 'Foreword', in Sayyed Abul Hasan 'Ali Nadwi, *Islam and the World: The Rise and Decline of Muslims and its Effect on Mankind*, Leicester: UK Islamic Academy, 2005, pp. i–x.

Rahnema, Ali (ed.), *Pioneers of Islamic Revival*, London: Zed, 2005.

——— *An Islamic Utopian: A Political Biography of Ali Shariati*, London: I.B. Tauris, 2000.

Ramadan, Tariq, 'The Way (Al-Sharia) of Islam', in Mehran Kamrava (ed.), *The New Voices of Islam: Reforming Politics and Modernity, A Reader*, London: I.B. Tauris, 2006, pp. 65–97.

Razi, Abu Bakr Muhammad Zakariyya, 'Spiritual Physick (al-Tibb al-ruhani)', in Seyyed Hossein Nasr with Mehdi Aminrazavi (eds), *An Anthology of Philosophy in Persia*, vol. 1, Oxford: Oxford University Press, 1999, pp. 355–364.

Redhead, Steve (ed.), *The Jean Baudrillard Reader*, Edinburgh: Edinburgh University Press, 2008.

Redhouse, J.W. (trans.), *The Diary of H.M. The Shah of Persia*, London: John Murray, 1874.

Reus-Smit, Christian, 'Liberal Hierarchy and the License to Use Force', *Review of International Studies*, vol. 31, no. 1, 2005, pp. 71–92.

Richardson, Michael, 'Enough Said', *Anthropology Today*, vol. 6, no. 4, 1990, pp. 16–19.

Ricoeur, Paul, *Time and Narrative*, vol. 1, London: The University of Chicago Press, 1984.

Rida, Muhammad Rashid, *Tarikh al-ustadh al-imam al-shaykh Muhammad 'Abduh*, vol. 1, Cairo: al-Manar, 1931.

—— al Wahabiyyun wa'l Hijaz, Cairo, 1344 (1925–1926).

Ridgeon, Lloyd (ed.), Religion and Politics in Modern Iran: A Reader, London: I.B. Tauris, 2005.

Ringer, Monica M., 'The Quest for the Secret of Strength in Iranian Nineteenth-Century Travel Literature: Rethinking Tradition in the Safarnameh', in Nikki R. Keddie and Rudi Matthee (eds), Iran and the Surrounding World, London: University of Washington Press, 2002, pp. 146–161.

Risse, Thomas, '"Let's Argue!" Communicative Action in World Politics', International Organization, vol. 54, no. 1, 2000, pp. 2–39.

Rodinson, Maxime, Muhammad: Prophet of Islam, London: I.B. Tauris, 2002.

Rothfels, Nigel, Savages and Beasts: The Birth of the Modern Zoo, Baltimore: The Johns Hopkins University Press, 2002.

Roy, Olivier, The Politics of Chaos in the Middle East, Ros Schwartz (trans.), London: Hurst, 2007.

—— Globalised Islam: The Search for a New Ummah, London: Hurst, 2002.

—— The Failure of Political Islam, Carol Volk (trans.), London: I.B. Tauris, 1999.

Ruggie, John Gerard, 'What Makes the World Hang Together? Neo-utilitarianism and the Social Constructivist Challenge', International Organization, vol. 52, no. 4 (1998), pp. 855–885.

Ruthven, Malise, Fundamentalism: The Search for Meaning, Oxford: Oxford University Press, 2004.

—— Islam in the World, London: Penguin, 1984.

Sacks, Jonathan, Dignity of Difference: How to Avoid the Clash of Civilisations, London: Continuum, 2003.

Safranski, Rüdiger, Nietzsche: A Philosophical Biography, London: Granta, 2003.

Saikal, Amin, Islam and the West: Conflict or Cooperation, London: Palgrave, 2003.

Said, Edward W., Reflections on Exile and Other Essays, Cambridge, MA: Harvard University Press, 2000.

—— 'The Clash of Definitions: On Samuel Huntington', in Edward Said Reflections on Exile and Other Essays, Cambridge, MA: Harvard University Press, 2000, pp. 569–590.

—— 'Shattered Myths' in A. L. Macfie (ed.), Orientalism: A Reader, Edinburgh: Edinburgh University Press, 2000, pp. 89–103.

—— Covering Islam: How the Media and the Experts Determine How We See the Rest of the World, London: Vintage, 1997.

—— Orientalism: Western Conceptions of the Orient, London: Penguin, 1995.

—— Culture and Imperialism, London: Vintage, 1993.

Salamé, Ghassan, 'The Middle East: Elusive Security, Indefinable Region', Security Dialogue, vol. 25, no. 1, 1994, pp. 17–35.

—— 'Islam and the West', Foreign Policy, no. 90, Spring 1993, pp. 22–37.

Salter, Mark B., *Barbarians and Civilization in International Relations*, London: Pluto, 2002.

Sardar, Ziauddin, *Postmodernism and the Other: The New Imperialism of Western Culture*, London: Pluto, 1998.

Sartre, Jean-Paul, *Critique of Dialectical Reason, Volume 1: Theory of Practical Ensembles*, Alan Sheridan-Smith (trans.), Jonathan Rée (ed.), foreword by Frederic Jameson, London: Verso, 2004.

Sayyid, Salman, *A Fundamental Fear: Eurocentrism and the Emergence of Islamism*, London: Zed, 1997.

Schirazi, Asghar, *The Constitution of Iran: Politics and the State in the Islamic Republic*, John O' Kane (trans.), London: I.B. Tauris, 1997.

Schluchter, Wolfgang, 'The Future of Religion', in Jeffrey C. Alexander and Steven Seidman (eds), *Culture and Society: Contemporary Debates*, Cambridge: Cambridge University Press, 1990, pp. 249–261.

Schluchter, Wolfgang, *Religion and America*, Mary Douglas and Steven M. Tipton (eds), Boston: Beacon Press, 1982.

Schmitt, Carl, *The Concept of the Political*, George Schwab (trans.), Chicago: University of Chicago Press, 2007.

Scholte, Jan Aart, 'The Globalisation of World Politics' in John Baylis and Steve Smith (eds), *The Globalisation of World Politics: An Introduction*, Oxford: Oxford University Press, 2001, pp. 13–30.

Schultz, Bud and Ruth Schultz, *The Price of Dissent: Testimonies to Political Repression in America*, Berkeley: University of California Press, 2001.

Schwab, Raymond, *La Renaissance Orientale*, Paris: Payot, 1950.

Shakespeare, William, *The Works of Shakespeare*, vol. 1, Howard Staunton (ed.), London: Routledge Warne & Routledge Farringdon Street, 1862.

Shani, Giorgio, 'Toward a Post-Western IR: The *Umma, Khalsa Panth*, and Critical International Relations Theory', *International Studies Review*, vol. 10, issue 4, Dec. 2008, pp. 722–734.

Shariati, Ali, 'Civilisation and Modernisation', in Lloyd Ridgeon (ed.), *Religion and Politics in Modern Iran: A Reader*, London: I. B. Tauris, 2005.

——— 'Humanity and Islam', in Charles Kurzman (ed.), *Liberal Islam: A Sourcebook*, Oxford: Oxford University Press, 1998.

——— *Man and Islam: Lectures by Ali Shariati*, Ghulam M. Fayez (trans.), Mashhad: University of Mashhad Press, 1982.

——— *On the Sociology of Islam: Lectures by Ali Shariati*, Hamid Algar (trans.), Berkeley: Mizan Press, 1979.

Sharif, M. M. (ed.), *A History of Muslim Philosophy: With Short Accounts of Other Disciplines and the Modern Renaissance in Muslim Lands*, vol. 2, Wiesbaden, Germany: Otto Harassowitz, 1966.

Shaw, David Gary, 'Modernity Between Us and Them: The Place of Religion Within History', *History and Theory*, vol. 45, issue 4, Dec. 2006, pp. 1–9.

Sheikh, M. Saeed, *Islamic Philosophy*, London: The Octagon Press, 1962.

Sherwood, Henry Nobel, 'The Formation of the American Colonization Society', *The Journal of Negro History*, vol. 2, no. 3, Jul. 1917, pp. 209–228.

BIBLIOGRAPHY

Shirazi, Mirza Saleh, *majmu'ah-e safarnamahha-ye Mirza Saleh Shirazi*, Gholam Hussein Mirza Saleh (ed.), Tehran: Nashr-e Tarikh-e Iran, 1364/1985.

Sijistani, Abu Ya'qub; *Kashf al-mahjub*, H. Corbin (ed.), Paris-Tehran: Institut Francais de Recherche en Iran, 1949.

Simberloff, Daniel, 'Non-native Species *Do* Threaten the Natural Environment!' *Journal of Agricultural and Environmental Ethics*, vol. 18, no. 6, Dec. 2005, pp. 595–606.

Ibn Sina, 'The Logic of the Orientals (Mantiq al-mashraqiyyin)', in Seyyed Hossein Nasr with Mehdi Aminrazavi (eds), *An Anthology of Philosophy in Persia*, vol. 1, Oxford: Oxford University Press, 1999, pp. 241–250.

——— 'The Healing: On time (al-Shifa)', in Seyyed Hossein Nasr with Mehdi Aminrazavi (eds), *An Anthology of Philosophy in Persia*, vol. 1, Oxford: Oxford University Press, pp. 268–270.

——— *Fontes sapientiae (Uyun al-hikmah)*, Abdurrahman Badawied (ed.), Cairo: no publisher, 1954.

Singer, Peter; *The President of Good and Evil: Taking George W. Bush Seriously*, London: Granta, 2004.

Skinner, Elliott P., 'Ethnicity and Race as Factors in the Formation of United States Foreign Policy', in Michael P. Hamilton (ed.), *American Character and Foreign Policy*, Grand Rapids, MI: William B. Eerdmans, 1986, pp. 87–136.

Smith, Adam, *The Wealth of Nations*, vol. 1, London: Dent, 1910.

Smith, Steve, 'The United States and the Discipline of International Relations: "Hegemonic country, hegemonic discipline"', *International Studies Review*, vol. 4, no. 2, Summer 2002, pp. 67–85.

——— 'The Discipline of International Relations: Still and American Social Science?', *British Journal of Politics and International Relations*, vol. 2, no. 3 (2000), pp. 374–402.

Soroush, Abdolkarim, *Reason, Freedom, and Democracy in Islam: Essential Writings of Abdolkarim Soroush*, Mahmoud Sadri and Ahmad Sadri (eds and trans.), Oxford: Oxford University Press, 2000.

Southern, R.W., *Western Views of Islam in the Middle Ages*, Cambridge: Harvard University Press, 1962.

Soya, Edward W., *Postmodern Geographies: The Reassertion of Space in Critical Social Theory*, London: Verso, 1989.

Spengler, Oswald, *The Decline of the West*, one volume edition, New York: Knopf, 1939.

Sweetman, J. Windrow, *Islam and Christian Theology*, part one, vol. 2, London: Lutterworth Press, 1955.

Swiney, Chrystie Flournoy, 'Racial Profiling of Arabs and Muslims in the US: Historical, Empirical and Legal Analysis Applied to the War on Terrorism', *Muslim World Journal of Human Rights*, vol. 3, issue 1, 2006, pp. 1–36.

Sykes, Mark, *Dar-Ul-Islam: A Record of a Journey Through Ten of the Asiatic Provinces of Turkey*, London: Bickers & Son, 1904.

Sylvest, Casper, '"Our passion for legality": International Law and Imperialism in Late Nineteenth-century Britain', *Review of International Studies*, vol. 34, no. 3, Jul. 2008, pp. 403–423.

Tavakoli-Targhi, Mohammad, *Refashioning Iran: Orientalism, Occidentalism and Historiography*, New York: Palgrave, 2001.

Thomassen, Lasse (ed.), *The Derrida-Habermas Reader*, Edinburgh: Edinburgh University Press, 2006.

Thompson, Michael J., (ed.), *Islam and the West: Critical Perspectives on Modernity*, Oxford: Rowman & Littlefield, 2003.

Tibi, Bassam, *Conflict and War in the Middle East. From Interstate War to New Security*, second edition, London: Macmillan, 1998.

——— *The Challenge of Fundamentalism: Political Islam and the New World Disorder*, Berkeley: University of California Press, 1998.

Tibi, Basssam. *Arab Nationalism. Between Islam and the Nation-State*, 3rd edition, Macmillan: London 1997.

Tocqueville, Alexis de, 'Second Letter on Algeria', reprinted in Michael J. Thompson (ed.), *Islam and the West: Critical Perspectives on Modernity*, Oxford: Rowman & Littlefield, 2003, pp. 139–151.

Tourneau, Roger Le, *Cités musulmanes d'Afrique du Nord*, Alger: La Maison de livre, 1957.

Toynbee, Arnold J., *Civilisation on Trial*, Oxford: Oxford University Press, 1948.

Trinh, Minh-ha T., *Women, Native, Other: Writing, Postcoloniality and Feminism*, Bloomington: University of Indiana Press, 1989.

Tripp, Charles, *Islam and the Moral Economy: The Challenge of Capitalism*, Cambridge: Cambridge University Press, 2006.

Tuck, Richard, *The Rights of War and Peace: Political Thought and the International Order from Grotius to Kant*, Oxford: Oxford University Press, 2001.

Turner, Bryan S., *Orientalism, Postmodernism and Globalism*, London: Routledge, 1994.

——— *Weber and Islam*, London: Routledge, 1974.

Tymieniecka, Anna-Teresa (ed.), *Islamic Philosophy and Occidental Phenomenology on the Perennial Issue of Microcosm and Macrocosm*, Dordrecht: Springer, 2006.

Vahdat, Farzin, 'Critical Theory and the Islamic Encounter with Modernity', in Michael J. Thompson (ed.), *Islam and the West: Critical Perspectives on Modernity*, Oxford: Rowman & Littlefield, 2003, pp. 123–138.

——— *God and Juggernaut: Iran's Intellectual Encounter with Modernity*, Syracuse: Syracuse University Press, 2002.

Vasquez, John A., *The Power of Power Politics: From Classical Realism to Neotraditionalism*, Cambridge: Cambridge University Press, 1999.

Veer, Peter van der, *Imperial Encounters: Religion and Modernity in India and Britain*, Princeton: Princeton University Press, 2001.

BIBLIOGRAPHY

Venn, Couze, *Occidentalism: Modernity and Subjectivity*, London: Sage, 2000.

Voegelin, Eric, *Political Religions*, New York: Edwin Mellin Press, 1986.

Waardenburg, Jaques *Muslims and Others: Relations in Context*, Berlin: Walter de Gruyter, 2003.

Waever, Ole, 'The Sociology of a not so International Discipline: American and European Developments in International Relations', *International Organization*, vol. 52, no. 4, Autumn 1998, pp. 687–727.

Waltz, Kenneth N., 'Reductionist and Systemic Theories', in Robert O. Keohane (ed.), *Neorealism and its Critics*, New York: Columbia University Press, 1985, pp. 47–69.

——— *Theory of International Politics*, New York: McGraw-Hill, 1979.

Walzer, Richard, *Greek into Arabic: Essays on Islamic Philosophy*, Cambridge, MA: Harvard University Press, 1962.

Ward, Julie K. and Tommy L. Lott (eds), *Philosophers on Race: Critical Essays*, Oxford: Blackwell, 2002.

Warren, Charles R., 'Perspectives on the "Alien" versus "Native" Species Debate: A Critique of Concepts, Language and Practice', *Progress in Human Geography*, vol. 31, no. 4, 2007, pp. 427–446.

Weber, Max, *General Economic History*, New York: Collier Books, 1961.

Wendt, Alexander, *Social Theory of International Politics*, Cambridge: Cambridge University Press, 1999.

'What We're Fighting For: A Letter from America', in David Blankenhorn, Abdou Filali-Ansary, Hassan I. Mneimneh, and Alex Roberts (eds), *The Islam/West Debate: Documents from a Global Debate on Terrorism, U.S. Policy, and the Middle East*, Oxford: Rowman & Littlefield, 2005, pp. 21–37.

White, Hayden, *Metahistory: The Historical Imagination in Nineteenth Century Europe*, Baltimore: Johns Hopkins Press, 1973.

Wiesel, Elie 'Stay Together Always', *Newsweek*, 16 Jan. 1995, p. 58.

Williams, Raymond, *Marxism and Literature*, Oxford: Oxford University Press, 1977.

Wittig, Monique, *The Straight Mind and Other Essays*, Boston: Beacon, 1992.

Wolff, Christian von, 'From *The Law of Nations Treated According to a Scientific Method*', in Chris Brown, Terry Nardin, N.J. Rengger, *International Relations in Political Thought*, Cambridge: Cambridge University Press, 2002, pp. 356–369.

Xenophon, *The Persian Expedition*, Rex Warner (trans.), London: Penguin 1949.

Yassin, Abd al-Salam, *Sur l'économie, préalables dogmatiques et régles chariques*, Rabat: Imprimerie Horizons, 1996.

Young, Robert J.C., *Postcolonialism: An Historical Introduction*, Oxford: Blackwell, 2001.

—————— 'Colonialism and the Desiring Machine', in Gregory Castle (ed.), *Postcolonial Discourses: An Anthology*, Oxford: Blackwell, 2001, pp. 74–98.

—————— *Torn Halves: Political Conflict in Literary and Cultural Theory*, Manchester: Manchester University Press, 1996.

—————— *Colonial Desire: Hybridity in Theory, Culture and Race*, London: Routledge, 1995.

—————— *White Mythologies: Writing, History and the West*, London: Routledge, 1991.

Zaman, Syed Badiuz, *Islamic Literature*, Lahore: No Publisher, 1956.

Zayd, Nasr Hamid Abu, *Reformation of Islamic Thought: A Critical Historical Analysis*, Amsterdam: Amsterdam University Press, 2006.

Zayd, Nasr Hamid Abu, *Rethinking the Qur'an: Towards a Humanistic Hermeneutics*, Utrecht: Humanistics University Press, 2004.

Žižek, Slavoj, *Violence: Six Sideways Reflections*, London: Profile Books, 2009.

—————— 'Why Heidegger Made the Right Step in 1933', *International Journal of Zizek Studies*, vol. 1, no. 4, 2008, pp. 1–43.

—————— *The Universal Exception: Selected Writings*, London: Continuum, 2006.

—————— Eric L. Santner and Kenneth Reinhard, *The Neighbor: Three Inquiries in Political Theology*, Chicago: The University of Chicago Press, 2005.

—————— 'Neighbors and Other Monsters: A Plea for Ethical Violence', in Slavoj Žižek, Eric L. Santner and Kenneth Reinhard, *The Neighbor: Three Inquiries in Political Theology*, Chicago: The University of Chicago Press, 2005, pp. 134–190

—————— *The Fragile Absolute or Why is the Christian Legacy Worth Fighting For?* London: Verso, 2000.

Zubaida, Sami, *Law and Power in the Islamic World*, London: I.B. Tauris, 2003.

Zulaika, Joseph and William A. Douglass, *Terror and Taboo: The Follies, Fables, and Faces of Terrorism*, London: Routledge, 1996.

Newspapers, E-Newsletters, Agencies, Journals, Periodicals etc.

Agence France Press (AFP)
Al-Ahram Weekly
Annals of the American Academy of Political and Social Science
Anthropology Today
Atlantic Monthly
bbc.co.uk/news
BBC Monitoring
bitterlemons-international.org
British Journal of Politics and International Relations
Bulletin of the School of Oriental and African Studies
Cambridge Review of International Affairs (CRIA)

BIBLIOGRAPHY

Christian Science Monitor
Commentary
CommonDreams.org
Common Ground News Network
Counterpunch
Critique: Critical Middle Eastern Studies
Cultural Anthropology
Cultural Critique
Diogenes
Etemad-e Melli
European Journal of International Relations
Financial Times
Foreign Affairs
Foreign Policy
Foreign Policy Analysis
Harvard Middle Eastern and Islamic Review
History and Theory
Inter Press Service (IPS)
International Affairs
International Journal of Middle East Studies
International Journal of Politics, Culture and Society
International Journal of Žižek Studies
International Organisation
International Security
International Sociology
International Studies Journal
International Studies Notes
International Studies Perspectives
International Studies Quarterly
International Studies Review
Iranian Studies
Islamic Republic News Agency (IRNA)
Jomhuri-ye Eslami
Journal of Agricultural and Environmental Ethics
Journal of Political Economy
Jyllands-Posten
Keyhan (Tehran)
London Review of Books
Millennium: Journal of International Studies
Monthly Review
Muslim World Journal of Human Rights
National Review
New German Critique
New Left Review
New York Daily Tribune

BIBLIOGRAPHY

New York Post
New York Review of Books
Progress in Human Geography
Radical Philosophy
Restoration Ecology
Reuters
Review of International Studies
Security Dialogue
Spiegel Online
Slate Magazine
The American Conservative
The Daily Star (Beirut)
The Daily Telegraph
The Guardian
The Harvard Theological Review
The Independent
The Journal of Negro History
The Lancet
The National Interest
The New Yorker
The New York Times
The Observer
The Times Literary Supplement
The Weekly Standard
Third World Quarterly
Vanity Fair

Selected Internet Sources

Benedict XVI, 'Three Stages in the Program of De-Hellenization', 12 Sept. 2006. Available at www.zenit.org [Last accessed 17 Jan. 2008].

Coleridge, Ernest Hartley (ed.) *The Works of Lord Byron, volume 6*, Ebook, The Project Gutenberg. Available at http://www.gutenberg.org/files/18762/18762–h/18762–h.htm [Last accessed 21 Jan. 2008].

Corn, M. Lynne, Eugene H. Buck, Jean Rawson, and Eric Fischer, 'Harmful non-native species: Issues for Congress III', *Congressional Research Service Report*, 8 April 1999. Available at http://ncseonline.org/NLE/CRSreports/Biodiversity/biodv–26.cfm [Last accessed 24 Jul. 2009].

Counterinsurgency, Headquarters: Department of the Army, December 2006. Available at http://www.usgcoin.org/library/doctrine/COIN-FM3-24.pdf [Last accessed 26 Dec. 2009].

Decker, Oliver, Katharina Rothe, Elmar Brähler, *Ein Blick in die Mitte—Zur Entstehung rechtsextremer und demokratischer Einstellungen*, Berlin: Friedrich Ebert Stiftung, 2008. Available at http://www.fes.de/rechtsextremis-mus/inhalt/studie.htm [Last accessed 12 Jun. 2009].

'Guidance for Non-Native Invasive Plant Species on Army Lands: Western United States', Public Works Technical Bulletin 200–1–18, Washington DC: U.S. Army Corps of Engineers, 13 Mar. 2003. Available at http://www.wbdg.org/ccb/ARMYCOE/PWTB/pwtb_200_1_18.pdf [Last accessed 12 Jun. 2009].

Lawrence, Thomas Edward (T.E.) *Letters*. Available at http://64.233.183.104/search?q=cache:WiCCq6iNi1gJ:telawrence.net/telawrencenet/letters/1924/240220_forster.htm+%E2%80%98self-satisfaction%E2%80%99+%E2%80%98hot+speed+on+a+motor+bike+lawrence+letters&hl=en&ct=clnk&cd=1&gl=uk [Last accessed 24 Sept. 2008].

No Blood, No Foul: Soldiers Accounts of Detainee Abuse in Iraq', *Human Rights Watch*, vol. 18, no. 3 (G¹, Jul. 2006. Available at http://hrw.org/reports/2006/us0706/ [Last accessed 14 Aug. 2007].

'The Invasive Non-Native Species Framework Strategy for Great Britain: Protecting our natural heritage from invasive species', Department for Environment, Food and Rural Affairs, 2008. Available at http://www.nonnatives-pecies.org/documents/Invasive_NNS_Framework_Strategy_GB_E.pdf [Last accessed 16 Jul. 2009].

'The Taguba Report: Article 15–6 Investigation of the 800th Military Police Brigade, March 2004', Available at http://news.findlaw.com/hdocs/docs/iraq/tagubarpt.html [Last accessed 18 Aug. 2007].

US Department of Defence, Office of Inspector General, 'Declassified Report on pre-war Intelligence on Iraq', Available at http://www.dodig.osd.mil/fo/Foia/ERR/Part2–07–Intel-04.pdf [Last accessed 27 Aug. 2007].

Wolf, Kenneth Baxter, *Christian Martyr's in Muslim Spain*, The Library of Iberian Resources Online, p. 59. Available at http://www.documentacatholi-caomnia.eu/03d/sine-data,_Wolf._Kenneth,_Christian_Martyrs_in_Muslim_Spain,_EN.pdf [Last accessed Jan. 2009].

INDEX

Abbasid Caliphate: growth of scientific research in, 74; institutionalisation of Islam under, 79; rise of, 236

Abduh, Mohammed, 104, 163, 238; and Lord Hartington, 103–5; co-founder of *al-urwa al-wuthqa* (The Indissoluble Link) (1884), 104; Grand Mufti of Egypt (1899), 162; writings of, 165, 239, 241

Abdul-Hamid II: Sultan of Ottoman Empire, 160

Achcar, Gilbert: 'clash of barbarisms', 17

Adams, Gerry: role in restructuring of political strategy of IRA, 15

Adorno, Theodor W., 295; and extended critique of maximal aesthetic value-based artwork, 295; and Negative Dialectics, 288, 297; critique of Enlightenment fostered attitudes, 129, 287; view of aims of Holocaust, 134; views of post-Auschwitz poetry, 298

Aeschylus, 37; *The Persians*, 33–4

al-Afghani, Sayyid Jamal-al-din, 81, 161, 163, 238; anti-imperialist activism of, 105; arguments with Ernest Renan in *Journal Des Débats* (1883), 104; background of,

160; co-founder of The Indissoluble Link (1884), 104; writings of, 165, 239, 241

Afghanistan, 160; Invasion of (2001), 3, 188, 251; Soviet Invasion of (1979–89), 251; War in, 22, 187, 210, 232, 283

Ahmadinejad, Mahmoud: invitation of controversial speakers to conference, 277; President of Iran, 277

Alexander of Macedonia, 36–7; and Darius, 37, 117; family of, 115

Algeria, 8; *Front Islamique du Salut* (Islamic Salvation Front) (FIS), 166

Ali, Tariq: 'clash of fundamentalisms', 17

Alighieri, Dante: *The Inferno*, 34, 72

al-Qaeda, 6, 242, 248, 251–3, 261, 277; aims of, 290; effect on domestic politics, 230; ideologues of, 82, 159; influence of, 232; personnel, 215; propaganda of, 230, 251; structure of, 268

American Civil Liberties Union: records requested by, 228

Amis, Martin: writings of, 272

Aquinas, Thomas: follower of St. Augustine of Hippo, 186

329

INDEX